JEWS AND THE MEDITERRANEAN

INDIANA SERIES IN SEPHARDI AND MIZRAHI STUDIES
Harvey E. Goldberg and Matthias Lehmann, *editors*

JEWS AND THE MEDITERRANEAN

Edited by
Matthias B. Lehmann and
Jessica M. Marglin

INDIANA UNIVERSITY PRESS

This book is a publication of

Indiana University Press
Office of Scholarly Publishing
Herman B Wells Library 350
1320 East 10th Street
Bloomington, Indiana 47405 USA

iupress.indiana.edu

© 2020 by Indiana University Press

All rights reserved

No part of this book may be reproduced or utilized in any form or by any means, electronic or mechanical, including photocopying and recording, or by any information storage and retrieval system, without permission in writing from the publisher. The paper used in this publication meets the minimum requirements of the American National Standard for Information Sciences—Permanence of Paper for Printed Library Materials, ANSI Z39.48-1992.

Manufactured in the United States of America

Cataloging information is available from the Library of Congress.

ISBN 978-0-253-04793-9 (hardback)
ISBN 978-0-253-04798-4 (paperback)
ISBN 978-0-253-04799-1 (ebook)

1 2 3 4 5   25 24 23 22 21 20

CONTENTS

Acknowledgments vii

Introduction: Jewish History in the Mediterranean, the Mediterranean in Jewish History / Jessica M. Marglin and Matthias B. Lehmann   1

1. Globalization or Culture: The Ancient Jews and the Mediterranean / Seth Schwartz   30

2. The New Melting Pot? Mediterraneanism and the Study of Jewish History / Jonathan Ray   49

3. Can We Speak of a Geographical Axis in Medieval Jewish Culture? / Andrew Berns   68

4. Jews and the Early Modern Mediterranean Slave Trade / Daniel Hershenzon   81

5. Religious Boundaries in Italy during an Era of Free Trade, 1550–1750: The Case of Livorno / Corey Tazzara   107

6. A Father's Consolation: Intracultural Ties and Religion in a Trans-Mediterranean Jewish Commercial Network / Francesca Bregoli   129

7. Soap and the Making of a Short-Distance Network in the Nineteenth-Century Adriatic / Constanze Kolbe   149

8. A Guide to the Jewish Mediterranean: *Le Guide Sam* and the Shaping of an Interwar Mediterranean Diaspora / Devi Mays   170

9 A New Myth of Coexistence? The Jewish
   Mediterranean Dream and the Three Ages of Nostalgia /
   Clémence Boulouque   191

Index   213

ACKNOWLEDGMENTS

THIS VOLUME GREW OUT OF A CONFERENCE HELD at the University of California, Irvine, and the University of Southern California in the spring of 2016. Clémence Boulouque conceived the conference and co-organized it with us, and we are grateful for her vision and her contributions to the discussions. We would like to thank the sources of funding that made this conference possible, including: the Teller Family Chair in Jewish History at UC Irvine; the UC Irvine Humanities Commons; the USC Casden Institute for the Study of the Jewish Role in American Life; the USC Dornsife College Office of the Dean; the UCLA Maurice Amado Program in Sephardic Studies; the UCLA William A. Clark Memorial Library; the UCLA Center for 17th and 18th Century Studies; and the UCI Department of History.

We would also like to thank the scholars who presented at this conference but did not contribute to this volume—their participation was crucial to the success of the conversations that sparked this book: Marina Rustow, Evelyne Oliel-Grausz, Joshua Schreier, Sarah Abrevaya Stein, Paris Papamichos Chronakis, Jonathan Decter, and Naomi Davidson. We would also like to thank the local scholars who chaired panels and attended the conference: Cavan Concannon, Ra'anan Boustan, Ian Coller, Claudia Moatti, and Aomar Boum.

We would also like to thank all those who made the publication of this volume possible. The entire team at Indiana University Press has been a pleasure to work with, and we particularly want to thank Dee Mortensen, our editor. Ashante Thomas, Rachel Rosolina, and Dave Hulsey all shepherded the book through various stages of production. We would also like to thank the two anonymous readers, whose comments improved the entire book.

JEWS AND THE MEDITERRANEAN

INTRODUCTION

Jewish History in the Mediterranean, the Mediterranean in Jewish History

Jessica M. Marglin
Matthias B. Lehmann

THE FIELD OF MEDITERRANEAN STUDIES HAS COME A long way since the German geographer Theobald Fischer (d. 1910) introduced the concept of the "Mediterranean region" as a distinct geographic area at the turn of the twentieth century.[1] Yet the field still grapples with some of the tensions and contradictions of this earlier work. Fischer's writings, for example, oscillate between a geographic determinism that assumes the primacy of certain timeless ecological conditions of "the Mediterranean" and a culturalist approach that sees the Mediterranean region as the cradle of Western civilization. While emphasizing the unity of the region, Fischer also, in a 1907 publication about the "Mediterranean peoples," presented a somewhat idiosyncratic classification of various groups in both religious and racialized terms—"Catholic Latin peoples," "Slavs of the southeast European peninsula," followed by Albanians, Greeks, Turks, Berbers, and Arabs, only to then present the subtotal of the overall population in the region divided into Muslims and Christians.[2] The tension between geography and culture, between Mediterranean unity and diversity, have continued to inform discussions among scholars in the field, just as the notion of the Mediterranean as a frontier separating the world of "Christendom" from that of "Islam" has persisted.[3] The political implications of the study of Mediterranean unity and diversity, on the other hand, were as clear to Theobald Fischer in the early twentieth century—the opening sentence of his essay on Mediterranean peoples notes that the "region for many years has stood in the foreground of international politics"[4]—as they are relevant today, in the face of the ongoing migration crisis that plays out on Europe's Mediterranean shores.

Theobald Fischer called Jews "one of the oldest people of the Mediterranean region" but had little else to say about them.[5] This relative absence of Jews from Mediterranean studies, too, has continued in much of the subsequent research, including, as we will see below, in the groundbreaking work of Fernand Braudel and, more recently, Peregrine Horden and Nicholas Purcell. On the other hand, Jewish historians have only quite recently begun to consider the Mediterranean as a framework for the study of Jewish history, though other paradigms—Sephardic versus Ashkenazi, the "Jews of Islam" versus the Jews of Europe, or the Jews of various empires and nation-states—continue to be dominant. The present volume is driven by two main questions: What can Jewish history contribute to the study of the Mediterranean? and What can Mediterranean studies contribute to scholarship on Jewish history? Focusing on the specificity of the Jewish experience, the essays that follow, by definition, emphasize human agency and culture over the ecological *longue durée* of Mediterranean history. Taking a Mediterranean perspective as a framework of analysis, however, they are able to move beyond an understanding of Jewish history that privileges identitarian contexts such as the "Jewish" or the "Sephardic diaspora," based on an assumed primacy of religious identity or notions of kinship, and at the same time to cut across the dividing lines separating the "Christian" from the "Muslim" Mediterranean, and one imperial or national space from another. Yet they also warn against an overly facile equation of Mediterranean connectivity and diversity with notions of cosmopolitanism, fluidity, and hybridity, and draw attention to the question of Jewish distinctiveness.

Jews in Mediterranean History

The field of Mediterranean studies is neither a discipline nor a version of area studies, such as Middle Eastern studies.[6] Mediterraneanists, as some might self-identify, do not agree on a methodological or analytical approach.[7] Nor do they necessarily even study the same part of the world; many books or articles use "Mediterranean" as a synecdoche for what is, in fact, only a part of the Mediterranean (Byzantium, the Iberian Peninsula, the Roman Empire, etc.).[8]

So what do we mean when we talk about Mediterranean studies? A useful starting point is to define the study of the Mediterranean along two axes. First, to study the Mediterranean—rather than, say, a part of the Mediterranean, or an empire that happens to be located in the Mediterranean—is to study the interaction between different religious, cultural, and/or political groups in and across the shores of the Mediterranean Sea. This is often accomplished by frameworks that cross regional boundaries (that is, studying Europe and the Middle East). Other Mediterraneanist studies are more localized, but with a focus on the interactions between a particular location and others (such as a history of Italy's interactions with Islamic empires in the Middle East and North Africa).

Second, to study the Mediterranean often involves an explicit engagement with what could be loosely defined as a Mediterranean canon. Three books stand out as having been particularly influential in shaping the historical discussion of the Mediterranean: the works of Henri Pirenne, Fernand Braudel, and Peregrine Horden and Nicholas Purcell.[9] Although these texts happen to be primarily historical, they have proved influential among social scientists and literary scholars as well.[10] And while not all scholars working on the Mediterranean engage explicitly with this canon, the influence of one or more members of this trilogy almost always hovers around current scholarship on the region. For our purposes, it is particularly important to note that each of these books relegates Jews to a relatively minor, and usually quite restricted, role in the drama of Mediterranean history.

Henri Pirenne (1862–1935) was a Belgian historian of medieval Europe; his contribution to Mediterranean studies is the eponymous Pirenne Thesis, outlined in his posthumous book *Mohammed and Charlemagne*, first published in French in 1937.[11] In this slender volume, Pirenne challenges the conventional narrative about the fall of the Roman Empire and the emergence of medieval Europe. He argues that the Barbarian invasions and the subsequent political collapse of the Roman Empire did not, in fact, shatter the cultural or economic unity of the Mediterranean. Pirenne instead points to the rise of Islam as the breaking point in late antiquity. With the expansion of the Islamic empire, "the old economic unity of the Mediterranean was shattered, and so it remained until the epoch of the Crusades. It had resisted the Germanic invasions; but it gave way before the irresistible advance of Islam."[12] For the field of Mediterranean studies, the particulars of Pirenne's thesis have perhaps been less influential than his vision of a unified Mediterranean, through which "the warm blood of ancient civilization . . . had continued to pulse into Western Europe" even after the disintegration of the Roman Empire.[13]

For Pirenne, Jews played a very specific, if relatively minor, role in the history of the early medieval Mediterranean: they were traders par excellence.[14] Jews constituted one of the foreign, "Oriental" elements (like Syrians and Greeks) that contributed to a particularly Mediterranean cosmopolitanism both before and after the rise of Islam.[15] Jewish merchants, he argues, remained in western Europe after the Barbarian invasions—the only group that continued to engage in commercial exchange.[16] After the Islamic conquests, Jews took up a position of middlemen linking East to West.[17] Post-Islamic European rulers cemented the association between Jews and commerce by coupling the words *Judaeus* (Jew) with *Mercator* (merchant) in the privileges allowing Jews to settle in Christian lands.[18] Moreover, Pirenne emphasizes that the "immense majority" of Jews were engaged "in lending money at interest" or that "many of them were slave-merchants"—a tendency they again preserved after the expansion of Islam.[19] Pirenne's pigeonholing of Jews as merchants specializing in the unsavory professions of usury and slave trading reflected contemporary historiographical narratives. Starting with German historians of the nineteenth century (both Jewish and non-Jewish), and further reinforced by Werner Sombart's 1911 book *The Jews and Modern Capitalism*, Jews became associated above all with the slave trade and international commerce, from the medieval period to the present.[20] More recent scholarship has demonstrated that the earlier association between medieval Jews and both slave traders and international commerce was exaggerated.[21] But the trope of Jews as cultural intermediaries—mentioned only once by Pirenne—became far more pronounced among later scholars such as Braudel, and has continued to exert influence in Mediterranean studies.

Fernand Braudel (1902–1985), in many ways heir to Pirenne, founded the field of Mediterranean studies with the publication of *La Méditerranée et le monde méditerranéen à l'époque de Philippe II* in 1949.[22] He spent ten formative years in Algiers (1923–1932), seeing the Mediterranean "from the opposite shore, upside down," where he began the research for what would become his magnum opus.[23] There, in 1931, he heard Pirenne lecture, which, in Braudel's words, "seemed prodigious to me; his hand opened and shut, and the entire Mediterranean was by turns free and locked in!"[24]

Braudel took from Pirenne a vision of the Mediterranean as a single region unified by culture and commerce. But unlike Pirenne, who saw this unity shattered by Islam, Braudel projected Mediterranean unity at least into the sixteenth century and in some ways beyond. Moreover, he based the cultural continuity of the Mediterranean not on the legacy of the Roman Empire, but on geography. Braudel is perhaps most famous for his three levels of historical time—the first, *la longue durée*, is shaped by climate and the environment and is "a history of constant repetition, ever-recurring cycles"; the second is the slow time of "economic systems, states, societies, civilizations, and . . . warfare"; and the third, *l'histoire événementielle*, is the history of (mere) events—of individuals, dates, and battles that had previously dominated historical writing (Pirenne being a notable exception).[25] According to Braudel, the ecological unity of the Mediterranean meant that the different peoples, states, and civilizations along its shores shared a "common destiny" over the *longue durée*.[26]

It is only in the second, heavily revised edition of *The Mediterranean* (from 1966) that Braudel added a section devoted to Jews. There, he astutely identifies the main drama of Jewish history, noting that Jews both adapted to their surroundings wherever they went and preserved their "basic personality"—a version of what Jewish historian David N. Myers sums up as Jews' ability to "adapt to new environments without losing a distinctive sense of cultural self."[27] Nonetheless, aside from this discussion, Jews appear relatively infrequently in the pages of *The Mediterranean*. And when they do, their religion is almost an afterthought; as with Christianity and Islam, Braudel refers to Judaism as a "civilization" rather than a religious tradition.[28]

Much like Pirenne, when Braudel did make room for Jews, it was to serve two particular roles in Mediterranean history. He associates them closely with commerce (although Braudel did not pigeonhole Jews as representatives of dubious practices like usury).[29] Because Jews had representatives everywhere, he argues, they "formed the leading commercial network in the world"; the connection between a transnational Jewish diaspora and commercial success still holds much currency in both scholarly and popular imaginations, though historians such as Francesca Trivellato have challenged the premise.[30] Above all, the Jews of Braudel's Mediterranean emerge as intermediaries *par excellence*. Due to the repeated expulsion of Jews from most of western Europe, Braudel explained, Jews ended up scattered throughout the Mediterranean. Thus, "willingly or unwillingly, the Jews were forced into the role of agents of cultural exchange."[31] They were also "born interpreters of all speech," exploiting their native multilingualism to become much-needed translators.[32] Braudel's picture of Jews as intermediaries in the Mediterranean—helping to connect the worlds of Islam and Christianity—was characteristic of persistent stereotypes about Jews' intimate ties to commerce. Yet such assumptions about Jews as merchants and intermediaries survived many more decades of historical scholarship. Only recently have medieval historians such as Michael Toch sought to discard the notion that "Jews were the proverbial long-distance traders connecting Europe with the Middle East and Muslim Spain," a notion tied to "contemporary (nineteenth- and twentieth-century) polemics and apologetics."[33]

A half century passed before anyone attempted to take up Braudel's mantle and write another synthetic study of the Mediterranean. In 2000, two British historians—Peregrine Horden, a medievalist, and Nicholas Purcell, a historian of the Roman Empire—coauthored *The Corrupting Sea: A Study of Mediterranean History*. The authors conceived of their work as both a response and a challenge to Braudel. Whereas Braudel had focused his study on the sixteenth century, Horden and Purcell wondered whether "such a work could have been written taking as its eponymous ruler an imperial potentate from Antiquity or the Middle Ages?"[34] Horden and Purcell's ambitious study became a second classic among Mediterraneanists.

The Corrupting Sea discards Braudel's premise that the cultural unity of the Mediterranean is founded on geographical similarity. Horden and Purcell argue that the distinctiveness of the Mediterranean is not a unified climate, or the ubiquity of grains, olives, and vineyards in close proximity to the sea, but rather the extreme diversity of landscape. Rather than a single Mediterranean geography, Horden and Purcell emphasize the dazzling variety of "microregions" that are quite distinct from one another. These microregions could not, in the pre-modern period, survive on their own; too often, the climatic conditions in one produced extremely low harvests, while nearby the yield was abundant. Each microregion thus had to rely on regular and intensive exchange with their more or less distant neighbors, often through "cabotage," short-distance coastal trade. The resulting "connectivity"—that is, "the various ways in which microregions cohere, both internally and also with one another"—is the second defining feature of Horden and Purcell's Mediterranean.[35] Their Mediterranean is distinctive because of the "paradoxical coexistence of . . . easy seaborne communications with a quite unusually fragmented topography of microregions."[36] Horden and Purcell use this specificity to insist on a distinction between history *of* the Mediterranean and history *in* the Mediterranean. Whereas history *in* the Mediterranean is "contingently Mediterranean"—it just happens to occur in the Mediterranean—history *of* the Mediterranean is "either of the whole Mediterranean or of an aspect of it to which the whole is an indispensable framework."[37]

In the tradition of the great Mediterraneanists who preceded them, Horden and Purcell are far more interested in economy than in religion or religious identity. In the dense pages of *The Corrupting Sea*—even more, perhaps, than in Braudel's work—individuals recede into the background, as do politics, class, gender, and the state. Accordingly, they have discarded older stereotypes about Jews (and other groups, such as Greeks) as merchants and intermediaries *par excellence*. This is in part related to their focus on small-scale commerce rather than the kind of international trade in luxury goods (spices, cloth) or grain that dominated the work of Pirenne and Braudel.

Nonetheless, the near-complete absence of Jews in *The Corrupting Sea* is striking. Even in Horden and Purcell's explicit discussions of religiosity, they find exceedingly few occasions to include Jews.[38] The chapter "The Geography of Religion" offers a Mediterranean-wide typology of religious practice. The authors trace how "the religious landscape . . . respond[s] to the social and economic aspects of Mediterranean geography . . . [and] will help us to understand the coalescence of the thousands of Mediterranean localities into some sort of unity."[39] Yet their focus is almost exclusively on the pagan, Christian, and Muslim Mediterranean. Jews are mentioned only three times, always in passing.[40] This is not always for lack of opportunity; for instance, in their discussion of pilgrimage, Horden and Purcell assert that "the journey to the local cult-place is easily attested from all periods of Mediterranean history." But aside from a passing mention of Jewish pilgrimage to Meiron, their analysis focuses exclusively on Christian and Muslim pilgrimage.[41] Jewish pilgrimage—known throughout the Mediterranean from antiquity to the present—is an afterthought compared with the mobility of what, for them, constitute more significant Mediterranean religions.[42]

In the nearly two decades since the publication of *The Corrupting Sea*, the study of the Mediterranean has positively exploded.[43] A number of noteworthy works eschew the search for unity championed by the Mediterraneanist canon, instead offering accounts of history that span the entire region. David Abulafia's *The Great Sea: A Human History of the Mediterranean* "aims to bring to the fore the human experience of crossing the Mediterranean or of living in the port towns and islands that depended for their existence on the sea."[44] Unlike Pirenne, Braudel, or Horden and Purcell, Abulafia does not seek any enduring unity or distinctiveness—economic, cultural, or geographical—in the Mediterranean.[45] What results is a comprehensive, if rather conventional, account of what happened on the "surface of the sea," an approach that is described by Horden and Purcell as an excellent example of history *in* the Mediterranean.[46] Accordingly, Abulafia pays attention to Jews as people who happened to live in the region and accordingly played a role in shaping its history.[47] Similarly, in *A Companion to Mediterranean History* edited by Horden and Sharon Kinoshita (a scholar of medieval Mediterranean literature), Fred Astren's chapter entitled "Jews" is a useful chronicle of Jews' presence in the Mediterranean. Astren, however, does not engage with the analytical or methodological themes outlined by the Mediterraneanist canon; his history, too, is one of Jews who happened to have lived *in* the Mediterranean.[48]

The ecological view of Mediterranean unity has of late been overshadowed by approaches that are more attuned to anthropological themes such as culture and discourse. Michael Herzfeld's work has been particularly influential in identifying the Mediterranean as a discursive construct. In the 1980s, he proposed the neologism "Mediterraneanism," an adaptation of Edward Said's term "Orientalism."[49] Herzfeld notes that northern Europeans view their southern neighbors with a mixture of contempt and fascination, not unlike Europeans' view of the Oriental other. Indeed, southern Europeans' proximity to North Africa and the Middle East makes them quasi-Oriental. Herzfeld argues that "claims of Mediterranean unity" represent "a global hierarchy of value in which 'Mediterranean' comes somewhere between 'modern' and 'primitive.'"[50] It is this idea of a discursive trope—rather than any actual unity, derived either from shared culture or shared ecology—that defines the Mediterranean for Herzfeld. Although Jews do not figure prominently in Herzfeld's analysis, his approach is potentially quite useful for thinking about intra-Jewish perceptions across perceived cultural or national lines.[51]

Also taking their cue from anthropology, a number of scholars eschew a search for a shared methodology in favor of a common emphasis on interaction and exchange as well as, in some cases, conflict and competition. This angle—which Horden dubs a "culturalogical" approach—has proven particularly appealing to medievalists and early modernists.[52] Medieval Iberian studies has also been heavily influenced by the culturalogical approach, given its long-standing emphasis on the interaction between Jews, Christians, and Muslims.[53] Models such as Américo Castro's *convivencia* (first proposed in 1948)—or Brian Catlos's modification "the convenience principle" (*conveniencia*)—continue to loom large in attempts to understand the history of interreligious and intercultural relations in the Mediterranean.[54]

On one end of the culturalogical spectrum are those scholars who view the premodern Mediterranean as a cosmopolitan space, "a region of cultural fluidity."[55] Their studies explore the ways in which religious and cultural frontiers were both regularly traversed and were blurry enough to accommodate symbiosis among seemingly different peoples. Brian Catlos, for instance, describes a "mutual intelligibility"[56] among the diverse peoples of the premodern Mediterranean; "a common understanding of the world in which they lived, a common framework for moral, political, and social action, and a common appreciation for how their experience in the world could be expressed through art, music and literature."[57] Here, Catlos echoes the approach prevalent among mid-twentieth-century anthropologists who identified a single Mediterranean culture based on concepts such as honor and shame.[58] Jews often figure prominently in these studies that emphasize exchange and/or hybridity. For instance, some scholars point to *conversos*—Jewish converts to Catholicism and their descendants, who often moved back and forth between identifying as Jews and identifying as Christians—as emblematic of the Mediterranean's porous religious borders.[59]

But a number of critics warn that overemphasizing cosmopolitanism elides important cultural and religious differences while in the process reifying the supposedly fixed units that came together as hybrids.[60] More recently, scholars have offered critiques of the hybridity/fluidity paradigm. Molly Greene's studies of relations among Ottoman Muslims, Orthodox Christians, and Catholics in the seventeenth-century eastern Mediterranean shine light on the interactions among religious groups. But Greene eschews the nostalgia that often colors histories of the Mediterranean, instead pointing out how religious differences (including among different types of Christians) could be sources of both cooperation and conflict.[61] Natalie Rothman and Francesca Trivellato's influential studies both emphasize that exchange and interaction were facilitated by clear demarcations between religious groups.[62] Indeed, these very exchanges contributed to solidifying interreligious boundaries. Trivellato writes against the stereotype of the Sephardic Jew as a marker of Mediterranean fluidity *par excellence*. Instead, she proposes the notion of "communitarian cosmopolitanism" to describe the ways in which clear boundaries between Jews and Catholics facilitated interreligious contact, both cultural and economic.[63]

Ultimately, the culturalogical approach leaves a central question unanswered: whether the interaction of cultures and religions in the Mediterranean is specific to this region—*of* rather than *in* the Mediterranean—as opposed to a local instance of a phenomenon observable throughout the world.[64] Many scholars are not bothered by this and are content to adopt the Mediterranean because it is "good to think with"—or at least better than the alternatives.[65] Indeed, perhaps the most persuasive aspect of this approach is to use the Mediterranean as an alternative to problematic and limiting geographical frameworks like Europe, Africa, and the Middle East; cultural zones like East and West; or reified religious categories like Christianity, Judaism, and Islam.[66] As such, in Horden's words, "Mediterranean scholarship is always, or should be, inherently, writing *against*—against other possible optics, or spatial frames."[67]

The Mediterranean in Jewish History

In *The Corrupting Sea*, Horden and Purcell pointed to four scholars they considered as their most important predecessors in the study of Mediterranean history, including the Jewish historian Shlomo Dov Goitein, whose magnum opus, *A Mediterranean Society*, appeared in five volumes between 1967 and 1988.[68] In reality, though, as Fred Astren has pointed out, Horden and Purcell made scant use of Goitein's massive study of the Jewish merchants and the medieval Mediterranean world that he saw reflected in the vast repository that is the documentary evidence of the Cairo genizah.[69] While Goitein's "people of the genizah" may have provided rich evidence to test Horden and Purcell's ideas about connectivity and the relation between ecology, redistribution of resources, and the interdependence of Mediterranean microregions in the eleventh and twelfth centuries, they saw him as someone writing a history *in*, but not a history *of*, the Mediterranean.[70]

The most widely cited (though not necessarily most widely read) work on the Mediterranean arguably remains Fernand Braudel's classic. As it happens, S. D. Goitein first began his work on the business letters and other historical documents from the Cairo genizah in collaboration with, and obtaining funding from, the *VIe section* of the École Pratique des Hautes Études in Paris, whose head at the time was none other than Braudel.[71] This connection notwithstanding, Goitein admits that he did not read Braudel's *La Méditerranée* until it appeared in paperback in English (1972), and nothing much came of the collaboration with the Parisian institute, as Goitein eventually chose to publish his major work in the United States. Peter Miller laments the *desencuentro* between the two major scholars of Mediterranean history, arguing that "Braudel's history would have been more compelling if he could have figured out how to accommodate the reality of human agency" of the kind that permeates the pages of Goitein's work and the latter's "more usable if he had been able to tell a story rather than curate individual documents."[72]

What was, in fact, Goitein's concept of "the Mediterranean"? In the first volume of *Mediterranean Society*, he raised the crucial question of "how far the spirituality and psychology of the Geniza people were specifically Jewish and to what extent they could be taken as characteristic for the time and area in general." Moreover, Goitein wondered "whether the various groups and individuals discernible in our records were representative of their countries of origin or domicile, of the world of Muslim civilization, or of the Mediterranean society as a whole." He promised to revisit the question in the "concluding chapter" of what he then anticipated as its third, and final, volume.[73]

In the event, the promised chapter that was to be entitled "The Mediterranean Mind" never materialized. By 1988, the "concluding chapter" had morphed into an entire, fifth, volume, but its focus had shifted. A disclaimer that appeared in the opening pages of the book, which came out three years after Goitein's death and had been curated by Abraham Udovitch, read: "The title originally planned for Chapter X, *The Mediterranean Mind*, was relinquished to avoid the erroneous assumption that the personality emerging from the Geniza documents is regarded as representative of a hypothetical human type common to the Mediterranean area."[74]

That was a bit of a climb-down from the confident assertion in 1968, when Goitein had maintained that "specific Jewish aspects" were not the main characteristic of the documents he was studying and that he was "even inclined to believe that, to a large extent, the Geniza records reflect Mediterranean society in general."[75] Still, Goitein's approach to the genizah documents throughout was predicated on the assumption that the "embeddedness" of the Cairene Jewish merchants in the society and culture of their time made it possible to draw broader conclusions from their example. Later historians, who, as Jessica Goldberg has pointed out, have often mined Goitein's research as if it were a primary source itself, sometimes uncritically accepted the equation between the "people of the geniza" and the wider Islamic world they inhabited—so much so that for the economic historian Avner Greif, the merchants of Goitein's study could become simply "the Maghribi traders," as if their status as members of a religious minority did not matter.[76]

With this, the slippage between "Mediterranean" and "Islamic" in Goitein's own work, and in that of subsequent historians, comes into focus. According to Goitein,

> during the High Middle Ages men, goods, money, and books used to travel far and almost without restrictions throughout the Mediterranean area. In many respects, the area resembled a free-trade community. The treatment of foreigners, as a rule, was remarkably liberal. The close connection among all parts of the Jewish diaspora, expressed in contributions to, and spiritual and organizational dependence upon, ecumenical religious authorities in faraway countries was not regarded by the governments of the various states concerned as an infringement on their sovereignty . . . At the root of all this was the concept that law was personal and not territorial.[77]

But if one of the key factors ensuring the unity of "the Mediterranean" was, in Goitein's estimation, the fact that "the same law was applied to the members of one religious community throughout the Mediterranean area,"[78] it is obvious that he was talking specifically about the *Muslim* Mediterranean, as clearly the legal situation of Jewish merchants would not have been identical everywhere around the Mediterranean basin, in both Islamic and Christian lands.[79] Thus, as Fred Astren has suggested, Goitein's Mediterranean, with its assumed Jewish-Islamic symbiosis of the eleventh and twelfth centuries, is really synonymous with what Marshall Hodgson dubbed the "Islamicate" world.[80]

The Mediterranean for Goitein, then, is a cultural Mediterranean, not one predicated on features of its environment and the topography and climate of its regions and microregions. In addition to the "conception that law was personal and not territorial" and "the consequences of the bourgeois revolution of the eighth and ninth centuries," Goitein argues that Mediterranean unity was based on the fact that "all these countries had a great and long-standing tradition in common. The fact that most of them had once been united within the confines of the Roman empire is perhaps of secondary importance. It is the cultural tradition, which begins with the ancient civilizations of Iraq, and even of Iran—for all these countries belong to the Mediterranean world—which counts." Like Pirenne before him, Goitein wondered when this unity had come to an end. Not until "the Islamic countries were taken over by intruders from the outside," he argues, "mostly from Central Asia and the Caucasus, who had no share in that tradition."[81]

The conflation of "Mediterranean" and "Islamic" (or "Islamicate") was thus explicit, which allowed Goitein to include Iraq and Iran in his vision of the Mediterranean because they, presumably, shared in the ancient Near Eastern and Hellenistic cultures that fed into medieval Islamicate civilization. Though

Goitein professed that he had no personal opinion on the Pirenne Thesis, for him it was not Barbarians destroying the Mediterranean of *pax romana*, nor the Muslim conquests of the seventh century, but the "invasion" of the Turkic peoples from central Asia that ended Mediterranean unity. What Pirenne and Goitein had in common was that both ultimately defined what they understood as the "Mediterranean" in political and cultural terms—for Pirenne, western Europe was "Mediterranean" when under Roman rule, just like Iran was "Mediterranean" for Goitein—and not, as Braudel or Horden and Purcell, in environmental terms.

While it lasted, the unified Mediterranean space of the genizah was, for Goitein, a veritable "free-trade community."[82] Though he acknowledged that the people of the genizah did not have a word for "Mediterranean" themselves, "as long as one traveled on the Mediterranean, one was, so to speak, within one's precincts and never beyond reach."[83] Goitein emphasized the ease of communication between the different parts of the Mediterranean at the same time as he noted that the letters preserved in the Cairo genizah clearly distinguished between various subregions ("the East," "the [Muslim] West," the "Land of the Romans"),[84] and he admitted that "despite the existence of a direct shipping line between Spain and Egypt, going east for a prolonged period meant a severe loosening or even severing of the ties with the people back home."[85]

In the end, Goitein's Mediterranean remains evocative rather than fully conceptualized. The distinction between "the world of Muslim civilization, or of the Mediterranean society as a whole," which he raised in the opening chapter of his monumental study, remains fuzzy. Yet it is precisely the perspective of Jewish history—during the period of the genizah, but not only then—that lends itself to explore the ways in which we might imagine, problematize, and historicize the notion of a distinct Mediterranean space and its relation to the religious cultures that shaped the lives of its inhabitants.

Perhaps the most fruitful recent reengagement with Goitein's Mediterraneanism is Jessica Goldberg's *Trade and Institutions in the Medieval Mediterranean*. Goldberg challenges the "two prominent and differing 'ecological' definitions of the Mediterranean offered by Braudel on the one hand and Horden and Purcell on the other." She sees evidence of neither Braudel's "eternal trinity of 'wheat, olives, and grapes,'" nor does she accept Horden and Purcell's model of the Mediterranean as a "collection of micro-regions." The genizah, she argues, demonstrates the existence of an agricultural "macro-ecology," whereas culture, not only immutable ecological conditions, influenced patterns of consumption and thus economic exchange.[86] At the same time, Goldberg shows, the Jewish identity of the genizah merchants mattered, as these traders displayed a "strong preference for conducting trade within their group." "Like institutions and infrastructures," she notes, "identities shaped economic geographies."[87] In the end, that leaves the question open whether there was, in fact, anything distinctly Mediterranean about the world inhabited by the "people of the genizah."

Beyond the medieval Islamic world, Joshua Holo looks at the diaspora of Byzantine Jews, spread out throughout the eastern Mediterranean, and the economic networks they established across political and religious boundaries up to the Fourth Crusade in the early thirteenth century. Holo's *Byzantine Jewry in the Mediterranean Economy* thus adds an important perspective that allows us to imagine a medieval (eastern) Mediterranean that is not coterminous with Islamicate society.[88]

While most studies in medieval Jewish history that explicitly invoke a (defined or assumed) Mediterranean context focus on economic history and trade, echoing the emphasis on the role of Jews as middlemen that appears so prominently in "general" histories of the Mediterranean, Sarah Stroumsa attempts something rather different in her *Maimonides in His World*. As the subtitle of her ambitious study—"Portrait of a Mediterranean Thinker"— suggests, hers is an attempt to locate the great medieval Jewish scholar and philosopher in the wider context of the Mediterranean world. For Stroumsa, this context manifests itself on three levels: first, Maimonides's own biography, which led him from Cordoba to Fez and on to Fustat (Old Cairo), and, second, the cosmopolitan character of his learning and literary oeuvre, which put him in conversation with a "multilayered, multifaceted Mediterranean legacy." Not only his philosophical writings but also his scholarship on Jewish law, Stroumsa argues, reveals how much Maimonides was immersed in the wider culture of his time, for example his encounter with Muslim legal scholarship (*fiqh*), and in particular, Almohad law.[89] The benefit of labeling the context of Maimonides's scholarship "Mediterranean" rather than "Islamic" lies, of course, in the fact that it avoids an artificial juxtaposition between "internal" Jewish and "external" Islamic knowledge. But it is especially on the third level, that of the reception history of Maimonides's writings, that the label "Mediterranean" is particularly useful. "Still wider than the parameters of Maimonides' biography," Stroumsa writes, "are the geographical parameters outlined by its literary output,"[90] namely with the translation of his Judeo-Arabic works into Hebrew and their reception in the Jewish communities in Christian Spain and southern France.[91] Maimonides, then, embodies a cultural exchange that involved the different religious traditions of the Mediterranean world and linked—through his biography, the cosmopolitan context of his own scholarship and the reception history of his writings—the Western with the Eastern and the Muslim with the Christian Mediterranean.

For Stroumsa, Maimonides marks the end of an era, and the translation of his works from Arabic into Hebrew points, in her reading, to the shifting balance of Jewish creativity away from the southern to the northern shores of the Mediterranean, from the Islamic world to Europe.[92] For Goitein, as we saw, the thirteenth century similarly saw the demise of an integrated, cosmopolitan Mediterranean—the Mamluks, he noted, "turned their backs to the Mediterranean" when they took control of Egypt in 1250.[93] These claims of a disruptive break may be exaggerated, but it is indicative of a shift away from the Mediterranean in Jewish historiography of the early modern and modern periods. There are plenty of studies, to be sure, of Jews in various countries along the Mediterranean shore, including an ever-growing body of scholarship on the Jews of Italy and the Ottoman Empire, yet little if any engagement with a wider Mediterranean context as such. Other approaches have dominated, for example the concept of "port Jews" first developed by Lois Dubin and David Sorkin. This "type" of Jewish community, prevalent in early modern port cities, anticipated the self-reforming ideology and acculturation into non-Jewish society usually associated with the Haskalah and the culture of the court Jews.[94] Moreover, the notion of an interconnected "Sephardic diaspora" came to define a great deal of early modern Jewish history—and with that, a turn away from the Mediterranean and toward the Atlantic.[95]

Modern Jewish history, on the other hand, has been compartmentalized into nation-states and empires—so much so that even inherently transnational topics like modern Jewish philanthropy have usually been rooted in a perspective that assumes the centrality of the nation-state and modern nationalism.[96] It is only in response to the rise of critical, post-Zionist scholarship on Israel and Israeli society that "Mediterraneanism" has reemerged on the scene, this time as a symbol of cosmopolitanism and as an alternative to binary juxtapositions of Europe versus Levant, West versus East, or Jew versus Arab.[97] As such, the emergence of *Yam Tikhoniyut* in Israeli public culture as well as academic discourse—note, for example, the establishment of the *Mediterranean Historical Review* at Tel Aviv University in 1986—often follows a political agenda that celebrates an image of Mediterranean cosmopolitanism and cultural symbiosis not altogether different from that imagined by S. D. Goitein decades earlier.[98] At the same time, of course, this Mediterraneanism allows Israelis to imagine themselves as part of something other than the "Middle East," eyes firmly set on the West.

In, or *Of*, the Mediterranean?

Elliott Horowitz has called Seth Schwartz's *Were the Jews a Mediterranean Society?* (2010) "the first major response to Horden and Purcell's two-volume *Corrupting Sea* by a scholar of Jewish society."[99] This characterization is somewhat misleading, however; as Schwartz points out in his contribution to the current volume, Horden and Purcell did not, in his estimation, "succeed in convincing us that 'connectivity' is *meaningfully definitional* in/of the world of the Mediterranean,"[100] and his argument does not in fact build on Horden and Purcell with their focus on "connectivity" and "cabotage." Instead, Schwartz draws on Mediterranean ethnography to develop an "ideal type," in the Weberian sense; for Schwartz, Mediterranean denotes a model of a reciprocity-driven social organization that he contrasts with a different model, the solidarity-based ideal promoted in the Hebrew Bible. He does not claim that the "ideal type" is representative of an empirical unitary Mediterranean ethos, but he argues—and it is here where he follows Braudel and Horden and Purcell—that for comparative purposes, it "makes good aprioristic sense" to compare across regions with "a shared ecology" and thus "to privilege Mediterranean ethnography" over other possible comparative models from very different contexts.[101]

Analyzing ideals of social organization in ancient and late antique Judaean writings through the lens of a Mediterraneanist ideal type, Schwartz offers a promising approach to link Jewish and Mediterranean studies: moving beyond Horden and Purcell's distinction of history *in* and *of* the Mediterranean, he is thinking *with* the Mediterranean, much as Kinoshita suggests we do.[102] Thinking *with* the Mediterranean makes it possible to treat the "great sea" not merely as an accidental context, a geographic space within which we can describe this or that Jewish community. Nor does it suggest that the particular ecology of the Mediterranean determines culture and social practice, in which case Jewish history could at best be illustrative of larger patterns of production and redistribution predicated on a particularly Mediterranean "fragmentation-plus-connectivity."[103] Instead, as Schwartz formulates it so compellingly here, we are "left to steer a course between the antimaterialist Foucauldian scheme in which discourse and *episteme* have unconstrained agency and ultramaterialist globalism in which the great patterns formed by the circulation of stuff are all that matter."[104]

Thinking *with* the Mediterranean thus allows scholars to reassert the historical specificity of the space in question, something that can be lost when the Mediterranean comes to denote a pattern of production and redistribution, or an ideal type of social organization. One Mediterraneanist, for example, has identified patterns of Mediterranean connectivity everywhere from the "neighboring Mediterranean" of the Sahara to the "Mediterranean of the North" (i.e., the North Sea and Baltic) and the "trans-Oceanic Mediterranean" (i.e., the Caribbean).[105] As useful as this kind of comparative approach might be, it ultimately fails to account for historical contingency and human agency. Once everything can be "Mediterranean," nothing really is.[106]

In the context of this volume, most of which focuses on the late medieval to the modern period, the Mediterranean emerges as a unique geography linking Jews, Christians, and Muslims. Thinking *with* the Mediterranean further invites a return to a more human scale, one in which individual actors take center stage. Yet moving away from studying Jews *of* the Mediterranean does not mean resigning oneself to merely telling the histories of people—Jewish and non-Jewish—who happened to live *in* the Mediterranean. Rather, Schwartz and the other contributors to this volume think about Jews *with* the Mediterranean—using the historiographical debates of Mediterranean studies to frame new approaches to the study of Jews. Two common themes emerge in the essays that follow: First, a number of contributions use their analysis of Jews to critique the emphasis on cosmopolitanism, fluidity, and hybridity in the Mediterranean. Second, many of the essays draw our attention to the question of Jewish distinctiveness in the context of the Mediterranean and beyond.

The study of Jews is particularly well suited to rethinking the purported fluidity and hybridity of identity, religion, and culture in the Mediterranean. As we have seen, many scholars have replaced Mediterranean essentialism—either Braudelian or anthropological—with an insistence on the Middle Sea as a space of religious and cultural cosmopolitanism. In response to this "hybrid" turn in Mediterranean studies, a number of essays in this volume argue that studying Jews refocuses our attention on the importance of religious boundaries, the preeminence of intrareligious ties over interreligious ones, and the limits of hybridity. They thus understand Jews as an example of what Natalie Rothman has described as "the medieval and early modern Mediterranean colonies [which] served as important laboratories for the elaboration of ethnic difference."[107] Challenging the conventional distinction between the medieval/early modern versus the modern Mediterranean, moreover, several chapters pursue this idea into the modern period as well.

The chapters that follow acknowledge the existence of networks that transcend religion. Yet many argue that such examples of "cosmopolitanism" must not overshadow the importance that both Jews and non-Jews attributed to religious difference. Jonathan Ray's discussion of Sephardic Jews in the medieval and early modern Mediterranean emphasizes that the vast majority of Jews lived most of their lives privileging their ties with other Jews. Ray suggests replacing hybridity with pluralism, which he argues is a more apt reflection of Jews' experience in the Mediterranean. He notes that even if a handful of elites found themselves deeply influenced by the culture of surrounding societies, the vast majority of Jews remained primarily identified with a single religious tradition—albeit one embedded in a plurality of other religions and cultures.

Moving forward a few centuries, Francesca Bregoli shows that even transnational Jewish merchants—so famous for their supposed cosmopolitanism—relied heavily on their close relationships with other Jews. Bregoli emphasizes the importance of intra-Jewish networks by analyzing letters sent among members of the Franchetti family, Italian merchants based in Tunis with agents stationed across the Mediterranean. Even if the Franchettis undoubtedly cultivated relationships with non-Jews and moved among a number of major cities, "this alleged 'cosmopolitanism' seems to have gone hand in hand with a strategic reliance on intra-Jewish ties and did not exclude deep mistrust of life in strange lands and fear of too close contacts with non-Jews, especially Christians."[108] For many Jews in the Mediterranean, these essays suggest, interreligious and cross-cultural connections did not outweigh their primary ties to fellow Jews.

Moreover, the preeminence of intra-Jewish ties persisted well into the modern period. Devi Mays's analysis of *Le Guide Sam*, a commercial guide to the Mediterranean published during the 1920s and 1930s, underscores a particularly Jewish vision of the interwar Mediterranean. Despite advertising itself as a general guide to "the Orient," the pages of the guides were filled almost exclusively with the names and contact information of Sephardic Jews. As Mays points out, "the underlying Jewishness of *Le Guide Sam* prompts us to rethink prevalent scholarly approaches to the modern Mediterranean, which often emphasize the cosmopolitanism or inter-religious nature of the region."[109]

The preeminence of intrareligious relationships suggests a deceptively simple observation about the Mediterranean: religion mattered. The myriad connections across cultures and religions did not reduce the importance of religious affiliation; on the contrary, if anything, such intercultural ties increased the significance of religious difference. In his discussion of the role of Jews in the seventeenth-century Mediterranean slave trade, Daniel Hershenzon shows that the religious affiliation of slaves, privateers, and ransomers determined the nature of slavery and captivity. Slaves were captured because of their religious alterity, and the rules governing who could own which slaves were based on religious identity. Thus "the possession and exchange of slaves [was] an important medium for the articulation and reconstitution of religious difference."[110]

Religious difference did not escape state authorities either. Corey Tazzara's discussion of religious tolerance and commerce in early modern Livorno emphasizes the state's insistence on firm interreligious boundaries. Despite being famous for issuing the Livornine edicts inviting Jews to settle in Livorno (and even allowing converts to revert from Catholicism to Judaism), the Medicis went to great lengths to prevent Catholics from mixing with Jews or other religious minorities. Comparing the Livornese model of toleration to the situation in the Ottoman Empire, Tazzara notes that it is impossible to speak of a particularly "Mediterranean" approach to religious diversity on the part of early modern governments: "There was no single Mediterranean model of *convivencia*."[111]

Despite the importance of barriers between religious groups, a number of contributors warn us against assuming the existence of a natural solidarity among all Jews in the Mediterranean. As Bregoli puts it, "intra-Jewish ties were essential, but they did not imply automatic cohesion or trust within the network."[112] Bregoli demonstrates that building this trust was hard work and relied in large part on Jewish ritual observance. The Franchetti patriarch exhorted his sons to display their adherence to Jewish practice in order to secure their reputation as good Jews and, therefore, as honest merchants. Ray points out that in addition to providing opportunities for transnational ties, the Sephardic diaspora created serious challenges among different kinds of Jews—often manifested in legal debates. Rather than presume a pan-Mediterranean Jewish unity, he encourages scholars to investigate "the interplay between long-distance networks and the power dynamics of local Jewish communities."[113] The particularities of Jews' experience in the Mediterranean was due not to their inherent commonality but rather to the ways in which different communities of Jews navigated the tension between local practices and translocal ties.

One might assume that the rise of Jewish nationalism in the late nineteenth and early twentieth centuries offered a way for Jews in the Mediterranean to transcend their differences. Zionism presented a form of common identity for many Jews who were otherwise divided by language, culture, and even ritual practice. Yet not everyone abandoned the significant differences among Jews in the Mediterranean for Zionism's pan-Jewish vision. As Mays shows, the *Guide Sam* insisted on the existence of concrete and even racial differences between Sephardic and Ashkenazi Jews in Palestine and beyond. "One of Zionism's key flaws, Lévy asserted, was the attempt to 'mix all these Jews in the same basket.'"[114] Sam Lévy's vision of trans-Mediterranean Jewish ties assumed the specificity of Sephardic identity. Even if many Jews in the Mediterranean relied mainly—if not exclusively—on intra-Jewish networks, such ties did not mean that all Jews got along seamlessly just because they were Jews.

While the Mediterranean was undoubtedly a privileged place of encounter among Jews, Christians, and Muslims, these interreligious relationships developed in the context of firm differences between religious groups. Nor did they displace the importance of intra-Jewish ties. The contributions to this volume suggest that focusing on Jews requires us to question the emphasis on fluidity and cosmopolitanism that has been prevalent among some scholars of Mediterranean studies. Ray's model emphasizing Mediterranean pluralism instead of hybridity might better reflect the multiplicity of religious and cultural identities in the Middle Sea without denying the importance of intrareligious networks and the maintenance of religious difference.

Thinking *with* the Mediterranean also makes us look differently at Jews, particularly by offering new perspectives on the age-old conundrum of Jewish distinctiveness. The questions Goitein asked about the genizah—whether its documents offered a narrow reflection of the Jewish societies from which they emerged or a broader portrait of a Mediterranean society that transcended religion—apply equally to subsequent periods. As Ray suggests, the history of Jews in the Mediterranean "must be read with and against studies that elucidate the uniqueness of the Jewish experience."[115] How different were the trajectories of Jews from those of other religious minorities—or indeed the majority population—and in what ways? What distinguished intra-Jewish networks from other intra- or interreligious ties? The essays in this volume engage with these questions, though by no means all conclude that Jews were unique. On the contrary, the extent to which Jews differed from their Christian and Muslim counterparts varied considerably across space and time.

A number of contributors remind us that it is precisely Judaism—and more specifically, religious observance—that made Jews' experience distinctive in the Mediterranean. Andrew Berns discerns a uniquely Jewish geography of the Mediterranean in medieval and early modern rabbinic legal texts concerning the commandment against wearing *sha'atenez*, a garment sewn with linen and wool. This supremely particularistic law reveals Jews' understanding of climatic differences among regions. Ultramontane European Jews developed a distinctive approach to the observance of *sha'atenez* from those of their coreligionists on the Mediterranean littoral based on the prevalence of certain types of vegetation. Even if most scholars have rejected the environmental unity of Braudel's Mediterranean, Berns shows that Jews' religious observance could in fact produce a distinctively Jewish Mediterranean geography.

In many ways, Jews were distinct from other religious minorities in the western Mediterranean. Hershenzon points out that Jews' participation in the slave trade was directly shaped by their status as religious others both in Spain and in North Africa. Christian and Muslim sovereigns relied on Jews to ransom slaves precisely because of their inherent alterity; North African Sephardic Jews were familiar with both Spanish and Maghribi culture, and yet their religious affiliation did not match either one. Because Jews did not share a religious persuasion with any of the political entities involved in the capture and ransoming of slaves, they served as a kind of neutral party. It was thus in large part their Jewishness that determined Jews' usefulness to rulers on both sides of the Mediterranean. Tazzara, meanwhile, shows that whereas Jews represented only one among a number of non-Catholic groups who had to be accommodated and regulated in the free port of Livorno, they also occupied a "privileged place... in the Catholic imagination."[116] Although the Livornine eventually applied to all non-Catholics, "forty-one of the patent's forty-four articles were pledges to Jewish immigrants."[117]

On the other hand, Constanze Kolbe's study of Jewish merchants in nineteenth-century Corfu argues that Jewishness had little to do with the short-distance trade networks that characterized this part of the Adriatic. Jewish merchants partnered with Christians and Muslims, as well as other Jews, to take advantage of the flexible borders between Corfu, the Ottoman Empire, and the new state of Montenegro. More than a common religion, "the post-Venetian heritage and the continued importance of Italian as the language of the market both in Corfu and northern Albania set the background against which trade flourished."[118] The kind of short-distance trade that characterized this microregion depended on "Jews, but not 'Jewishness'"[119]—a distinction that could easily apply to a number of studies of Jews in the Mediterranean.

Some of the essays presented here reflect the recent "economic turn" in Jewish history and focus on commerce and the circulation of stuff.[120] This is not to say, however, that they privilege a "materialist" over a cultural-discursive analysis. The commercial histories told in the chapters by Bregoli and Kolbe, for example, present culturally embedded narratives that posit the Jewishness of the economic networks that they explore as a central question, though they arrive at rather different conclusions. As they demonstrate, Jewish as well as interethnic commercial networks crisscrossing various subregions within the Mediterranean might emerge as a function of a particular commodity or be established on the basis of kinship. Religious identity mattered, but it was not predictive of the networks that Jews and others created.

Clémence Boulouque, finally, turns our attention to the existence of a discursive Jewish Mediterranean. Following Michael Herzfeld's argument that the Mediterranean exists as a discursive construct, Boulouque traces the emergence of various myths of the Jewish Mediterranean. In the second half of the twentieth century, Jewish authors began constructing an image of their lives in the Mediterranean that was saturated with loss. They thus turned "the Jewish Mediterranean into a nexus of nostalgia."[121] Though related to the narratives about Jews' symbiotic coexistence with Muslims and Christians in the Mediterranean—particularly the myth of a golden age of *convivencia* in medieval Iberia—the modern myth of a Jewish Mediterranean emerges from the imperial context of the early twentieth century. Even as Jews have ceased to live in most parts of the Mediterranean, they have left behind a discursive Mediterranean that is, perhaps, even more real than any historical Jewish Mediterranean could be. As the writer Albert Cohen put it, the Mediterranean existed in the minds of the Jews who inhabited its shores: "If I was by the sea, I was sure that the Mediterranean before me was also inside my head—not a picture of the Mediterranean but the Mediterranean itself, minute and salty inside my head, in miniature but real."[122]

The search for a "real" Mediterranean—Jewish or otherwise—is not, of course, the goal of this volume. Perhaps the only real Mediterranean is the discursive one suggested by Herzfeld and evoked by Jewish authors born on the shores of the Middle Sea. In bringing together essays on the Jewish experience that think with the Mediterranean, we seek not to determine some essential Jewish Mediterranean. On the contrary, the essays in this volume emphasize that there was no single Jewish experience of the Mediterranean. While in some cases, Jews' distinctiveness led them to construct particularly Jewish spaces or networks, in others their religious identity mattered little in shaping their encounters with Jews and non-Jews. Nor was there a typical "Mediterranean" Jew; the essays in this volume call into question the tropes of Jewish history thought to epitomize the Mediterranean, such as hybridity, cosmopolitanism, and symbiosis. These case studies instead emphasize the primacy of religious and cultural difference, made only more important in the multiplicity and diversity of the Mediterranean context. The point of this volume is not to identify the "real" Mediterranean. Rather, it seeks to demonstrate that for historians of Jews, the Mediterranean is still useful to think with.

JESSICA M. MARGLIN is Associate Professor of Religion and Law at the University of Southern California, where she holds the Ruth Ziegler Early Career Chair in Jewish Studies. She earned her PhD from Princeton and her BA and MA from Harvard. Her book, *Across Legal Lines: Jews and Muslims in Modern Morocco*, was published by Yale University Press in 2016.

MATTHIAS LEHMANN is Professor of History at the University of California, Irvine, where he holds the Teller Family Chair in Jewish History. His publications include *Ladino Rabbinic Literature and Ottoman Sephardic Culture* (Indiana University Press, 2005), *Emissaries from the Holy Land* (Stanford University Press, 2014), and as coauthor with John Efron and Steve Weitzman, *The Jews: A History*, 3rd ed. (New York and London: Routledge, 2019).

Notes

1. The "Mediterranean region" (rather than the Mediterranean as a body of water) is "a conception the world owes to [Theobald] Fischer," as the 1922 edition of the *Encyclopaedia Britannica* noted: *Encyclopaedia Britannica*, 12th edition (London: The Encyclopaedia

Britannica Company, 1922): vol. 31, 75. Theobald Fischer's publications included *Beiträge zur physischen Geographie der Mittelmeerländer* (Leipzig: Fues, 1877); *Der Ölbaum: Seine geographische Verbreitung, seine wirtschaftliche und kulturhistorische Bedeutung* (Gotha: Justus Perthes, 1904); *Mittelmeerbilder: Gesammelte Abhandlungen zur Kunde der Mittelmeerländer* (Leipzig: Tuebner, 1908); "The Mediterranean Peoples," *Smithsonian Institution Annual Report* 1907: 497–521.

2. Fischer, "The Mediterranean Peoples," 519.

3. See, for example, the critical appraisal of the field by Molly Greene, "The Mediterranean Sea," in *Oceanic Histories*, ed. David Armitage, Alison Bashford, and Sujit Sivasundaram (Cambridge: Cambridge University Press, 2018), 134–55; see also Judith E. Tucker, "Introduction," in Judith E. Tucker, ed., *The Making of the Modern Mediterranean: Views from the South* (Berkeley: University of California Press, 2019), 1–15.

4. Fischer, "The Mediterranean Peoples," 497.

5. Fischer, *Mittelmeerbilder*, 399. This is the only reference to Jews in the volume.

6. The difference in large part between Mediterranean and Middle East studies has to do with the history of these respective pursuits, particularly of their funding; Middle East studies (like Slavic, East Asian, and Latin American studies programs) has its roots in regional politics—particularly the interests of the American government during the Cold War; on this history, see Zachary Lockman, *The Making of Middle East Studies in the United States* (Stanford, CA: Stanford University Press, 2016). Mediterranean studies, by contrast, never received such extensive funding and did not lead to the constitution of departments or centers in universities.

7. Peregrine Horden, "Introduction," in *A Companion to Mediterranean History*, ed. Peregrine Horden and Sharon Kinoshita (Chichester, UK: Wiley Blackwell, 2014), 1–7, at 4. A recent useful overview of Mediterranean historiography can be found in Greene, "Mediterranean."

8. Peregrine Horden and Nicholas Purcell, "The Mediterranean and the 'New Thalassology,'" *The American Historical Review* 111, no. 3 (2006): 722–40, at 730; Horden, "Introduction," 4. The exception is the study of the Roman Empire, which did, in fact, expand across most of the Mediterranean.

9. Any attempt to define a "canon" of Mediterranean studies might be considered by some as incomplete. We exclude books that cover the entire geographical scope of the Mediterranean but that are rarely cited as methodological or analytical models, such as John Julius Norwich, *The Middle Sea: A History of the Mediterranean* (New York: Vintage, 2007). David Abulafia, *The Great Sea: A Human History of the Mediterranean* (New York: Oxford University Press, 2011), discussed below, is often cited as an important chronological account of Mediterranean history but has not been particularly influential as a methodological or analytical approach. Horden and Purcell identify the work of Mikhail Rostovtzeff, a historian of ancient Greece and Rome whose first influential book, *The Social and Economic History of the Roman Empire*, was published in 1926, as among the "most influential figures in the twentieth-century historiography of the Mediterranean" (Peregrine Horden and Nicholas Purcell, *The Corrupting Sea: A Study of Mediterranean History* [Oxford: Blackwell, 2000], 31). But this book rarely appears in the studies of postclassical Mediterranean history and thus is omitted from our discussion.

10. See, for example, the work of Sharon Kinoshita, Michael Herzfeld, and Naor Ben-Yehoyada, to name just a few.

11. Henri Pirenne, *Mahomet et Charlemagne* (Paris: Félix Alcan, 1937); Henri Pirenne, *Mohammed and Charlemagne* (London: Allen and Unwin, 1939).

12. Pirenne, *Mohammed and Charlemagne*, 166.

13. Peter Brown, "'Mohammed and Charlemagne' by Henri Pirenne," *Daedalus* 103, no. 1 (1974): 27.

14. As opposed to Christians and Muslims, who together shaped the destiny of western Europe, Jews merely continued "hawking articles of value of Eastern origin" despite the death of international trade (Pirenne, *Mohammed and Charlemagne*, 250).

15. Pirenne notes that Marseille was "a cosmopolitan city" (Ibid., 95), although he does not, in fact, use this word to describe the Mediterranean more broadly. Pirenne noted that both Syrians and Jews were found in all the cities of the ancient Mediterranean and that together they provided "the Oriental influence which made itself felt at the same period in the art and the religious thought of the period" (19; see also 82, 96, 103).

16. Ibid., 174, 250, 255.

17. "The intermediary was no longer the sea but Spain; and through Spain the Jews were in touch with the powers of Musulman Africa and Baghdad" (Ibid., 258).

18. Ibid., 255.

19. Ibid., 85. See also 99, 115. Werner Sombart was particularly influential in associating Jews with capitalism and moneylending: Werner Sombart, *Die Juden und das Wirtschaftsleben* (Leipzig: Duncker, 1911), esp. 192–93.

20. Sombart, *Die Juden und das Wirtschaftsleben*. Sombart's study was in large part a response to Weber's *The Protestant Ethic and the Spirit of Capitalism* (first published in 1905), but it also reflected antisemitic stereotypes current at the time. Toni Oelsner, "The Place of Jews in Economic History as Viewed by German Scholars," *The Leo Baeck Institute Year Book* 7 (1962): 183–212.

21. Oelsner, "Jews in Economic History"; Michael Toch, "Jews and Commerce: Modern Fancies and Medieval Realities," in *Il ruolo economico delle minoranze in Europa, secc. XIII-XVIII*, ed. Simonetta Cavaciocchi (Florence: Le Monnier, 2000), 43–58; Michael Toch, "The Jews in Europe, 500–1050," in *The New Cambridge Medieval History*, ed. P. Fouracre (Cambridge: Cambridge University Press, 2005), 555–59. For an updated economic history of this period that does not consider Jews solely in their roles as merchants or slave traders, see Michael McCormick, *Origins of the European Economy: Communications and Commerce, A.D. 300–900* (Cambridge: Cambridge University Press, 2001).

22. Fernand Braudel, *La Méditerranée et le monde méditerranéen à l'époque de Philippe II* (Paris: Colin, 1949). A second, heavily revised edition was published by the same press in 1966 and was translated into English as *The Mediterranean and the Mediterranean World in the Age of Philip II* (London: Collins, 1972).

23. Fernand Braudel, "Personal Testimony," *The Journal of Modern History* 44, no. 4 (1972): 448–67, at 450.

24. Ibid., 452. Both Pirenne and Braudel did much of their thinking about the Mediterranean in German prison camps. Pirenne was a prisoner in Germany from 1916 until the end of World War I, and it was there that he "emphasized, for the first time, the close relation that existed between the conquests of Islam and the formation of the mediaeval Occident" (Jacques Pirenne, "Preface," in Pirenne, *Mohammed and Charlemagne*, 9). Braudel was a prisoner in 1940–1945, where he wrote the dissertation that became *The Mediterranean* (Braudel, "Personal Testimony," 453). It was, perhaps, in the midst of intense war among

European nation-states that these authors began to think about the Mediterranean as a trans- or supranational space.

25. Braudel, *The Mediterranean*, 20–21.

26. Ibid., 14.

27. Ibid., 803; David N. Myers, *Jewish History: A Very Short Introduction* (New York: Oxford University Press, 2017), xxiii.

28. The section on Jews is entitled "One Civilization against the Rest; The Destiny of the Jews" (Braudel, *The Mediterranean*, 802–26). Braudel's understanding of Judaism as a "civilization" is also apparent in his refusal to distinguish between practicing Jews on the one hand and Christians of Jewish descent on the other (that is, conversos or descendants of conversos)—a discussion that also only appears in the second edition: ibid., 640–42.

29. Ibid., 145, 629, 640–42, 726–28, 814–16, 820. This is similarly the case in the first edition: see, for example, Braudel, *La Méditerranée*, 113, 617–18, 898–99, 989. Curiously, the index of the English translation does not have an entry for Judaism (nor for Christianity, or Islam—though it does have one for Protestants); "Juifs" are listed in the index of the first edition but not, curiously, in that of the second (which does, however, have an entry for "Jewish merchants").

30. Braudel, *The Mediterranean*, 816. In her study of Sephardic merchants from Livorno in the eighteenth century, Trivellato argues that Livornese Jews relied heavily on extra-Jewish networks for their commercial success (Francesca Trivellato, *The Familiarity of Strangers: The Sephardic Diaspora, Livorno, and Cross-Cultural Trade in the Early Modern Period* [New Haven: Yale University Press, 2009]). For an example of scholarship that perpetuates this view of Jewish cosmopolitanism, see Yuri Slezkine, *The Jewish Century* (Princeton: Princeton University Press, 2006).

31. Braudel, *The Mediterranean*, 811. This characterization is not nearly as apparent in the first edition.

32. Ibid., 809.

33. Toch, "The Jews in Europe," 555.

34. Horden and Purcell, *The Corrupting Sea*, 1.

35. Ibid., 123.

36. Ibid., 5.

37. Ibid., 2.

38. Indeed, the index to *The Corrupting Sea* does not contain an entry for Judaism (although it does have ones for Christianity and Islam).

39. Ibid., 406. Their discussion does not, however, adequately address the question of what is uniquely Mediterranean about religion in the region; for a discussion of this, see Greg Woolf, "A Sea of Faith?" *Mediterranean Historical Review* 18, no. 2 (2003): 126–43, at 135.

40. Horden and Purcell, *The Corrupting Sea*, 407, 422, 446. There is a passing reference to the Talmud on p. 449, but not a discussion of Jews.

41. Ibid., 446. This focus is also made particularly clear on p. 457.

42. On Jewish pilgrimage, see, for example, Yoram Tsafrir, "Jewish Pilgrimage in the Roman and Byzantine Periods," in *Akten des XII. Internationalen Kongresses für Christliche Archäologie*, ed. E. Dassmann, K. Thraede, and J. Engemann (Münster: Aschendorffsche Verlagsbuchhandlung, 1995), 369–76; Issachar Ben-Ami, *Saint Veneration among the Jews in Morocco* (Detroit: Wayne State University Press, 1998); Josef W. Meri, *The Cult of Saints among Muslims and Jews in Medieval Syria* (Oxford: Oxford University Press, 2002).

Similarly, Horden and Purcell's work does not fully account for the Ottoman Empire's role in the Mediterranean; on this, see Tucker, "Introduction," 10.

43. This is evidenced in journals, articles, edited collections, and monographs; see, for example, Horden, "Introduction," 3.

44. Abulafia, *The Great Sea*, xxx. Abulafia already used the approach he takes in *The Great Sea* in an earlier edited volume: David Abulafia, ed. *The Mediterranean in History* (Los Angeles: J. Paul Getty Museum, 2003).

45. Indeed, he divides his book into five different "Mediterraneans," from antiquity to the present.

46. Abulafia, *The Great Sea*, xxv. Horden and Purcell were, in fact, referring to Abulafia's earlier edited volume, which applied the same arguments and methodology: Horden and Purcell, "The New Thalassology," 732.

47. See, for instance, his discussion of Jews in Ostia Antica (212) or of Zionism and the state of Israel (592–96, 616–20).

48. Fred Astren, "Jews," in *A Companion to Mediterranean History*, ed. Sharon Kinoshita and Peregrine Horden (Chichester, UK: Wiley Blackwell, 2014), 392–408.

49. See Michael Herzfeld, *Anthropology through the Looking Glass: Critical Ethnography in the Margins of Europe* (Cambridge: Cambridge University Press, 1984), 64. For a more detailed discussion, see Michael Herzfeld, "Practical Mediterraneanism; Excuses for Everything, from Epistemology to Eating," in *Rethinking the Mediterranean*, ed. W. V. Harris (Oxford: Oxford University Press, 2005), 45–63.

50. Ibid., 50.

51. See, for instance, Daniel J. Schroeter, "Orientalism and the Jews of the Mediterranean," *Journal of Mediterranean Studies* 4, no. 2 (1994): 183–96; Joëlle Bahloul, "The Sephardic Jew as Mediterranean: A View from Kinship and Gender," *Journal of Mediterranean Studies* 4, no. 2 (1994): 197–207.

52. Peregrine Horden, "The Maritime, the Ecological, the Cultural—and the Fig Leaf: Prospects for Medieval Mediterranean Studies," in *Can We Talk Mediterranean?*, ed. Brian A. Catlos and Sharon Kinoshita (London: Palgrave Macmillan, 2017), 65–79, at 72–76. For this approach, see also a number of chapters in Horden and Kinoshita's *A Companion to Mediterranean History*, especially Karla Mallette, "Lingua Franca"; Stephen Epstein, "Hybridity"; Brian Catlos, "Ethno-Religious Minorities"; and Maria Couroucli, "Shared Sacred Places." Brian Catlos and Sharon Kinoshita's Mediterranean Seminar, founded in 2007, has been particularly influential in nurturing this approach: see Brian A. Catlos and Sharon Kinoshita, eds., *Can We Talk Mediterranean?* (London: Palgrave Macmillan, 2017). See also Adnan A. Husain, "Introduction: Approaching Islam and the Religious Cultures of the Medieval and Early Modern Mediterranean," in *A Faithful Sea: The Religious Cultures of the Mediterranean, 1200–1700*, ed. Adnan A. Husain and K. E. Fleming (Oxford: Oneworld, 2007), 1–26, as well as the other chapters in this volume; Tijana Krstić, *Contested Conversions to Islam: Narratives of Religious Change in the Early Modern Ottoman Empire* (Stanford, CA: Stanford University Press, 2011).

53. See, for example, Michelle M. Hamilton and Núria Silleras-Fernández, "Iberia and the Mediterranean: An Introduction," in *In and Of the Mediterranean: Medieval and Early Modern Iberian Studies*, ed. Michelle M. Hamilton and Núria Silleras-Fernández (Nashville: Vanderbilt University Press, 2015), ix–xxvii, esp. xiv–xvi.

54. Américo Castro, *España en su historia : cristianos, moros, y judíos* (Buenos Aires: Losada, 1948); Brian Catlos, "Contexto social y 'conveniencia' en la Corona de Aragón.

Propuesta para un modelo de interacción entre grupos etno-religiosos minoritarios y mayoritarios," *Rivista d'Història Medieval* 12 (2002): 220–35.

55. Horden, "Introduction," 5. See, for example, Eric R. Dursteler, *Venetians in Constantinople: Nation, Identity, and Coexistence in the Early Modern Mediterranean* (Baltimore: Johns Hopkins University Press, 2006).

56. Brian A. Catlos, *Muslims of Medieval Latin Christendom, c. 1050–1614* (Cambridge: Cambridge University Press, 2014), 509.

57. Brian A. Catlos, "Why the Mediterranean?" in *Can We Talk Mediterranean?*, ed. Brian A. Catlos and Sharon Kinoshita (London: Palgrave Macmillan, 2017), 1–17, at 11.

58. See, for example, John George Péristiany, ed. *Honour and Shame: The Values of Mediterranean Society* (London: Weidenfeld and Nicolson, 1966). For a critique, see Horden and Purcell, *The Corrupting Sea*, 461–529; Naor Ben-Yehoyada, "Mediterranean Modernity?" in *A Companion to Mediterranean History*, ed. Sharon Kinoshita and Peregrine Horden (Chichester, UK: Wiley Blackwell, 2014), 107–21, at 110–13.

59. See, for example, Dursteler, *Venetians in Constantinople*, 18–19.

60. See, for example, Horden, "The Maritime," 73–76; Greene, "Mediterranean," 150.

61. Molly Greene, *A Shared World: Christians and Muslims in the Early Modern Mediterranean* (Princeton: Princeton University Press, 2000); Molly Greene, *Catholic Pirates and Greek Merchants: A Maritime History of the Mediterranean* (Princeton: Princeton University Press, 2010).

62. Natalie E. Rothman, *Brokering Empire: Trans-Imperial Subjects between Venice and Istanbul* (Ithaca, NY: Cornell University Press, 2011); Trivellato, *Familiarity of Strangers*. See also Hussein Fancy, *The Mercenary Mediterranean: Sovereignty, Religion, and Violence in the Medieval Crown of Aragon* (Chicago: University of Chicago Press, 2016). On this turn, see Greene, "Mediterranean," 149–52.

63. See, for example, Trivellato, *Familiarity of Strangers*, 50, 73.

64. See in particular Sharon Kinoshita, "Negotiating the Corrupting Sea: Literature in and of the Medieval Mediterranean," in *Can We Talk Mediterranean?*, ed. Brian A. Catlos and Sharon Kinoshita (London: Palgrave Macmillan, 2017), 33–47, at 46. Catlos makes a stronger claim for Mediterranean uniqueness: Catlos, "Why the Mediterranean?," 5–6.

65. Kinoshita, "Negotiating the Corrupting Sea," 46.

66. Catlos, "Why the Mediterranean?," 1.

67. Horden, "The Maritime," 71. See also Kinoshita's essay in the same volume.

68. S. D. Goitein, *A Mediterranean Society: The Jewish Communities of the Arab World as Portrayed in the Documents of the Cairo Geniza*, 5 vols. (Berkeley: University of California Press, 1967–1988). A cumulative index was published as S. D. Goitein and Paula Sanders, *A Mediterranean Society*, vol. 6 (Berkeley: University of California Press, 1993). The other three scholars mentioned by Horden and Purcell are Mikhail Rostovtzeff, Henri Pirenne, and Fernand Braudel. See Horden and Purcell, *The Corrupting Sea*, 31–39.

69. Fred Astren, "Goitein, Medieval Jews, and the 'New Mediterranean Studies,'" *Jewish Quarterly Review* 102, no. 4 (2012): 513–31, at 519.

70. Horden and Purcell, *The Corrupting Sea*, 35.

71. The story of Goitein and his complicated relation with the EPHE is told by Peter Miller, "Two Men in a Boat: The Braudel-Goitein 'Correspondence' and the Beginning of Thalassography," in *The Sea: Thalassography and Historiography*, ed. Peter Miller (Ann Arbor: University of Michigan Press, 2013), 27–59; and Peter Miller, "*From Spain to*

India becomes *A Mediterranean Society*: The Braudel-Goitein 'Correspondence' Part II," *Mitteilungen des kunsthistorischen Instituts in Florenz* 56, no. 1 (2014): 113–35.

72. Miller, "Two Men in a Boat," 28. Miller's ungenerous characterization of Goitein simply "curating individual documents" echoes a common critique of his work; Jacob Neusner, for example, called it "a work of description, not of analysis, let alone synthesis." As Jessica Goldberg points out, such a reading of Goitein misses that, in fact, "almost every sentence in the book is a miniature argument hidden as a statement of fact." See Jessica Goldberg, "On Reading Goitein's *A Mediterranean Society*: A View from Economic History," *Mediterranean Historical Review* 26, no. 2 (2011): 171–86, at 172–73. Peter Miller argues that the stakes were even higher and that, if it had not been for the "failed meeting of Braudel and Goitein," "one could envision a very different shape to both the Jerusalem School and to the Annales School." Ibid., 52.

73. Goitein, *Mediterranean Society*, vol. 1 (1967), 74.

74. Goitein, *Mediterranean Society*, vol. 5 (1988), v.

75. S. D. Goitein, *Studies in Islamic History and Institutions* (Leiden: Brill, 1968), 246.

76. Jessica Goldberg, *Trade and Institutions in the Medieval Mediterranean: The Geniza Merchants and Their Business World* (Cambridge: Cambridge University Press, 2012), 28. See Avner Greif, *Institutions and the Path to the Modern Economy: Lessons from Medieval Trade* (Cambridge: Cambridge University Press, 2006).

77. Goitein, *Mediterranean Society*, vol. 1, 66.

78. Ibid., 68.

79. That, of course, is the premise of Mark Cohen, himself a scholar of the Cairo genizah in what Phillip Lieberman dubs the "Princeton school" of genizah studies, in *Under Crescent and Cross: The Jews in the Middle Ages* (Princeton, NJ: Princeton University Press, 1994), especially chapters 3, 4, and 5. For Lieberman's discussion of the "Princeton school," see Phillip I. Ackerman-Liberman, *The Business of Identity: Jews, Muslims, and Economic Life in Medieval Egypt* (Stanford, CA: Stanford University Press, 2014), 27–41.

80. Astren, "Goitein, Medieval Jews, and the 'New Mediterranean Studies,'" 521.

81. Goitein, *Studies in Islamic History and Society*, 301.

82. Goitein, *Mediterranean Society*, vol. 1, 61 and passim.

83. Ibid., 42.

84. Ibid., 43.

85. Ibid., 69. Jessica Goldberg emphasizes this point: "while connections between Egypt and the distant west (Morocco and Spain) waxed and waned in the period 1000–1150, they were never common or humdrum." Goldberg, "On Reading Goitein's *A Mediterranean Society*," 176.

86. Goldberg, *Trade and Institutions in the Medieval Mediterranean*, 342–43.

87. Ibid., 28–29. Phillip Ackerman-Lieberman, *The Business of Identity*, likewise emphasizes the importance of taking the genizah merchants' Jewish identity seriously.

88. Joshua Holo, *Byzantine Jewry in the Mediterranean Economy* (Cambridge: Cambridge University Press, 2009).

89. Sarah Stroumsa, *Maimonides in His World: Portrait of a Mediterranean Thinker* (Princeton, NJ: Princeton University Press, 2009), 13–14. This is the emphasis in Mark Cohen's recent study of Maimonides in the context of medieval Islamic law and society: Mark R. Cohen, *Maimonides and the Merchants: Jewish Law and Society in the Medieval Islamic World* (Philadelphia: University of Pennsylvania Press, 2017).

90. Stroumsa, *Maimonides in His World*, 10.
91. Ibid., 23.
92. Ibid., 23.
93. Goitein, *Mediterranean Society*, vol. 1, 38. Holo's account of the Byzantine Jewish diaspora likewise ends with the Fourth Crusade and the sacking of Constantinople in 1204.
94. Lois Dubin, *The Port Jews of Habsburg Trieste: Absolutist Politics and Enlightenment Culture* (Stanford, CA: Stanford University Press, 1999); David Sorkin, "The Port Jew: Notes toward a Social Type," *Journal of Jewish Studies* 50 (1999): 87–97.
95. To cite just two important examples, see Jonathan Israel, *Diasporas within a Diaspora: Jews, Crypto-Jews and the World of Maritime Empires (1540–1740)* (Leiden: Brill, 2002); Richard Kagan and Philip Morgan, eds., *Atlantic Diasporas: Jews, Conversos, and Crypto-Jews in the Age of Mercantilism, 1500–1800* (Baltimore: Johns Hopkins University Press, 2009). For a renewed emphasis on the Mediterranean dimension of the early modern Sephardic diaspora see Jonathan Ray, *After Expulsion: 1492 and the Making of Sephardic Jewry* (New York: NYU Press, 2013). Other historians have focused on "connectivity" in early modern Jewish history, moving beyond specific countries or regions, but while much of their geographic emphasis may focus on the Mediterranean region, these studies are not framed analytically in Mediterraneanist terms. See, for example, David Ruderman, *Early Modern Jewry: A New Cultural History* (Princeton, NJ: Princeton University Press, 2010); Matthias Lehmann, *Emissaries from the Holy Land: The Sephardic Diaspora and the Practice of Pan-Judaism in the Eighteenth Century* (Stanford, CA: Stanford University Press, 2014).
96. The continued centrality of a national or imperial framework is already signaled in the titles of seminal studies such as Aron Rodrigue, *French Jews, Turkish Jews: the Alliance Israélite Universelle and the Politics of Jewish Schooling in Turkey, 1860–1925* (Bloomington: Indiana University Press, 1990); Lisa Moses Leff, *Sacred Bonds of Solidarity: The Rise of Jewish Internationalism in Nineteenth Century France* (Stanford, CA: Stanford University Press, 2006); Abigail Green, *Moses Montefiore: Jewish Liberator, Imperial Hero* (Cambridge, MA: Belknap, 2012).
97. See Alexandra Nocke, *The Place of the Mediterranean in Modern Israeli Identity* (Leiden: Brill, 2009).
98. Gideon Libson, "Hidden Worlds and Open Shutters: S. D. Goitein between Judaism and Islam," in *The Jewish Past Revisited*, ed. David Myers and David Ruderman (New Haven, CT: Yale University Press, 1998), 163–98; Steven Wasserstrom, "Apology for S. D. Goitein: An Essay," in *A Faithful Sea: The Religious Culture of the Mediterranean, 1200–1700*, ed. Adnan Husain and K. E. Fleming (Oxford: Oneworld, 2007), 173–98.
99. Elliott Horowitz, "Scholars of the Mediterranean and the Mediterranean of Scholars," *Jewish Quarterly Review* 102, no. 4 (2012): 477–90, at 489. See Seth Schwartz, *Were the Jews a Mediterranean Society? Reciprocity and Solidarity in Ancient Judaism* (Princeton, NJ: Princeton University Press, 2010).
100. This volume, 31; italics in the original.
101. Schwartz, *Were the Jews a Mediterranean Society?*, 25.
102. Kinoshita, "Negotiating the Corrupting Sea," 46.
103. For the phrase "fragmentation-plus-connectivity" as a summary of Horden and Purcell's approach, see Nicholas Purcell, "The Boundless Sea of Unlikeness? On Defining the Mediterranean," *Mediterranean Historical Review* 18, no. 2 (2003), 9–29, at 13.
104. This volume, 45.
105. David Abulafia, "Mediterraneans," in *Rethinking the Mediterranean*, ed. W. V. Harris (Oxford: Oxford University Press, 2005), 64–93.

106. The proliferation of "Mediterraneans" in this approach recalls Rogers Brubaker's critical analysis of the shifting (and inflationary) use of the term *diaspora*, which, as he argues, is applied so broadly that it is best understood not as describing a historically specific, bounded entity but rather as a "category of practice." Rogers Brubaker, "The 'Diaspora' Diaspora," *Ethnic and Racial Studies* 28 (2005): 1–19.

107. Rothman, *Brokering Empire*, 8.

108. This volume, 130.

109. This volume, 172.

110. This volume, 82. See also Daniel Hershenzon, "The Political Economy of Ransom in the Early Modern Mediterranean," *Past and Present* 231 (2016): 61–95.

111. This volume, 122.

112. This volume, 142.

113. This volume, 53.

114. This volume, 182.

115. This volume, 56.

116. This volume, 108.

117. This volume, 111.

118. This volume, 164.

119. This volume, 164.

120. On the economic turn in Jewish historiography, see, for example, Derek Penslar, *Shylock's Children: Economic and Jewish Identity in Modern Europe* (Berkeley: University of California Press, 2001); Jonathan Karp, *The Politics of Jewish Commerce: Economic Thought and Emancipation in Europe, 1638–1848* (Cambridge: Cambridge University Press, 2008); Sarah A. Stein, *Plumes: Ostrich Feathers, Jews, and a Lost World of Global Commerce* (New Haven, CT: Yale University Press, 2008); Trivellato, *The Familiarity of Strangers*; Jerry Muller, *Capitalism and the Jews* (Princeton: Princeton University Press, 2010); Gideon Reuveni, ed., *The Economy in Jewish History: New Perspectives on the Interrelationship between Ethnicity and Economic Life* (New York: Berghahn, 2011); Rebecca Kobrin, ed., *Chosen Capital: The Jewish Encounter with American Capitalism* (Bloomington: Indiana University Press, 2012); Rebecca Kobrin and Adam Teller, eds., *Purchasing Power: The Economics of Modern Jewish History* (Philadelphia: University of Pennsylvania Press, 2015); Eliyahu Stern, *Jewish Materialism: The Intellectual Revolution of the 1870s* (New Haven, CT: Yale University Press, 2018), and others.

121. This volume, 192.

122. Albert Cohen, *The Book of My Mother* (New York: Archipelago Books, 2012), 33.

1

GLOBALIZATION OR CULTURE

The Ancient Jews and the Mediterranean

Seth Schwartz

IAN MORRIS DESERVES CREDIT FOR NOTING THAT THE neo-Braudelian Mediterraneanism of the most influential and controversial book on the Mediterranean since Braudel, Peregrine Horden and Nicholas Purcell's *The Corrupting Sea*, owes something to its having been formulated in the era of globalization, just as its precursor among ancient historians in influence and controversy, Moses Finley's *The Ancient Economy*, can be read as a product of the age of the Cold War.[1] Horden and Purcell imagine a world in constant flux, in which objects and people pullulate ceaselessly, not simply along established and stable trade routes, à la Braudel, but "everywhere." Such boundaries—physical, political, and cultural—as existed were necessarily laboriously constructed, shifting, highly contingent, and porous. Contemplation of them helps us understand little about the people who lived around the sea. By contrast, Finley's world was characterized by staticity: people and objects stayed put because the effort and expense involved in mobility were too great for it to be a meaningful option. Most people in Finley's world necessarily lived lives shaped by primordial social institutions and fixed cultural identities. Morris's presentist reading of these classics (significantly, he attempted no such reading of Braudel), though reductive, helps us understand the enthusiastic reception of the books but also the resistance they encountered.

It is worth emphasizing that Morris's extrapolation from the two books of basic cultural histories of the region is essentially hypothetical. Neither Finley nor his antagonists wasted much ink on cultural history per se, though Finley to be sure relied on a theory—derived from Karl Polanyi but given heft by his juxtaposition of Polanyi's ideas with readings of classical texts[2]—about some of the cultural norms of a tiny segment of the Greco-Roman elites, imagined as unitary, hegemonic, and practically uncontested by the other inhabitants of his world ("the ancient world," whose boundaries are at least as vague as those of Braudel's Mediterranean world). I have discussed elsewhere the problems that Finley's cavalier treatment of such matters caused him (and have taken the further speculative step of trying to relate them to his struggles with his Jewishness).[3] Horden and Purcell's approach to culture requires a different sort of treatment, but it may be said that since both camps are trying to construct models of the behavior of goods in a large system (however squeamish Horden and Purcell may be about this), both tended to regard culture as more or less insignificant ornamentation on a structure whose weight is carried by the girders and beams of exchange and distribution of tangible *stuff*. To the extent that they deal with culture, they tend—in accordance with Morris's description—toward moderate structural determinism: the idea that culture is generated by and straightforwardly reflects socioeconomic structures.

Morris correctly objected to Horden and Purcell that their model fails precisely at the task historical models are supposed to perform: it gives us no sense of scale. For all their criticism of Braudel's impressionism, Horden and Purcell end up in the same trap, if anything, rather deeper in; imagining a world of "connectivity," they do not adequately address questions of its frequency and volume, its social and geographical penetration, its modulation over time. They do not, in sum, succeed in convincing us that "connectivity" is *meaningfully definitional* in/of the world of the Mediterranean, meaningful in the strong sense of trumping all other categories of analysis (as they would wish) as opposed to modestly supplementing them.

Nevertheless, it is reasonable to suppose that, at some periods, the Brownian motion of goods enabled correction of an economy characterized by chronic shortage. There is one proviso, though: the participants in this "connective" economy had to live close enough to navigable waterways, especially the coast of the sea, to make casual redistribution of this sort—whether it took the form of small-scale trade ("*cabotage*"), gift exchange, or piracy—productive. This is a simplification that errs in its excessive functionalism but perhaps not by *too* large a margin.

How did those living away from the shore cope with the chronic shortage that is the defining ecological constraint of so many areas in the Mediterranean basin? Would it not have been through highly localized and cellular redistribution, as Finley argues? There remains plenty of evidence that for casual exchange, even in the High Roman Empire, such cells tended to extend no more than twenty-five miles from a putative central point. On the other hand, there was a third economy in the Roman world, in addition to the connective economy of the immediate coast and the cellular economy of the hinterlands. This economy was generated not by agricultural shortage but by surplus: by state/elite demands for it in the form of taxes and rents, by rising populations whose upper strata consumed imported luxury goods that were arguably trivial as a percentage of the Roman economy as a whole but were significant in gross quantity. Under Roman rule, then, if not before, and not for many centuries after, there was a small, inchoate, but definitely extant globalizing economy overlaying and influencing the enduring, local, cellular, and "primitive" economy made famous by Finley. And this economy was focused on the coast and enabled by the sea and by its accessibility to other seas (the Black, the Atlantic, and the Indian Ocean by means of a difficult but in some periods domesticated route overland from the Nile Valley to the Red Sea).[4] Here it partly coexisted with and partly superseded the Purcellian economy of *cabotage*. But because it depended on the state's extraction of taxes and the elites' extraction of rents far from the sea, the proto-globalizing economy of the High Empire was more truly globalizing than that of the seacoast *caboteurs*. To sum up, we may—inspired by Finley, Horden and Purcell, and finally by Keith Hopkins[5]—posit, in a consciously reductive act of extreme schematization, three distinct but interdependent economies in the Roman world: the allegedly immemorial economy of *cabotage*, serving the redistributive needs of inhabitants of the narrow coastal strip—probably of little economic significance in the High Roman Empire but important as a vector for the circulation of goods and culture earlier and later;[6] the localized, cellular economies of the hinterlands away from the coasts and the major river valleys; and the proto-globalizing economy generated by state demands, the rise of an elite class requiring imported goods supplied by long-distance trade, and so on. In historical terms, needless to say, this last economy proved the most fragile.

Jews

Jews are, so far, missing in this account. Even before the discoveries of the Cairo genizah, Jews played a role in the historiography of the medieval counterpart of the globalizing, Mediterranean-focused economy just adumbrated. Furthermore, it would not have been hard even then—indeed, in the absence of the richly complex information the genizah provided, it was all too easy—to trace the diffusion of Jewish texts and norms along trade routes, initially from Iraq and Palestine across the Mediterranean and thence (shades of Braudel) across the Alps. The sketchy or fanciful narratives in medieval Jewish texts ("The Tale of the Four Captives" recorded in the *Sefer Ha-Qabalah* of Abraham ibn Daud; the story of the northward emigration of the Kalonymids from Italy; the westward journey of Aaron of Baghdad, recounted in *Megillat Ahima'az*) provided some apparent evidence.[7] Furthermore, somewhat later, the pervasiveness of Jewish networks, necessarily integrated to some extent into their host societies, played some role in the development of mercantilism and of late medieval–early modern proto-capitalism, apart from the fact that in the Middle Ages and later, Jews often served as vectors for the circulation not just of stuff and capital but also of ideas and practices, even of food habits, in the expanded Braudelian Mediterranean (matters perhaps changed only when in the course of the seventeenth century the demographic center of gravity shifted from Venice/Salonika/Istanbul, with northern and western extensions, to Amsterdam, Prague, Krakow, and points north and east).[8]

For Roman antiquity, by contrast, we have very little information about the participation of Jews in the proto-global economy, though that does not mean there was none, notwithstanding Josephus's claim that the Jews, in contrast to the Greeks, were an inland people averse to trade (*Against Apion* 1.60). Some of the preconditions for a role in quasi-globalizing trade surely existed: as in the Middle Ages, the presence of a large (though unknown) number of Jews in Mesopotamia and the well-attested mobility of Jews between Mesopotamia and the west could have created the firm foundation for a prominent Jewish role in trade between the Roman and Parthian Empires and points farther east. For a time under the Julio-Claudians (reigned 27 BCE–68 CE), the highest-ranking trade official in Egypt was Alexander, brother of the Jewish philosopher and essayist Philo of Alexandria, who may have supervised, among other things, trade between the Roman Empire and the Persian Gulf/Indian Ocean.[9] Prominent Jews in Palestine (members of the Herodian family) and Egypt (again, we know only about Philo's family) during the early empire were well-enough connected in the Roman metropolis to have access to large quantities of credit and capital on demand (Josephus, *Antiquities* 18.159–60; 165). Yet it seems overwhelmingly likely that such participation in the Roman version of the globalizing economy was the province of only a tiny handful of Jewish individuals—members of the two intermarried families of Philo and the Herodians, both of which included members whose ties to Judaism lapsed as they were incorporated into the general Roman aristocracy—and then only before the period of the Jewish revolts (66–135 CE); after these revolts, it is only in the fourth century that we hear again of Jews rich enough to be involved.[10] But by then the Roman economy was shrinking and retreating—deglobalizing. In the interim (135–350 CE), we know of not a single Jew who possessed senatorial or equestrian wealth (a minimum of 600,000 sesterces). We have no way of knowing how many possessed curial wealth (150,000). Membership in one of the elite classes—the top 1 percent of the Roman Empire—was presumably a precondition for participation in the globalizing economy, which few Jews seem to have met.[11]

By contrast, despite what we can speculate was some sense of group solidarity, we cannot by any means be certain that Jews in the early empire in

Palestine, Syria, Asia Minor, Greece, Libya, and Italy enjoyed meaningful internal economic and social integration, beyond the fact that before 70 CE some sent or brought money or goods to Jerusalem.[12] Communal expenditure, to extrapolate from the exiguous shreds of surviving evidence, was overwhelmingly local, and no translocal institutions existed to foster Jewish trade, as far as we are aware. One of the main contributors to the mobility that was the foundation of later medieval and early modern Jewish integration—the wave of expulsions that began in England before 1290 and ended only in the eighteenth century—was not a factor in antiquity. To be sure, there was a vaguely comparable period, between the outbreak of the first Jewish revolt and the quelling of the last (66–135 CE), but the conditions under which Jews were transported from, or fled, Palestine, Egypt, Libya, and elsewhere in that period (often as slaves) may not have favored the creation or persistence of economic ties between the *disjecta membra*.

Furthermore, Jews in the pagan, and even for the most part in the Christian, Roman Empire were not forced into dealing with capital, as in medieval and early modern Europe, and could own land or work land owned by others without restriction, an important brake on their mobility and their creation of significant intercommunal ties. The only places where we have fairly decent evidence about Jewish occupations are Palestine and the Egyptian countryside (but not Alexandria); Jews were mostly farmers. They were not all ipso facto capital-poor and so are as likely to have consumed luxuries and engaged in some commerce as any other agrarian subjects of Rome, but they had no special connection to the globalizing economy nor any unusual external pressures casting them off their land and into the world of local small-scale finance, as in early modernity. Our truly paltry evidence for the occupations of town-dwelling Jewish residents of Syria, Asia, Greece, Italy, and so on suggests that few even of these Jews were plugged in to translocal networks; they were artisans, shopkeepers, small traders—thus, embedded in local cellular economies.

All this said, there is some evidence for some limited flow of items, not only from a Judaean center toward a diasporic periphery nor from the periphery to the center (primarily before the year 70) but also within diasporic networks; by late antiquity, Jewish communal life was assuming a standardized form almost certainly due in part to its spread through such networks (which encompassed Jews who continued to live in northern and coastal Palestine)—centered on the synagogue and on a presumably increasingly standardized text of the Greek Bible, adopted by Christian communities, too, among other things. A shift to Hebrew began at the transition to the Middle Ages. The fact that the process of communal standardization took centuries (from about 300 to perhaps 700) argues that the flow of ideas through the networks was exceedingly slow and irregular and thus that the "networks" were so flaccid that network theory may not constitute a particularly useful way to approach the phenomenon.[13]

"Mediterranean Culture"

If we cannot think of Jews as meaningful participants in an ancient Mediterranean economy of whatever scale, either because they weren't or because we lack sufficient information—and conversely, cannot make much use of models of the Mediterranean economy to make sense of ancient Jewish history—then can ancient Jews contribute at all to a "Mediterraneanist" project?

As every reader of this volume can see, "Mediterranean history," in more or less theorized forms, chugs on, a beneficiary of globalization, as noted above, and of a concomitant interest in a revived network theory (not to mention the attractions of doing one's research in Italy or Spain, to name two items on an unfortunately shrinking list). Mediterranean anthropology, by contrast, seems well past its prime except in some of the less enlightened corners of religious studies. To extrapolate from a brief search on JSTOR—confirming what anyone familiar with the topic would have guessed—the field was in steep decline by 1990. One could even argue that the search for meaningful and definitive cultural continuities across the region was stillborn; the classic early treatments, which generated the short-lived industry, for example the volume edited by John G. Peristiany or John Davis's book on Pisticci, never seriously argue that the Mediterranean basin constituted a single distinctive cultural zone, despite their titles.[14] Their enthusiastic epigones briefly promoted this idea, and Michael Herzfeld among others soon crushed it, though it should be noted that the idea that the Mediterranean basin might indeed have constituted one or, more likely, two or more fuzzy and loosely organized cultural zones in some periods is not necessarily invalid; it simply lacks utility as an interpretive tool.[15]

Nevertheless, I have argued that it is precisely anthropology—including but not limited to Mediterranean anthropology—and not Mediterranean history that can help us make sense of the ancient Jews. This is so in several ways. Notwithstanding Herzfeld's strictures, there may be some occasional and local utility in citing cases from Mediterranean ethnography for the sake of comparison.[16] For example, I found it illuminating to learn from John Davis about land tenure patterns in mid-twentieth-century rural southern Italy because careful consideration of them tended to problematize the simplistic assertions of Bible and rabbinics scholars of social historical bent about land tenure patterns in the similar ecologies of ancient Palestine. The patchwork patterns of southern Italy; the complexity and improvisational quality of personal landholding arrangements that entailed individuals being simultaneously owners, renters, seasonal laborers, and shopkeepers; and the fact that plots of land constantly changed hands—a situation to some extent dictated by environmental constraints—cannot, to be sure, simply be translated to ancient Palestine. Nevertheless, Davis's account does provide us with a salutary warning about what the spotty and often idealizing ancient literary evidence may fail to tell us. I might as well have learned the same lesson from an ethnography of rural India, but there is something to be said for drawing one's comparisons from places with similar ecologies and geographies, even if one does not automatically believe in the pervasive significance of the *longue durée*. This is particularly true in the environmentally constrained case of land tenure. In sum, Mediterranean ethnographic comparison may be sporadically useful especially when it introduces skepticism and complexity in a field that otherwise tends, in the hands of some of its practitioners, to positivism and unselfconscious simplification. Ethnographic comparison should be welcomed provided it blocks facile synthesis.

Redistributive Institutions

Chronologically and logically prior to my dip into Mediterranean ethnography came my immersion in a certain mode of social history. This brings us back to Finley, because I wished to write for the ancient Jews the type of social and economic history I learned about in the intellectual environment of late-twentieth-century Cambridge, suffused as it was with post-Marxism, Weber, the ethos of the "Past & Present School," and structural functionalist social theory; mediated through Keith Hopkins in my immediate environment; and still strongly influenced by the recently deceased Sir Moses Finley. (Post-structuralism, by contrast, was of peripheral importance except among a small group of classicists.) I wished to write about the sorts of social—not religious—institutions that bound ancient Jewish society. My first, juvenile, attempt was inspired not by Mediterranean ethnography but by a controversial account of life in a twentieth-century village in northern China.[17]

But I subsequently came to grasp that there was remarkably little evidence in Jewish texts for the existence of such institutions; even an ostensibly descriptive writer like Josephus barely noticed them and provided little more than sporadic hints of their existence (which I and a few others mined, to be sure).[18] In light of the perspicuity of such institutions in the Hellenistic and Roman worlds more generally, their invisibility—almost never noted by modern Jewish historians and literary scholars because they are so often mired in internalism—suddenly struck me as glaringly problematic. As Horden and Purcell noted, the dry-farming economies of the Mediterranean basin were fragile; self-sufficiency may have been an ideal for some of the inhabitants of the region, but it was rarely attainable, at any rate not consistently. In the Hebrew Bible it is represented as a state the Israelites achieved only on those infrequent occasions when they collectively heeded divine commands. This was, then, an economy of shortage, and those who lived in its grip needed compensatory strategies. Purcellian connectivity, as we have seen, has many shortcomings as an explanatory tool. Among them is vagueness, since connectivity covers a great range of social practices. But we can infer some specificities from historical evidence. Redistribution within clan structures is one possibility; in some premodern societies, wherever they may be situated, it is often the most important. How important it was for the ancient Jews was a question I did not address and still cannot answer. Martin Goodman may conceivably have been right to argue that it was of declining importance in the later Hellenistic and Roman periods.[19] On the other hand, the silence of the sources is not probative, and the issue needs to be reexamined.

For the Hellenistic world and earlier, we know a great deal about the importance of formal friendships in the creation and maintenance of redistributive networks, and in the Roman world, about the importance of patron-client relations.[20] In both environments, in urban contexts, these subtly different relationships might take the form of what modern historians call euergetism, a kind of hybrid of patronage and the ideology of the civic community: wealthier citizens or political leaders contribute disproportionately to public expenses and are rewarded with expressions of communal gratitude—honorary inscriptions and statues expressing the citizenry's loyalty to and affection for its benefactor (*euergetes* in Greek, hence "euergetism").[21] A certain modulation of honor, in the sense of the clout enjoyed by people in advantageous positions in social hierarchies rather than in the ethnographic sense made famous by Julian Pitt-Rivers or Michael Herzfeld[22]—the aggressive masculine pride said to be a crucial feature of the construction of the male self in many parts of the world (including the Mediterranean)—played a crucial role in maintaining these social institutions. While these can all be mapped onto Mediterranean ethnography to some extent, there is little point in claiming that some particularly Mediterranean situation either generated them or can explain them. They are historically and culturally specific solutions to problems generated by a particular type of agrarian regime, which happens to have existed in parts—especially in the non-African parts of the southeastern cell—of the Mediterranean basin, among other places.

Did the Jews Have Friendship, Patronage, and Euergetism?[23]

As noted above, Jewish texts maintain a peculiar silence about redistributive social institutions based on reciprocity. This is demonstrably *not* because such institutions were entirely unknown to their authors because, for example, the

Jews possessed fully adequate alternatives. The relationship between God and Israel is commonly described in biblical texts in language drawn from the Near Eastern counterparts of such institutions: God is the lord and Israel his vassal. Lords and vassals are bound by mutual obligation but also by love—a key theme in the book of Deuteronomy but also in neo-Assyrian vassalage treaties. Formal friendship is familiar to every reader of the Book of Samuel, since David and Jonathan were bound by a *berit ahavah*—a covenant of friendship/love: indeed, one of the differences between Near Eastern and Greek friendship is that the former was contractual, as in the biblical tale, whereas the latter, though laden with ritual and ceremonial elements, was not. It seems reasonable to suppose that formal friendship—in its interethnic version (which Greeks called *xenia*), an institution well attested all over the Iron Age eastern Mediterranean—lies behind the idyll of the Judahite Boaz and the Moabite Ruth. This is what would have made it possible for Boaz's kinsmen to take refuge in Moab during a famine.[24] Both cases, as well as the strongly affective nature of the relationship of God and Israel both in Deuteronomy and in many of the prophetic books, show that contracts/covenants do not preclude emotions. On the contrary, the fact that the mutual obligations were spelled out may have shifted the focus of such relationships from the individual act of reciprocity (fraught, perilous, and attention-sapping, as we learn from the Roman handbook on the subject, Seneca's *De Beneficiis*) to the affective content of the relationship. The language of institutionalized reciprocity in familiar ancient Near Eastern forms is easy to find in the Hebrew Bible, but only rarely is it used to describe relations between Israelites, and it is mentioned in the legal *pericopae* of the Pentateuch only to restrain the institutions or prohibit them altogether.

This is not an isolated tendency of some biblical passages but a pervasive theme of ancient Jewish literature. The ancient Jewish text that is most informative about institutionalized reciprocity is the *Wisdom of Ben Sira*, composed, presumably at Jerusalem, shortly after 200 BCE. In mood and style, *Ben Sira* owes much to the somber realism of earlier Israelite wisdom, especially to Proverbs—whose language it extensively borrows—but also to Ecclesiastes, though *Ben Sira* is far more pious. *Ben Sira* provides many gnomic discussions of relations of social dependency, subtly modernized: he no longer writes in ancient Near Eastern style of contractual friendship and vassalage but of emotionally cooler but less legalistic Greek-style formal friendship and of something similar to what would be called in a Roman context *patrocinium* (patronage) or *clientela*. Perhaps this shift explains *Ben Sira*'s obsession with these relationships—the shift away from contractual relationships left *Ben Sira*'s audience uncertain and anxious. In this sense *Ben Sira* is parallel to the one Greek text he is almost certain to have known—the first book of the

Theognidea, a Greek wisdom text of the archaic period (ca. sixth century BCE) full of mildly paranoid advice about how to cope with friendships and alliances in the new world of the emerging *polis*, where older oligarchic social institutions were under threat.

Ben Sira regarded friendship and patronage as necessary evils. Seneca, by contrast, was aware of the perils of such relationships but promoted them as vehicles of the great virtue of liberality, one of the foundations of society. For Ben Sira, they are mainly dangerous, tending inexorably to degenerate into betrayal and oppression. Only the man who is wise, which in Ben Sira's thought is equivalent to God-fearing, can manage such relationships successfully. *Ben Sira* thus repeatedly juxtaposes two incommensurable value systems in a way that has confused modern analysts of the text. These have persistently tried to determine whether wisdom (practical advice on relationships and sensitive social occasions) or piety is primary for Ben Sira, without considering the possibility that what matters is the juxtaposition of the two, however clumsily performed.

There are similar ambivalences in later texts. As noted, Josephus is largely (though not completely) silent about the role of patronage, friendship, and similar institutions in Jewish history, in contrast to, say, his younger Roman aristocratic contemporary Tacitus, whose history of the early Roman Empire is among other things a record of the shifting friendships, alliances, and betrayals among the Roman elites. Beyond that, Josephus explicitly claims that the Jews of Judaea rejected the practices associated with Roman-style euergetism, had no use for the idea of honor, and expected their rulers to perform *mitzvot*, not provide benefactions, and when they did as expected the Jews felt gratitude not to the ruler but to God.

The Palestinian rabbis likewise were indifferent or hostile to the cultures of civic benefaction and embraced the concept of patronage but only for the purpose of extolling God as the only patron a Jew truly needs (Y. Berakhot 5:1; in other scattered passages the Palestinian Talmud acknowledges that a human patron might sometimes help). In this way they "Romanized" a core theological element of the Hebrew Bible, transforming God, in this pericope at least, from lord into patron. *Ben Sira* argues that more honor (another concept treated mainly with hostility in biblical texts, when it is mentioned at all, except with respect to God) inhered in fear of God than in the possession of riches and social clout. The Palestinian Talmud is in some passages more extreme, arguing that honor inheres *only* in piety/Torah. The rabbis' view was thus somewhat different from the complete rejection of honor Josephus attributed to the Jews. But elsewhere, they seem rather untroubled by the notion that honor inheres in wealth and were willing to deploy the language of euergetism strategically, as a way of encouraging Jews to perform the *mitzvot* of supporting the poor and communal endeavors. This slippage between charity and euergetism (attested also among contemporary Christians) would have a fateful impact on Jewish communal life forever after.

Ambivalence about these common features of an ambient culture of reciprocity—and I emphasize that in some aspects this culture was fully native to Judaea and is not to be confused with "Hellenism"[25]—is thus one of the hitherto unsuspected features that distinguishes much ancient Jewish literature from much Greek and Roman literature. Whether we can take the speculative leap and talk about Jewish culture in general, not just literature (which is atypical by the very fact of its having been written, in a society in which we must suppose literacy rates to have been low), is less clear. But Jerusalemite archaeology of the later Second Temple period, devoid as it is of statuary and honorary inscriptions, seems to show that Josephus did not completely misrepresent the culture of Herodian and post-Herodian Jerusalem, not to speak of Judaea as a whole, Galilee, or the diaspora. If there was a culture of euergetism in first-century Jerusalem, it did not follow patterns that Roman rule had elsewhere already done much to standardize.

How are we to explain this? To produce an explanation, I drew not on Mediterranean ethnography in particular but on the anthropology and sociology of exchange. I posited that there existed in "agro-literate" regimes two ways of conceptualizing social organization.[26] One way, in the manner of Aristotle and the Stoics, but resonating with classic theories of the gift extrapolated from preliterate societies, valorized reciprocal exchange.[27] The other way might downplay reciprocal exchange in recognition of its competitive nature and oppressive potential; instead it embraced corporate solidarity based on shared loyalty to some set of ideas or beliefs. In the first system, one is loyal to those to whom one is bound by personal relationship—one's kinship and patronage networks, for example. Such networks may be clustered into larger entities. The Stoics, for example, valorized relationships established by reciprocal exchange because they promoted the solidarity of humanity as a whole, leaving open the question of how societies should be organized in practice. But the Torah (like Plato) regarded such a construction of society with suspicion or even hostility. For the Torah, Israel was indeed, as already suggested, bound to its God in a relationship of reciprocal exchange, but Israelites were supposed to feel for one another a sense of loyalty and dedication without consideration of family relationships or of gift-derived social ties. It can be argued that some of the Torah's most distinctive rules are meant to devalorize the kinship and patronage network or even render it unnecessary. The prohibition of interest on loans to poor Israelites, and the other poor relief laws, the more or less severe limitations placed on debt bondage, the septennial cancelation of debts and the periodic redistribution of land (however unrealistic in practice), all gesture toward an egalitarian ideal in which redistribution is institutionalized at the level of the state. These laws are meant to preclude the formation of relationships of personal dependency between Israelites. This is stated almost explicitly in Leviticus 25's version of the laws restricting debt bondage: "For the children of Israel are my slaves," God says, not meant to be enslaved to one another (v. 55; cf. v. 42).

I argued, in sum, that the core ideological commitments of the Jews were shaped by a sharp and probably self-conscious aversion to institutionalized *human* social relationships based on reciprocal exchange. By contrast, they imagined their relationship with their national god in the conventional terms of social reciprocity. The Israelites' shared commitment to this "covenantal" relationship was the content of their corporate solidarity. But the Israelites' social ideals were in some respects unrealizable. The most radical pentateuchal law—return of all land to its original holders every fifty years—would, if put into practice, have ensured that land never became concentrated in the hands of acquisitive individuals, forcing others into relationships of dependency (whether the dependency took the form of tenancy, bondage, or clientele). But the law was framed in such a way as to make it impossible to impose a priori: it required every Israelite to return to his original Mosaic allotment. But, of course, there were no original Mosaic allotments, and even if there had been, the law makes no allowances for patrilineal families that had grown in size or passed out of existence and so on. It is consciously utopian. And how could the more realistic cancelation of debt every seven years be imposed? Couldn't creditors find ways of circumventing the rule even before the *prozbol* loophole allegedly introduced by Hillel (M Gittin 4.3; M Shevi'it 10.3)? Likewise the prohibition of charging interest to poor Israelite brethren: What state apparatus ever existed to enforce compliance/nonevasion, or indeed, to enforce adherence to poor relief laws more generally? Finally, even if these laws had been successfully imposed, or their importance so completely internalized that Israelites observed them without state coercion, would they have had more than a symbolic impact on the real-life economy of shortage? In other words, to what extent did they actually fulfill their manifest purpose of suppressing the proliferation of institutionalized relationships of dependency among Israelites/Jews?

The answer must be that real-life ancient Jewish societies and communities exhibited highly varied types of tensions between these conflicting principles of social organization. Ben Sira informs us that in Hellenistic Jerusalem the culture of reciprocity-based, honor-fueled social dependency was flourishing but that an effort was afoot to complicate it by transforming piety even in the absence of wealth into a source of social clout and honor. By contrast, in

Roman Jerusalem and Judaea more generally—though we know little about patronage—the standardized Roman version of euergetism, which was one of the building blocks of the imperial administration since it was vital for sustaining the friendly relations between the imperial center, local elites, and broad segments of the subject population, was apparently ineffective, as Josephus says. This is not the only reason for the disastrous features of the relations between Rome and the Jews of Palestine, but it is an important one not hitherto given its due. The peculiar features of Judaean Jewish culture turn out to have been highly consequential in that they shaped social and political relations in ways that proved dysfunctional for the Jews.

In other times and places, there were different sorts of compromises. Steven Weitzman argues that Philo's acceptance of the standard norms of reciprocity was complete and untroubled, but the evidence for this consists exclusively of Philo's apologetic insistence (which Josephus shared with him) that the Jews do not in fact dishonor the emperor by failing to participate in the normative reciprocations of imperial euergetism—sacrifice to emperors, erection of statues, and so on. This seems to confirm rather than refute my position and ignores the political context in which Philo was writing: a crisis in the relations between Egyptian Jews and the state that anticipated the Judaean crisis by thirty years. Like Josephus, Philo was engaging in apologetics and/or wishful thinking. The correct evidence for Weitzman's argument would have been the dedicatory inscriptions from Hellenistic Egypt, all advertising their loyalty to the ruling Ptolemaic dynasty in standard epigraphic style. But the Hellenistic rulers, unlike their Roman successors, were perforce euergetic pluralists. They had no notion of state citizenship and never expected cultural uniformity from their subjects. They did not demand *isotheoi timai* ("quasi-divine honors," in other words, cult and a statue) and were content to have their different groups of constituents celebrate their loyalty and gratitude in a variety of ways (the exception being the Seleukid king Antiochus IV). For Jews to reject all expressions of loyalty to the state would have been suicidal, a fact that did not prevent some Jews from doing so three times under Roman rule, but never under Hellenistic rule except in the anomalous administration of King Antiochus. In truth, Weitzman is right to say that I neglected Philo, but as far as I can determine, there is nothing in the Philonic corpus that contradicts my model—and how could there be, since my model is meant as an analytic tool, not a predictive one? What the results of such an analysis would be remains to be seen.

The Jewish religious community, as it began to take shape in late antiquity (300–700 CE), constitutes another response to the tension between the Torah's antireciprocal norms and the economically, socially, and politically validated norms of institutionalized reciprocity. It is primarily in small groups that the

Torah's social vision had the best chance of realization in a premodern environment. Thus, the Dead Sea community and the Jewish (and soon enough "gentile") sectarian communities who formulated and transmitted the very earliest Christian doctrines preserved in the earliest strata of the Gospels and the Epistles of Paul embraced a radical version of this vision, characterized by a highly pronounced sense of egalitarian solidarity, sharing of property to a greater or lesser extent, and rigid rules of social interaction unrelated to general Greco-Roman ideas about politesse, deference, and honor. Local communities developed certain similar features. Like sectarian communities, they applied loaded biblical language to themselves—the late antique local community was called a *qahal*, or, in Greek sometimes, *laos* (= *'am*), or, simply, Israel; the Dead Sea community applied the unusual biblical term *yahad* to itself but also Israel; Christian communities were *ekklesiai*, the equivalent of the biblical *'edot*, another word used by Jewish communities. And they, too, at least for a time, might call themselves Israel. Though the history of the development is obscure, they seem to have developed ways, more or less effective, of providing support to poor constituents: redistribution came to be a fundamental function of the local community, if it was not from the start. They also placed piety at their center: charitable gifts were called *mitzvot*, funds were raised, sometimes slowly and laboriously, to construct monumental synagogues. The rabbis described/prescribed a culture of what the anthropologist Marshal Sahlins called pooling, a type of generalized reciprocity typical of solidary communities that in principle did not produce patronage networks[28]: consoling mourners was, to be sure, a commandment, but the rabbis demanded that a husband who refused to permit his wife to console mourners provide her with the sum stipulated in her *ketubbah* (in other words, divorce her, divorce being regarded in many rabbinic texts as a kind of manumission from servitude). This was so not because he was interfering with her performance of a *mitzvah* but because, "when her dead was laid out before her, no one would come to console her" (Y. Ketubbot 7.5, 31b). In other words, the rabbis recognized the reality that the quasiegalitarian system of the community could not sustain "free-riders."

There were still more pronounced adaptations of reciprocity present as well. Indeed, both Jewish and Christian local communities adopted characteristic practices from the euergetic culture of the late Roman city. The dedicatory and honorary inscription, eschewed in first-century Jerusalem, became a standard feature of the charitable gift. While a small minority of inscriptions from both synagogues and contemporaneous churches honors donors "whose names God alone knows," most honor donors by name. In many places, the leading benefactors presumably wielded disproportionate influence (we know next to nothing about the relations between individual late antique communities and the state: intermediaries were indubitably important and then as later were not necessarily identical with communal leaders).[29] Yet while ancient communities were in some respects euergetistic in structure, there remained a strong sense of the agency, importance, and dignity of the community. Inscriptions frequently honored very modest donors (unlike those associated with Roman municipal euergetism) or donors of very small items. Synagogue epigraphy often commemorates not just anonymous donors but also gifts given by the *qahala qadisha* as a whole. What we do not know, in the absence of any documentary evidence beyond a few hundred inscriptions, is how far this ideological tension influenced the actual governance of local communities. In other words, it is entirely possible that in practice local religious communities operated as straightforward euergetic systems and that the communitarian ethos suggested by elements of the epigraphical record was "symbolic"—that it affected people's subjective experience of the community or expressed a set of ideals tacitly acknowledged to be unrealizable but did not affect patterns of expenditure.

This is overwhelmingly likely to have been the case in some places and at some times. But it is implausible to suppose that no local Jewish community ever tried hard enough to live up to its egalitarian ideals that patterns of expenditure were invariably left untouched by them. And the same argument may be applied to earlier periods as well. We can be tolerably certain that in many times and places Jewish societies were much more "normal" than surviving literature, which is often prescriptive and idealizing, would lead us to think. Brent Shaw demonstrated that in the prolonged period of strife during the simultaneous collapse of the Hasmonean dynasty and the Roman Republic, the people of greater Judaea fell back on reciprocity: they rushed into the clientele of warring strongmen without hesitation derived from religious scruples and without priestly status or sectarian affiliation playing any apparent role in constituents' loyalty to their patrons. Even Josephus, who was very reluctant to depict Jews behaving in this way, let it slip that this was in fact happening (*Jewish Antiquities*, books 13–14).

Conclusion: No Mediterranean?

With all the appropriate caveats, I do not doubt that for some periods Mediterranean history is a viable if not in itself entirely satisfactory option. I continue to think that Braudel in particular is required reading for any historian of the region, of whatever period (but especially premodernity). This is so because *The Mediterranean and the Mediterranean World* is so packed with information and acute observation that though Braudel must, for example, never be used by ancient historians simply to plug informational gaps, almost everything we write about has some counterpart in Braudel's account that can be brought into fruitful dialogue with our material. The same is true of the best Mediterranean ethnography. It does not follow from this that we should allow our comparative efforts to stop at wherever the borders of the Mediterranean world are supposed to be, but ecological continuities should be given their due.

I have adopted on the whole a somewhat different approach, extracting from anthropological and social theoretical literature an "ideal type" of social organization, with variegated counterparts in the actual history of the Mediterranean basin—and elsewhere—and used this as an analytic tool. It has helped me uncover some fundamentally important but hitherto scarcely recognized features of ancient Israelite and Jewish cultures. One can in broad terms believe in the heuristic utility of structural-functionalist interpretation while recognizing its limitations. The Jews' normative social ideologies contained elements, meant to enhance in-group solidarity, which were drastically dysfunctional. In premodern conditions, in the absence of a strong state, poor-relief measures are very unlikely to have suppressed completely the need for more reliable redistributive institutions, even if these were, as seems to have been the case, somewhat devalorized. Furthermore, the stronger the emphasis on in-group solidarity, the stronger is the sense of hostility to outsiders. But without *some* integration into the world outside the Jewish community, the Jews' corporate existence would have been impossible; they needed to cope with rulers and neighbors, and outside Palestine, there was a structural need for Jews to maintain good relations with their hosts, apart from the obvious fact that willy-nilly they would be economically integrated into their broader polities. Yet in some times and places, Jews were willing to embrace their dysfunctional norms fully. Those who did so in the context of sectarian communities (and even these could not survive without some measure of integration in the nonsectarian world) could come closer to realizing Israelite social ideals than nonsectarians, and some such communities endured for centuries. In other cases, the corporate ideology-driven decision not to integrate, the rejection of regionwide social institutions, led to disaster, or at least contributed to it. At moments when ideology and culture—allegedly mere superstructure both for Marxizing structural-functionalists and for their heirs, the new globalists—acquire agency, structural functionalism breaks down. We are thus left to steer a course between the antimaterialist Foucauldian scheme in which discourse and *episteme* have unconstrained agency and ultramaterialist globalism in which the great patterns formed by the circulation of stuff are all that matter. From the ancient Jews we can learn about something larger than the Mediterranean.

SETH SCHWARTZ is the Lucius N. Littauer Professor of Classical Jewish Civilization, and professor of history and classics, at Columbia University. He is the author of *Imperialism and Jewish Society, 200 BCE to 640 CE* (Princeton, 2001), *Were the Jews a Mediterranean Society?* (Princeton, 2010), and *The Ancient Jews, from Alexander to Muhammad* (Cambridge, 2014).

Notes

1. Ian Morris, "Mediterraneanization," in *Mediterranean Paradigms and Classical Antiquity*, ed. Irad Malkin (London: Routledge, 2005), 30–55. On the debt of area studies to globalization see also Peregrine Horden and Nicholas Purcell, "The Mediterranean and the 'New Thalassology,'" *American Historical Review* 111, no. 3 (2006): 722–40.

2. Karl Polanyi, *The Great Transformation* (New York: Farrar and Rinehart, 1944). For his understanding of precapitalist societies, Polanyi drew on the ethnographies of exchange of Marcel Mauss and Bronislaw Malinowski, not to mention Max Weber.

3. Seth Schwartz, "Finkelstein the Orientalist," in *Finley and Politics*, ed. William V. Harris (Leiden: Brill, 2013), 31–48.

4. See Andrew Wilson, "Red Sea Trade and the State," in *Across the Ocean: Nine Essays on Indo-Mediterranean Trade*, ed. Federico De Romanis and Marco Maiuro (Leiden: Brill, 2015), 13–32.

5. Keith Hopkins, "Rome, Taxes, Rents and Trade," *Kodai: Journal of Ancient History* 6/7 (1995/6): 41–71, reprinted in *The Ancient Economy*, ed. Walter Scheidel and Sitta von Reden (Edinburgh: Edinburgh University Press, 2002), 190–230. This revises an article first published in 1980.

6. For an updating and refinement of this model see Walter Scheidel, "The Shape of the Roman World: Modeling Imperial Connectivity," *Journal of Roman Archaeology* 27, no. 1 (2014): 7–32; and note the important and drastic qualification of Brent Shaw, "A Peculiar Island: Maghrib and the Mediterranean," in *Mediterranean Paradigms and Classical Antiquity*, ed. I. Malkin (London: Routledge, 2005), 93–125, concerning North Africa: the relatively few permanently settled locations on the coast from Libya west should be thought of as, in effect, islands, separated from their neighbors by great distances, situated in a larger region too arid for most agriculture. From the perspective of the *très longue durée*, Shaw provides excellent evidence that North Africa was mostly outside Horden and Purcell's zone of connectivity. The rise of the Punic world and the subsequent prosperity of Roman North Africa reflect not traditional connectivity but precisely the intrusion of politics—proto-globalizing imperial politics that had developed a knack for large-scale extraction and distribution beyond the "connective zone."

7. See Fred Astren, "Jews," in *Companion to Mediterranean History*, ed. Peregrine Horden and Sharon Kinoshita (London: Wiley, 2014), 392–408.

8. Braudel himself assigned such roles to the Jews: Fernand Braudel, *The Mediterranean and the Mediterranean World in the Age of Philip II*, 2 volumes (New York: Harper and Row, 1972–1973), 2:802–26.

9. If this is what his title "alabarch" means; there is also papyrological evidence that he oversaw the Egyptian estates of Antonia, daughter of Marc Antony and mother of the emperor Claudius. See Eric Gardner Turner, "Tiberius Julius Alexander," *Journal of Roman*

Studies 44 (1954): 54–64; Alexander Fuks, "Marcus Julius Alexander," *Zion* 13/14 (1948): 10–7. An inscribed statue base from Rhodes may provide further evidence for the broad mercantile connections of Philo's family, though the editors' restoration of the text is debatable: *L'Année Epigraphique* 2010 (2013): #1614a-b.

10. The Tiberian patriarchs attained senatorial rank sometime in the fourth century, which implies possession of considerable wealth. For a recent account of the patriarchal dynasty featuring a salutary focus on money, see Alan Appelbaum, *The Dynasty of the Jewish Patriarchs* (Tübingen, Germany: Mohr Siebeck), 2013.

11. On the absence of Jewish senators, and of Palestinian and Arabian senators more generally, see Glen Bowersock, "Roman Senators from the Near East," in *Studies on the Eastern Roman Empire*, ed. Glen Bowersock (Goldbach, Germany: Keip, 1994), 141–60. On elite status as precondition for participation in the globalizing economy in the High Empire see Walter Scheidel and Steven J. Friesen, "The Size of the Economy and the Distribution of Income in the Roman Empire," *Journal of Roman Studies* 99 (2009): 61–91.

12. This highly attenuated version of Jewish globalization—attenuated since among other things pilgrims from afar probably always constituted a small minority of the total number of pilgrims and a minuscule proportion of Jews, however defined, living in the diaspora—was very short-lived (after 20 BCE to 66 CE), rendered possible by Herodian construction and brought to an end by the outbreak of the Great Revolt. Nevertheless, its importance for the transmission of cultural capital from Judaea to other Jewish communities was probably considerable. In economic terms, the flow was basically unidirectional, toward Jerusalem. For an important attempt to model the economic impact, see Hayim Lapin, "Feeding the Jerusalem Temple: Cult, Hinterland and Economy in First Century Palestine," *Journal of Ancient Judaism* 8, no. 3 (2017): 410–53.

13. See Seth Schwartz, *Imperialism and Jewish Society, 200 B.C.E. to 640 C.E.* (Princeton, NJ: Princeton University Press, 2001), 179–289.

14. John G. Peristiany, ed., *Honor and Shame: The Values of Mediterranean Society* (Chicago: University of Chicago Press, 1966); John Davis, *People of the Mediterranean: An Essay in Comparative Social Anthropology* (London: Routledge, 1977).

15. Michael Herzfeld, *Anthropology through the Looking Glass: Critical Ethnography in the Margins of Europe* (Cambridge: Cambridge University Press, 1987).

16. Michael Herzfeld, "Practical Mediterraneanism: Excuses for Everything from Epistemology to Eating," in *Rethinking the Mediterranean*, ed. William V. Harris (Oxford: Oxford University Press, 2005), 45–63.

17. Controversial at least in part because of the author's sympathy for the Communist revolution: William Hinton, *Fanshen: A Documentary of Revolution in a Chinese Village* (New York: Monthly Review Press, 1966). In its first half it provides a vivid account of life in a near-subsistence, dry-farming, wheat-based agricultural regime. The paper inspired by it was Seth Schwartz, "Josephus in Galilee: Rural Patronage and Social Breakdown," in *Josephus and the History of the Greco-Roman Period: Essays in Memory of Morton Smith*, ed. Fausto Parente and Joseph Sievers (Leiden: Brill, 1994), 290–308.

18. For example, Brent Shaw, "Tyrants, Bandits, and Kings: Personal Power in Josephus," *Journal of Jewish Studies* 44, no. 2 (1993): 176–204.

19. Martin Goodman, *Rome and Jerusalem: The Clash of Ancient Civilizations* (London: Penguin, 2007), 221–31.

20. On formal friendship the standard work is Gabriel Herman, *Ritualised Friendship and the Greek City* (Cambridge: Cambridge University Press, 1987); on Roman patronage, see Richard Saller, *Personal Patronage under the Early Empire* (Cambridge: Cambridge

University Press, 2002). Both books emerged from the atelier of Finley and suffer from a similar excess of functionalist explanation.

21. See Paul Veyne, *Bread and Circuses: Historical Sociology and Political Pluralism* (London: Penguin, 1990) (French original, 1976).

22. See Julian Pitt-Rivers, *People of the Sierra* (London: Weidenfeld and Nicholson, 1954), and Michael Herzfeld, "Honour and Shame: Problems in the Comparative Analysis of Moral Systems," *Man*, New Series 15, no. 2 (1980): 339–51.

23. The following section compresses and updates my *Were the Jews a Mediterranean Society?: Reciprocity and Solidarity in Ancient Judaism* (Princeton, NJ: Princeton University Press, 2010).

24. See Seth Schwartz, "Conversion to Judaism in the Second Temple Period: A Functionalist Approach," in *Studies in Josephus and the Varieties of Ancient Judaism: Louis H. Feldman Jubilee Volume*, ed. Shaye J. D. Cohen and Joshua J. Schwartz (Leiden: Brill, 2007), 223–36.

25. Contrast the misinterpretation in Steven Weitzman, "Mediterranean Exchanges: A Response to Seth Schwartz's 'Were the Jews a Mediterranean Society?'" *Jewish Quarterly Review* 102, no. 4 (2012): 491–512.

26. "Agro-literate" was introduced by the social theorist Ernest Gellner in his influential *Nations and Nationalism* (Ithaca, NY: Cornell University Press, 1983).

27. Marcel Mauss, *The Gift: The Form and Reason for Exchange in Archaic Societies*, trans. W. D. Hall (New York: Norton, 1990) (French original, 1925); and Bronislaw Malinowski, *Argonauts of the Western Pacific* (London: Routledge, 1922).

28. See Marshall Sahlins, *Stone Age Economics* (Chicago: Aldine Press, 1972), 188.

29. Tessa Rajak and David Noy, "Archisynagogoi: Office, Title, and Social Status in the Greco-Jewish Synagogue," *Journal of Roman Studies* 83 (1993): 75–93.

2

THE NEW MELTING POT?

Mediterraneanism and the Study of Jewish History

Jonathan Ray

THE CURRENT DISCOURSE ON MEDITERRANEANISM, INCLUDING THE "NEW Thalassology," to use Peregrine Horden and Nicolas Purcell's phrase, has led to an understanding of human geography that emphasizes the literally and metaphorically fluid nature of the Mediterranean world. In the hands of an ever-widening circle of scholars from a variety of disciplines, Mediterraneanism has come to represent something of a new moral geography, replacing and forcefully contradicting older, negative notions of a shared culture of honor and shame. In the new paradigm, the Mediterranean Sea itself is seen as fostering a natural connectivity and mobility that resonated within the cultures that developed along its shores. Mediterraneanism thus provides the perfect counterpoint to the bounded, ethnocentric model of nation-states that are now the markers of an outdated historiographic paradigm.

The case of Mediterranean Jews, however, presents us with something of an interesting dilemma. What are we to make of a people who, for most of their history, were translocal, mobile, and culturally hybrid—that is, quintessentially "Mediterranean"—and yet also members of a notoriously bounded, even clannish, society—a self-styled "chosen" nation (albeit without a state)? Throughout his long and productive career, S. D. Goitein sought to resolve the incongruity of Mediterranean Jewry by making their society paradigmatic to his Mediterranean model and in so doing dissolving any significant differences between Jewish and non-Jewish binaries. His formative work on medieval Jews continues to exert an influence on the field of Jewish studies, echoing in discussions of early modern "port Jews," Jewish cosmopolitans, and others who effectively transcended the narrow confines of their Jewish identities.[1] Even Maimonides, perhaps the most emblematically "Jewish" figure to generations of Mediterranean Jews, and a communal leader that vehemently attempted to distinguish Jews from their neighbors, has been reimagined in recent years as a representation of Mediterranean cosmopolitanism.[2]

Nonetheless, the integration of Jews into Mediterranean studies may not be as simple as declaring their inherent cosmopolitan bona fides. To be sure, Jews in the premodern Mediterranean and elsewhere were continuously adopting and adapting elements of their surrounding cultures. Yet, for all but a small handful of elites, this process of cultural amalgamation never truly altered their association with a very particular religious heritage and the legal, social, and spiritual communities that it produced. Therefore, the experience for most Mediterranean Jews is perhaps better characterized by the notion of religious and ethnic pluralism, rather than cosmopolitanism, as it is most often understood.[3] The question, then, is not whether premodern Jews exhibited elements of what may be called a shared Mediterranean ethos—for surely evidence of such cross-cultural connectivity is plentiful—but how we are to evaluate the ultimate impact of these traits on Jewish history and society. To this end, I would like to consider the applicability of Mediterraneanism to Jewish studies by addressing some of its underlying assumptions and the associated implications of these assumptions for the study of Jewish history.

The distinction between pluralism and cosmopolitanism that I have raised recalls the work of the American Jewish philosopher and cultural critic Horace Kallen.[4] It is now over one hundred years since Kallen published his seminal essay "Democracy versus the Melting Pot"—a milestone that indicates the longevity of this debate. Kallen's interest was in distinguishing between the goal held by immigrant groups of preserving core elements of their distinctive cultural characteristics within the American setting and the goal of attaining a deeper social integration, or assimilation, in which those elements were largely lost. With regard to a Mediterranean turn in Jewish historiography, we might think in terms of a similar distinction between a cosmopolitan transnational Jewry that exemplifies many of the characteristics of Mediterranean societies or a distinctively Jewish culture that operated within a Mediterranean context but that was more significantly shaped by discrete, internal factors.[5] I would like to emphasize that to resist the allure of melting-pot cosmopolitanism, in which specific religious identities are sublimated or ignored, does not signal the acceptance of myopic and exclusionary "nationalism." A focus on religious pluralism, for instance, carries with it the notion of being part of a multiethnic or multireligious society without devaluing the importance of those individual components of that society. In many ways, this paradigm recalls the notion of unity-out-of-diversity emphasized by Horden and Purcell as a key characteristic of the premodern Mediterranean.⁶ Similarly, internally bounded or "national" identities and cosmopolitanism need not be viewed as mutually exclusive. Kwame Anthony Appiah makes reference to a "rooted cosmopolitanism" that can simultaneously situate people within a particular group, as well as beyond it, in fruitful ways.⁷

Moreover, while I acknowledge that the field of Mediterranean studies offers new vistas onto the nature of Jewish history, I nonetheless caution against presenting a narrative of that history that discounts its protagonists' conscious pursuit of cultural and religious distinctiveness. It is not my intention to identify general problems with the Mediterranean as a heuristic tool. An extensive literature already exists on this subject, and the incisive objections of its leading voices will no doubt be given careful consideration by those in Jewish studies who seek to apply a Mediterranean model to their own research.⁸ Instead, I wish to address a few issues with specific reference to the field of Jewish studies. These include the temptation to privilege what we might call the "Mediterranean" aspects of Jewish society to the exclusion of other facets and the role that Judaism and Jewish identity played in the lives of early modern Mediterranean Jews.

The establishment of the Sephardic diaspora during the late medieval and early modern periods offers several opportunities for the application of a Mediterranean framework to the study of Jewish history. The various forms of connectivity that have become an abiding hallmark of the new Mediterraneanism can also be seen as playing an integral role in shaping early modern Jewish society in the region. With regard to the latter, connectivity was, notably, born of necessity in response to cataclysmic ruptures within Jewish communal life. As a sea that helped carry Jewish refugees along established shipping lanes and as a broader, albeit delimited, region that promoted connectivity between the peoples who settled in its ports, the Mediterranean served as more than just the stage on which the formation of the Sephardic diaspora played out. It was an integral factor in the formation of the Sephardic diaspora and the rise of early modern Sephardic trading networks.⁹

As is well known, Jewish participation in trans-Mediterranean trade intensified following the expulsion of the Jews from Spain in 1492, as did the migration and general travel along these same maritime routes. Much of this trade was centered on the eastern Mediterranean, as Venice and the Ottoman Empire each rose to power, and stretched southward to the ports of the Gulf of Aden and eastward to India.¹⁰ The impressive system of economic and social networks established by the early modern Sephardim often functioned as sociopolitical units, offering mutual aid and some of the other services that were traditionally provided by local *kehillot*. These networks were, in many ways, better suited to respond to the needs of such a peripatetic society than the institutions of local congregational communities. For centuries, these networks linked the Sephardim of the Mediterranean to those in northern Europe, the Americas, and beyond. And beginning in the eighteenth century, Livornese merchants helped to breathe new life into the older web of Spanish and Portuguese networks, just as the latter were beginning to lose their long-standing ties to their Iberian homeland. The highly mobile and transnational character of Sephardic society throughout the early modern period reaffirms many of the current historiographic claims of Mediterranean studies and suggests that family groups and scholarly circles shaped that society as much as the structures of the local Jewish community or the attitudes of the non-Jewish cultures in which the Sephardim lived.[11]

However, there is a problem in privileging the transnational ties among Sephardic merchants over other aspects of their lives or over the lives of Mediterranean Jews who were not engaged in long-distance trade. In her work on the Jews of colonial Algeria, Sarah Abrevaya Stein reminds us that, by neglecting some of the smaller and more marginalized groups that do not fit the general narrative of the field, we hazard the inadvertent reiteration of certain problematic themes and perspectives.[12] This observation is, I think, quite applicable to the general historiography on Mediterranean Jews, where there has been a tendency to represent the Jewish merchant as the archetype of the Jewish community. This is, perhaps, to be expected given the available documentation, especially for the Middle Ages, where the Cairo genizah has played such a formative role in our image of both Jewish and Mediterranean history. Yet, as Mark Cohen and others have shown, medieval Mediterranean Jewish communities were filled with poor, sedentary, and distinctly uncosmopolitan Jews.[13] For the early modern period as well, it is important to bear in mind that these far-flung mercantile networks should not be taken as synonymous with "Jewish," or even Sephardic, society. Rather, those Jews who were active in mercantile or intellectual networks across the Mediterranean and beyond it were able to draw upon the wealth and political connections these networks provided them in order to enhance their power within their home communities—a phenomenon that simultaneously marginalized and subordinated other Jews.

Thus, with regard to transnational connections, we should bear in mind that many Jews were left out of these systems and that this exclusion played an important role in shaping the relationship between those inside and those outside of these networks. Put another way, it would be helpful to ask how transnationalism and cosmopolitanism within the Sephardic or broader Jewish world served to exclude certain Jews and contributed to a ramified Jewish society. The need to recognize the limits and implications of the so-called Mediterranean aspects of Jewish societies should not be underestimated. In discussing the composition of Mediterranean port cities, David Abulafia claims that enclosed living quarters for merchants of the same ethnic and religious minorities "only enhanced the solidarity and sense of community that held these merchants together."[14] Perhaps. And yet such proximity, whether voluntary or forced, could also enhance competition, suspicion, and strife. If we are to make a case that Mediterranean Jewish society presents an example of diversity within unity built upon a series of connectivities, we must nonetheless remain open to instances in which diversity acted as a foil to unity, leading to friction and factionalism within the Jewish world.[15] Here, the notions of interdependence and unity-through-fragmentation emphasized by scholars like Horden and Purcell can help inform our thinking about Jewish history, as long as we are willing to think openly about the full meaning of that interdependence.[16]

I would argue that investigating the interplay between long-distance networks and the power dynamics of local Jewish communities is more fruitful than merely identifying evidence of Jewish transnationalism itself.[17] We now possess many fine studies of the Sephardic diaspora broadly conceived as well as studies of local Jewish communities around the early modern Mediterranean. Yet thus far, relatively little attention has been paid to the mutual influence of these different arenas. How, in other words, did these so-called Mediterranean dimensions of Jewish history—however we choose to define them—impact the social, political, and religious character of regional and local Jewries? How did they shape political affiliation, poor relief, and attitudes toward religious tradition?[18] Following these questions should lead us to a fuller understanding of what Sephardic trading networks—or the port cities in which many Sephardim lived—meant, not just for those active in these networks but also for those who were excluded and marginalized. Furthermore, awareness of colonialism, subalterns, and the processes of disenfranchisement should sensitize us not only to the plight of the direct victims of certain mechanisms (such as slaves) but also to those whom the mechanism bypasses and excludes.[19]

Perhaps one of the ways we can profitably use the concept of the Mediterranean in Jewish studies is to rethink how Jewish society was transnational and how it was local or regional in character. The ideal model for the Sephardic diaspora, or for Mediterranean Jewry in any period, is neither a cosmopolitan "melting pot" nor a fully insulated Jewish society that developed along in its own historical trajectory. Rather, we need to be alert to how these two general orientations of Jewish life were in tension with and ultimately shaped each other.[20] The formation of the Sephardic diaspora and the concurrent migrations of other Jewish groups into and around the early modern Mediterranean represent something of a revival of the Mediterranean society depicted by S. D. Goitein for the High Middle Ages. While Jews also migrated beyond the shores of the Mediterranean, the region itself and the travel lanes that circulated within and across it did give rise to a tighter-knit Jewish community than had existed in the later Middle Ages. These new bonds were built out of necessity, as the intense mobility of early modern Jews—both forced and voluntary—greatly challenged the stability and natural solidarity of Jewish society at the local level. The peripatetic nature of Jewish society in the early modern Mediterranean can be understood as simultaneously bolstering the formation of trans-regional Jewish networks and provoking local sociopolitical instability. Indeed, these two features of Mediterranean Jewish society during this period were interdependent. Heightened connectivity among Jews of different cities fostered transregional networks while simultaneously exacerbating instability within their local Jewish communities.

Evidence of this can be seen in the relationships that bound together the great rabbinic decisors of the sixteenth-century Levant. These scholars appear to have been involved in trade and were thus organically connected to the networks of travel and communication that aided in the maintenance of a rabbinic "Republic of Letters."[21] In addition to aiding the circulation of knowledge with regard to Jewish law, kabbalah, philosophy, and science, rabbinic networks also functioned as pathways for bolstering power and authority within the scholar's local community. Using these networks as a means to assert power became especially relevant during the late medieval and early modern period, as the dislocation and resettlement of large numbers of Jews wreaked havoc on Jewish communal organization and the already precarious authority of Jewish leaders. Once the political bonds of local Jewries were torn asunder, they were not easily reconstructed. The process of communal formation—or reformation—often brought to light the divergent interests of Jewish leaders and those they sought to lead. While most displaced Jews fervently clung to their native religious and cultural practices, many were nonetheless quite hesitant to formally associate themselves with communal institutions in their new lands of settlement. This created serious problems for rabbinic authorities who sought to regulate all aspects of Jewish observance as well as for those self-styled communal leaders who were charged by Muslim and Christian authorities with collecting Jewish taxes. In the early modern Mediterranean, Sephardic political life was marked by power struggles between leading families and between this fractious leadership and the recalcitrant masses that often resisted their communal council's efforts at fiscal and moral control.[22] In such times of communal volatility, the social importance of rabbinic networks increased. Group solidarity among rabbinic colleagues and their students served to mark these elites off from other Jews and to bolster their authority. Sephardic scholars, in particular, used these networks of intellectual exchange and mutual support to vie for influence with other rabbis and to further distinguish themselves as a group from the Jewish masses.[23]

The expulsion of 1492 and the subsequent peregrinations of Sephardic Jews across the Mediterranean also prompted a more direct involvement in the religious life of Jerusalem and its environs. Although the Jews of medieval Spain had held the Holy Land in high esteem, Jerusalem remained for them a distant symbol rather than a place of actual religious interaction and involvement. After 1492, greater geographical proximity to the Levant facilitated Sephardic Jews' ability to lend financial and charismatic support to study houses in Jerusalem and Safed. In the early Sephardic diaspora, rabbinic leaders such as Isaac Sholal, Moses and Solomon Alashkar, Levi ibn Habib, and Jacob Berab all took an active interest in these study centers of the Holy Land, maintaining close ties to them even if they settled in Egypt.[24] Sholal, the last Nagid of Egypt, was an important patron for yeshivot in Jerusalem. In turn, the students he supported wrote to others in Italy, singing Sholal's praises.[25] Such scholarly networks linked the Jewries of Egypt, Italy, and the land of Israel through a web of financial support, honors, and praise that served to extend the authority of leading scholars far beyond their home communities. Again, while this is not new to this period, the power of such links does appear to have intensified, becoming an important feature of Mediterranean Jewish life.

The same rabbinic networks that became bulwarks for Levantine yeshivot became the cause, and generally the means of resolving, intellectual conflicts. The dispute between Levi ibn Habib and Jacob Berab and their respective supporters over the possible reinstitution of the ancient form of rabbinic ordination (*semikhah*) is perhaps the most notorious example of the use of wide-ranging scholarly networks to bolster one's authority in a given locale or situation, but it was hardly unique.[26] Egyptian rabbis such as Moses Alashkar were asked to lend their gravitas in support of other leading scholars in Corfu, Tunis, Salonica, and Candia (Crete).[27] Similarly, when Egyptian notables Solomon Alashkar and Jacob ibn Tibbon became embroiled in a local dispute, they appealed to their rabbinic networks for support. Joseph Caro, Moses Trani, and other scholars from Safed joined the quarrel in an effort to resolve the matter.[28]

How are we to evaluate the relative Jewish and Mediterranean characteristics of these networks? A Mediterraneanist perspective might go as follows: early modern cabotage and travel routes throughout the Mediterranean gave rise to port cities characterized by what Henk Driessen has called a "striking ethnic plurality," of which early modern Jews formed a vital component.[29] Building on the widespread assertion that these port cities nurtured religious tolerance and cultural hybridity, Jewish historians have argued that this cosmopolitan ethos also fostered the proliferation of a particular Jewish social type throughout the

Mediterranean and beyond—that of the "port Jew."[30] From sea currents and mercantile routes to the pluralistic trading centers they created came the fruit of Mediterranean cosmopolitanism and hybridity, a particular social and cultural character that developed out of the religious and ethnic plurality and eventually came to transcend the individual elements of that pluralistic milieu. There is a sense in this literature that Mediterranean cosmopolitanism eventually began to wane with the advent of modern nationalism as diversity became uncoupled from connectivity. As Driessen notes, people "began to see themselves increasingly as citizens of mutually exclusive nations."[31] This stance serves to reaffirm the existence of a premodern, prenationalist Mediterranean in which transnational Jewish networks can be comfortably set. However, we need not read Mediterranean phenomena of connectivity and encounter merely as foils to contemporary religious and nationalist tensions. Rather, just as the history of piracy has been treated as part of the history of economic exchange, so too must we acknowledge that connectivity also aided in the propagation of plague, war, and violence, and a subsequent wariness of outsiders. In this same vein, discussions of translocal networks and the circulation of ideas should not focus on harmonious developments to the exclusion of missionary zeal and the assertion of religious orthodoxy, important notions that flowed along these same Mediterranean routes.

Current scholarly interest in the hybridities, connectivity, and general cosmopolitanism represented by Mediterraneanism—like an older generation's interest in a "melting pot" society—appears to be motivated by our desire to transcend older nationalist histories as well as by a more popular need to respond to some of the political tensions of our time. By pointing out commonalities among religious and cultural groups, we are able to argue for a more inclusive narrative of Jewish history that firmly locates Jews within the societies in which they lived. The move toward a Mediterranean studies approach to Jewish history thus holds a great deal of promise for the connection of its subjects to new conceptual categories and broader scholarly themes. Indeed, as the underlying motivation for this volume indicates, there exists a marked interest in the integration of the Jewish experience into the broader narrative of the Mediterranean.

Yet the danger of such an approach is the potential for Jews as a subject to become shorn of any characteristics that would render them distinct—most notably, Judaism. In order for studies that treat Jews as Mediterraneans to have any real scholarly value, they must be read with and against studies that elucidate the uniqueness of the Jewish experience. Mediterraneanism, like the associated notions of cosmopolitanism and cultural hybridity, presumes the existence of something concretely Jewish that can be expanded, blurred, or transcended.

For all the discussion about the importance of agency and the postcolonial efforts to understand marginalized groups such as the Jews on their own terms, the primary objective of this historiographic turn toward inclusion has been to understand premodern Jews in light of their relationship to the host societies in which they lived. The question of whether or not Jewish history forms a field of academic inquiry in its own right is a subject discussed at length elsewhere, and I will not address it here.³² Rather, I accept that the relationship between Jews and their neighbors is a topic worthy of greater investigation and illumination, and I suggest that our efforts to understand the nature of interfaith relations in the medieval and early modern Mediterranean first require us to possess a nuanced understanding of the internal composition of Jewish society. Whatever moments of encounter Jews had with Muslims and Christians—and for certain sectors of the Jewish community these might have been plentiful—they were still quantitatively outnumbered and qualitatively overshadowed by contacts and encounters with other Jews. Their lives were lived, by and large, in Jewish spaces and defined by their relationships with other Jews. As Phillip Ackerman-Lieberman has noted with regard to the lives of the Mediterranean Jews found in the genizah documents, these were essentially "Jewish merchants and traders whose counterparties were Jewish, whose agreements were initiated and maintained by Jewish courts, and whose commercial practices may well have been structured to express an affinity for or even loyalty to the rules and norms of Jewish law."³³ Here, in fact, is an opportunity to borrow a bit of theory from the field of Mediterranean studies. Defending his use of the Mediterranean as a cohesive unit of study, a *tertium genus* to supersede the older division between Europe and the Middle East, Peregrine Horden has argued that the region ultimately represents "a large zone of net introversion: an area within which internal contacts are overall . . . more numerous, dense or durable than external ones."³⁴ The very same sort of characterization can be made with regard to the Sephardic diaspora and other Jewish communities of the early modern Mediterranean. That is, for all our interest in cross-cultural contacts and interfaith encounters, most interactions and communications in which early modern Mediterranean Jews engaged were with their parents, their spouses, their neighbors, and other members of their most immediate community—that is to say, other Jews.³⁵ Mercantile, kinship, and social networks represented important subsets of the Sephardic and greater Mediterranean Jewish diaspora, but in nearly all cases the Jewish element of these networks remained paramount.

As with the centering of Jews within their own historical narrative, so too the importance of Judaism in this narrative should not be undervalued. For many working in Jewish studies, the question of how to best integrate their research into larger historical narratives and fields of academic inquiry remains a methodological concern. It is not uncommon for critics to view the relative marginalization of Jewish history within the academy as being self-imposed, the result of unnecessarily parochial interests of Judaica scholars.[36] With regard to the confluence of Mediterranean and Jewish studies, however, we need not look upon the focus on religion, or the recognition of religious difference, as being intellectually retrograde or out of step with the larger trends in the academy. On the contrary, recent scholarship has begun to criticize the unnecessarily dismissive stance within much of the academy with regard to the role of religion in the premodern world. Writing on the medieval Mediterranean, Hussein Fancy cautions against reducing the Middle Ages to "a period of incomplete or frustrated secularism."[37] We might take to heart the same notion with regard to the repositioning of Jews and Judaism within Mediterranean studies.[38] Religion and specific religious identities did matter for the subjects we study. Beyond the theological meaning inherent in religious belief and practice, we can also speak of religion as a cultural force that gave meaning to the individual and collective lives of Jews. The cultural meaning of Judaism and of its various subsets—Sephardic, Ashkenazic, Mustarab, Romaniote, and so on—was central to Jewish self-understanding in the medieval and early modern periods.

Moreover, the geographic mobility of Mediterranean Jews also created opportunities for mobility between religious communities. Indeed, the peripatetic character of Sephardic Jewry between the fifteenth and seventeenth centuries offered new opportunities for self-fashioning and the creation of new categories of identity. As the Sephardim moved in and out of Muslim and Christian societies, they retained their older religious designations as Jews but simultaneously developed and emphasized newer economic and cultural identities. This is particularly notable for those Jews who had lived as Conversos—or Christians of Jewish ancestry—in Spain and Portugal before escaping Iberia and reverting openly to Judaism in North Africa, the Ottoman Empire, and even Counter-Reformation Italy. That these Sephardim often privileged ethnic, linguistic, familial, and intellectual identities over and against strictly religious ones also raises some interesting questions. They routinely eschewed standard religious categories in favor of invented terms such as "Levantines" or "Ponentines"—categories that loosely mapped onto "Spanish Jews" and "Hispano-Portuguese Conversos" (or former Conversos) and that deftly deflected questions of religious identity. At other times, the Sephardim also presented themselves as "Spaniards," "Spanish-speakers," or "men of the (Spanish and Portuguese) nation" rather than as Jews or Christians. Indeed, some Sephardim attempted to avoid committing to a religious tradition. Spanish and Portuguese Conversos who settled among the Sephardic communities of Italy and the Ottoman Empire often displayed a reticence to revert permanently to Judaism. Some lived as Jews in these regions but then as Christians when they returned to Iberia to trade, while others behaved publicly as Christians and privately as Jews. Belief that many Conversos readily took advantage of financial and political opportunities that were denied to professing Jews often led many Jews to reject their efforts to revert to Judaism, an attitude that ran counter to the repeated assertions of most rabbis.[39] Even as religious identity was contested, it remained central to Jewish self-understanding, and the Jews' status and movement within the larger society was primarily determined and limited by the common recognition of that identity.

While the centrality of religion in the construction of Mediterranean communal identities may seem somewhat obvious to many scholars working in Jewish studies, I think that there is a real possibility for a Mediterranean approach to undervalue Judaism per se. In their magisterial volume, *The Corrupting Sea*, Horden and Purcell see the Mediterranean as being comprised of micro regions that are the result of locally determined intersections of geography, climate, and human presence. This paradigm might well have led them to challenge the notion of the Jews as the prototypical Mediterranean society that transcended the influence of local factors. Unfortunately, the authors have almost nothing to say about Jews or, for that matter, about Christianity, Islam, and the notion of religious communities in general.[40] Indeed, one of the hallmarks of much of the new research on the Mediterranean is that religion is either ignored or reduced to its most basic anthropological categories: a need for ritual, a belief in a transcendent God or gods, and so on. The distinguishing particularities that characterized and separated each religion—between Judaism and Islam for instance, or between one form of Judaism and another—are often nonexistent. Even when Mediterranean studies scholarship addresses distinct religions as such, the tendency is to focus on hybridity, convivencia, and connectivity rather than the ways in which each group understood itself as unique.[41] I have long found this reticence to analyze both religion as a phenomenon and religions as operative conceptual communities to be puzzling and, with regard to the history of the Jews, quite problematic. It is simply hard to accept that the specific religious culture to which premodern people belonged was really so unimportant. For many of us working on premodern Jewish societies, as well as anyone aware of the importance of religious identities in the postcolonial Mediterranean, the notion of a Mediterranean world devoid of specific religious affiliations and tensions seems strikingly simplistic.[42]

Similarly, there has been a noticeable scholarly trend aimed at de-Judaizing Jews (or Israelis) by portraying them as more integrationist, more hybrid "Mediterraneans." Israeli historians have tended to think of their own national identity as one with deep roots in the Mediterranean region, conceiving of Jews and Israelis as historically native to the area, now coming home. Yaacov Shavit notes that scholars of Israeli and Jewish history have tried to re-read their "national" histories as "Mediterranean" since at least the 1970s.[43] Their detractors have rejected this trend, seeing Israelis as outsiders who are conspicuously, even criminally, out of place in the Mediterranean littoral. Other, less polemical, observers have argued that the Israeli concept of Mediterranean-ness and its analogues (Levantine-ness, *Yam Tikhoniyut*, *Mizrahiyut*, etc.) can simultaneously evade, embrace, and conceal categories of identity.[44] Such questions of Israeli authenticity and belonging intersect with Horden and Purcell's well-known model that seeks to distinguish being intrinsically "of" the Mediterranean region and not merely "in" it. Are Israeli Jews really foreign transplants playing at being Mediterranean—the result of modern European and Zionist fantasies that "orientalized" all Jews? Or are they correct in claiming a level of normativity with regard to their Mediterranean-ness? The controversial and contested nature of such disputes makes the prospect of avoiding questions of religious identity very appealing. When Jews, Muslims, and Christians—in all their various denominations and subethnic groups—can be viewed through the lens of a shared Mediterraneanism, debates about relative authenticity and belonging can be dismissed altogether. And yet, attractive as such trends may be, they are ultimately unconvincing. For Jewish studies in particular, emphasis on a shared cultural legacy cannot fully conceal the fact that, since the Middle Ages, Judaism was the key defining marker for all but the most elite Jews. Jewish society, however else we may choose to define it, was inextricably bound up with Judaism for most of its long history. As we contemplate the relative benefits of reading Jewish history through a Mediterraneanist lens, it is important not to lose sight of the religious factor in the premodern world and to explore how and why religious identities were invoked, ignored, or constructed and concealed.

Finally, I would like to briefly address the question of the regnant categories or "labels" used in reference to Mediterranean Jewry. The use of a Mediterranean frame for the analysis of Jewish studies can enable us to rethink and potentially transcend categories in Jewish studies that may unnecessarily limit our perceptions of Jewish identities and allegiances. It can raise questions about the utility of dividing the Jewish world into Sephardim and Ashkenazim—itself an extension of the larger historiographic division between "East and West"—or of similar binaries that juxtapose Sephardim and Mizrahim, colonial and indigenous, and so on.[45] Recent scholarship in Jewish studies has already made great strides toward revising the older historiography that separates the history of European Jewry from that of the Jews of the Muslim world. In addition to research that focuses on the Jews as a pan-Mediterranean society per se (à la Goitein), a variety of localized studies on Jewish communities around the early modern and modern Mediterranean suggest that the differences between Europe and the Middle East were not as stark as has often been assumed.⁴⁶ I would only add that rethinking such categories is also an opportunity to recognize the role that they have played in Jewish history. Before we jettison identitarian labels such as Sephardic or Mizrahi—problematic as these may be—we might pause to consider how and why these labels have been embraced, especially by those on the fringes of these societies. Such terms, no less than Mediterranean (or Levantine, to mention yet another popular construct) have provided otherwise disenfranchised Jews a means to establish a sense of communal belonging and to strengthen their cultural and religious identity.⁴⁷ More recently, terms that construct religious identities, such as *Dati*, *Haredi*, or even "Jewish," have often served the same ends. Thus, we might become more acutely aware of how various labels have offered a way in to communal history from which many Jews have often been economically, politically, and socially marginalized.⁴⁸

The current Mediterranean turn in historiography will no doubt find new ways to read old data and narratives with this latest set of tools and lenses. Nevertheless, it remains to be seen if our findings will be any less romanticized than those of earlier generations of scholars. In adopting a Mediterraneanist approach to Jewish studies, we would do well to heed the various notes of caution sounded by many working in that field. Paolo Giaccaria and Claudio Minca see a tendency within Mediterranean studies to create "a sort of (imagined) topography that too often essentializes it as a mythical space," and Simone Pinet warns against the uncritical use of the Mediterranean as a category of analysis, especially when it "presents itself so frequently as (morally) superior to other modes/lens, etc." This alarm at the potential popularity of a mythic Mediterranean also prompts Henk Driessen to wonder if the very notion of connectivity and fluidity has begun to taint our reading of the premodern Mediterranean world. He raises the question as to whether the characterizations of Mediterranean port cities as sites of a clear and distinct cosmopolitanism are anything more than "nostalgic celebrations by elites of a lost world that never really existed."⁴⁹ Scholars of Jewish studies would do well to heed such caveats against idealizing Mediterranean identity. In order for the methodological approaches of Mediterranean studies to truly enhance the field of Jewish studies, treatments of the Jews as "Mediterraneans" will have to be read against studies that elucidate the uniqueness of the Jewish experience.

The competing discourses on the Mediterranean are as different as the subject is enduringly popular. These varying approaches to Mediterranean studies have given rise to what Giaccaria and Minca call "conflictual and contradictory narratives [that] tend to penetrate each other, rendering the definition of a Mediterranean cultural space not only paradoxical, but also impossible."⁵⁰

In brief, we cannot agree on a definition of what "Mediterranean" means, and yet we cannot stop using it as a theoretical and heuristic tool. The "Mediterranean" as an interpretive category of historical and cultural markers is, then, endlessly elastic—expanding to become what we want and need it to be. Asking whether or not Jewish history can benefit from being viewed through the lens of the "Mediterranean" seems to beg a larger question—or questions—regarding our motivating concerns. If we wish to focus on a Jewish Mediterranean that is fundamentally cosmopolitan, mobile, and hybrid, there is much evidence to support such a stance and much good that it can offer.[51] But in order for us to avoid exchanging one set of overly romanticized notions for another, we need to probe a bit more deeply into the meaning and resonance of this "Mediterranean" character. If we are able to do so, following both the Mediterranean and the non-Mediterranean threads of Jewish history has the potential to lead us to a better understanding of the internal composition of Jewish society, past, present, and future.

JONATHAN RAY is the Samuel Eig Professor of Jewish Studies at Georgetown University. He is the author of *The Sephardic Frontier: The Reconquista and the Jewish Community in Medieval Iberia* (Cornell University Press, 2006) and *After Expulsion: 1492 and the Making of Sephardic Jewry* (NYU Press, 2013).

Notes

1. On Goitein as a bridge between Jewish and Mediterranean studies see Gideon Libson, "Hidden Worlds and Open Shutters: S. D. Goitein between Judaism and Islam," in *The Jewish Past Revisited: Reflections on Modern Jewish Historians*, ed. David N. Myers and David B. Ruderman (New Haven, CT: Yale University Press, 1998), 163–98; Steven M. Wasserstrom, "Apology for S. D. Goitein: An Essay," in *A Faithful Sea: The Religious Cultures of the Mediterranean, 1200–1700*, ed. Adnan A. Husain and Katherine E. Fleming (Oxford: Oneworld, 2007), 173–98; Fred Astren, "Goitein, Medieval Jews and 'The New Mediterranean Studies,'" *Jewish Quarterly Review* 102, no. 4 (2012): 513–31; and Peter N. Miller, "Two Men in a Boat: The Braudel-Goitein 'Correspondence' and the Beginning of Thalassography," in *The Sea: Thalassography and Historiography*, ed. Peter N. Miller (Ann Arbor: University of Michigan Press, 2013), 27–59.

2. Sarah Stroumsa: *Maimonides in His World: Portrait of a Mediterranean Thinker* (Princeton, NJ: Princeton University Press, 2009).

3. These terms are not completely stable. In some of the current literature on Mediterraneanism, ethno-religious pluralism can be both aligned with and in opposition to cosmopolitanism. See, for instance, E. Natalie Rothman, "Interpreting Dragomans: Boundaries and Crossings in the Early Modern Mediterranean," *Comparative Studies in Society and History* 51, no. 4 (2009): 771–800, at 771–72. Generally, though, cosmopolitanism

stands as a marker of having transcended the bounded cultures and allegiances of national, ethnic, or religious groups.

4. On Kallen see Daniel Greene, *The Jewish Origins of Cultural Pluralism: The Menorah Association and American Diversity* (Bloomington, IN: Indiana University Press, 2011); Susanne Klingenstein, *Jews in the American Academy 1900-1940: The Dynamics of Intellectual Assimilation* (New Haven, CT: Yale University Press, 1991); and Milton R. Konvitz, ed., *Legacy of Horace M. Kallen* (Cranbury, NJ: Associated University Presses, 1987). On the continued echoes of Kallen's terminology in Israeli society see Daniel Gutwein, "From Melting Pot to Multiculturalism: Or, the Privatization of Israeli Identity," *Israeli Identity in Transition*, ed. Anita Shapira (Westport, CT: Praeger, 2004), 215–31; Henriette Dahan-Kalev, "The 'Mizrahim': Challenging the Ethos of the Melting Pot," in *Who's "Left" in Israel?*, ed. Dan Leon (Brighton: Sussex Academic Press, 2004), 161–67; and Shlomo Avineri, "The Theory and Practice of Pluralism in Israel," in *Perspectives on Israeli Pluralism*, ed. Kitty O. Cohen and Jane S. Gerber (New York: Israel Colloquium, 1991), 17–22.

5. Or, to follow Andrew C. Hess in his critique of Braudel, we might think of the Jewish Mediterranean in terms of "the patterns of both unity and diversity that lie beneath the surface of events," *The Forgotten Frontier: A History of the Sixteenth-Century Ibero-African Frontier* (Chicago: Chicago University Press, 1978), 1.

6. Peregrine Horden and Nicholas Purcell, *The Corrupting Sea: A Study of Mediterranean History* (Oxford: Blackwell, 2000), 396–400. To be sure, Horden and Purcell's work is more focused on geographical diversity than religious or cultural diversity, as I note below. Nevertheless, I believe that several of the paradigms they develop with regard to the premodern Mediterranean do have resonance for the study of the region's cultural and religious history, including Jewish history.

7. Kwame Anthony Appiah, "Cosmopolitan Patriotism," *Critical Inquiry* 23, no. 3 (1997): 617–39, at 618.

8. A sense of this growing literature can be found in Michael Herzfeld, "The Horns of the Mediterraneanist Dilemma," *American Ethnologist* 11, no. 3 (1984): 439–54; John Marino, "Mediterranean Studies and the Remaking of Pre-Modern Europe," *Journal of Early Modern History* 15, no. 5 (2011): 385–412; Paolo Giaccaria and Claudio Minca, "The Mediterranean Alternative," *Progress in Human Geography* 35, no. 3 (2010): 345–65; and the collected studies presented in William V. Harris, ed., *Rethinking the Mediterranean* (Oxford: Oxford University Press, 2005).

9. Arnold Franklin, "Relations between Nesi'im and Exilarchs: Competition or Cooperation," in *Esoteric and Exoteric Aspects in Judeo-Arabic Culture*, ed. Benjamin Hary and Haggai Ben-Shammai (Leiden: Brill, 2006), 301–21; Elinoar Bareket, "Jewish Inter-Communication in the Mediterranean Basin in the Eleventh Century as Documented in the Correspondence of 'Eli ben 'Amram," *European Journal of Jewish Studies* 2, no. 1 (2008): 1–19.

10. On genizah documentation of Jewish contacts from the Adriatic to India, see Abraham David, "The Role of Egyptian Jews in Sixteenth-Century International Trade with Europe: A Chapter in Social-Economic Integration in the Middle East," in *"From a Sacred Source:" Genizah Studies in Honor of Professor Stefan C. Reif*, ed. Ben Othwaite and Siam Bhayo (Leiden: Brill, 2010), 99–126, at 103–4.

11. On Sephardi families see Julia R. Lieberman, ed., *Sephardi Family Life in the Early Modern Diaspora* (Waltham, MA: Brandeis University Press, 2011); Christopher H. Johnson et al, ed., *Transregional and Transnational Families in Europe and Beyond: Experiences since the Middle Ages* (New York: Berghahn Books, 2011); and Edgar Morin, *Vidal and His Family:*

From Salonica to Paris: The Story of a Sephardic Family in the Twentieth Century (Brighton: Sussex Academic Press, 2009).

12. Sarah Abrevaya Stein, "The Field of In Between," *International Journal of Middle East Studies* 46, no. 3 (2014), 581–82.

13. See Mark R. Cohen, *Poverty and Charity in the Jewish Community of Medieval Egypt* (Princeton, NJ: Princeton University Press, 2005), as well as the documents collected by the same author in *The Voice of the Poor in the Middle Ages: An Anthology of Documents from the Cairo Geniza* (Princeton, NJ: Princeton University Press, 2005).

14. David Abulafia, "Mediterranean History as Global History," *History and Theory* 50, no. 2 (2011): 220–28, at 225.

15. David Abulafia, *The Mediterranean in History* (London: Thames and Hudson, 2016), 19.

16. Horden and Purcell, *The Corrupting Sea*, part 4.

17. An older example of Jewish intellectual networks being used to foster local political goals can be seen in the case of Joseph ibn Abitur and the struggle for succession of Jewish communal leadership in al-Andalus. Jonathan Ray, "The Jews of al-Andalus: Factionalism in the Golden Age," in *Jews and Muslims in the Islamic World*, ed. Zvi Zohar (Bethesda, MD: University Press of Maryland, 2013).

18. On Mediterranean Jewish networks and poor relief, see Cohen, *The Voice of the Poor in the Middle Ages*, 47–67; Francesca Trivellato, *The Familiarity of Strangers: The Sephardic Diaspora, Livorno, and Cross-Cultural Trade in the Early Modern Period* (New Haven, CT: Yale University Press, 2009), 23, 49, 66, and 94; and Miriam Bodian, "The 'Portuguese' Dowry Societies in Venice and Amsterdam: A Case Study in Communal Differentiation within the Marrano Diaspora," *Italia* 6 (1987): 30–61. See also Yaron Ayalon, "Poor Relief in Ottoman Jewish Communities," in *Jews, Christians, and Muslims in Medieval and Early Modern Times*, ed. Arnold Franklin, Roxani Eleni Margariti, Marina Rustow, and Uriel Simonsohn (Leiden: Brill, 2014), 77–82. Francesca Trivellato has shown that methods of poor relief could serve to marginalize some while supporting others. In the Livornese context, methods of poor relief reinforced boundaries between Ashkenazim and Sephardim. Trivellato, *The Familiarity of Strangers*, 94.

19. Jessica L. Goldberg, "Friendship and Hierarchy: Rhetorical Stances in Geniza Mercantile Letters," in *Jews, Christians, and Muslims in Medieval and Early Modern Times*, ed. Arnold Franklin, Roxani Eleni Margariti, Marina Rustow, and Uriel Simonsohn (Leiden: Brill, 2014), 273–86, shows the intricate relationship between connection and exclusion.

20. Matthias Lehmann, *Emissaries from the Holy Land: The Sephardic Diaspora and the Practice of Pan-Judaism in the Eighteenth Century* (Stanford, CA: Stanford University Press, 2014).

21. Abraham David, "The Role of Egyptian Jews," 111; and Meir Benayahu, "Genizah Documents on the Commercial Business of Ha-Ari and on His Family Members in Egypt," in *Sefer Zikaron le-ha-Rav Yitshak Nissim*, vol. 4 (Jerusalem: Yad ha-Rav Nissim, 1985), 225–53 [in Hebrew].

22. Jonathan Ray, *After Expulsion: 1492 and the Making of Sephardic Jewry* (New York: New York University Press, 2013), ch. 5.

23. Simha Goldin, "'Companies of Disciples' and 'Companies of Colleagues': Communication in Jewish Intellectual Circles," in *Communication in the Jewish Diaspora: The Pre-Modern World*, ed. Sophia Menache (Leiden: Brill, 1996), 127–38, at 133; and Elisheva Carlebach, "Rabbinic Circles as Messianic Pathways in the Post-Expulsion Era," *Judaism* 41, no. 3 (1992): 208–16, at 209.

24. In 1509, Sholal wrote a *takkanah* that exempted Levantine scholars from taxes, perhaps as a means of drawing more scholars to the region. Abraham David, *To Come to the Land: Immigration and Settlement in 16th-Century Eretz-Israel* (Tuscaloosa: University of Alabama Press, 1999), 81, 83.

25. David, *To Come to the Land*, 80.

26. Jacob Katz, "The Dispute between Jacob Berab and Levi ben Habib over Renewing Ordination," *Binah* 1 (1989): 119–41; and Robert M. Cover, "Bringing the Messiah through the Law: A Case Study," in *Religion, Morality and the Law*, ed. J. Roland Pennrock and John W. Chapman (New York: NYU Press, 1988), 201–17.

27. Moses ben Isaac Alashkar, *Sefer She'elot u-teshuvot Maharam Alashkar* (Sudilkov: Bi-defus Y. Madpis, 1834), nos. 3, 20, 25, 48, and 99.

28. David, *To Come to the Land*, 83. This dynamic became a notable feature of rabbinic networks for centuries. For the nineteenth-century Mediterranean, see Jessica M. Marglin, "Mediterranean Modernity through Jewish Eyes: The Transimperial Life of Abraham Ankawa," *Jewish Social Studies* 20 (2014): 34–68.

29. Henk Driessen, "Mediterranean Port Cities," *History and Anthropology* 16, no. 1 (2005): 132; and also Dieter Haller, "The Cosmopolitan Mediterranean: Myth and Reality," *Zeitschrift für Ethnologie* 129, no. 1 (2004): 29–47, at 30.

30. See the collections of essays in David Cesarani, ed., *Port Jews: Jewish Communities in Cosmopolitan Maritime Trading Centres, 1550–1950* (London: Frank Cass, 2002); and David Cesarani and Gemma Romain, eds., *Jews and Port Cities, 1590–1990: Commerce, Community and Cosmopolitanism* (London: Vallentine Mitchell, 2006). On the early modern Sephardic context in particular, see Matthias Lehmann, "A Livornese 'Port Jew,' and the Sephardim of the Ottoman Empire," *Jewish Social Studies* 11, no. 2 (New Series) (2005): 51–76.

31. Driessen, "Mediterranean Port Cities," 134. It remains to be seen how this narrative might apply to premodern Jews, who already possessed clear, if complex, notions of a shared "national" culture, history, and destiny long before the rise of modern states and their nationalist identities.

32. For three distinct approaches to the question, see Moshe Rosman, *How Jewish Is Jewish History?* (Portland, OR: Littman Library, 2007); Seth Schwartz, *Were the Jews a Mediterranean Society? Reciprocity and Solidarity in Ancient Judaism* (Princeton, NJ: Princeton University Press, 2009); and *The Faith of Fallen Jews: Yosef Hayim Yerushalmi and the Writing of Jewish History*, ed. David N. Meyers and Alexander Kay (Waltham, MA: Brandeis University Press, 2014).

33. Phillip Ackerman-Lieberman, *The Business of Identity: Jews, Muslims and Economic Life in Medieval Egypt* (Stanford, CA: Stanford University Press, 2014), 48.

34. Peregrine Horden, "Mediterranean Excuses: Historical Writing on the Mediterranean since Braudel," *History and Anthropology* 16, no. 1 (2005): 25–30, at 29–30.

35. This observation need not force us toward the same conclusions of Jacob Katz and others who argued that such external contacts were either unimportant or, worse, outright obstacles to the Jews reaching their full potential as a people. Jacob Katz, *Exclusiveness and Tolerance: Studies in Jewish-Gentile Relations in Medieval and Modern Times* (New York: Schocken, 1962).

36. See the discussions in Rosman, *How Jewish Is Jewish History?*; Aaron Hughes, "Jewish Studies Is Too Jewish," *The Chronicle Review*, March 28, 2014, B4-5; and the essays on "American Jewish History and American Historical Writing" in *American Jewish History* 95, no. 1 (2009).

37. Hussein A. Fancy, *The Mercenary Mediterranean: Sovereignty, Religion and Violence in the Medieval Crown of Aragon* (Chicago: Chicago University Press, 2016), 129–30, following the work of Steven Justice and Brad Gregory.

38. Categories such as Jew, Christian, Muslim, and Spain, Portugal, Maghreb, dar al-Islam, and so on are not mere modern fabrications but indeed existed and had importance in the premodern world. They represent an important potential contribution to the way in which people conceived of their own identity and their place in the world.

39. Dora Zsom, "'But the names of the Wicked will Rot' (Prov. 10:7): Names used by Conversos in the Responsa Literature," *Hispania Judaica Bulletin* 8 (2011): 193–213, and Dora Zsom, "The Return of the Conversos to Judaism in the Ottoman Empire and North Africa," *Hispania Judaica Bulletin* 7 (2010): 335–47.

40. Fred Astren, "Goitein, Medieval Jews and the New Mediterranean Studies," *Jewish Quarterly Review* 102, no. 4 (2012): 523.

41. Adnan A. Husain and K. E. Flemming, eds., *A Faithful Sea: The Religious Cultures of the Mediterranean, 1200–1700* (Oxford: Oneworld, 2007); and Abulafia, "Mediterranean History as Global History," 226–27.

42. In the field of anthropology, distinct religious and ethnic categories remain marginal objects of research for most scholars working on the Middle East and North Africa. Seteny Shami and Nefissa Naguib, "Occluding Difference: Ethnic Identity and the Shifting Zones of Theory on the Middle East and North Africa," in *Anthropology of the Middle East and North Africa: Into the New Millennium*, ed. Sherine Hafez and Susan Slyommovics (Bloomington, IN: Indiana University Press, 2013), 23–46.

43. Yaacov Shavit, "Mediterranean History and the History of the Mediterranean: Further Reflections," *Journal of Mediterranean Studies* 4, no. 2 (1994): 313–29.

44. Alexandra Nocke, *The Place of the Mediterranean in Modern Israeli Identity* (Leiden: Brill, 2009), 167–68, 177–84. For a sense of how Mizrahi Israelis complicate debates over Israeli-ness, Mediterranean-ness, and authenticity, see Harvey E. Goldberg and Chen Bram, "Sephardic/Mizrahi/Arab-Jews: Reflections on Critical Sociology and the Study of Middle Eastern Jewry within the Context of Israeli Society," in *Studies in Contemporary Jewry* 22 (2007): 227–56.

45. Harvey E. Goldberg, "From Sephardi to Mizrahi and Back Again: Changing Meanings of 'Sephardi' in Its Social Environments," *Jewish Social Studies* 15, no. 1 (2008): 165–88; Joshua Schreier, "The Creation of the 'Israélite Indigène': Jewish Merchants in Early Colonial Oran," *Journal of North African Studies* 17, no. 5 (2012): 757–72; and Sarah Abrevaya Stein, "Dividing South from North: French Colonialism, Jews, and the Algerian Sahara," *Journal of North African Studies* 17, no. 5 (2012): 773–92.

46. A sampling includes the essays collected in *Ottoman and Turkish Jewry: Community and Leadership*, ed. Aron Rodrigue (Bloomington, IN: Indiana University Press, 1992); Minna Rozen, *A History of the Jewish Community in Istanbul: The Formative Years, 1453–1566* (Leiden: Brill, 2002); Minna Rozen, "Collective Memories and Group Boundaries: The Judeo-Spanish Diaspora between the Lands of Christendom and the World of Islam," *Michael* 14 (1997): 35–52; Kenneth R. Stow, "Corporate Double Talk: Kehillat Kodesh and Universitas in the Roman Jewish Sixteenth Century Environment," *Journal of Jewish Thought & Philosophy* 8, no. 2 (1999): 283–301; and José Alberto Rodrigues da Silva Tavim, *Os judeus na expansão portuguesa em Marrocos durante o século XVI: origens e actividades duma comunidade* (Braga, Portugal: APPACDM Distrital, 1997).

47. See the mission statement of the recently inaugurated *Journal of Levantine Studies*. All these terms are problematic, to be sure, but a perfect label for such communal identities may well elude us. As Seth Schwartz has noted regarding the term *Judaism*, "no one has yet come up with a word other than Judaism for what Judaism is." Seth Schwartz, "How Many

Judaisms Were There? A Critique of Neusner and Smith on Definition and Mason and Boyarin on Categorization," *Journal of Ancient Judaism* 2, no. 2 (2011): 208–38, at 227, n. 51.

48. On the problematic nature of the quasi-geographical terms *Mediterranean*, *Orient*, and *Levant*, see Alexandra Nocke, *The Place of the Mediterranean in Modern Israeli Identity* (Leiden: Brill, 2009).

49. Giaccaria and Minca, "The Mediterranean Alternative," 346–47; Driessen, "Mediterranean Port Cities," 135; and Simone Pinet, "Between the Seas: Apolonio and Alexander," in *In and of the Mediterranean: Medieval and Early Modern Iberian Studies*, ed. Michelle Hamilton and Núria Silleras Fernández (Nashville: Vanderbilt University Press, 2015), 75–98, at 76. See also Michael Herzfeld, "Practical Mediterraneanism: Excuses for Everything from Epistemology to Eating," in *Rethinking the Mediterranean*, ed. William V. Harris (Oxford: Oxford University Press, 2005), 45–63.

50. Giaccaria and Minca, "The Mediterranean Alternative," 348.

51. Abulafia, "Mediterranean History as Global History," 221.

3

CAN WE SPEAK OF A GEOGRAPHICAL AXIS IN MEDIEVAL JEWISH CULTURE?

Andrew Berns

IN THE LANDS SURROUNDING THE MEDITERRANEAN SEA in the later Middle Ages, Jews energetically debated the way in which certain plants were grown and how to identify them properly. These debates drew their heat from a legal requirement: the Bible prohibited Jews from donning garments containing both linen and wool (*sha'atenez*), and rabbis and writers throughout the post-biblical period strove to understand and honor that law. Proper observance of this stricture required precise identification of plant fibers; a false identification might lead Jews to transgress a scriptural proscription. We possess legal writings from Spain, Venetian Crete, and the Italian peninsula composed during the thirteenth, fourteenth, and fifteenth centuries that struggle to distinguish hemp from flax: the former, mixed with wool, would not necessarily constitute a violation of the *sha'atenez* prohibition; the latter would. These legal texts illuminate the botanical knowledge of medieval Jewry and expose the social and economic pressures they faced.

The sources also reveal an agricultural axis that divided southern from northern Europe. Southern European Jews lived in areas where hemp was not easily distinguished from flax. Accordingly, they were scrupulous in their avoidance of hemp. Conversely, northern European Jews at this time were confident in their ability to differentiate flax from hemp and were more permissive in their use of hemp with wool. These discrepancies in the interpretation of religious law point to a geographical cleavage in Jewish culture and provide a vantage point from which we are able to enrich current debates about the Mediterranean's agricultural and ecological unity.

Historians and geographers have long discussed the degree to which the Mediterranean region is characterized by a consistent climate and uniform growing conditions. Questions of Mediterranean unity versus disunity mark the historiography of the premodern Mediterranean. The chief antagonists in this debate are Fernand Braudel, who argued for overarching Mediterranean unity, and Nicholas Purcell and Peregrine Horden, who contend that disunity prevails in the Mediterranean region. Famously, Braudel stressed the Mediterranean's cultural and ecological unity.[1] Conversely, in their "ecologizing" approach, Horden and Purcell emphasize that microregions characterize the Mediterranean. In *The Corrupting Sea* they write that the "determining capacity of the environment was weak" and insist that microregions can be more intensely connected to others far away than to neighboring regions.[2] Horden and Purcell argue that Braudel's broad brushstrokes are overly simplified at best and false at worst.

The customs, laws, and debates of premodern Jews provide a perspective from which we can freshly reassess this decades-old controversy. The clothes Jews wore, the tailors they employed to sew them, and the identification of the plants that provided the raw materials for that raiment all indicate a spatial border: the Jewish legal texts examined in this chapter divide ultramontane Europe from Mediterranean Europe. Sources from the Hellenic territories of the Venetian Republic, chiefly Crete; the Italian Peninsula; and Spain display similar patterns of botanical cultivation and nomenclature. An assessment of those similarities enables us to draw a longitudinal line near the northern littoral of the Mediterranean. South of that line, Jewish communities followed consistent precedents regarding the observation of the *sha'atenez* prohibition. North of that line, in ultramontane Europe, different growing conditions led to a divergent understanding of what the Bible and its rabbinic exponents meant by "linen." The jurisprudential controversies surrounding an arcane law and its quotidian application help us see more than just what Jews grew, bought, and wore; it helps us see that, for Jews at least, the Mediterranean meant something concrete in botanical terms. Though Braudel's thesis addressed the entire Mediterranean—including North Africa and the Levant—this modest contribution identifies Jewish notions of botanical unity across select parts of the Mediterranean.[3] Braudel's work, like that of Horden and Purcell, deemphasizes religion, particularly Judaism. As Jessica Marglin and Matthias Lehmann point out in their introduction to this volume, "Jews appear relatively infrequently in the pages of *The Mediterranean*. And when they do, their religion is almost an afterthought; as with Christianity and Islam, Braudel refers to Judaism as a 'civilization,' rather than a religious tradition."[4] This chapter puts one facet of Judaism—the interpretation of a Mosaic law concerning sartorial practices—at the center rather than the periphery of Jewish concerns. In doing so my contribution aims to ground Horden and Purcell's notion of "religious landscape" in the specific, lived experience of medieval Mediterranean Jewry.[5]

Throughout the diaspora some Jews took care not to conjoin garments that contain both wool and linen (*sha'atenez*). The prohibition derives from two biblical verses. The first, in Leviticus, states, "Neither shall there come upon thee a garment of two kinds of stuff mingled together." The second, in Deuteronomy, is more precise: "thou shalt not wear a mingled stuff, wool and linen together."[6] The biblical word for wool (*tzemer*) is unambiguous and does not present problems of translation or identification. The second fiber (*pishtim*) is more problematic. Often translated as "linen," it can also mean flax.

In the entire medieval Jewish world, the combination of wool with linen/flax was illicit. For devout Jews in modern times it still is. In the Middle Ages problems frequently arose in regions that grew hemp. Even though wool and flax were easily distinguished, hemp and flax were not. In most growing areas, hemp was understood to be a different species than linen/flax.[7] But in Crete, for example, the opposite was the case: hemp was conflated with linen/flax and therefore forbidden to be used as thread to sew a woolen garment (see table 3.1).

The difficulty was not unique to Crete; as one scholar of medieval textiles observed, "the cultivation, manufacture, and uses of canvas [hemp] so closely resembled those of flax [that] these two textiles may be considered virtually interchangeable."[8] Hemp was far from a specialty or luxury product. On the contrary, it was, in the words of two environmental historians of the Middle Ages, "the most vital vegetable fiber in Europe until about 1300" as well as "the source of the region's linen cloth."[9]

While problems distinguishing hemp from linen may not have been unique to Crete, those problems took on additional urgency because of the prominence of textile manufacture and trade. The production of textiles and garments, especially but not exclusively silk, was, along with tanning and dyeing, among the most popular professions practiced by the Jews throughout Byzantium.[10] One expert on Byzantine Jewry goes so far as to say that the textile industry "was the mainstay of economic life for the Jewish community."[11] Accordingly, Crete is a good place to explore controversies about the identification and use of plant fibers.

Table 3.1. Depiction of various places' stance on the combination of wool with linen/flax.

Wool (צמר)	+	Flax (פשתים)	=	A forbidden mixture everywhere
Wool (צמר)	+	Hemp (קנבוס)	=	A permitted mixture in many places
Wool (צמר)	+	Hemp (קנבוס)	=	A forbidden mixture on Crete

There are additional reasons to focus on Crete. Of all of Venice's Hellenic territories, Crete hosted the largest Jewish population.[12] The documentation, accordingly, is rich. In the years following the Fourth Crusade (1204) and the Venetian conquest of the Mediterranean's fifth-largest island, historical sources that shed light on Jews' lives become more abundant. One of the best sources we have for Jewish life on Crete is a collection of lay ordinances assembled by the sixteenth-century rabbi and historian Elia Capsali and published in the middle of the twentieth century by Elias Artom and Umberto Cassuto as *Takkanot Kandiyah*.[13] The *Takkanot Kandiyah* reflect many aspects of Jewish life on Crete: liturgical, administrative, financial. They also demonstrate the extent of Jewish involvement in agriculture and testify to the presence of rural Jewish populations. These documents indicate that Cretan Jews herded cattle, goats, and sheep; produced and sold cheese; and puzzled over the botanical nomenclature of fibers used to sew garments.

One ordinance from 1363 states that Jews should not buy hemp threads, on the grounds that hemp is generally mistaken as flax; therefore, its use with wool would constitute a forbidden mixture in violation of Leviticus's proscription. The authors of this ordinance declare that "a garment of wool and linen together may not come upon them, unless with careful examination and testing, for the love of the most high God. They may not buy threads presumed to be hemp, but which in fact are flax. Their hands should not be stretched forth to provide a place for Satan in this matter. Accordingly, the man who does so presumptuously will be sentenced to hell. Therefore we decree that all Jews [must] seek out a Jewish tailor to sew their garments."[14]

Here the lay leadership of Crete rules that the plant known as hemp (*canvus*) is identical to flax and thereby constitutes a forbidden mixture when joined with wool. There are two ways to understand this statement: as a legal stringency regarding the *sha'atenez* prohibition or as confusion on Crete as to what actually constitutes flax. Either way, the language of the text is forceful and indicates that the writers of the ordinance worried that their community might take this matter lightly: "their hands should not be stretched forth to provide a place for Satan in this matter." Proper observance of this law was taken seriously on Crete.

Debates about botanical nomenclature were not mere legalistic squabbles; they resulted in social changes. In order to properly honor a sartorial stricture, Cretan Jews were enjoined to shift their business practices and to alter their domestic arrangements. "Therefore we decree," the ordinance goes on, "that all Jews seek out a Jewish tailor to sew their garments." Even so, provision was made for alternative arrangements that would have marked consequences for future generations: "If a Jewish tailor cannot be found, and if he requires a

Christian tailor to sew for him a woolen garment, the Jew should bring the Christian tailor to his house and [the Christian tailor] should sew for him in the domain of the Jew, so that he may see with his own eyes that [the Christian tailor] not reinforce a flax garment with woolen ones, or [use] threads of flax to sew [a garment of] wool."[15]

The need to ensure proper observance of the biblical prohibition concerning *sha'atenez* resulted in the lodging of Christian tailors in Jewish homes. Apparently the authors of this ordinance foresaw that there would be a deficit of qualified Jewish tailors, or, perhaps as likely, that Jews would seek the services of an expert seamster, regardless of his religion. Because the restriction concerning *sha'atenez* was rooted in a biblical prohibition, its observance was taken very seriously. "The sages recalled," the ordinance's authors remind us, "that one who sees a forbidden mixture in his garment should remove it, even in the public marketplace."[16] In other words, a Jew was expected to suffer the ill effects of public embarrassment so as not to transgress a biblical commandment. To avoid this, the Cretan lay leadership decreed that "gentile artisans shall sew garments for Jews in Jewish homes."[17]

On Crete in the Middle Ages, it was not unusual for people of one religion to hire workers or apprentices and even lodge them in their own homes.[18] In fact, the practice became highly common among Cretan Jews. What is unusual is that in the space of only a few generations, the Jewish leadership of Crete abruptly reversed its ruling. In 1363, they encouraged—or at least allowed—Jews to host and board gentile tailors in their homes. A legal requirement led to a social practice: inviting Christians into Jewish homes to perform a job. That, in turn, posed halakhic problems: by the early years of the sixteenth century, the situation was viewed as an intolerable threat to the community.

In 1518, about five generations after the 1363 ordinance, Elia Capsali (who originally assembled the *Takkanot Kandiyah* that were eventually published in 1943) proposed a legal reform concerning the widespread practice of Jews hosting gentiles. Capsali sets the scene in dramatic fashion: "and it was that day, the second of Ḥeshvan in the year 1518, the week of the pericope Noah [Genesis 6:9 to 11:32], I, a mere boy, alone among all the people in the house of my father's family . . . was required to explicate and investigate the affairs of our community, may its Rock protect it and may it thrive!"[19] In 1518, Capsali was either thirty-four or thirty-five years old and certainly not a "boy" (*tzaʻir*) any longer. The invocation of youth is meant to stress his humility, especially in the context of his illustrious family. "Young and old were there," Capsali informs us, "wishing to know what Israel should do. I looked into doors, into the doors of some of the Jewish artisans who are found among us, such as tailors and cobblers." What the rabbi and historian saw was an affront to his sensibilities. Peering into the homes and shops of his community's tailors and cobblers, Capsali noted:

> They had taken gentiles for themselves, whomever they chose, and settled them securely in their homes, in their courtyards and castles.[20] They are not afraid of what our sages of blessed memory said—do not give up the idea of divine retribution [when you see sinners prosper].[21] They also do not harken their hearts to the law of our authority, the exalted government of Venice, who decreed in their wisdom that gentiles shall not regularly be found serving [Jews] in Jewish homes, for many reasons, and under penalty of a monetary fine: he shall pay as the judges determine.[22]

Cretan Jews, living as they did in a Venetian colony, were subject to the authority of Venice's Jewish leadership. Capsali's remarks indicate that Venetian rabbis noted and forbade the widespread practice of gentile apprentices and laborers working in Jewish homes.[23] The Jews of Crete failed to heed Venice's authority. The punishment Capsali proposed was a fine—the legally sanctioned punitive measure for this category of offense.

Capsali's focus here is on his community's disobedience of Venetian authority. Later on his tone shifts, and his language becomes more caustic and condemnatory: he slides into moral opprobrium. "From this day forward," the Cretan rabbi harangued his congregants, "no one from among our people, man or woman, foreigner or resident, near or far, whoever he may be, from the artisans mentioned above, shall increase his sin and add evil to his evil."[24] Nor shall Jews "be permitted ever again to take gentile attendants to remain all day long within the community to serve him." Hiring and harboring gentile "attendants" was not only an affront to Venetian decrees; it was morally unacceptable to invite non-Jews "within the community."[25]

These ordinances demonstrate the significance of agricultural practices and of botanical knowledge. In the 1360s, Cretan Jewish authorities scolded their community about laxity in the observance of the biblical commandment not to sew wool and linen together. In order to ensure proper respect for this law, they allowed Jews to engage gentile tailors with one proviso: that Jews lodge them in their homes in order to supervise them more attentively. So far as we know, Cretan Jews did exactly that: by the 1510s, their practice of hosting gentile tailors and cobblers was so common that it earned condemnation from Venetian jurists. A seemingly insignificant gaffe (confusing one plant and its thread for another) led to social intercourse and thence to the violation of a prohibition. Properly identifying plants was essential to medieval Jews.

Long before these Cretan ordinances were promulgated, Greek-speaking Jewry acquired a reputation for legal rigor with regard to the observance of the *sha'atenez* prohibition. More specifically, the tendency of Jews throughout the

Hellenic world, including Crete, to equate hemp with flax was noted by jurists and compilers in other settings. For example, the thirteenth-century Roman writer Tzidkiyahu ben Avraham Anav, better known as Tzidkiyahu ha-Rofe, criticized Greek Jews' tendency to be "overscrupulous" in this matter. If we cast our gaze back in time from the fourteenth to the thirteenth century, and west from Crete to the Italian peninsula, we see how issues related to textiles—not only their manufacture but also the harvesting and preparation of their raw materials—play a role in medieval Jewish life and law.

In *Shibbole ha-Leket* (*Ears of Gleaning*), his popular collection of legal teachings, Tzidkiyahu ha-Rofe wrote a section on laws of *kilayyim* ("diverse kinds").[26] He observed that this is notoriously difficult material: "I myself know that the laws of *kilayyim* are somewhat jumbled, because the tractate *Kilayyim* has no *gemara*, and those *mishnayot* are not clear to us as are the other tractates. We are like blind men finding our way down from the *arubbah*," literally the aperture in the roof of a villa. By this, Tzidkiyahu meant that interpreters could only reach the truth by chance.

To Tzidkiyahu ha-Rofe, Greek interpreters of Jewish law were excessively stringent about *sha'atenez*. In his work he cited Rabbi Moses Cohen "in the land of Greece."[27] Tzidkiyahu reports that Cohen had heard that some people in Greece had forbidden the use of hemp with wool, thinking that hemp is the same as flax.[28] Tzidkiyahu refutes this view, insisting that it is a widely accepted practice throughout the Jewish world to wear woolen garments sewn with hemp. "Let us return to our subject," the Roman scholar writes, "to the overscrupulous ones who hesitate on this matter, those who slander the earlier authorities who treated this matter in a lenient fashion since the days of their forefathers in all the lands of the diaspora: Germany, France, England, and Provence, for all of them wear wool sewn with hemp. No one had second thoughts in the matter."[29]

This geographical grouping suggests an agricultural demarcation in medieval Jewish life. Italy, the areas controlled by the Byzantine Empire, and Spain are all conspicuously missing from this list. This indicates that northern Europeans lived in a place with divergent agricultural practices—or simply had different botanical traditions according to which hemp and flax were sharply differentiated. Even though Provence has roughly five hundred kilometers of shoreline on the Mediterranean, growing conditions there were fundamentally different from those in more southerly locales. The Italian peninsula, Crete, and Spain (as we shall see) formed a unified biome, at least to a number of medieval Jews who wrote about *sha'atenez*. Since these texts originate in ultramontane as well as Mediterranean environments, they cannot definitively resolve the persistent debate within Mediterranean studies concerning whether or not the region is characterized by ecological unity or disunity (Braudel versus Horden and Purcell). Still, they do point to the importance of place in Jewish law and culture and suggest that in the lands washed by the Great Sea, Jews interpreted their laws—and their natural environments—differently than did their coreligionists elsewhere.

Tzidkiyahu ha-Rofe's brief discussion of the complex laws of *kilayyim* show that he was aware of how Jewish customs differ according to local and regional conditions. This passage in *Shibbole ha-Leket* demonstrates a dividing line between Jewish diasporas. The observance of the *sha'atenez* restriction varied from northern to southern Europe. That variation indicates one of two possibilities: either agricultural practices were different in southern versus northern Europe or there were shifts in botanical nomenclature—what was known as "hemp" in one place may actually have been flax in another. Either way, Tzidkiyahu's geographical taxonomy suggests an agricultural axis in Jewish life.

This thirteenth-century Roman writer is not the only Jew of the later Middle Ages who knew how important geography was to Jewish agricultural laws. In Spain at the beginning of the fourteenth century, Asher ben Yeḥiel (d. 1327), better known as "Rosh," authored an undated *responsum* concerning the threads being sewn into Jews' garments.[30] Unfortunately, the original question does not survive; we have only the response: "Whereas concerning what you wrote, that you heard there is a custom in Narbonne to be stringent regarding sewing, that is sewing garments acquired from gentiles: you do not know on what they base this practice. Know that this is a regional issue (*ki ha-davar talui be-ḥiluk mekomot*). There is a place where one only finds hemp, and in such a place there is no need for a leniency concerning sewing."

Here Rabbi Asher emphasizes that different Jewish communities have divergent practices concerning the *sha'atenez* prohibition. In a place where one finds only hemp, one need not be stringent concerning *sha'atenez* because it is permissible to sew hemp together with wool. In an area that abounds in flax, however, one would have to be careful. The Spanish rabbi's ruling is justified by his knowledge of the different growing regions throughout the Jewish diaspora:

> However in these places [Narbonne and its environs] the majority is flax, and you would have to be lenient concerning sewing, and have them sew with hemp. Regarding what you asked, if the gentile [who sews the garment] makes an informal statement "that which I sell is sewn with hemp" [and may therefore be trusted concerning the content of the thread] I am accustomed to always rule not to believe him. For it is known to every gentile that Jewish tailors go around in search of villages [where they may] buy thread made of hemp to sew with it, for it [hemp] is not commonly found, as flax is. Therefore one ought to suspect that the gentile improves the value of his merchandise by saying that it is hemp, and we should not believe him.

Rabbi Asher's response shows how economic issues are closely connected to regional customs and the identification of plants: whether or not to trust a gentile merchant who claims to sew with hemp depends on where that transaction takes place and what is normally grown in that area. Rosh's response also signals that Jews traveled to country towns in order to buy hemp thread: hemp was made in the countryside and sold in fairs there.

This should not surprise us, as Spanish Jews were considerably attached to the land and its products; they farmed extensively. Particularly during and after the *Reconquista*, when they were rewarded for their services in support of Christian conquerors with tracts of land, they settled in rural areas.[31] As Salo Baron wrote with regard to Spain, "her great fertility, the character and density of her population, which made the suburban type of farming highly remunerative, and the prolonged friendly relations with both the Muslim and Christian regimes, encouraged more Jews there than probably in any other country of the world to own and cultivate land."[32] To choose only one example: during the fifteenth century in the Aragonese city of Huesca, Jews were widely known to be "for the most part cultivators of fields and vineyards."[33] For Spanish Jews, as for their coreligionists in Italy and on Crete, the laws of *sha'atenez* were far from bookish abstractions; they related to agricultural, economic, and social realities that medieval Jews experienced on a daily basis.

Asher ben Yeḥiel, who emigrated to Toledo from his native Cologne, was aware of the differences between places. How to observe the *sha'atenez* prohibition depended on the predominance of hemp as opposed to flax in a certain region—or how botanical nomenclature was decided upon and deployed. As the cases from Crete and Spain demonstrate, what was called hemp in one place may not necessarily have been *cannabis sativa*.

Conclusion

This chapter has shown that Jewish texts can shed light on current debates in Mediterranean historiography concerning the ecological unity or disunity of the region. As we saw at the outset, Braudel (and those in his wake) maintains that the Mediterranean region is characterized by ecological consistency. Horden and Purcell, on the contrary, stress that the Mediterranean is not an ecologically stable category: microclimates are more significant than any overarching climatic coherence. Jewish texts from the later Middle Ages draw a clear distinction between Mediterranean and ultramontane Europe. Seth Schwartz has issued a helpful proposal: that we move beyond Horden and Purcell's distinction between history "in" and "of" the Mediterranean and instead think "with the Mediterranean."[34] As Marglin and Lehmann observe in their introduction to this volume, thinking "with the Mediterranean" allows scholars to "reassert the historical specificity of the space in question," which can be lost when the Mediterranean "comes to denote a pattern of production and redistribution, or an ideal type of social organization."[35] In this chapter my focus has not been on production, redistribution, or social organization in the premodern Mediterranean. When those issues do arise among the Jewish communities I consider here, they are outcomes of a more fundamental reality: land, soil, and what nature suffers to grow.[36]

As we have seen, Jewish jurists, commentators, and communal leaders from this period recognized that the Mediterranean had its own biome.[37] This led them to distinguish between different regions marked by their own legal and customary traditions. Those traditions were influenced, if not determined, by geography. Writing about late antiquity and the early Middle Ages, Michael Toch has observed that the north and the south are not part of one Jewish world. Toch notes that there is no "unified Jewish world of trade," as certain scholars have assumed; a more constructive model would distinguish between Mediterranean Europe and northern Europe.[38] The sources in this chapter demonstrate that Toch's analysis—and his geographical axis—can be extended forward in time, into the later Middle Ages. The regionalism identified in this chapter does pertain to a particular Jewish legal trope; the geographical taxonomy of legal writings on *sha'atenez* may not have been recognizable to contemporary Christians or Muslims, let alone to future scholars. Still, the fact that an axis may be traced between the western Mediterranean and ultramontane Europe is significant and tempers the applicability of Horden and Purcell's widely accepted argument for microregionalism in the Mediterranean.

The texts examined here originated in Spain, Italy, and Venetian Crete. Environmental and geographic factors may not be the only ones that link these places; earlier historians have stressed social and economic connections that are not necessarily dependent on geography. Salo Baron, for example, folds two of these settings (Spain and Italy) together and notes that "the masses of Jews" residing there "must, of necessity, have had a much more diversified economic structure, which included some forms of farming, the prime occupation of their non-Jewish neighbors." Agriculture in these places was facilitated by a "great emphasis laid upon vineyards, orchards and truck gardens which could be cultivated in the vicinity of the Jews' urban or suburban homes."[39] But geographic factors were important too. In the later Middle Ages, Jews were united and divided by laws and customs concerning the plants that grew in the ground. Jews in Mediterranean Europe adhered to botanical nomenclature that distinguished their religious observances from those of their northern European peers. This suggests a degree of unity in Mediterranean Europe—at least in Jewish botanical, legal, and sartorial life.

ANDREW BERNS is an associate professor of history at the University of South Carolina. His research investigates the intellectual and cultural history of Jews in the medieval and early modern Mediterranean, especially Italy and Spain. His book *The Bible and Natural Philosophy in Renaissance Italy: Jewish and Christian Physicians in Search of Truth* was published by Cambridge University Press in 2015 and won the 2016 Howard R. Marraro Prize from the American Catholic Historical Association.

Notes

1. Fernand Braudel, *The Mediterranean and the Mediterranean World in the Age of Philip II*, 2 vols. (Berkeley: University of California Press, 1995), 1:14.

2. Peregrine Horden and Nicholas Purcell, *The Corrupting Sea: A Study of Mediterranean History* (Oxford: Blackwell, 2000), 3–4.

3. Jessica Goldberg has offered a thoughtful and constructive alternative to Braudel, as well as to Horden and Purcell, and has proposed that the Mediterranean "has its zones of agricultural macro-ecology." Although the sites Goldberg points to—the Nile Valley, parts of Sicily, and the Ifrīqiyyan plain—are considerably more circumscribed than the settings I consider in this chapter, one could view the Mediterranean regions discussed in this chapter's legal source material as a macro-ecological zone. See Goldberg, *Trade and Institutions in the Medieval Mediterranean: The Geniza Merchants and Their Business World* (Cambridge: Cambridge University Press, 2012), 343.

4. See "Introduction" (this volume, 5), and Braudel's *The Mediterranean*, 2: 802–26 for the section "One Civilization against the Rest; The Destiny of the Jews."

5. Horden and Purcell, *The Corrupting Sea*, 406: "the religious landscape ... respond[s] to the social and economic aspects of Mediterranean geography ... [and] will help us to understand the coalescence of the thousands of Mediterranean localities into some sort of unity." As Marglin and Lehmann point out ("Introduction" [this volume, 24 n. 39]) Horden and Purcell do not adequately address the question of what is uniquely Mediterranean about religion in the region. For more on this see Greg Woolf, "A Sea of Faith?," *Mediterranean Historical Review* 18, no. 2 (2003): 126–43, at 135.

6. Leviticus 19:19; Deuteronomy 22:11 (JPS translation).

7. In Linnaean classification the difference goes beyond species to the genus of the plants. Hemp is *cannabis sativa*; flax is *linum usitatissimum*.

8. Michael Hodder, "Flax," in *Dictionary of the Middle Ages*, ed. Joseph Strayer (New York: Scribner, 1982–1989), 5: 83–84.

9. Ronald Edward Zupko and Robert Anthony Laures, *Straws in the Wind: Medieval Urban Environmental Law: The Case of Northern Italy* (Boulder, CO: Westview Press, 1996), 87. Flax's importance was by no means restricted to Europe; Jessica Goldberg has shown the centrality of flax to the commercial interests of genizah merchants in the eleventh-century Islamicate world: see her *Trade and Institutions*.

10. Jacoby, "The Jews in the Byzantine Economy (Seventh to Mid-Fifteenth Century)," in *Jews in Byzantium*, ed. Robert Bonfil, Oded Irshai, Guy G. Stroumsa, and Rina Talgam (Leiden: Brill, 2011), 229.

11. Steven Bowman, *The Jews of Byzantium (1204–1453)* (Tuscaloosa: University of Alabama Press, 1985), 119.

12. Israel Lévi, "Les Juifs de Candie," *Revue des Études Juives* 26 (1893): 198–208. For a more detailed study see Joshua Starr, "Jewish Life in Crete under the Rule of Venice," *Proceedings of the American Academy for Jewish Research* 12 (1942): 59–114. Most recently see the work of Rena N. Lauer, *Colonial Justice and the Jews of Venetian Crete* (Philadelphia: University of Pennsylvania Press, 2019).

13. Elias S. Artom and Humbertus M. D. Cassuto, eds., *Takkanot Kandiyah ve-Zikhronoteha* (*Statuta Iudaeorum Candiae eorumque memorabilia*) (Jerusalem: Mekitze Nirdamim, 1943). Henceforth *TK*. The most recent work on these ordinances is Martin Borysek, "*Takkanot Kandiyah*: A Collection of Legislative Statutes as a Source for the Assessment of Laymen's Legal Authority in a Jewish Community in Venetian Crete" (PhD diss., Cambridge University, 2015). I thank Dr. Borysek for sharing his work with me.

14. *TK* #41, p. 33.

15. *TK* #41, p. 33.

16. BT *Yoma* 69a; BT *Betzah* 14b.

17. *TK* #41, p. 33.

18. Elisabeth Santschi, "Contrats de travail et d'apprentissage en Crète vénitienne au XIVe siècle d'après quelques notaires," in *Schweizerische Zeitschrift für Geschichte* 19 (1969): 34–74; Sally McKee, "Households in Fourteenth-Century Venetian Crete," in *Speculum* 70, no. 1 (1995): 27–67.

19. *TK* #74, 78–80: 79.

20. Cf. Numbers 31:10.

21. *Pirke Avot* 1:7

22. *TK* #74, 78–80: 79.

23. For contemporary sources from Venice and the Veneto, several of which express misgivings about Venetian Jewry's moral uprightness, see Robert Bonfil, "Aspects of the Social and Spiritual Life of the Jews in the Venetian Territories at the Beginning of the Sixteenth Century," *Zion* 41 (1976): 68–96 [in Hebrew].

24. Cf. Job 34:37.

25. *TK* #74, 78–80: at 80. Other communal ordinances (*takkanot*) from the Italophone world of this period express similar reservations about Jews congregating with non-Jews. See Louis Finkelstein, *Jewish Self-Government in the Middle Ages* (New York: Jewish Theological Seminary, 1924), 290–94.

26. See Leviticus 19:19.

27. No one has confidently identified Rabbi Moses Cohen.

28. It is worth noting that Moses of Greece himself is quoted as being opposed to the equation flax=hemp and that Rabbi Ephraim of Regensburg took a more stringent position and did equate the two. See Tosafot to BT *Zevaḥim* 18b, s.v. *ve-Ema*, and BT Yoma 12b. Rabbi Ephraim claimed that the *kanvus* in the *Mishnah* is a different species. I am grateful to Pinchas Roth for this reference.

29. Menahem Hasida, ed., R. Tzidkiyahu ha-Rofe (Tzidkiyahu ben Avraham Anav), *Shibbole ha-Leket* (Jerusalem: [no publisher given], 1968), 77.

30. Rosh, *She'elot u-Teshuvot* (Vilna, 1885), 2:7.

31. Abraham Neuman, *The Jews in Spain: Their Political, Social, and Cultural Life during the Middle Ages* (Philadelphia: Jewish Publication Society of America, 1948), 1:277, no. 18;

Yitzhak Baer, *A History of the Jews in Christian Spain*, trans. Louis Schoffman (Philadelphia: Jewish Publication Society, 1961–1966), 1: 188.

32. Salo Baron, *A Social and Religious History of the Jews* (New York: Columbia University Press, 1952), 4: 159.

33. Juan Piqueras Haba, "Los judíos y el vino en España: siglos XI–XV, una geografía histórica," *Cuadernos de Geografía* 75 (2004): 17–41, at 20: "pro magna parte laboratores sive cultivatores agrorum et vinearum."

34. Seth Schwartz, *Were the Jews a Mediterranean Society? Reciprocity and Solidarity in Ancient Judaism* (Princeton, NJ: Princeton University Press, 2010).

35. Jessica Marglin and Matthias Lehmann, "Introduction" (this volume, 15).

36. I borrow this phrase from Mart A. Stewart, *'What Nature Suffers to Groe': Life, Labor, and Landscape on the Georgia Coast, 1680–1920* (Athens: University of Georgia Press, 1996).

37. The argument of this chapter challenges Michael Herzfeld's suggestion that the Mediterranean exists not as a real place but as a discursive space. See Michael Herzfeld, "Practical Mediterraneanism; Excuses for Everything, from Epistemology to Eating," in *Rethinking the Mediterranean*, ed. William V. Harris (Oxford: Oxford University Press, 2005), 45–63.

38. Michael Toch, *The Economic History of European Jews: Late Antiquity and the Early Middle Ages* (Leiden: Brill, 2013), 251.

39. Baron, *A Social and Religious History of the Jews*, 5: 37. See also Jessica Goldberg's argument that "economic geographies" were also "a function of culture": Goldberg, *Trade and Institutions in the Medieval Mediterranean*, 345.

4

JEWS AND THE EARLY MODERN MEDITERRANEAN SLAVE TRADE[1]

Daniel Hershenzon

BETWEEN 1450 AND 1700, THE NUMBER OF CHRISTIANS and Muslims captured and enslaved across the Mediterranean was equal to, and perhaps even greater than, the number of sub-Saharans enslaved on the Atlantic.[2] Slavery was one of the central early modern interfaces for the Spanish Empire, Morocco, and Ottoman Algiers, and it thus offers an excellent vantage point from which to examine the implications of a Mediterranean framework for Jewish studies. The slave trade was pervasive—it was both vast and extremely complex. Muslims and Christians, the dominant political actors in the world of slavery, enslaved and were enslaved by one another. Jews constituted a third confessional group involved in the slave trade—although they were inherently non-state actors. Like members of other ethno-religious groups, Jews captured, enslaved, owned, sold, and redeemed captives, both Muslim and Christian. Jews too were captured by Christian and Muslim pirates and enslaved, although the number of Christian and Muslim captives that Jews trafficked far exceeded the number of Jews that were enslaved.

Mediterranean slavery was a cross-cultural form of commerce in which religion mattered.[3] Slaves' religious identities made them unique commodities; they were at once objects and subjects and thus capable of converting of their own volition or being converted. Their singularity transformed them into religious boundary markers. In the complex system of slavery, its actors, Christian, Jewish, and Muslim, were bound to distinct exchange regimes—sets of prohibitions and permissions that determined who they could exchange and what transactions they could employ. For example, Moroccan Jews were not allowed to own Muslim slaves, and Spanish Jews could not enslave Christians, only redeem them. The distinct but overlapping exchange regimes, which included additional limitations, made the possession and exchange of slaves into an important medium for the articulation and reconstitution of religious difference. In the Atlantic world, on the other hand, slavery lost the power to articulate religious difference. Over the course of the second half of the seventeenth and in the eighteenth century, slaves came to be defined mostly in racial rather than in religious terms.

This chapter argues that Mediterranean slavery and the rules regulating the slave trade gave visibility to Jews' status as members of an ethno-religious minority and formed an important site in which this status was debated, manipulated, and reproduced. It demonstrates this argument by exploring the role played by the Jews of Spanish Oran and Moroccan Tétouan in the Mediterranean slave trade—capturing, enslaving, owning, selling, and ransoming humans—from roughly the 1580s to the 1670s.[4] A Mediterranean framework—combining comparative and connected historical perspectives—and a commodity-sensitive approach reveal that the slave trade functioned in similar ways across confessional lines;[5] namely, Jews were bound to comparable but reversed exchange regimes in Muslim and Christian cities across the Mediterranean. Approaching Jewish history from the perspective of the slave trade demonstrates the degree of Jews' imbrication with the societies in which they lived. At the same time, paying close attention to the religious identity of the commodities that Jews traded—in the case of this chapter, slaves—as well as to the rules that regulated this commerce, shows how Jews' involvement in the slave trade and in commercial life was predicated upon their exclusion. By becoming actors in the slave trade, Jews' minority status was affirmed. Yet, this status was flexible rather than fixed, and Jews played a part in negotiating and defining its boundaries.

In recent years, the theme of bondage has garnered much attention from scholars of the early modern Mediterranean.[6] We now understand much better the nature of slavery across the sea; the mechanisms of capture, enslavement, and ransom; and how the system created a multiplicity of unintended links between Christian and Muslim polities in the western Mediterranean. With a few notable exceptions, scholars have shied away from examining the active role Jews played in the trade and have narrowed their focus to Jewish captives and Jewish ransom mechanisms.[7] This approach is part of a larger trend, still prominent in studies of early modern Maghribi Jews, of studying Jewish history from an exclusively Jewish perspective.[8] A Mediterranean perspective—namely, an examination of the relations between Jews and the slave trade from a regional rather than a confessional or national perspective—offers a way to complement an internalist framework and reinsert Jews into broader historical trends.

One of the difficulties in writing a history of the early modern Maghrib from a Mediterranean perspective comes from the state of the field and the absence of North African documental corpora similar to those made available by European administrative archives.[9] Currently, Spanish archives offer the best access for studying the interactions between Christians, Jews, and Muslims in the western Mediterranean. Therefore, this chapter brings together sources from Spanish state and private archives and libraries, Spanish published chronicles, rabbinic *responsa*, and Muslim fatwas. I begin by setting the geopolitical scene and by introducing the main actors—redeeming friars, North African Jewish traders, and Mediterranean rulers. The second and third sections examine the kinds of exchange of captives and slaves in which Jews were involved and how these exchanges were shaped by Jews' minority status while in turn reconstituting it. To stress the flexibility of these exchange regimes and Jews' status articulated by these regimes, the third section also compares Oran and Tétouan to other cities across the Mediterranean. The final section focuses on a particular instance of captivity of Muslims and Christians as an example of the dynamics that transformed the relations between North African Jews and their rulers.

Captivity and Ransom in the Early Modern Mediterranean

Scholars estimate that in the four centuries from 1450 to 1850, between two million and three million Muslims and Christians were taken captive and enslaved in the Mediterranean.[10] Only a few captives obtained their liberty in return for a payment, by swapping with other slaves, or through flight. Unlike the Atlantic slave system, in the Mediterranean, captive and slave markets coexisted and were interrelated. Captivity and slavery were nonexclusive dimensions and stages in the life of bonded individuals. Victims of maritime piracy could be sold either as slaves to masters who sought to benefit from their slaves' labor or as captives to merchants who bought them as a shrewd investment. Yet, some captives labored as slaves while waiting for their ransom fee to be paid. Some slaves managed to arrange their ransom after years of enslavement, becoming de facto captives.

The redemption of captives in the Middle Sea is mostly associated with the orders of redemption—the Order of Our Lady of Mercy (Mercedarians) and the Order of the Holy Trinity (Trinitarians)—established at the turn of the thirteenth century in France and Aragon, respectively.[11] However, the friars were never alone in the ransom scene, which they shared with Christian, Muslim, and Jewish merchants who also freed captives across the Muslim-Christian border in late medieval Iberia. As ransom agents, friars and merchants differed in significant ways. Ransom via merchants was costly, but merchants could free captives faster than the friars. Redemption via the orders was much cheaper but slow—in the seventeenth century, the friars arrived in Maghribi cities on average only once every three years.¹² Friars and merchants also differed in how they understood the purpose of their activities. For the orders of redemption, captives were Christians at risk of conversion to Islam under duress, and redeeming them meant saving their souls. Their activity was based on a sense of obligation among group members. Captives were members of a confessional group, as Catholics, and of a political community, as Castilians, Catalans, or Portuguese. In this sense, imperially regulated ecclesiastic redemption was based on communal solidarity. In contrast, for merchants, ransom was a secondary activity generating direct and indirect profits. For Muslims, ransom was also a religious duty, yet institutions similar to the religious orders did not develop in the Maghrib. Muslim captives who wished to reunite with their families had to rely on Christian, Jewish, and Muslim merchants or arrange their swap for Christian captives.¹³ During the seventeenth century, however, Muslim rulers became increasingly involved in redeeming their subjects, an activity that they used to claim spiritual guardianship, much like their Christian counterparts.¹⁴

The Christian conquest of Granada in 1492 and subsequent Castilian and Portuguese conquests in North Africa redrew the geography of ransom. Between 1504 and 1508, the Portuguese took Tangiers, Agadir, and Safi. The Castilians conquered Mers El-Kebir in 1505; the Peñón de Vélez de la Gomera in 1508; Oran in 1509; and Béjaïa, Tripoli, and the Peñón of Algiers in 1510. Most of these forts were soon lost, but a few remained under Spanish control for centuries and became bases for enslaving raids and the main providers of Muslim slaves for Spanish slave markets. Another effect of moving the Christian-Muslim frontier southward was that freeing captives now required crossing the Mediterranean, making the whole enterprise more costly and complicated.

During most of the sixteenth century, the majority of those captured lost their liberty in spectacular naval battles between the Ottoman and Spanish imperial fleets. In 1581, when the Ottoman and Spanish Empires signed a truce and turned their backs to the Mediterranean, the world of captivity and ransom was transformed once again. Corsairs replaced imperial fleets, small-scale raids became endemic, the number of captives increased, and the pattern of capture was spread throughout the year and across the sea. In response, the Spanish crown turned the religious orders into de facto royal agencies, making ransom a royal prerogative. The king helped finance ecclesiastical rescue expeditions and bureaucratized their procedures. The crown also imposed its ransom agenda on the friars, including ordering them to redeem soldiers before all others.

The move of the frontier toward the Mediterranean also separated Christian merchants from Jewish and Muslim merchants, subjected both groups to distinct exchange and mobility regimes, and reshaped their relations with Trinitarians and Mercedarians and with Mediterranean rulers. Officially, the Spanish crown prohibited trade with infidels, grounding its position in canon law and ideology. But in practice, Spanish trade with North Africa became routine in the seventeenth century. Redeeming captives became a way of legitimating this trade, perceived as immoral. Christian merchants who sought licenses to trade with the Muslim Maghrib had to declare that they would not trade in war materials. Moreover, they had to agree to use their profits to ransom Christians rather than invest in goods to be sold back in Spain.[15] The merchants' relative freedom to travel to North Africa and their access to captives' kin in Iberia allowed them to participate in the ransom market. They also came to compete with the friars for control of ransoming.

While the geopolitical transformations of the long sixteenth century turned Christian merchants into the friars' competitors, they also made Jewish and Muslim merchants into the friars' allies. After the expulsion of the Spanish Jews in 1492 and the Moriscos (Spanish Muslims and their descendants forced to convert to Christianity) between 1609 and 1614, Jews and Muslims who wanted to enter the Iberian Peninsula needed a permit from the Inquisition, the governors of the Spanish garrisons in the Maghrib, or a royal council. Such authorization was required for Spanish, Moroccan, and Algerian Jews, both for Jewish residents of Muslim cities and for members of the Jewish communities that settled in the Spanish fort towns of North Africa. Jews' limited access to Spain meant that they did not threaten the image the friars carefully crafted of ecclesiastic redemption expeditions as the only path to freedom. And Jewish merchants had local contacts, mastered Arabic and Ottoman Turkish, and had resources and skills, which provided them with access not granted to the friars. Teaming up with these Jews created less friction than collaborating with Christian merchants and allowed the friars to claim symbolic credit in Spain for captives that Maghribis had redeemed on their behalf.

Redeeming Christian Souls

Friars and Jewish merchants from Spanish and Muslim cities in the Maghrib worked together to ransom Christian captives on a regular basis. These Jewish merchants often framed their activity using the same vocabulary as the friars—namely, as the redemption of Christian souls; however, for them their involvement was a source of revenue, a justification for engaging in lucrative trade with Spaniards, and a way of obtaining political protection and power. Given that the Catholic kings had expelled the Jews from Spain in 1492, the collaboration between Spanish friars and Jews could seem surprising. And yet the partnership was not a secret. The crown benefited from and protected the

Jewish communities of Oran, Ceuta, Tangiers, Larache (Al-Araish), and other fort towns, and thus tacitly approved limited collaboration with Jews, including Jewish subjects in the service of their Muslim rulers.[16]

How did this Christian-Jewish partnership look on the ground? The well-studied case of the Jewish community of Oran, the largest and most important Spanish fort town in the Maghrib, offers a good example.[17] The community settled in the city almost immediately after its Spanish occupation and lived there until expelled in 1669. Jews' linguistic skills; mastery of Spanish, Moroccan, or Ottoman administrative repertoires; and contacts across frontiers, all of which allowed them to rescue Christian captives, were important factors in the decision to allow their settlement. Soon their role and contacts in regional commerce and the provisions they supplied to the city became essential. Jews served the city's authorities as linguistic intermediaries, spies, and scouts, and as food suppliers and moneylenders. After some decades, however, a few Christians in Oran learned Arabic and offered competing services.[18] At this point, the Jews' position was no longer only a function of their resources, and they constantly had to convince the authorities that they were indispensable for the garrison.

The leading families of the Jewish community of Oran, the Sasportases and the Cansinos, participated directly and indirectly in the ransom of Christian captives. They donated large sums of money for ransom deals that individuals negotiated and made generous gifts to the Mercedarian convent in Oran. In fact, the Mercedarians in Oran felt so indebted to the Sasportas family that in 1653 Diego de Majares and Juan Trevinos, brothers in the Mercedarian convent in town, faked municipal documents in an attempt to help the family in its struggles against the governor-general, probably in gratitude for favors granted by Sasportas family members to Christian captives.[19] But Jews also actively rescued Christians, taking advantage of their social networks that stretched across the Maghrib. There was a rough geographic division of labor between the two families: the Sasportases had better links in Fez and Marakesh, the Cansinos in Tlemecen and Algiers.[20] The power and contacts of these families were known among Spaniards. Pedro de Bricuela, a captain in the *Armada del mar Océano* who was captured in 1614 and taken to Algiers, sent a petition to the Council of War. Bricuela pleaded with the members of the council to ask Yaho Sasportas, via the governor of Oran, to assist with his ransom.[21] Similarly, in 1621, in one of the unsuccessful attempts to ransom the Trinitarian Bernardo Monroy, imprisoned in Algiers, the Sasportas family agreed to donate ten thousand ducats for his rescue.[22] The Sasportases and Cansinos facilitated the ransom of Christian captives until the expulsion of the Jewish community from Oran in 1669.

Yaho Sasportas offers insight into the relational nature of Jews' position as intermediaries. A letter he sent to the king of Spain in September 1612 demonstrates that he practiced careful "impression management."²³ Sasportas, whose family lent large sums of money to the governors of Oran, asked the king to increase his salary. When his request was denied, he asked the royal magistrates

> to put into His Majesty's consideration that the main riches he [Yaho] has with which to serve [his king] are His Majesty's protection and grace. And if the people of his nation, of which he and his father are the leaders in these garrisons, as well as the Moors, his friends and allies with whom he corresponds and has a friendship, see him [Yaho] return with empty hands and without His Majesty's order to bestow on him some of His Majesty's grace, they will be suspicious and consider him [Yaho] to lack the protection and favor of his majesty. Since they [the Jews and the Moors] do not judge things for what they are but only for their visible effects, they might stop providing him with intelligence and corresponding with him the way they used to.²⁴

Sasportas's standing at the Spanish court was partly based on the contacts he nurtured among Muslims. However, he reminded the king that these contacts were in turn based on how people in Algiers and in other cities gauged his position at the Spanish court. In order for Sasportas to maintain his position among Muslims, he had to demonstrate that his position in Madrid was solid and that the king supported him and his family. Sasportas's pleas also reflect that despite the long duration of Jewish life in the *presidio*, the community's existence was never formally grounded and had to be constantly secured by the Jews, whose status remained that of royal vassals dependent on the crown's goodwill.

Moroccan Jews also partook in redeeming Christian captives, almost always in collaboration with the friars. Jacob Crudo, a merchant from Tétouan, had commercial links in Algiers and even as far as Annaba (today in the northeast of Algeria), and the ransom deals he cut may have stretched as far east and north as Livorno.²⁵ He worked with the Mercedarians, lodging them in Tétouan when they came to buy captives in 1590 and 1596. He and other Jews served the friars as linguistic interpreters and commission agents, bought the goods the friars brought from Spain—providing them with cash necessary for ransom—and negotiated better prices and deals on their behalf. As a result of the contacts Crudo nurtured with the friars and other Spaniards, when the Inquisition arrested him in 1596 as he wandered the streets of Seville "dressed in a Christian habit and dealing and trading out in the open thus causing a great scandal," he could present warm letters of recommendation from the duke of Medina-Sidonia, who was the Captain-General of the *Armada del mar Océano*, and from two Mercedarian brothers whom he had helped in Tétouan.²⁶ By the end of 1596, Crudo was back in Tétouan dealing again with the Mercedarians.

Yehuda Malachi (or Judas Malaqui, as the Spanish sources spell his name) offers a different model. He was a merchant from Chefchaouen in the Rif mountains of northwest Morocco and one of the suppliers of the Peñón de Vélez, a Spanish fort in Morocco. Malachi appears in the sources for the first time in 1585, when he was detained upon his arrival in Málaga. He was eventually released as he carried a valid letter of safe conduct issued by the commander of the Peñón de Vélez. The purpose of Malachi's visit was to collect money owed him on account of a number of boys and girls whom he had already rescued and who were being held on his behalf in custody in Tétouan.[27]

Malachi left a later archival mark in an account he submitted in 1589 to the crown in which he described his success: "In the journey I have just executed, I brought nineteen captives, among them five women and four babies, two of whom are nursing at the breast."[28] By stressing the captives' sex and tender age, Yehuda Malachi alluded both to Christian fears of captives' conversion to Islam—children and women were perceived as being more susceptible to conversion—and to redemption as a way of saving souls. However, ransom for him was not a socio-religious duty but rather an economic transaction yielding profits. In 1589, he made an offer to the Spanish crown, hoping to become its exclusive ransom agent in the Maghrib. He promised to "get all the Christian captives from all of Barbary and Algiers ... [and] ... to bring them to whatever location your highness asks me for two thirds of the price it would cost anyone else ransoming them, be they [from] the Holy Trinity or from our Lady of Mercy."[29] Malachi openly competed with the Trinitarians and Mercedarians for their share of the ransom market and their funds, confidently stressing that he could redeem captives from places to which the friars had no access and asking to be paid from their resources: "and these women and children I got out of the house of the King of Fez; and not one of those who ransom [captives] could ransom them for any price; and together with these I brought ten men with the intention that they will pay me from the alms of the redemption of captives of the [Holy] Trinity and the [our Lady of the] Mercy."[30] Philip II continued to employ the friars as redeemers, but Malachi's success and the cost-to-revenue ratio he offered convinced the king to nominate him as official royal ransom agent, a position he occupied until at least the end of 1595.

Malachi's eagerness to monopolize the ransom market hints at the profitability of this activity. But his interest in the occupation was not limited to financial gains alone. For Malachi and for other Spanish and Moroccan Jews, ransoming Christians yielded indirect benefits in the form of legitimation and permission to trade with Spain. When he was arrested in Málaga in 1585, Malachi claimed he was "well-known" in the Peñón de Vélez and had "many friendship[s] and business and that he provided there many services to his majesty provisioning the residents with many kinds of food supplies and gifts for the sick in time of hunger and need [and] providing many important reports, risking his life and ransoming captives with his efforts at very moderate prices."[31]

He lists two kinds of activities: Provisioning the fort occurred in the marketplace and yielded direct profits. Giving alms, providing intelligence services, and saving captives were costly activities that bore minimal profits, if any, but justified Malachi's participation in other moneymaking activities. His involvement in the Christian economy of salvation never became his main trade, but it provided critical support to the rest of his business.

Ransom greased the wheels of commerce and simultaneously had political implications. Spanish and Moroccan Jewish ransomers enjoyed the protection of the king of Spain and the sultan of Morocco, respectively. Redeeming Christians joined translating and interpreting as activities that made the Sasportases and the Cansinos competent political actors in Oran, where they formed power coalitions with Christians and meddled in the city's politics.[32] Moreover, for a century and a half the king protected the Jewish community in Oran from continual attempts to expel it. Moroccan sultans, interested in increasing commerce between Morocco and Europe, supported Jewish traders and when necessary interceded on their behalf at the Spanish court.[33] In September 1608, for example, Mawlay Zaydan, the sultan of Morocco, asked Phillip III to help a Jewish Moroccan merchant who had lent ransom money to Spaniards captured in Morocco but had never been repaid.[34] It is unclear if the Spanish king acquiesced, but a year earlier the Inquisition had responded positively to a similar request from two Moroccan Jewish merchants, likely with the approval of the sultan.[35]

While both Spanish and Moroccan Jews ransomed Christian captives, their relation to these captives was diametrically opposed. Spanish Jews in North Africa benefited from assisting in the ransom of Christians and charged commission for their efforts, but they never owned or were allowed to own Christians as slaves. The prohibition was grounded in a long tradition of papal bulls and church council decisions dating back to Christianity's first centuries.[36] If Muslim slaves owned by Jews converted to Christianity, the Jews had to free them—in contrast to Christian slave owners, who could and usually continued to own their slaves even after the latter's conversion.[37] These prohibitions articulated and reinforced Jews' status as minority subjects bound to particular strictures.

Jewish Slave Owners and Slave Traders

Jews were not just intermediaries but also slave traders; they were party to transactions in which slaves changed hands. The limitations that shaped their engagement in the slave market were a function of the relation between Jews' religious identity and their rulers' religious identity. Simultaneously, Jews' involvement in and exclusion from slave-related transactions gave visibility and affirmed the difference in religion between them and their sovereign as well as their status as members of a minority group. In this regard, Spanish and Moroccan Jews occupied similar positions in relation to their respective authorities and to the slave trade. Jews in Spanish cities ransomed Christians but could not sell them as slaves or own them. In contrast, they ransomed, enslaved, and owned Muslims. Jews in Muslim cities could ransom, enslave, and own Christians. Crudo and Malachi had owned for years some of the Christians they sold to the friars. Moroccan Jews probably also rescued Muslim captives, but they could not own or sell them as slaves. The relations of Moroccan and Spanish Jews to Christians and to Muslims were bound by similar privileges and limitations; Jews in Muslim cities were *dhimmis* (protected non-Muslims living under Muslim rule), while those in Spanish cities were royal vassals whose precarious existence fully depended on the king's will. But the practical outcomes diverged. The exchange regimes that governed their engagement in the slave market and that operated as a medium to challenge, expand, and reproduce their status as Jews become clearer when we take a second look at the Jewish communities of Tétouan and Oran.

Members of the Jewish community of Tétouan sold captives to the friars during most of the ransom expeditions the religious orders sent to Ceuta, a Portuguese garrison that became part of the Spanish Empire in 1580. During the first two-thirds of the seventeenth century, Morisco families over which sultans had little control governed Tétouan.[38] Piracy, the slave trade, and the ransom of Christians were a major source of income for the city, whose economy boomed at the beginning of the seventeenth century.[39] The short distances between Ceuta and Gibraltar (eighteen miles) and between Ceuta and Tétouan (twenty-two miles) made the garrison an ideal base for exchanging captives and other goods. The friars would arrive in Ceuta, where they would leave their ransom money with the governor, and then travel to Tétouan to negotiate the ransom; subsequently Tetouanites would transfer the captives to Ceuta.

One Jewish family is repeatedly mentioned in records the friars composed during the first three-quarters of the seventeenth century.[40] Members of the Mejía family (also spelled in the sources as Mejías, Mexía, Mexías, and Megías) served the governors of Tétouan as interpreters for most of the century, and at least one family member, Joseph (José) Mejía, served as the governor's secretary in the 1650s and 1660s, one of the highest administrative posts in the city.[41] It is likely that Tetouanite Jews redeemed Muslim Tetouanites enslaved in Ceuta and in Spain on behalf of the slaves' kin. Members of the Mejía family straddled the boundary between Ceuta and Tétouan, spending much of their time at a residency in Ceuta. They also served the friars as interpreters, lodged them in Tétouan, and worked as their commission agents, buying captives on their behalf. Joseph Mejía's divided life—between Ceuta and Tétouan—probably assisted his efforts to maintain the appearance crucial to his standing among Muslims and Christians, as a person well connected to both sides.

Tetouanite Jews monopolized the mediation between Muslims and Christians and controlled a significant share of the ransom market. Members of the Mejía family sold captives owned by the Tetouanite political elite and the city merchants, but Jews also owned and sold their own captives, whom they bought in anticipation of the rescue expeditions of the friars. In 1612, 10 percent of all the captives the Mercedarians ransomed from Tétouan belonged to Moses (Moisés) Mejía and another Tetouanite Jew. In 1614 and again in 1615, the same Moses Mejía owned about 15 percent of the captives that the friars purchased, and in 1640, Joseph Mejía owned 6 percent of the captives redeemed. While the Mejías were the most involved members of the Jewish community, others also owned and sold slaves. For example, in 1579, Jacob Crudo, whom we have already encountered, Mordechai (Mordafay) Alia, and Abraham Manasseh (Menagí) owned 25 percent of the captives that the friars had redeemed.[42] In other words, Moroccan Jews actively bought and sold Christians just like their Muslim counterparts. Their share of the captive market was a function of the administrative positions they occupied and of their relation to the city's rulers.

Tetouanite Jews who sold slaves and captives were also bound to a particular exchange regime. Legal prohibitions regarding *dhimmis* had existed in the Muslim world at least since the ninth-century Pact of 'Umar (some scholars date this text to the seventh century), the document that served as a blueprint for regulating the relations between Muslims and their Jewish and Christian protected subjects. Further legislation on the matter from as early as the eleventh century forbade Jews from owning or selling Muslim slaves.[43] Unlike Muslim slave owners, who could continue to own their converted slaves, Jews whose Christian slaves had converted to Islam were legally obliged to emancipate these slaves or sell them to Muslims. For early modern Muslims, the idea that slaves had a religious identity that determined who could and who could not own them was obvious. In his *The Clear Standard*, the most influential collection of fatwas in the early modern Islamic west, Aḥmad ibn Yaḥyā al-Wansharīsī (1430 or 1431–1508) cites a fatwa that compares *dhimmis*' obligation to sell their slaves who had converted to Islam with their obligation to sell copies of the Qur'an they might have obtained to Muslims.[44] According to this stance, the religious identity of converts to Islam was as clear as that of the Qur'an.

Christian and Muslim prohibitions on slave owning resembled one another, but in practice there were differences. Unlike Christians, who sought to convert their slaves and often baptized them soon after their capture, Maghribi Muslims were reluctant to let Christian slaves convert to Islam.[45] Converted slaves were decommoditized because Christians refused to redeem them—unlike Muslims who ransomed Muslim slaves who were forcibly converted to Christianity—and their conversion meant financial loss for their owners.[46] Another reason for which Muslim slave owners preferred not to force their Christian slaves to convert to Islam was that owners of Muslim slaves in Spain could avenge these forced conversions by compelling their Muslim slaves to convert to Christianity.[47]

Examining the involvement of the Jews of Oran in the trafficking of Muslims further demonstrates how their status was shaped, in part, by a unique exchange regime. During the early modern period, Oran was the most important Spanish conduit of Muslim slaves to Spain, and its soldiers captured thousands of Muslims, mostly children and women, in attacks on hostile Berber tribes.[48] In the 1630s, a Spanish observer indicated the importance of the slave trade for the Jewish and Christian residents of the garrison.[49] In the nine attacks conducted between mid-1568 and the end of 1570, the Spaniards took 1,282 men, women, and children captive.[50] On March 10, 1645, Spanish soldiers returned to the city with 106 captives; nine months later they took a further 175 captives.[51] It appears that the annual number of attacks increased during the seventeenth century. Between 1661 and 1666, military forces led seven or eight attacks each year. The majority of the captives taken were soon ransomed and returned to their campsite; others were sold in the local slave market, ending up as slaves of residents of the garrison or sent to the Spanish slave markets of Andalusia.

The same skills that allowed the Jews of Oran to be efficient mediators in the ransom of Spaniards strategically positioned them for the trading of Muslim slaves. Members of the Jewish community participated in every aspect of that trade: scouting attacks, verifying that the victims were not protected by peace agreements with the Spaniards, dividing the booty, drawing up ransom agreements, and owning and selling captives as slaves. Powerful families like the Cansinos, Sasportases, and Maques employed a number of Muslim slaves in their households, and it seems as if during the century and a half of Jewish presence in Oran, the number of slaves owned by Jews exceeded the number of members of the Jewish community, which from the end of the sixteenth century counted between four hundred and five hundred individuals.[52]

The prominence of Jews in the slave market stemmed from their linguistic skills and began with their role in enslavement enterprises, where they served as interpreters and often as scouts. The slaving contracts the governor of Oran drew up with Jacob Cansino and Yaho Sasportas in the mid-seventeenth century acknowledge the men's importance. According to these agreements, the interpreters were to receive seven *doblas* for each slave captured and four slaves if a hundred or more were taken captive in the attack.⁵³ Jews continued to operate as intermediaries in the negotiations between owners and captives over the ransom agreements. These agreements stipulated the price or number of sub-Saharan slaves for which the captive would be swapped, the number of payments, and due dates. Often captives were allowed to leave a family member as a hostage and depart from Oran to collect alms with which to pay the ransom fee. If the ransom fees were not settled on the payment date, the captive or the captive's substitute hostage would be sold at auction in the slave market.

Legal suits that fell under the governor's jurisdiction and concerned slaves show that Jews were also party to such agreements. Fifteen cases involving Rabbi Abraham Cansino and his slaves occurred between March 13, 1656, and April 7, 1660.⁵⁴ The captives had all failed to settle their ransom fees on the payment date. Like other Jewish and Muslim slave owners, Cansino hurried to sell his debtor captives in the slave market. The reasons for the rush must have been economic, for, in theory at least, captives who were waiting for their ransom to arrive were not supposed to work and so incurred costs for their owners.

* * *

The exchange regimes to which Jews were bound were based on long-term historical traditions, and yet they were not set in stone. To the contrary, Christians, Jews, and Muslims all sought to shape and manipulate these regimes—and such struggles were not unique to the Jews of Oran or Tétouan. Archival records from the crown of Aragon document a decline in Jewish slave owning between the thirteenth and fifteenth centuries, the result of concern at the possibility of sexual relations between Jews and their Christian servants and of legislation that forced Jews to free their slaves upon the slaves' conversion to Christianity.⁵⁵ Fearing the loss of their investment, Jews purchased fewer slaves and sold slaves they already owned. However, Christians who had slaves to sell and Jews who wished to own slaves devised creative formulae that left both sides satisfied. For example, a Christian might give a slave to a Jew as collateral for a supposed large loan that was to be repaid over a ten-year period. The loan, however, was no more than a legal fiction, and the parties agreed that should the slave convert to Christianity and be freed, the Christian agreed to continue to repay the loan and not to demand compensation for the slave.⁵⁶

Even when Jews had been granted official permission to own slaves, their right to do so was contested. Christian opponents of the Jewish community of Oran repeatedly accused Jews of discouraging their slaves from converting, hoping to limit Jews' entitlement to own slaves. One strategy Jews employed to counter such accusations was to summon a priest to baptize slaves on their deathbed.⁵⁷ In 1660, when the governor-general banned Jews from owning slaves and forced them to sell the slaves in their possession, the king's representative in the municipal council proposed to the community leaders that a blind eye might be turned in return for a hefty bribe. The negotiation failed, but this royal officer still only implemented the order selectively. When the magistrates took Jacob Cansino's female slave, they handed her to a poor resident who lived in front of Cansino's house—and the slave continued to serve in the Cansino household.[58] Similarly, Livornese Jews' right to own slaves, granted to them in 1591 and 1593 by the grand duke of Tuscany, was contested several times in the seventeenth and eighteenth centuries.[59] Christians suspected that they pressured their slaves not to convert to Christianity, and in 1673 it was mandated that a priest interview Jews' slaves to detect and prevent such schemes. In the 1680s, the grand duke encountered fierce opposition when he sought to reverse his ancestor's decision and limit Livornese Jews' right to own slaves.[60]

Although the sources provide no evidence of similar struggles in Tétouan, Jews and majority group members were involved in such debates elsewhere in the Maghrib and more broadly in the Muslim world. According to Melchor de Zúñiga, a captive-turned-redeemer and an acute observer of life in Algiers in the first half of the seventeenth century, Algerian Jews used their connections to Muslim patrons in order to circumvent the prohibition against purchasing Christian captives. These Muslim patrons bought Christian captives on their Jewish clients' behalf. When the Jewish owners wanted to sell their captives for a ransom, the Muslims initiated the negotiation with the captives and invited the Jewish owners to participate as if they were no more than commercial brokers.[61] Medieval and early modern Jewish *responsa* from the Ottoman Empire were vocal about Jews' right to own slaves and the authorities' position on the issue.[62] In fact, despite the opposition expressed by the Pact of Umar and by fatwas, in sixteenth-century Egypt, Palestine, and Syria, the prohibition on slave owning—including in some cases ownership of Muslim slaves!—was bypassed by payments of special taxes, bribes, and legal fictions of the kind we have encountered in medieval Aragon and early modern Algiers.[63] These tensions and their documentation suggest that the prohibitions that governed Jews' possession and trading of slaves could be manipulated in accordance with local contexts and power struggles between Jews and majority group members.

Frictions and Transformations

Jews were not only *local* but also *regional* actors in the political economy of slavery and ransom, and the role they played in the cross-regional slave trade placed them in potential opposition to Maghribi rulers. On occasion, this tension was brought into sharp relief, temporarily transforming the relations between friars, Jews, and rulers, and thus the world of slavery.

Occasionally, Jews—mostly subjects of Muslim cities—bought Christian captives in Algiers and traveled with them hundreds of miles west to Tétouan, where they sold the captives to the friars. For example, in March 1608, Turkish, Arab, and a few Jewish merchants left Algiers on an English ship with captives they had purchased and headed for Tétouan, from where the captives were to be delivered to the Mercedarians, who were waiting in Ceuta.[64] The archive provides further evidence that the practice was fairly common. Since the friars arrived in Maghribi cities such as Algiers infrequently, the opportunity to buy captives from Algiers for the price of a redemption expedition to Ceuta-Tétouan was appealing.

This practice stood in sharp contrast to the interests of Algerian rulers, who wanted the friars to visit Algiers as frequently as possible in order to ransom the captives that the pashas were interested in selling. On September 2, 1608, for example, the Algerian Divan (the governing council) ordered merchants "not to take Christian [captives] to Tétouan under any circumstances . . . because [the merchants taking them] are the reason that the Spanish Trinitarians and Mercedarians do not arrive in this city [Algiers] and that the pasha is losing his fees."[65] Unlike the Mercedarians and Trinitarians, who during their visits in Algiers were fully dependent on the pasha's hospitality and bound to buy the captives he wished to sell, Jews' and Muslims' linguistic skills and local contacts allowed them to bypass the pasha's and Divan's attempts to regulate the ransom market. The very skills and contacts that made Jews desirable allies for the friars in North Africa made them into the competitors for the rulers in Algiers. Yet, the evidence suggests that as long as the market share of these merchants was limited, the authorities in Algiers either came to accept their participation or failed to curb it.

The status quo was shaken at the end of the first decade of the seventeenth century, when the Algerian Divan ordered the arrest of three Trinitarian friars and 130 captives the friars had already redeemed. The Divan was reacting to news that Fatima, a ten-year-old Algerian girl captured by Genoese forces in 1608, sold into slavery in Livorno, and ransomed by her father a few months later, had been forced to convert to Christianity in Corsica, where the ship that was about to return her to her parents was temporarily anchored. Algiers refused to release the Trinitarians and their redeemed captives before the Corsicans let Fatima leave for Algiers. Imperial logic dictated the Algerian decision to arrest Spanish friars rather than Genoese or Corsican priests. Genoa had been a Spanish satellite since 1528, and Corsica was a Genoese colony. Detaining the Trinitarians was a strategy designed to pressure the king of Spain to force Genoa to arrange the girl's immediate release. But after her conversion, the Christians could not legally or morally hand her back to her parents. The Algerian effort to bring the affair to an end failed, as did multiple attempts to ransom the Trinitarians or swap them for Muslim captives held in Spain. Fatima was married to a Christian in Corsica and never returned to Algiers, while the Trinitarians died in their prison cells in Algiers.[66]

The affair led Spain to formalize and expand its collaboration with Jews and Muslims, thereby transforming long-standing informal relations between the friars, slave traffickers, and Mediterranean rulers. Hearing of the arrest, Phillip III ordered a halt to all ecclesiastic ransom expeditions to Algiers unless the Trinitarians were freed. For its part, Algiers froze the release of Spanish captives until Fatima was freed. In the meantime, Algerian corsairs continued to capture Spaniards. The latter's kin begged the friars for help and pressured the king to assist them.[67] In 1612, in an attempt to solve the impasse, the king allowed the friars to commission a French captain in Ceuta or Gibraltar to sail to Algiers with Jewish and Muslim merchants, who would use their local contacts to purchase Spaniards on behalf of the friars and transfer them to Tétouan.[68] This ransom channel was not new, but now the king made it official. The king continued to issue and reissue such permits at least until 1627, when the Mercedarians returned to Algiers (the Trinitarians returned to the city only in 1650).

As a result, Jews and Muslims, the paradigmatic others of Spanish Catholicism, took over the friars' market share and gained a monopoly on the rescue and redemption of Spanish bodies and souls. The friars did not like the power gained by Jewish merchants. In reference to the monopoly of Jews over ransom from Algiers, one Mercedarian wrote in 1618 that "it does not seem advisable, nor will it ever be, that the redemptions be executed by intermediaries, especially not by Jews," who are "great in sticking their nose into other people's business, and always great at turning every event into a business matter."[69] However, banned from traveling to Algiers, teaming up with Jews and Muslims was the only way friars could rescue Spanish captives from that city.

The new modus operandi enhanced the power of North African merchants and thus actualized the potential tension between these merchants and North African authorities. Jewish and Muslim commercial networks were vibrant and potent prior to the conversion of Fatima and the imprisonment of the Trinitarians, which was why Spain decided to incorporate them into the royal ransom apparatus. Once the crown legitimated the partnering, however, Maghribi merchants came to control a greater portion of the ransom market. Their increased influence served Spain but posed a threat to Maghribi authorities and hindered their attempts to pressure Spain to release Fatima—as long as local merchants helped Spain bypass the embargo on the trade in captives, Algiers could not achieve its goals.

In response, Algiers tightened its attempts to regulate ransoming, doing all it could to prevent local merchants from meddling in the ransom market. In 1613, the government obstructed a Mercedarian attempt to commission intermediaries to free captives on their behalf.[70] In September 1614, Algiers intercepted the frigate of a Muslim merchant who was on his way to Tétouan with thirty-three Christians he intended to sell there to the friars; the merchant was executed, and the captives were imprisoned again.[71] And in 1618, Algiers prevented local go-betweens from selling captives to the Trinitarians. In comparison to the measures taken before 1609, now the Algerians were much more reluctant to allow intermediaries to operate counter to their prohibitions.[72] Similarly, once the friars announced to the authorities in Tétouan that from then on they were to spend the bulk of their funds on captives from Algiers, the Tetouanites protested and sought to subvert their plan.[73]

Before Fatima's conversion and the imprisonment of the friars, Mediterranean rulers perceived Jewish and Muslim merchants and ecclesiastical ransom institutions as complementary options. The forced conversion and the arrest of the captives brought the tensions inherent in the relation between Maghribi Jews and their rulers to the fore, transforming the nature of their relationship. Now, redemption via the religious orders and ransom via intermediaries came to be perceived as mutually exclusive alternatives.

Conclusion

Possession of slaves, and slave trafficking even more so, could be read as signs of social and economic integration. Such a reading is in line with the position that holds that commerce often led to cultural toleration, allowing Jews to integrate into the larger societies among which they lived.[74] Recently, Francesca Trivellato has stressed that while this was often true, it is still crucial to historicize the relation between trade and tolerance.[75] The case of Oran and Tétouan shows that Jews owned and traded slaves; in fact, it seems as if Jews were disproportionally represented in the slave market in both cities. In this sense, Maghribi Jews were more involved in the slave market than Jews elsewhere in the Mediterranean.[76] Doubtlessly, their involvement in the slave trade, their possession of slaves, and their struggles over the right to own slaves reflect the degree to which Jews were imbricated with the Christian community of Oran and the Muslim community of Tétouan. Simultaneously, buying, owning, and selling slaves affirmed Jews' otherness as well as their status as members of a minority group in contradistinction to Muslims and Christians. This affirmation was articulated in the exchange regimes that shaped Jewish involvement in the slave trade and distinguished Jews from their neighbors.

In 1999, Lois Dubin and David Sorkin introduced the notion of "port Jews."[77] According to Sorkin, port Jews were elite members of Sephardic merchant communities in Mediterranean and Atlantic port cities invited to settle by rulers who wished to promote trade and believed Jews would speed up the local wheels of commerce. Jewish port communities were organized as merchant corporations or voluntary associations rather than as autonomous communities subject to Jewry laws. Their members developed a unique ethnic identity, understood their Judaism to be fully compatible with the larger cultures in which they lived, and mastered both vernacular languages and Hebrew.

Members of the Jewish communities of Oran and Tétouan shared some of these defining features. They were Sephardic, spoke a host of vernacular languages, and lived in ports whose rulers favored commerce and believed Jews contributed to it. But in contrast to Sorkin's port Jews, the Jews of Oran and Tétouan lived in communities subject to Jewry laws. Finally, while elite members of the community were often fully immersed in the larger culture of their host societies—Jacob Cansino, the royal interpreter in Oran between 1634 and 1666, quoted the New Testament and Cervantes in the letters he exchanged with the Spanish bureaucracy—they continued to form a repressed minority group.[78]

North African Jews, then, do not fit Sorkin's definition of "port Jews," but their engagement with the slave trade sheds new light on Jewish communities that fit the concept better. For example, the Jewish community of Livorno was one whose members shared "an extensive array of rights"—to a degree that suggested "emancipation could also be regarded as the outgrowth of developing commercial cities and societies."[79] However, just as in Oran and Tétouan, the participation of Livornese Jews in the slave trade and the fact they owned slaves reflected assimilation and privileges but simultaneously marked and reproduced Jews' status as minority-group members. As Trivellato has argued, in some cases cross-confessional commerce was predicated on the production of clear religious boundaries.[80] In port cities across the Mediterranean, slavery shaped the religious boundaries that enabled Jews to participate in the slave trade, a form of cross-confessional commerce. Slavery was a system that reflected and reproduced the social order. A commodity-sensitive approach shows how slavery constituted slaves as socially inferior. But in the Mediterranean, slavery also constituted a portion of slave traffickers as subaltern.

Slavery did not simply reproduce religious difference and status but also allowed for limiting, preserving intact, or expanding the privileges associated with Jews' status. In other words, religious difference—as reflected in privileges related to slave owning and trading—was flexible rather than essential. The malleability of Jews' status manifested itself in the multiplicity of arrangements regarding slaves that Jews and others negotiated. Slavery continued to operate as a medium for the negotiation of sellers and buyers' status as long as slaves' religious identity mattered. The system began changing in the second half of the seventeenth- and eighteenth-century Atlantic world, in which all slaves were sub-Saharans and in which slavery was racialized in a process that undermined slaves' religious identity. Calvinist clergy, and to a lesser degree government officials, in Surinam, Dutch Brazil, and New Nederland as well as in English colonies still sought to limit Jews' right to possess slaves or to employ them on Sundays, but their efforts were in vain.[81] By then the identity of slaves as commodities was mostly racial, and as such, the commercial exchange of slaves between Christians and Jews was not cross-cultural trade anymore.

Jews' subaltern status was constituted in relation to an array of Mediterranean cross-boundary mobilities—capturing, enslaving, and redeeming—between cities and settlements in the Maghrib and across the Mediterranean as well as in relation to Christians and to Muslims. To properly historicize the construction of Jews' status requires a Mediterranean framework understood here as a connected historical perspective combined with a comparative frame. On the one hand, this framework accounts for mobilities across political and religious boundaries at the heart of the slave trade. On the other, it stresses the contingency of the relations these forms of mobility shaped by comparing different cities and regions across the sea.

DANIEL HERSHENZON is an Associate Professor in the Department of Literatures, Cultures, and Languages at the University of Connecticut. His book *The Captive Sea: Slavery, Commerce, and Communication in Early Modern Spain and the Mediterranean* (University of Pennsylvania Press, 2018) explores the seventeenth-century entangled histories of Spain, Morocco, and Ottoman Algiers, arguing that captivity and ransom of Christians and Muslims shaped the Mediterranean as a socially, politically, and economically integrated region.

Notes

1. Danna Agmon, Francesca Bregoli, Ofer Dynes, Mercedes García Arenal, Molly Warsh, Anya Zilberstein, the volume's editors, and the press's two anonymous readers have read earlier versions of this chapter and have provided helpful feedback for which I am grateful.

2. Salvatore Bono, "La schiavitù nel Mediterraneo moderno. Storia di una storia," *Cahiers de la Méditerranée*, LXV (2002): 1–16; and "Slave Histories and Memories in the Mediterranean World: A Study of the Sources (Sixteenth-Eighteenth Centuries)," in *Trade and Cultural Exchange in the Early Modern Mediterranean: Braudel's Maritime Legacy*, ed. Maria Fusaro, Colin Heywood, and Mohamed-Salah Omro (London: Tauris Academic Studies, 2010), 97–115; Alex Borucki, David Eltis, and David Wheat, "Atlantic History and the Slave Trade to Spanish America," *American Historical Review*, 120 (2015): 433–61; Robert

Davis, "Counting European Slaves on the Barbary Coast," *Past and Present*, 172 (2001): 87–124; Michel Fontenay, "Il mercato maltese degli schiavi al tempo dei Cavalieri di San Giovanni (1530–1798)," *Quaderni Storici*, 107 (2001): 391–413; Paul Lovejoy, "The Volume of the Atlantic Slave Trade: A Synthesis," *Journal of African History*, 23 (1982): 494–500; Raffaella Sarti, "Bolognesi schiavi dei 'turchi' e schiavi 'turchi' a Bologna tra cinque e settecento: alterità etnico-religiosa e riduzione in schiavitù," *Quaderni Storici*, 107 (2001): 437–74; Alessandro Stella, *Histoires d'esclaves dans la Péninsule Ibérique* (Paris: Editions de l'École des Hautes Études en Sciences Sociales, 2000), 78–79.

3. For an important discussion of this perspective, see Leor Halevi, "Religion and Cross-Cultural Trade: A Framework for Interdisciplinary Inquiry," in *Religion and Trade: Cross-Cultural Exchanges in World History, 1000–1900*, ed. Francesca Trivellato, Leor Halevi, and Cátia Antunes (Oxford: Oxford University Press, 2014), 24–61, here 54–61. See also Molly Greene, *Catholic Pirates and Greek Merchants: A Maritime History of the Mediterranean* (Princeton, NJ: Princeton University Press, 2010).

4. In this chapter, I am referring to Jews living under Spanish rule in North Africa as *Spanish Jews* and to Jews living under Muslim rule as *Moroccan Jews*. Possibly, a few of these Spanish Jews were indigenous to North Africa, while many Moroccan Jews, known as *Megorashim* (expelled), perceived themselves and were perceived by others as Sephardic.

5. In this sense, the chapter follows the first of two axes defining the study of the Mediterranean according to the volume's editors: "to study the interaction between different religious, cultural, and/or political groups in and across the shores of the Mediterranean" (Introduction, 2). However, I broaden this axis to include not only cross-boundary interactions but also comparisons among religious, cultural, and political regimes.

6. For a review of the field, see Daniel Hershenzon, "Towards a Connected History of Bondage in the Mediterranean: Recent Trends in the Field," *History Compass*, 15–8 (2017): 1–13.

7. On Jews as slave owners and slave traders in the Mediterranean, see Bernard Vincent, "Juifs et esclavage à Oran," in *Entre el Islam y Occidente: los judíos magrebíes en la Edad Moderna*, ed. Mercedes García-Arenal (Madrid: Casa de Velázquez, 2003), 245–52; Renzo Toaff, "Schiavitù e schiavi nella Nazione Ebrea di Livorno nel Sei e Settecento," *La Rassegna Mensile di Israel* 51 (1985): 82–95; and Jonathan Schorsch, *Jews and Blacks in the Early Modern World* (Cambridge: Cambridge University Press, 2004). On Jewish slave traffickers in the Atlantic world, see Schorsch, *Jews and Blacks in the Early Modern World*; Eli Faber, *Jews, Slaves, and the Slave Trade: Setting the Record Straight* (New York: NYU Press, 1998). On what the Hebrew sources had to say on the phenomenon, see Simha Assaf, "Slavery and the Slave-Trade among the Jews during the Middle Ages (from the Jewish sources)," *Tsiyon* 4 (1938/39): 91–125, and *Tsiyon* 5 (1939/40): 271–80 [in Hebrew]. On redeeming Jewish captives, see Daniel Carpi, "The Activities of the Officials of the Sephardic Jewish Congregation in Venice for the Redemption of Captives (1654–1670)," *Tsiyon* 68 (2003): 175–222 [in Hebrew]; Minna Rosen, *The Mediterranean in the 17th Century: Captives, Pirates, and Ransomers* (Palermo, Italy: Quaderni Mediterranea Ricerche Storiche, 2016), 37–64; Giuseppe Laras, "La 'compagnia per il riscatto degli schiavi' di Livorno," *La rassegna mensle di Israel* 38, no. 7/8 (1972): 87–130; Eliezer Bashan, *Captivity and Ransom in Mediterranean Jewish Society (1391–1830)* (Jerusalem: University of Bar Ilan Press, 1980) [in Hebrew]. I thank Ofer Ashuali for sharing a draft of his dissertation on Jewish ransoming ("An Analysis of the Negotiation of Ransom of Jewish Captives in the Pre-Modern Period" [in Hebrew]), which he is about to defend at the University of Tel Aviv.

8. Generally speaking, there is very little research on early modern Jewish communities of the Maghrib in their broader context; see David B. Ruderman, *Early Modern Jewry: A New Cultural History* (Princeton, NJ: Princeton University Press, 2010), 12. For two notable exceptions, see Mercedes García Arenal and Gerard Wiegers, *A Man of Three Worlds: Samuel Pallache, a Moroccan Jew in Catholic and Protestant Europe* (Baltimore: John Hopkins University Press, 2003); and Emily Benichou Gottreich, "Of Messiahs and Sultans: Shabbatai Zevi and Early Modernity in Morocco," *Journal of Modern Jewish Studies* 12 (2013): 184–209.

9. On what Maghribi archives offer for early modern Mediterranean history, see Leïla Maziane, *Salé et ses corsaires (1666–1727): Un port de course marocain au XVIIe siècle* (Caen, France: Presses Universitaires de Caen, 2007), 16–17; Abdelhamid Henia, "Archives ottomans en Tunisie et histoire régionale," in *Les Ottomans au Maghreb à travers les archives locales et méditerranéennes*, ed. Abdelhamid Henia, Abderrahman el Moudden, and Abderrahim Benhadda (Rabat, Morocco: Université Mohammed V, Faculté des lettres et des sciences humaines, 2003), 241–55, here 246–47; Mercedes García Arenal, *Ahmad al-Mansur: The Beginning of Modern Morocco* (New York: Oneworld, 2009), 144; Daniel J. Schroeter, *The Sultan's Jew: Morocco and the Sephardi World* (Stanford, CA: Stanford University Press, 2002), xiii; Fatiha Loualich, "In the Regency of Algiers: The Human Side of the Algerine Corso," in *Trade and Cultural Exchange in the Early Modern Mediterranean: Braudel's Maritime Legacy*, ed. Maria Fusaro, Colin Heywood, and Mohamed-Salah Omro (London: Tauris Academic Studies, 2010), 69–96.

10. For estimates on Christian and Muslim slaves see footnote 2. For estimates on sub-Saharan slaves in Iberia, see Stella, *Histoires d'esclaves dans la Péninsule Ibérique*; on sub-Saharan slaves in the Maghrib, see Ralph A. Austen, "The Mediterranean Islamic Slave Trade out of Africa: A Tentative Census," *Slavery and Abolition* 13 (1992): 214–48 and Ralph A. Austen, "The Trans-Saharan Slave Trade: A Tentative Census," in *The Uncommon Market: Essays in the Economic History of the Atlantic Slave Trade*, ed. Henry A. Gemery and Jan S. Hogendorn (New York: Academic Press, 1979), 23–76.

11. James William Broadman, *Ransoming Captives in Crusader Spain: The Order of Merced on the Christian-Islamic Frontier* (Philadelphia: University of Pennsylvania Press, 1986); Andrés Díaz Borrás, *El miedo al Mediterráneo: La caridad popular valenciana y la redención de cautivos bajo poder musulmán 1323–1539* (Barcelona: CSIC, Institución Milá y Fontanals, Departamento de Estudios Medievales, 2001); Jarbal Rodriguez, *Captives and Their Saviors in the Medieval Crown of Aragon* (Washington, DC: The Catholic University of America Press, 2007).

12. José Antonio Martínez Torres, *Prisioneros de los infieles: Vida y rescate de los cautivos cristianos en el Mediterráneo musulmán [siglos XVI–XVII]* (Barcelona: Ediciones bellaterra, 2004), 42–43.

13. Giovanna Fiume, "Redimir y rescatar en el Mediterráneo moderno," *Darssana*, 23 (2015): 54–77; and Daniel Hershenzon, "'[P]ara que me saque cabesa por cabesa . . .': Exchanging Muslim and Christian Slaves across the Mediterranean," *African Economic History* 42 (2014): 11–36.

14. Peter Kitlas, "Al-Miknāsī's Mediterranean Mission: Negotiating Moroccan Temporal and Spiritual Sovereignty in the Late Eighteenth Century," *Mediterranean Studies* 23 (2015): 170–94, esp. 179–88.

15. Wolfgang Kaiser, "La excepción permanente: Actores, visibilidad y asimetrías en los intercambios comerciales entre los países europeos y el Magreb (siglos XVI–XVII)," in

Circulación de personas e intercambios comerciales en el Mediterráneo y en el Atlántico (siglos XVI, XVII, XVIII), ed. José Antonio Martínez Torres (Madrid: CSIC, 2008), 171–89; Rafael Benítez, "La tramitación del pago de rescates a través del reino de Valencia," in *Le commerce de captifs: Les intermédiaires dans l'échange et le rachat des prisonniers en Méditerranée, XVe-XVIIIe siècle*, ed. Wolfgang Kaiser (Rome: École Française de Rome, 2008), 193–217; and Natividad Planas, "Conflicts de competence aux frontiers: Le contrôle de la circulation des homes et des marchandises dans le royaume de Majorque au XVIIe siècle," *Cromohs* 8 (2003), 1–14.

16. On the Jews of Oran, see Jean-Frédéric Schaub, *Les juifs du roi d'Espagne* (Paris: Hachette Littératures, 1999). On the same community but also on other Jewish communities in Spanish North Africa, see Jonathan Israel, "The Jews of Spanish North Africa, 1600–1669," *Transactions of the Jewish Historical Society of England*, XXVI (1979): 71–86; Jonathan Israel, "The Jews of Spanish Oran and Their Expulsion in 1669," *Mediterranean Historical Review* 9 (1994): 235–55.

17. Schaub, *Les juifs du roi d'Espagne*; Israel, "The Jews of Spanish North Africa, 1600–1669"; and Beatriz Alonso Acero, *Orán-Mazalquivir, 1589–1639: una sociedad española en la frontera de Berbería* (Madrid: CSIC, 2000).

18. Claire Gilbert, *The Politics of Language in the Western Mediterranean c. 1492–c. 1669: Multilingual Institutions and the Status of Arabic in Early Modern Spain* (unpublished PhD diss. Princeton University, 1992), 139–66.

19. Schaub, *Les juifs du roi d'Espagne*, 94–95

20. Schaub, *Les juifs du roi d'Espagne*, 55, 78, and 89.

21. Archivo General de Simancas (hereafter AGS), *Guerra Antigua*, Leg. 811, 15.1.1616.

22. AGS, *Estado*, Leg. 1950, 16.10.1621.

23. On "impression management" see Erving Goffman, *The Presentation of Self in Everyday Life* (New York: Anchor Books, 1959).

24. "Pone en consideración a vuestra majestad, que el mayor caudal que tiene para poder acudir a su servicio es el amparo y favor de vuestra majestad, y la gente de su nación de quien su padre y el son caveças en aquellas plaças, y los moros sus amigos y aliados con quien tiene correspondencia y amistad biéndole bolver sin que se aya hecho con el ningún demostración ni que vuestra majestad le ha mandado hazer merced juzgaran como gente de confiada que le falta el amparo y favor de vuestra majestad, pues no miran las cosas por lo que ellas son sino por los effectos que ben, y será posible no le acudiesen con los avisos ni tuviesen con el la correspondencia que solían," AGS, *Guerra Antigua*, Leg. 786, Fol. 83, 9.8.1612.

25. Crudo had commercial relations with Sima di Giuseppe Levi, a Jewish merchant active in Algiers and Livorno at the turn of the century, whom he met in Annaba; see Vittorio Salvadorini, "Traffici e schiavi fra Livorno e Algeria nella prima decade del '600," *Bollettino Storico Pisano* 51 (1982): 67–104, at 88.

26. "[Y] vuelto en esta ciudad anda en habito de cristiano y trata y contrata en ella con mucha publicidad de que ha dado mucho escándalo." Archivo Histórico Nacional (hereafter AHN), *Inquisición*, Leg. 2952, 5.8.1597 and AGS, *Guerra Antigua*, Leg. 487, fols. 213–215, 15.7.1597.

27. AGS, *Guerra Antigua*, Leg. 181, fol. 19, 1585.

28. "En este biaxe que al presente he hecho, he traído diez y nueve captivos en ellos cinco mugeres y quatro niños dos al pecho de sus madres y dos de siete años," AGS, *Guerra Antigua*, Leg. 271, fol. 304, 1589.

29. "[T]raer a todos los cristianos captibos que de toda la Berbería y Argel se me pidieren de cualquier estado . . . los quales ofrezco a poner en la parte donde vuestra majestad

me señalare la terçia parte menos que los que otro ninguno rescatare aunque sean de la Sanctísima Trinidad y Merced" (Ibid.).

30. "Estas mugeres y niños saqué de cassa del rrey de Fez y ninguno de los que van a rescatar por ningún preçio los pudieron rescatar y con estos truxe diez honbres con yntençión que se me pagarían de las limosnas de rredempçión de captivos de la Trinidad o de la Merced" (Ibid.).

31. "[Y] que en aquella fuerça es muy conoscido donde tiene mucha amistad y trato y en ella hecho mucho servicios a su majestad ha ydo socorrido la gente con muchas cosas de comer y regalaos para enfermos en tiempo que estaban con mucha hambre y necesidad y dado avisos muy ymportantes con mucho riesgo de su vida y rescatado cautivos con su yndustria en muy moderados precios" AGS, *Guerra Antigua*, Leg. 181, fol. 19, 1585.

32. Schaub, *Les juifs du roi d'Espagne*.

33. In his *Crónica de Almançor*, the Portuguese António de Saldaña describes how Al-Mansur asked the European merchants in his realm to write home, telling "how well he treated them" (o bom trato lhes fazia). This policy "provoked the arrival in Marrakech of many Italians, Spaniards, French, English and Flemish that filled those kingdoms with such a quantity of commodities" (que foi ocasito de se irem pera Marrocos muitos italianos, espanhois, franceses, ingreses e framengos que encheram aqueles reinos de todas as mercadorias em tanta cantidade), António de Saldanha, *Crónica de Almançor, Sultão de Marrocos (1578–1603)*, ed. António Dias Farinha (Lisbon, Portugal: Instituto de Investigação Científica Tropical, 1997), 31. On the measures Al-Mansur took to attract merchants to Morocco, see also García Arenal, *Ahmad al-Mansur: The Beginning of Modern Morocco* ([Oxford: OneWorld, 2009]), 111–15.

34. Mercedes García-Arenal, Fernando Rodríguez Mediano, and Rachid El Hour, *Cartas marruecas: Documentos de Marruecos en archivos españoles (siglos XVI-XVII), Estudios árabes e islámicos; Monografías; 3* (Madrid: CSIC, 2002), 222–23.

35. The two Moroccan Jewish merchants asked for papers that would allow them to enter Spain in order to sue Portuguese nobles formerly captive in Morocco to whom they had lent ransom money that had never been repaid. The Inquisition acknowledged their legal rights in the matter and issued two passports for them; see AHN, *Inquisición*, Leg. 1592, 25.7.1607. Cf. Martínez Torres, *Prisioneros de los infieles*, 120. In 1695 and 1696, Hadji Ahmed ben al-Hadji, Dey of Algiers, exchanged letters with the Spanish authorities regarding an Italian merchant who had committed to ransom Algerians from Naples but failed to do so, see Biblioteca Nacional de España (hereafter BNE), Mss. 5065/1.

36. Amnon Linder, *The Jews in the Legal Sources of the Early Middle Ages* (Detroit: Wayne State University Press; Jerusalem: Israel Academy of Sciences and Humanities, 1997).

37. Bernard Vincent, "Juifs et esclavage à Oran," 250–51.

38. On the early modern history of Tétouan, see Guillermo Gozalbes Busto, *Los Moriscos en Marruecos* (Granada: T. G. Arte, 1992); Abderrahim Yebbur Oddi, *El gobierno de Tetuán por la familia Al-Naqsis (1597–1673)* (Tétouan, Morocco: Imprenta del Majzen, 1955); Jean-Louis Miège, "Consuls et négociants à Tétouan, 1681–1727," in *Titwan hilal al-qarnayn 16 wa-17: 'amal Nadwat Titwan Hilal al-Qarnayn 16 wa-17 ; 9, 10, 11 mars 1995* (Titwan, Morocco: Kulliyat al-Adab wal-'ulum al-Insaniya: Al-majmu'a al-Hadariya li-Madinat Titwan, 1996), 109–49; and Jean-Louis Miège, M'hammad Benaboud, and Nadia Erzini, *Tétouan. Ville andalouse marocaine* (Paris: CNRS Editions, 1996), 12–73. On the political history of Morocco in the period, see B. A. Mojuetan, "Legitimacy in a Power State: Moroccan Politics in the Seventeenth Century during the Interregnum," *International Journal of Middle Eastern*

Studies 13 (1981): 347–60; and R. Mantran, "North Africa in the Sixteenth and Seventeenth Centuries," in *The Cambridge History of Islam*, ed. P. M. Holt, K. S. Lambton, and Bernard Lewis, vol. 2A (Cambridge: Cambridge University Press, 1977), 238–65, at 239–48.

39. Hicham Louah, "Aspects de l'économie tétouanaise," in *Actes du colloque: Aspects de la mémoire de Tanger et de Tétouan (18–20 February 1993)* (Tétouan, Morocco: La faculté des lettres et des sciences humaines de Tétouan, 1994), 177–82.

40. Very little has been published on the early modern history of the Jewish community of Tétouan; see Juan Bautista Villar Ramírez, *Tetuán en el resurgimiento judío contemporáneo (1850–1870): Aproximación a la historia del judaísmo norte africano* (Caracas, Venezuela: Editorial Arte, 1985), 15–33, and Juan Bautista Villar Ramírez, *La judería de Tetuán, 1489–1860* (Murcia, Spain: Universidad de Murcia, 1969), 15–39.

41. Gozalbes Busto, *Los Moriscos en Marruecos*, 141.

42. Martínez Torres, *Prisioneros de los infieles*, 99.

43. Bernard Lewis, *Race and Slavery in the Middle East: An Historical Enquiry* (New York: Oxford University Press, 1990), 8–9.

44. Halevi, "Religion and Cross-Cultural Trade: A Framework for Interdisciplinary Inquiry," 57–58. For the fatwa, see Aḥmad ibn Yaḥyā al-Wansharīsī, *La pierre de touche des fétwas de Ahmad al-Wanscharīsī* in *Archives Marocaines. Publication de la mission scientifique du Maroc*, ed. and trans. Émile Amar, vol. 12 (Paris: E. Leroux, 1908–1909), 200–1.

45. On the conversion of Muslim slaves in Oran, see Juan Jesús Bravo Caro, "El reflejo de la esclavitud del Mediterráneo en los registros parroquiales oraneses," in *Orán: Historia de la corte chica*, ed. M. Á. De Bunes Ibarra and B. Alonso Acero (Madrid: Ediciones Polifemo, 2011), 143–72.

46. For cases of Maghribis making efforts to redeem Muslims who were baptized, see Daniel Hershenzon, *The Captive Sea: Slavery, Communication and Commerce in Early Modern Spain and the Mediterranean* (Philadelphia: University of Pennsylvania Press, 2018), 130–31.

47. Daniel Hershenzon, "Plaintes et menaces réciproques: captivité et violence religieuses dans la Méditerranée du XVIIe siècle," in *Les Musulmans dans l'histoire de l'Europe. Tome 2. Passages et contacts en Méditerranée*, ed. Jocelyne Dakhlia and Wolfgang Kaiser (Paris: Albin Michel, 2013), 441–60.

48. Between May 3, 1661, and May 6, 1662, the governor sent 107 slaves, the majority of whom were women, children, and infants (the mean age was seventeen, the median sixteen); see Biblioteca Francisco Zabálburo, *Collección Altamira*, D. 1–20, 22.

49. Fernando Jiménez de Gregorio, "'Relación de Orán,' por el Vicario D. Pedro Cantero Vaca (1631–1636)," *Hispania: Revista Española de Historia* 85 (1962): 81–117, here 107.

50. Bernard Vincent, "Juifs et esclavage à Oran," in *Entre el Islam y Occidente: Los judíos magrebíes en la Edad Moderna*, ed. Mercedes García-Arenal (Madrid: Casa de Velásquez, 2003), 245–52.

51. AGS, *Guerra y Marina*, cartas, Leg. 1600, 10.3.1645 and Leg. 1598, 10.12.1645.

52. About 7.5 percent of the entire population of the city—around six thousand people including slaves and soldiers lived in the city; Schaub, *Les juifs du roi d'Espagne*, 30, and Israel, "The Jews of Spanish North Africa," 71. In the premodern period the possession of slaves was as common among Jews as among Muslims and Christians; see Assaf, "Slavery and the Slave-Trade among the Jews during the Middle Ages (from the Jewish sources)."

53. Israel, "The Jews of Spanish North Africa," 78. On the division of loot, see the eyewitness testimony of Diego Suárez Montañés, *Historia del Maestre último que fue de*

Montesa y de su hermano Don Felipe de Borja: la manera como gobernaron las memorables plazas de Orán y Mazalquivir, Reinos de Tremecén y Ténez, en África, ed. Miguel Ángel de Bunes Ibarra and Beatriz Alonso Acero (Valencia: Institució Alfons el Magnànim, 2005), 290–91.

54. On the relation between business, money, credit, and rabbis, including community rabbis, see Natalie Zemon Davis, "Religion and Capitalism Once Again? Jewish Merchant Culture in the Seventeenth Century," *Representations* 59 (1997): 56–84.

55. Rebecca Winer, "Jews, Slave-Holding, and Gender in the Crown of Aragon circa 1250–1492," in *Cautivas y esclavas: El tráfico humano en el Mediterráneo*, ed. Aurelia Martín Casares and María Cristina Delaigue (Granada: Editorial Universidad de Granada, 2016), 43–60.

56. Ibid.

57. Bernard Vincent, "Juifs et esclavage à Oran," 250–51.

58. Schaub, *Les juifs du roi d'Espagne*, 54–55.

59. On the Jewish community of Livorno, see Francesca Trivellato, *The Familiarity of Strangers: The Sephardic Diaspora, Livorno, and the Cross-Cultural Trade in the Early Modern Period* (New Haven, CT: Yale University Press, 2009); Francesca Bregoli, *Mediterranean Enlightenment: Livornese Jews, Tuscan Culture, and Eighteenth-Century Reform* (Stanford, CA: Stanford University Press, 2014); and Matthias Lehmann, "A Livornese 'Port Jew' and the Sephardim of the Ottoman Empire," *Jewish Social Studies* 11 (2005): 51–76.

60. Toaff, "Schiavitù e schiavi nella Nazione Ebrea di Livorno nel Sei e Settecento."

61. Pancracio Celdrán Gomariz, ed. *Judíos, moros y cristianos en la ciudad de Argel (según un manuscrito inédito de Melchor de Zúñiga, 1639)* (Madrid: Ediciones del Orto, 2012), 249–50. There were two Jewish communities in the city: a local one who suffered extreme repression and another formed by French and Italian Jews who participated openly in all aspects of commerce including ransoming. See Antonio de Sosa, "Topography and History of Algiers," in *An Early Modern Dialogue with Islam: Antonio de Sosa's Topography of Algiers (1612)*, ed. María Antonia Garcés (Notre Dame, IN: University of Notre Dame Press, 2011), 181–83. On the community as it emerges from Jewish documents, see Menachem Weinstein, "The Jewish Communities in Algeria between the Years 1300–1830" (PhD diss., Bar-Ilan University, Ramat Gan, 1974) [in Hebrew].

62. Assaf, "Slavery and the Slave-Trade among the Jews during the Middle Ages (from the Jewish Sources)," here 110–23.

63. Ruth Lamdan, "The Holding of Maidservants in the Jewish Community in Israel, Syria and Egypt in the Sixteenth Century" [in Hebrew] in *Days of the Moon: Chapters in the History of the Jews in the Ottoman Empire*, ed. Minna Rozen (Tel Aviv: The University of Tel Aviv, 1996), 355–71; and Ovadia Salame, "Slaves in the Ownership of Jews and Christians in Ottoman Jerusalem" [in Hebrew], *Cathedra* 49 (1989): 63–75.

64. Hershenzon, *The Captive Sea*, 174–75.

65. AGS, *Estado*, Leg. 210, 2.9.1608. "A le mandado la aduana que de ninguna manera lleve cristianos a Tetuán . . . de los que han comprado los mercantes, porque ellos son causa que las dichas limosnas dEspaña no vengan a esta ciudad y que el baxa pierde sus derechos."

66. AGS, *Estado*, Leg. 1882, Fol. 266, 10.29.1618.

67. The Mercedarian Pedro de Medina claimed that "porque muchas personas graves de esta corte le an pedido rescatarse algunos cautivos que el pressente están en Argel y ofrecieron limosnas y adjutorios para ello" (AGS, *Guerra Antigua*, Leg. 767, 3.9.1612). The second lieutenant Domingo Pérez petitioned the Council of War to help him ransom his

nephew from Algiers; see AGS, *Guerra Antigua*, Leg. 768, 11.9.1612. María de Hierro, possibly following instructions from Medina, specifically petitioned the council to allow Medina to execute his plans. She was hoping to ransom her husband, who was held captive in Algiers; see AGS, *Guerra Antigua*, Leg. 767, 4.2.1612.

68. AGS, *Guerra Antigua*, Leg. 767, 3.9.1612.

69. José Antonio Gari y Siumell, *La orden redentora de la Merced ó sea historia de las redenciones de cautivos cristianos realizadas por los hijos de la orden de la Merced* (Barcelona: Imprenta de los herederos de la Viuda Pla, 1873), 287–88.

70. AGS, *Guerra Antigua*, Leg. 785, 2.28.1613.

71. AGS, *Estado*, Leg. 255, 20.9.1614.

72. AGS, *Estado*, Leg. 255, 20.9.1614.

73. BNE, Mss 3,870, Apud Gozalbes Busto, *Los Moriscos en Marruecos*, 278. For a description of the uproar that erupted in 1614 once the plans of the Mercedarians became public, see BNE, Mss 12078, Fol. 160. See also Gari y Siumell, *La orden redentora*, 283.

74. David Sorkin, "The Port Jew: Notes towards a Social Type," *Journal of Jewish Studies* 50 (1999): 87–97. For a critique, see C. S. Monaco, "Port Jews or a People of the Diaspora? A Critique of the Port Jew Concept," *Jewish Social Studies* 15 (2009): 137–66.

75. Trivellato, *The Familiarity of Strangers*, 73.

76. While evidence of Jews who owned slaves abounds, there is significantly less evidence of Jewish slave traders. For examples not mentioned in the chapter, see Assaf, "Slavery and the Slave-Trade among the Jews during the Middle Ages (from the Jewish sources)," 100–1, 114–19, 272–73, and 277–80; and Toaff, "Schiavitù e schiavi nella Nazione Ebrea di Livorno nel Sei e Settecento," 93–95.

77. Sorkin, "The Port Jew: Notes towards a Social Type"; and Lois Dubin, *The Port Jews of Habsburg Trieste: Absolutist Politics and Enlightenment Culture* (Stanford, CA: Stanford University Press, 1999).

78. Schaub, *Les juifs du roi d'Espagne*, 112–24.

79. Sorkin, "The Port Jew: Notes towards a Social Type," 97.

80. Trivellato, *The Familiarity of Strangers*.

81. Schorsch, *Jews and Blacks in the Early Modern World*, 55–61.

5

RELIGIOUS BOUNDARIES IN ITALY DURING AN ERA OF FREE TRADE, 1550–1750

The Case of Livorno

Corey Tazzara

THE MEDITERRANEAN HAS PLAYED A SURPRISING ROLE IN the conceptualization of religious boundaries in early modern Europe.[1] The philosopher Will Kymlicka contrasted an idealized model of the millet system in the Ottoman Empire, which emphasized communal rather than personal autonomy, with modern or liberal toleration, grounded in the rights of the individual. Kymlicka's model of the millet system was in turn extended to much of Europe by the historian Benjamin Kaplan, who saw it as the product of ad hoc negotiations between Protestants and Catholics. For Kaplan, a variety of practices kept Christian communities distinct from one another and made mutual coexistence possible despite ongoing antagonisms—such as separate churches, power-sharing arrangements, and formal boundaries between jurisdictions. By an act of historiographical wizardry, the management of religious minorities in the Ottoman Empire migrated to interconfessional Europe.[2]

The millet model implies the boundedness of religious communities. It is interesting, therefore, that while the millet was colonizing European historiography, recent scholarship on the Mediterranean has emphasized the unboundedness of communities—the fluidity of personal identity and the porousness of social groups.[3] This body of research repudiates any account that treats Christendom and Islam as "warring" civilizations, as Braudel did, or of Jews as "one civilization against the rest."[4] Instead, it emphasizes collaboration between polities and social or cultural mixing at the ground level. Its emblematic figure is the boundary crosser. Instances include Marranos who "used their Jewishness instrumentally," according to the demands of the situation, and Greek Orthodox individuals who circulated (not without friction) between the eastern and western Mediterranean.[5] Other examples include the dragomans in Istanbul, Venice, and other cities. Social integration could be especially pronounced among elites. Consider the case of the Venetian patrician Andrea Gritti. Gritti fathered three sons by an Ottoman Greek woman and became personal friends with Sultan Bayezid II and Grand Vizier Ahmed Paşa. These connections did not prevent Gritti's election to the dogeship—although his political enemies complained that "a man with three bastards in Turkey cannot be Doge."[6]

We are in the presence of a peculiar problem, in which some historians have emphasized the construction of boundaries between Christians of different confessions (i.e., barriers where one might have expected their absence) at the same time that others have emphasized the erasure of boundaries between different Mediterranean peoples (i.e., fluidity where one might have expected boundaries). This article adjudicates between these perspectives by focusing on the Italian port of Livorno, which has figured differently in both historiographies. It generally employs the methods of social analysis, but it will also consider how the concept of social boundaries can help explain the complex culture of the boundary crosser.[7]

Part one begins by laying out the rationale for the toleration of Jews and other religious minorities in late Renaissance Italy. This section reveals the privileged place that Jews had in the Catholic imagination. Parts two and three examine the social mechanisms employed to maintain appropriate religious boundaries as well as their overall efficacy. Here, the ideological distinctions that separated Jews from other religious minorities tended to break down: all were subject to similar forms of social disciplining. The fourth section sketches the impact of commercial toleration on Enlightenment programs of liberal toleration. It suggests that marketplace norms tended increasingly to serve as a model for other social arenas. And the final section assesses the limits of coexistence in the Mediterranean world. It disputes the extension of the millet model even to Italy, let alone to northwestern Europe, and it urges a more contextual analysis of religious toleration in the early modern Mediterranean. This approach accounts for stark differences in the treatment of Jews in the Iberian Mediterranean in comparison to the Italian Mediterranean, despite shared commitments to Catholicism; and it also explains why, despite similar methods for managing religious minorities, commercial toleration had a different legacy in Europe than in the Ottoman Empire.

Commercial Toleration in Early Modern Italy

The most influential economic theorist of the Renaissance was Giovanni Botero. In his *On the Greatness of Cities* (1588), Botero explained that urban life depended on a city's capacity to draw citizens together in the pursuit of industry and commerce. Like others before and after, Botero saw commerce as part of the divine plan: "For His Divine Majesty, willing that men should mutually embrace each other as members of one body, divided in such sort His blessings as to no nation did he give all things, to the end that others having need of us, and contrariwise we having need of others, there might grow a community, and from a community love and from love and unity between us."[8] Botero advocated light fiscal burdens, low customs duties, and incentives for immigration. He praised the Ottoman Empire for receiving into its fold those whom Catholic persecution had driven from their homelands. He also condemned Ferdinand and Isabella's expulsion of the Jews, for instance, as well as the effort to drive Protestants out of France and Italy. "Let us add to the aforesaid that the difference and enmity between the Mohammedans and us depriveth us in a manner of the commerce of Africa, and of the most part of the trade of the Levant."[9]

Although Botero was cognizant of the commercial benefits of toleration, he was by no means an advocate of the unconditional acceptance of religious others. He asserted that "religion and the worship of God" was a powerful force behind urban growth. Conversely, he warned rulers against nursing heresies within their realms:

> For such are the ruins of kings, the plague of kingdoms, the scandal of Christianity, the sworn enemies of the Church, nay rather of God, against whom, to the imitation of the ancient giants, they build up a new tower unto Babel which shall breed and bring unto them in the end confusion and utter ruin.... If this place would suffer it I could easily show that the greatest part of the loss of states and ruins of Christian princes have proceeded of this accursed variance in religion, through the which we are disarmed and deprived of the protection and favour of Almighty God, and have thrust into the hands of the Turks and Calvinists the weapons and the scourges of God's Divine justice against us.[10]

His insistence on orthodoxy is not to be seen as a contradiction or even a tension in Botero's thought. Instead it is meant as an injunction: commercial toleration must proceed, yes, but within an institutional framework that leaves the social and religious order intact.

Italian regimes intensified their search for foreign merchants in the final decades of the sixteenth century, just as Botero began to theorize the practice. But a much earlier decree establishing the Jewish ghetto in Venice makes explicit the anxiety surrounding commercial toleration. While the 1516 decree begins by noting the economic needs that impelled the city to welcome Jews, it hurried on to detail the rules of dress, conduct, and legal status that were to distinguish them from Christian residents. As the text explained, "no God fearing subject of our state would have wished them ... to disperse throughout the city, sharing houses with Christians and going wherever they choose by day and night, perpetrating all those misdemeanors and detestable and abominable acts which are generally known and shameful to describe."[11] Only clear religious boundaries could preserve the Republic of Venice as it embarked on its project of commercial toleration.

The legal regime governing religious minorities was fairly incoherent in Venice and elsewhere in Italy, varying greatly from city to city, a hodgepodge of ad hoc measures. But on the whole, early modern Italy underwent an unprecedented degree of liberalization along two key axes during the long seventeenth century: openness to foreigners and reduction in customs barriers. The vehicle for these changes was an institution known as the free port. Free ports were places where merchants of any nationality or religious affiliation were free to trade on equal terms and where taxes on maritime trade had been reduced to a minimum. Although the road to liberalization was long and tortuous, by 1740 all major ports in the peninsula were free ports of some kind. Whether this situation was good for Italy was hotly contested: a Neapolitan commercial writer, Carlo Broggia, accused Italian states of "prostituting" their commerce to foreigners, and another denounced the institution as a false idol.[12] What is certain is that the new policies of hospitality raised pressing questions of how to manage foreign religious communities—Jews at first, but ultimately Protestants, Orthodox, and even Muslim communities.[13]

Livorno was the greatest of Italy's free ports. Founded ex nihilo by the Medici grand dukes of Tuscany, Livorno soon became "one of the most famous places for trade in all Christendom."[14] Its port traffic increased dramatically over the early modern period; between 1676 and 1720, Livorno probably had more long-distance connections than any port in the Mediterranean. The city owed its growth to its generous customs regime and a multifaceted program of ethno-religious toleration. We will examine these policies momentarily, but it is worth noting at the outset their success. By 1642, Livorno had at least ten Italian and thirty-three French commercial houses, neither of which posed a religious threat, but it also had eighty Jewish merchant houses, ten English, ten Dutch, and seventy-six other houses—mostly Italian but also those of Armenian and Greek Orthodox merchants. Communities themselves were much larger than these figures indicate; for instance, the English community comprised some one hundred people in the mid-seventeenth century between merchants, mariners, and artisans. The Jewish community was the largest, reaching about two thousand members by the middle of the seventeenth century and four thousand by the end of the Ancien Régime. To the French traveler Charles De Brosses, Livorno's "streets seemed to be a veritable masquerade and the language that of the Tower of Babel."[15]

The Mechanisms of Social Discipline

Livorno had a deceptively clear framework for religious toleration. In 1591, the grand duke issued a letter patent called the Livornina (reissued in slightly modified form in 1593). Although the primary audience was Sephardic Jews, the patent was addressed generally to merchants of every nation, including Turks, Moors, Armenians, and Persians. All merchants were granted safe conduct against debts contracted before their settlement in Livorno, freedom from prosecution for crimes committed outside of Tuscany, and housing loans. There were personal tax exemptions as well, including the right to exercise a trade without paying guild fees. But forty-one of the patent's forty-four articles were pledges to Jewish immigrants. Some were oriented toward integrating Jews into the life, especially the business life, of the city. Thus, the Livornina granted Jews freedom of movement, the ability to dress without an identifying sign, and the rights to carry arms, practice any profession, purchase real estate, and open shops in any part of the city. On the other hand, several provisions were intended to maintain the religious boundaries of the community. The Livornina guaranteed Jewish immigrants access to kosher meat and confirmed their right to observe holy days. Further provisions shielded them from Catholic conversion efforts and protected them from slander, insult, and violence. And finally, the regime delegated supervision of the minutiae of community life to local leaders, who were authorized to set up a self-governing body for regulating the internal religious and judicial affairs of the community. In effect, the Jewish community of Livorno became a miniature protectorate of the Tuscan state.[16]

Although the Livornina was orientated toward Jews, its principles came to encompass all religious minorities in the port.[17] I shall pass over the details whereby the Livornina came to serve as the basic constitution of the free port, noting only that it also functioned as a model for other port cities in the Italian peninsula, hence its significance as a case study. Instead, I shall categorize the principal mechanisms that maintained religious boundaries in the port as criminalization, spatialization, cultural distinction, and delegation. As these mechanisms were in operation simultaneously and reinforced one another, I shall examine them individually before considering their overall efficacy.

Criminalization is the simplest mechanism for maintaining religious boundaries. It denotes certain practices as illegal and then vows to take judicial action against violators. Undoubtedly, Livorno had a reputation from its earliest days as "a nest of evil people, without a conscience, without faith in their words, and without shame in their actions."[18] But certain things were outlawed even in this den of iniquity. Sexual relations between Jews and Christians were prohibited; indeed, it was illegal for a Jew to keep a Christian servant or nurse, although this law was often ignored; as the city's governor explained, "when it concerns girls of a young age [we] have always closed our eyes."[19] Forced conversions of all kinds, but especially of Jews and Muslim slaves, were prohibited, and the conversion of publicly owned slaves was outright discouraged. And finally, the public celebration of Protestant rituals from baptism to burial was sternly forbidden. Indeed, incognito Anglican ministers were expelled from the port in 1645, 1649, 1666, 1668, and 1670.[20] Unlike some cities in Germany and the Netherlands, the Medici regime was not prepared to tolerate clandestine Protestant churches in Livorno, let alone open ones. This situation led to widespread dissimulation. For instance, as the governor explained to the grand duchess in 1622, "the Flemish who reside here live with great circumspection, [they] do not set a poor example, [and they] comport themselves, at least apparently, as good Catholics and without any ostentation of being heretics."[21] "Turning a blind eye" to religious realities was a cliché of official life in Livorno.[22]

One problem with criminalization as a mechanism is that it is information intensive. A regime has not only to be aware of a violation but also have access to enough evidence to convict and punish transgressors. In addition, criminalization operates only post facto; a criminal situation might go on for weeks, months, or years before authorities learn of it. Fortunately for scrupulous believers, one response to the problem of criminalization—committing one's crimes in marginal places—fed into another mechanism of boundary maintenance: spatialization.

Spatialization kept religious communities and their ritual activities separate from the life of the Catholic majority. Much spatialization was voluntary. Since this mechanism was ubiquitous, a few examples will suffice. Thus, although Livorno had no ghettos and no residential houses like the Fondaco dei Turchi in Venice, religious communities tended to cluster together around their place of worship. When the fledgling Sephardic community completed its synagogue in 1607, for instance, Jews settled in the nearby streets, particularly on the Via degli Ebrei, later called Via della Sinagoga, Via della Scuola, or as it remains today, Via del Tempio. These toponyms identified this neighborhood as the de facto Jewish quarter.[23] Reasons of security and convenience presumably motivated this pattern of settlement. Prohibitions against Christians cohabiting with Jews further reinforced spatial segregation.[24]

More coercive spatialization occurred in the *bagno*, a building for imprisoning slaves and forced laborers near the center of the city. The bagno—which recalls similar slave quarters in Algiers and Malta—typically contained between one and two thousand residents. Yet religious boundaries were maintained even in the bagno, where Catholics, Protestants, and Muslims had separate quarters and where four mosques tended to the religious needs of Muslims.

This concession was not issued in the spirit of toleration but rather reciprocity, "because the Turks also allowed Christians to have secret churches in their *bagnos*," as one Capuchin traveler from Sicily explained.[25]

And finally, there was ritual spatialization. The French traveler Maximilien Misson reported that "Protestants marry aboard English, Dutch, Danish, and other ships that meet in the port, and there they baptize their children"; he also noted that the Protestants had their own cemetery outside the city walls.[26] Protestants found a way to maintain their rites only by recourse to spaces outside the precincts of the city—a satisfying compromise, since it enabled Protestant merchants to stay in business in Livorno while allowing the city to keep its Catholic purity intact. Conversely, consider how the boundaries between Latin and schismatic Greeks were not enforced until 1757, when the two groups were ordered to worship in different churches. This indicates the effort to suppress religious division by enforcing spatial unity.[27]

Spatialization had different motives, ranging from coercion in the case of the bagno, to security and convenience in the case of the Jewish quarter, to ritual fulfillment for the Protestants aboard their ships or in their extramural cemetery. The degree of official connivance in these spatial solutions also varied. But in all cases, spatialization served to maintain religious boundaries by physically separating religious minorities from those central spaces dominated by Catholics. Thus, the description of the Fondaco dei Turchi as "totally exceptional" in Europe is true in an architectural sense but problematic as a summary of hospitality between the Muslim and Christian worlds. Spatial division was common throughout Italy.[28]

A third mechanism for maintaining religious boundaries was cultural distinction. Livorno, despite its cosmopolitan makeup, celebrated its Catholic identity in many ways. Its most famous piece of art was the Statue of the Four Moors, which depicted four shackled Muslims writhing in agony. This was an incongruous image for a free port, perhaps, but it reminded viewers of the grand duke's enterprises against Muslim shipping, and the same exploits were frescoed onto the walls of the main buildings in Livorno for all to admire.[29] Dietary practices were also an important means of distinguishing Catholics and Protestants and for ferreting out dissimulators (not to mention distinguishing both from Jews and Muslims).[30] Then there was the public life of the city, with its festivities and parades, such as after a severe earthquake, when the Livornesi proceeded through the streets bearing the image of the Virgin Mary.[31] And—lest these artistic and ritual spectacles left anyone in doubt as to the religious identity of the city—communal officeholding was only open to Catholics. In all these ideological niceties, Livorno was typical of Counter-Reformation cities throughout Italy, but in Livorno they probably also reinforced the self-awareness of

Catholics and reminded non-Catholics of their precarious position as religious minorities. Livorno was known as the "paradise of the Jews" to many Europeans, but it was a paradise that the Jews shared with a Catholic majority whose lower classes were animated by a ferocious anti-Judaism. Perhaps the consciousness of religious distinction explains why religious imagery was exceptionally common in the homes of middling-class Christians in Livorno.[32]

The Medici regime was unable to intervene regularly and effectively in the lives of its subjects; power flowed through chains of intermediaries, each of whom was pursuing his own ends. This situation handicapped information flows between the capital of Florence and the port of Livorno. One revealing token of informational incapacity was that neither the central government nor local officials knew for certain the laws that governed the presence of foreigners in Livorno; so much for the clear legal framework described above. In a squabble that broke out in 1644 when a group of creditors had a ship captain imprisoned, the customs director revealed that he routinely issued ad hoc exemptions. When pressed further on the issue, he made a blanket appeal to the informal traditions of the free port: "the custom is that even our enemies the Turks have enjoyed and continue to enjoy the freedom of this port."[33] This episode is an extreme example of the central government's obtuseness, and by the late seventeenth century, the regime did have more well-defined ideas about foreign hospitality. But plenty of evidence indicates that officials in Florence were the last to find out about what was happening in the port city.

What kept governance from collapsing into chaos was the practice of delegation, whereby the Medici regime granted a large measure of internal autonomy to ethno-religious communities in the port. We have already seen that the Livornina authorized Jews to establish their own formal community. Other groups in the port came to be organized around their consuls, and the regime negotiated with such consuls over a wide variety of affairs, not merely matters of commerce or diplomacy. So obvious did this solution seem that even the slaves in the bagno got their own "mercantile slave boss" to help manage the economic and other activities of the slave population.[34] Several historians have likened these arrangements to the millet system in the Ottoman Empire; I shall revisit this question in the conclusion.[35]

The practice of delegation concentrated power in the hands of intermediaries who were scrupulous about regulating their own community's affairs, above all its religious affairs. Or to put it another way: the regime delivered the maintenance of religious boundaries to those individuals who had the greatest incentives for protecting them.[36] For example, the regime was well aware that not all Greeks in Livorno were Uniate with the Roman Catholic Church; many were Orthodox. And yet it compelled the Orthodox to worship alongside their Uniate cousins inside a single Church of the Holy Annunciation (until 1757). Even though one inquisitor's report concluded in 1699 that members of the Greek Church were "barely Catholics," the regime resisted prying into the community's affairs as long as Uniate Greeks managed to put a lid on community scandal.[37] Similar dynamics were at play in the Armenian and Jewish communities, each of which the regime treated as a single group although they were rent by terrible ethnic, religious, and class divisions.

These delegates—consuls and national deputies, translators and religious officials—are sometimes described as boundary crossers, as people able to straddle multiple spheres or cultivate flexible identities. Undoubtedly, but such figures are to be seen not only as boundary crossers but also as boundary enforcers, as those liminal individuals who made possible the general maintenance of religious boundaries. This way of conceiving of boundary crossers indicates that they were central rather than peripheral figures in the social landscape; they were not on the margins at all. It also helps explain why they were a numerically restricted phenomenon. Their presence was contingent on maintaining the very boundaries they defied—and helped define. Whatever psychological implications their rare positions entailed, they were profoundly embedded in the social realities in the early modern Mediterranean.[38]

Between Society and the Marketplace

It should be apparent that these four mechanisms operated in tandem. How well did they work? Here we run into a question about what metric best captures the boundedness of communities. Religious endogamy is a standard measure, and while there were a handful of marriages between non-Catholics and Catholics, especially between Protestant merchants and Catholic women, they were by no means common.[39] On the other hand, fear of sexual relations between Christians and Jews (and to a lesser extent, between Christians and Muslims) was rampant in official documents; how often the act itself occurred is impossible to ascertain. A few documents suggest that johns preferred to visit prostitutes from their own ethno-religious community.[40] On the other hand, it is known that the prohibition against Jews having Christian women as servants was widely flouted. It is hard to imagine that all such relationships were chaste, and archival evidence suggests that at least some Jewish masters exploited their Christian servants with as much gusto as masters elsewhere. One Jew, Abram Costa, was notorious for frequenting Christian prostitutes despite the hefty fines he had to pay.[41] There is also evidence of more consensual relations between Jews and Christians. The sexual cordon that in theory separated Christians from Jews was not impermeable, although long-term domestic partnership seems to have been rare.

Likewise with conversion. It goes without saying that Catholics could not convert out of the Roman Catholic Church, leaving aside the case of New Christians (who were permitted to revert to Judaism in Livorno). Between 1677 and 1713, there were forty-six conversions of Ottoman Muslims to Catholicism—about one per year, though sixteen occurred in 1688 alone as part of a mass baptism.[42] Among Jews, there were several dozen conversions to Catholicism during the long seventeenth century, although more archival work remains to be done. The fragmentary Inquisition records indicate that there were 380 "reconciliations" with the Catholic Church between 1574 and 1785: almost two per year. Of these, about a third were renegades who had previously converted to Islam, and about 60 percent were Protestant in origin. Thus, something like one Protestant per year was reconciled to the Church.[43]

The Livornina protected Jews against the pressure to convert, and the regime stuck by its commitments on this score. The paucity of Protestant conversions is ironic, however, since one justification for toleration in Livorno worked out between the Papacy and the Medici concerned the possibility of just such conversion. For instance, the Jesuit Caludio Sacripandi proposed in 1610 "that the heretic English Protestants, especially the nobles, that arrive here be tolerated so long as they not give scandal in public and that one has hope for their probable conversion."[44] Yet in practice the regime made few efforts to convert heretics and infidels until late in the seventeenth century. Even then it upheld obstacles to conversion, especially regarding age. When the eleven-year-old English girl Anna Gravier sought to convert to Catholicism in 1764, shortly after the death of her father, she was shipped back to her mother in England. But her two older sisters, eighteen and fifteen years old, were not prevented from converting.[45]

Such conversions as did occur often took place as part of family conflicts over issues of marriage and patrimony. Conversion was the "nuclear option," when other moves in the social game had been abandoned. That is, it occurred when the stakes in play were so high that an individual was willing to sacrifice one's ties (at least temporarily) by summoning outside forces—Church and State. These institutions could offer inducements in the face of family opposition, such as dowries for girls who converted.[46] Sometimes, conversions were a prelude to more substantial forms of integration—such as that of Richard Thornton, who became a naval captain for the grand duke and eventually served as the English consul in the port, or a few Jewish converts who went on to serve in the Catholic priesthood.[47]

But perhaps sex and conversion set the bar too high; we might instead consider whether ethno-religious groups mixed socially when the stakes were lower. New Christians and Jews certainly socialized in the early seventeenth century, as for example when a few were caught reciting a play together in Spanish.[48] Elite

Christians sometimes attended Jewish ceremonies such as marriages and circumcisions; the reverse situation—of Jews attending Christian festivities—was quite rare, however, suggesting that the practice reflected an exercise of religious and class privilege.[49] The coffeehouses that began to proliferate in the second half of the seventeenth century might have become a venue for interfaith sociability, but here too, ethno-religious groups preferred to frequent their own distinct establishments "to play common games, or to talk and spend time," as the governor put it in the mid-eighteenth century.[50] Meaningful intellectual exchange between Jewish and Catholic intellectuals did not take place until the 1730s—when the norms associated with Enlightenment would begin to overdetermine such relations.[51]

Another way to get at this question is to consider where religious boundaries mattered the least. The answer: the dockyards, where sailors and stevedores mingled in a half-drunken stupor; and the Piazza Grande at the center of the city, where merchants struck their business deals; or the barbershops, where Muslim slaves sold their services to Jews and Christians alike.[52] Take John Evelyn's 1644 description of the harbor:

> Here, especially in this piazza, is such a concourse of slaves, Turks, Moors, and other nations, that the number and confusion is prodigious; some buying, others selling, others drinking, others playing, some working, others sleeping, fighting, singing, weeping, all nearly naked, and miserably chained. Here was a tent, where any idle fellow might stake his liberty against a few crowns, at dice, or other hazard: and, if he lost, he was immediately chained and led away to the galleys, where he was to serve a term of years, but from whence they seldom returned; many sottish persons, in a drunken bravado, would try their fortune in this way.[53]

Archival records confirm the promiscuous socializing, at times violent, that occurred at the docks.[54]

Merchants tended to do their socializing in the Piazza Grande, which the German painter Georg Christoph Martini referred to as a kind of stock exchange. "The merchants have their own gathering place at the end of the Via Grande, where the porticos make it possible to stay covered in case of bad weather, and where they discuss their affairs. This is called 'visiting the piazza,' and it's almost like visiting the Bourse."[55] Like Martini, who loved watching the *passeggiata* of "men of various nations," virtually every traveler noted the ethno-religious parade that occurred in the Piazza Grande—Persians, Armenians, Arabs, Levantines, North Africans, and Jews elicited the greatest commentary and often appear in visual materials.[56] It remains to be determined whether merchants in Livorno were more likely to engage in contractual relations with religious others than merchants elsewhere. But conversation and exchange was undoubtedly common.[57]

These considerations suggest that Livorno's experiment with cross-cultural trade was a success by Botero's criteria: our four mechanisms of division successfully promoted commerce between ethno-religious groups while upholding the religious boundaries that kept their communities separate. Such arrangements could probably have gone on indefinitely had not a wave of reforms swept through Italy beginning in the late eighteenth century and continuing through the Napoleonic era. There was no inherent tendency for commercial toleration to spill over into liberal cosmopolitanism in port cities such as Livorno.

Commerce, Toleration, and the Invention of Liberalism

In *The Passions and the Interests*, the economist Albert Hirschman demonstrates how "gentle commerce," *doux commerce*, was a common theme of cultural discourse from the late seventeenth century on. In 1669, in an edict making Marseilles into a free port, Jean-Baptiste Colbert declared that "commerce is the fittest means for conciliating the various nations and keeping the most opposed spirits within a good and mutual correspondence, bringing and spreading abundance by the most innocent of paths."[58] As the word *innocent* suggests, this discourse was critical of aristocratic ideals, with all their capacity for bloodshed—a capacity that enlightened Europeans remembered with horror when thinking upon the wars of religion that sullied the sixteenth and seventeenth centuries. The further civilizing claims made on behalf of commerce are therefore of special interest. A few years later, Jacques Savary linked Colbert's point to a theory of international trade hailing back to late-antique sources (and which for that matter Botero had also endorsed): "[Divine Providence] has not willed for everything that is needed for life to be found in the same spot. It has dispersed its gifts so that men would trade together and so that the mutual need which they have to help one another would establish ties of friendship among them. *This continuous exchange of all the comforts of life constitutes commerce and this commerce makes for all the gentleness of life.*"[59]

The civilizing effects of commerce went on to become one of the clichés of the Enlightenment, propounded most famously by Montesquieu in France and the historian William Robertson in Britain.[60] It remains an important dogma among modern liberal peace theorists too, for whom commerce fosters honesty, prudence, and empathy among individuals engaged in trade; at the level of society it allegedly promotes toleration of others, including religious others.[61] The implications for toleration are clear: people put away their knives to pursue common economic interests, and in doing so other boundaries between ethno-religious groups declined and eventually collapsed.

Alas! Liberal toleration never proceeded alongside commercial toleration in the narrow sense. "Nowhere in Europe . . . can we trace a linear correlation between mercantilist policies of toleration and the legal and social acceptance of Jews."[62] As our case study of Livorno indicates, what was true for Jews was true of other ethno-religious minorities. Italian regimes were aware of the economic benefits of toleration, but they were anxious to prevent the corrosive effects commerce supposedly entailed. State authorities and their delegates policed a number of social, cultural, spatial, and legal boundaries whose existence—far from impeding commerce, as one might expect in light of liberal theory—owed precisely to the effort to promote commercial expansion. Mercantilist toleration represented the will to participate in international trade without undermining the social order. To that extent, the form of toleration that took root in Christian countries was substantially different from that which flourished in (for instance) the Ottoman Empire, where toleration was *part* of the social order.

And yet, Martini's reference to the Piazza Grande as a stock exchange, a *bourse*, helps us follow the thread of toleration beyond Livorno itself. For from the mid-seventeenth century on, the stock exchange became a showcase for religious toleration in action, and by the Enlightenment it was a model to be imitated and extended to the rest of society. Here is what Voltaire said: "Take a view of the Royal Exchange in London, a place more venerable than many courts of justice, where the representatives of all nations meet for the benefit of all mankind. There the Jew, the Mahometan, and the Christian transact together as tho' they all professed the same religion, and give the name of Infidel to none but bankrupts. There the Presbyterian confides in the Anabaptist, and the Churchman depends on the Quaker's word. And all are satisfied."[63] The link between toleration and commercial growth was hardly new; it was already commonplace when Giovanni Botero set pen to paper in the late Renaissance. What does seem new, in the works not only of Voltaire but also of many other writers, is the conviction that such toleration ought to be a model for interconfessional relations in society as a whole, enabling "men [to] live together like citizens of the world, associated by the common ties of humanity," as one put it in 1673.[64]

Indeed, the Piazza Grande in Livorno or the Royal Exchange in London modeled social relations for eighteenth-century thinkers. This observation is one indication that liberal toleration proceeded by extending the structure of commercial exchange to other, hitherto protected realms, to religion and marriage, to society and intellectual life. The rise of "voluntary exchange" as an ideal not just for commerce but for all of society bears the ultimate responsibility for dismantling the religious boundaries of early modern Europe. Adam Smith recommended that religion be treated like any commodity on the free market:

> The interested and active zeal of religious teachers can be dangerous and troublesome only where there is, either but one sect tolerated in the society, or where the whole of a large society is divided into two or three great sects. . . .

> But that zeal must be altogether innocent where the society is divided into two or three hundred, or perhaps into as many thousand small sects, of which no one could be considerable enough to disturb the public tranquility. The teachers of each sect, seeing themselves surrounded on all sides with more adversaries than friends, would be obliged to learn that candour and moderation which is so seldom to be found among the teachers of those great sects ... [this] might in time probably reduce the doctrine of the greater part of them to that pure and rational religion, free from every mixture of absurdity, imposture, and fanaticism, such as wise men have in all ages of the world wished to see established.[65]

For Smith, just as monopoly led to reduced supply and higher prices, so too did the monopoly of a religious establishment intensify intolerance.

The rise of liberal toleration reflected a basic reordering of hitherto separate social realms according to mercantile norms; that is, most of life was subjected to the ethical and legal rationale underlying voluntary exchange. So if liberal peace theorists are correct that liberal norms make for toleration, it is not because commerce makes for empathy and understanding or because the pursuit of wealth spills over into other social arenas. Instead, it appears that toleration was initially formulated in the context of a limited sphere, that of commerce, which was already structured by contractual norms and became even more so during the seventeenth and eighteenth centuries. This model of commercial toleration succeeded so well that some thinkers saw contractualism as a panacea for other social ills, above all that of religious fanaticism.[66] The irony, of course, is that commercial toleration was initially developed within a religious framework that had long sought to regulate the limits of contractual freedom.

"Mediterranean Toleration" and Toleration in the Mediterranean

Structured and coercive toleration was the norm in early modern Italy. Just as free ports were controlled intrusions of the free market into a society otherwise bent on controlling the movement of goods, so too were they places of toleration in states that otherwise enforced religious unity. While Italian regimes could not uphold religious boundaries perfectly, they were successful enough that illicit mixing never threatened their ideological program or the Catholic social order.

Was the Italian situation typical elsewhere in the Mediterranean? It is worth beginning with a comment about method. Enforcing religious boundaries was costly. State power was strongest in the major cities, where efforts at policing boundaries—as well as opportunities for mixing—were most intense. Boundaries were more porous outside of the cities and in frontier regions. This difference between center and periphery is worth emphasizing, since fluidity in the borderlands tells us as much about the limits of state power as it does about the nature of religious identity. Borderlands have little bearing on the problem of coexistence within the same urban environment, however, which is the focus of the comparisons offered here.[67]

Some features of the toleration regime in Livorno were typical throughout Mediterranean cities. The practice of community delegation was a common solution to interfaith management—obvious examples include the autonomy of the Greek Orthodox and Jewish communities in Ottoman cities, not to mention the pockets of consular extraterritoriality enjoyed by certain European Christians, such as French Catholics. These arrangements are sometimes described as the millet system, but that term lends too much coherence to the policy. Delegation made sense given the limits of bureaucratic power in the Ottoman Empire, which exploited identity markers such as religious affiliation to facilitate the exercise of power.[68] Settlement patterns likewise indicate that interconfessional spatialization was common in Mediterranean cities. In Istanbul, for instance, ethno-religious groups tended to cluster around specific neighborhoods, even within the diverse district of Galata—the center of Frankish settlement in the port, but also hosting Jews, Muslims, and Armenians. Relations could be tense; when the Venetian *bailo* attempted to open his house's ceremonial portal, some two thousand Turks protested outside, shouting, "come Muslims to defend the cause of the religion against a *Giaur* [infidel]."[69] The Ottoman dynasty also employed elaborate means for underscoring the empire's Islamic legitimacy, from the construction of mosques and other monuments, to the organization of civic festivals, to the protection of the hajj. Religious boundaries clearly mattered in the Ottoman Empire.[70]

Yet it is inappropriate to extend the free port model to the eastern Mediterranean. While the Ottoman Empire was not economically obtuse—it engaged in economic imperialism in the Mediterranean as well as the Indian Ocean—it did not predicate its treatment of foreigners on a calculus of commercial utility. Rather, the empire's hospitality to religious minorities had roots in long-standing Islamicate practices as well as in the process of Ottoman expansion, which incorporated large numbers of Jews, Catholics, and Orthodox Christians directly into the polity. Even the *'ahdname* (capitulation agreements) conformed, from the Ottoman perspective, more to a political than an economic logic.[71] Accordingly, the mechanism of criminalizing various kinds of relationships or practices was less pervasive in the Ottoman Empire than in Italy. The periodic suppression of the Shi'a and other heterodox groups was generally linked to the Safavid political menace, at least notionally. There was no permanent body for snuffing out heterodox beliefs typical of the Catholic inquisitions. And although sanctions for illicit sex between Christian men and

Muslim women could be severe, including the gruesome exemplary punishments that early modern regimes knew so well how to stage, Ottoman officials were not unusually zealous executors of this law. On the whole, the Ottoman state took a less militant approach to policing religious boundaries than most regimes in confessional Europe.[72]

We should not be misled by common solutions to common problems, then. Although the exigencies of managing interfaith relations throughout the Middle Sea suggested a common repertoire of strategies and tactics, they were embedded in starkly different political and social milieus. If Kymlicka's distinctions have heuristic value in helping to clarify our concept of religious liberty in the modern West, the application of his model to past societies risks obscuring the historical peculiarities of commercial toleration. It also ignores the role that commercial toleration played in creating the modern autonomous individual that Kymlicka himself contrasts with the millet system. To emphasize the peculiarities of commercial toleration means distinguishing not only between the Mediterranean and Europe but also between parts of the Mediterranean such as the Spanish sphere, where toleration arrangements were precarious at best, especially for Jews and Muslims; to north-central Italy, where commercial toleration was common; and to the Ottoman Empire, where toleration was an integral aspect of the imperial order.[73] There was no single Mediterranean model of *convivencia*.

COREY TAZZARA is an Associate Professor of History at Scripps College. His first book, *The Free Port of Livorno and the Transformation of the Mediterranean World*, was published by Oxford University Press in 2017. He is the editor (with Paula Findlen and Jacob Soll) of *Florence after the Medici: Tuscan Enlightenment, 1737–1790* (Routledge, 2019). His next monographic project will deal with the seventeenth-century Roman traveler and orientalist Pietro Della Valle.

Notes

1. I would like to thank Carlos Grenier, Daniel Hershenzon, and the volume editors, Matthias Lehmann and Jessica Marglin, for their helpful comments toward improving this article.

2. Will Kymlicka, "Two Models of Pluralism and Tolerance," *Analyse & Kritik* 13 (1992): 33–56; Benjamin J. Kaplan, *Divided by Faith: Religious Conflict and the Practice of Toleration in Early Modern Europe* (Cambridge, MA: Harvard University Press, 2007), 240–41. Kymlicka's conception of the millet relies principally on Benjamin Braude and Bernard Lewis, eds., *Christians and Jews in the Ottoman Empire: The Functioning of a Plural Society*, 2 vols. (New York: Holmes & Meier, 1982). Kaplan emphasizes that the model is an ideal type and must be cautiously applied to historical material, Ottoman or otherwise.

3. See Eric R. Dursteler, *Venetians in Constantinople: Nation, Identity, and Coexistence in the Early Modern Mediterranean* (Baltimore: Johns Hopkins University Press, 2006), 19, 60, 104–5. For other influential treatments, see Tijana Krstić, *Contested Conversions to Islam: Narratives of Religious Change in the Early Modern Ottoman Empire* (Stanford, CA: Stanford University Press, 2011); and E. Natalie Rothman, *Brokering Empire. Trans-Imperial Subjects between Venice and Istanbul* (Ithaca, NY: Cornell University Press, 2012).

4. Fernand Braudel, *The Mediterranean and the Mediterranean World in the Age of Philip II* (Berkeley: University of California Press, 1995), 759, 802.

5. Quoted by Dursteler, *Venetians in Constantinople*, 19. On the Greeks, see Molly Greene, *Catholic Pirates and Greek Merchants: A Maritime History of the Mediterranean* (Princeton, NJ: Princeton University Press, 2010).

6. Quoted in Lucette Valensi, *The Birth of the Despot: Venice and the Sublime Porte* (Ithaca, NY: Cornell University Press, 1993), 19. Dursteler provides examples of elite socializing in *Venetians in Constantinople*, 174–79.

7. It is worth recalling that social network analysis was designed in part to bypass the problems of reifying social identity. That is why I have made patterns of interaction (sex, marriage, conversion, socializing, and commerce) the main object of analysis in this paper. See Francesca Trivellato, *The Familiarity of Strangers: The Sephardic Diaspora, Livorno, and Cross-Cultural Trade in the Early Modern Period* (New Haven, CT: Yale University Press, 2009), 163.

8. Giovanni Botero, *On the Greatness of Cities*, in *The Reason of State and On the Greatness of Cities*, trans. D.P. Waley/Robert Peterson (New Haven, CT: Yale University Press, 1956 [1606]), 1:10. On Botero, see Romain Descendre, *L'état du monde: Giovanni Botero entre raison d'état et géopolitique* (Geneva: Droz, 2009); and Corey Tazzara, *The Free Port of Livorno and the Transformation of the Mediterranean World* (Oxford: Oxford University Press, 2017), ch. 1.

9. Botero, *On the Greatness of Cities*, II:II; see too ibid., II:I.

10. Botero, *On the Greatness of Cities*, II:III.

11. David Chambers and Brian Pullan, eds., *Venice: A Documentary History 1450–1630* (Toronto: University of Toronto Press, 2001), 338. Among a vast bibliography, see Benjamin Ravid, *Economics and Toleration in Seventeenth Century Venice* (Jerusalem: The American Academy for Jewish Research, 1978); Rothman, *Brokering Trade*, 49–53. For a translated firsthand account with extensive notes, see *The Autobiography of a Seventeenth-Century Venetian Rabbi: Leon Modena's Life of Judah*, ed. Mark R. Cohen (Princeton, NJ: Princeton University Press, 1988).

12. Carlo Antonio Broggia, *Trattato de' tributi, delle monete, e del governo politico della sanità* (Naples: Pietro Palombo, 1743), 104; Antonio Genovesi, *Delle lezioni di commercio o sia d'economia civile* (Naples: I Fratelli Simone, 1765), vol. 1, 319.

13. Tazzara, *The Free Port of Livorno*, ch. 8.

14. Thomas Mun, *England's Treasure by Forraign Trade* (New York: Macmillan, 1895 [1664]), 24–25.

15. Charles de Brosses, *Lettres familières écrites d'Italie en 1739 et 1740* (Brussels: Editions Complexe, 1995), 125. The demographic figures are from Elena Fasano Guarini, "La popolazione," in *Livorno e Pisa: due città e un territorio nella politica dei Medici: Livorno, progetto e storia di una città tra il 1500 e il 1600* (Pisa: Nistri-Lischi and Pacini, 1980), 199–215, at 212; Lucia Frattarelli Fischer and Stefano Villani, "'People of Every Mixture.' Immigration, Tolerance and Religious Conflicts in Early Modern Livorno," in *Immigration and Emigration*

in Historical Perspective, ed. Ann Katherine Isaacs (Pisa: Pisa University Press, 2007), 93–107; and Trivellato, *The Familiarity of Strangers*, 54.

16. Lucia Frattarelli Fischer, *Vivere fuori dal ghetto. Ebrei a Pisa e Livorno (secoli XVI–XVIII)* (Turin: Silvio Zamorani, 2008), 36–43; and Tazzara, *The Free Port of Livorno*, chs. 1 and 2. For the relationship between the Inquisition and the Medici state, see now in addition to Frattarelli Fischer, Brett Auerbach-Lynn, "'Addomesticare' gli inquisitori, costruire la libertà. Lo stato mediceo e il Sant'Uffizio a Pisa e Livorno, 1591–1655," in *La città delle nazioni: Livorno e i limiti del cosmopolitismo (1566–1834)*, ed. Andrea Addobbati and Marcella Aglietti (Pisa: Pisa University Press, 2015), 51–91.

17. Although see the quote by Flavio Guglielmi from ca. 1668, in Frattarelli Fischer, *Vivere fuori dal ghetto*, 226–27.

18. "Vero è che Livorno è un nido di persone di malaffare, senz'anima nella loro conoscenza, senza fede nella parola, senza vergogna nelle attioni." Archivio di Stato di Venezia, Senato Secreta, Dispacci degli Ambasciatori, 61, f. 74, dispatch by Giovanni Ambrogio Sarotti of May 7, 1652, as quoted by Stephanie Nadalo, "Constructing Pluralism in Seventeenth Century Livorno: Managing Religious Minorities in a Mediterranean Free Port (1537–1737)" (PhD diss., Northwestern University, 2013), 26 n. 15.

19. Quoted in Frattarelli Fischer, *Vivere fuori dal ghetto*, 240. The quote is from 1664.

20. See the works of Stefano Villani, especially "'Cum scandalo catholicorum . . .'. La presenza a Livorno di predicatori protestanti inglesi tra il 1644 e il 1670," *Nuovi studi livornesi* VII (1999): 9–58.

21. Quoted by Fischer, *Vivere fuori dal ghetto*, 208.

22. Archivio di Stato di Firenze (ASF), Mediceo del Principato (MP), 1814, ins. 1, f. 14; ASF, Archivio Serristori, 435, unpaginated, dated June 21, 1664, quoted by Frattarelli Fischer, *Vivere fuori dal ghetto*, 240. Although persecution of non-Catholics intensified in the decades before the Interdict of 1606–1607, this form of commercial toleration was also common in Venice. See John Jeffries Martin, *Venice's Hidden Enemies: Italian Heretics in a Renaissance City* (Baltimore: Johns Hopkins University Press, 2004), ch. 7; Rothman, *Brokering Empire*, 44, chs. 3 and 4. For the interdict itself, see Filippo de Vivo, *Information and Communication in Venice: Rethinking Early Modern Politics* (Oxford: Oxford University Press, 2007), ch. 5.

23. Aldo Lucchese, *Stradario storico della città e del Commune di Livorno* (Livorno, Italy: Belforte Grafica, 1973); Frattarelli Fisher, *Vivere fuori dal ghetto*, 185–206; Frattarelli Fisher, "Proprietà e insediamento ebraici a Livorno dalla fine del Cinquecento alla seconda metà del Settecento," *Quaderni Storici* 54, no. 19 (1983): 879–96; Frattarelli Fisher, "Tipologia abitava degli ebrei a Livorno nel Seicento," *Rassegna Mensile di Israel* 50 (1984): 583–605.

24. See the decree from the ASF, Auditore Riformagioni, 32, f. 421, 7/26/1620, quoted by Nadalo, "Negotiating Pluralism," 194.

25. Quoted by Romain Rainero, *Il Congo agli inizi del Settecento nella relazione di p. Luca da Caltanissetta* (Florence: La Nuova Italia, 1972), 117. Local authorities even claimed that they helped impose *shari'a* on Muslim slaves by punishing those who drank alcohol: Franceso Pera, *Curiosità livornesi inedite o rare* (Livorno, Italy: Giusti, 1888), 117–18. Typically, relations between officials and the slaves of the Bagno, when they were not simply repressive, often took a transactional form: slaves paid extensive bribes to officials in exchange for a host of petty favors. See Cesare Santus, "Crimini, violenza e corruzione nel Bagno di Livorno," in *La città delle nazioni: Livorno e i limiti del cosmopolitismo (1566–1834)*, ed. Andrea Addobbati and Marcella Aglietti (Pisa: Pisa University Press, 2015), 93–107.

26. Maximilien Misson, *Nouveau Voyage d'Italie*, vol. III (The Hague: Henry van Builderen, 1698), 268–69. The Dutch cemetery was officially authorized in 1695, from a plot of land bought in 1683. On the English cemetery, see Matteo Giunti and Giacomo Lorenzini, eds., *Un archivio di pietra: l'antico cimitero degli inglesi di Livorno* (Pisa: Pacini, 2013).

27. Guido Bellatti Ceccoli, "Voci dall'oriente: Arabi cristiani e musulmani a Livorno in età moderna," in *Livorno 1606-1806: Luogo di incontro tra popoli e culture*, ed. Adriano Prosperi (Turin: Umberto Allemandi, 2006), 418–29: 422.

28. Cf. Kaplan, *Divided by Faith*, 305.

29. Danilo Matteoni, *Livorno* (Bari, Italy: Laterza, 1985), 29–30, 37; Elena Fasano Guarini and Danilo Matteoni, "L'Ufficio della Fabbrica," in *Livorno e Pisa: due città e un territorio nella politica dei Medici: Livorno, progetto e storia di una città tra il 1500 e il 1600* (Pisa: Nistri-Lischi e Pacini, 1980), 149–51. On the *Quattro Mori*, see Mark Rosen, "Pietro Tacca's Quattro Mori and the Conditions of Slavery in Early Seicento Tuscany," *The Art Bulletin* 97, no. 1 (2015): 34–57.

30. Barbara Donati, *Tra inquisizione e granducato. Storie di inglesi nella Livorno del primo seicento* (Rome: Edizioni di storia e letteratura, 2010), 119–20.

31. ASF, MP, 2163, f. 29, 05/14/1646, Ludovico da Verrazzano to Domenico Pandolfini.

32. Menzone, "L'Arte," in *Livorno 1606-1806: Luogo di incontro tra popoli e culture*, ed. Adriano Prosperi (Turin: Umberto Allemandi, 2006), 461–92, at 461–63. The paradise quote is in Michel Guyot de Merville, *Voyage historique d'Italie* (The Hague: Chez M.G. de Merville, 1729), 555–56.

33. Quoted by Corey Tazzara, "Managing Free Trade in Early Modern Europe: Institutions, Information, and the Free Port of Livorno," *The Journal of Modern History* 86, no. 3 (2014): 493–529, at 495.

34. See Lucia Frattarelli Fischer, "Il bagno delle galere in 'terra cristiana,'" *Nuovi Studi Livornesi*, 8 (2000): 69–94.

35. See, for example, the *premessa* in Andrea Addobbati and Marcella Aglietti, eds., *La città delle nazioni*, 20.

36. See Krstić, *Contested Conversions*, 148ff.

37. Lucia Frattarelli Fischer, "Alle radici di una identità composita. La 'nazione' greca a Livorno," in *Le iconostasi di Livorno, patrimonio post-Bizantino* (Pisa: Pacini, 2001), 49–61, at 55.

38. See Rothman, *Brokering Empire*, 14 and 18; and more generally, chs. 2 and 5.

39. Notwithstanding the rumors about which the Pisan inquisitor complained in 1622: Frattarelli Fischer, *Vivere fuori dal ghetto*, 208.

40. For example, Archivio di Stato di Livorno (ASL), Capitano poi Governatore poi Auditore (CGA), 2602, vol. 2, f. 302.

41. Frattarelli Fischer, *Vivere fuori dal ghetto*, 242. On the other hand, the eminent Jewish prostitute Perla appears to have had no Christian johns.

42. Calogero Piazza, *Schiavitù e guerra dei barbareschi. Orientamenti toscani di politica transmarina (1747-1768)* (Milan: Giuffré, 1983), 95–96.

43. Stefano Villani, "Dalla Gran Bretagna all'Italia: narrazioni di conversione nel Sant'Uffizio di Pisa e Livorno," in *La città delle nazioni: Livorno e i limiti del cosmopolitismo (1566-1834)*, ed. Andrea Addobbati and Marcella Aglietti (Pisa: Pisa University Press, 2015), 109–26, at 101–2. Villani also notes that about ten (total, not by percentage) were Greek and Armenian Orthodox, and about fifteen were Jewish *conversos*.

44. Quoted by Barbara Donati, *Tra inquisizione e granducato*, 175. Filippo Ganucci, the first bishop of Livorno, also spoke in 1806 of bringing the peoples of the city from darkness into light.

45. Stefano Villani, "Donne inglesi a Livorno nella prima età moderna," in *Sul filo della scrittura. Fonti e temi per la storia delle donne a Livorno*, ed. Lucia Frattarelli Fischer and Olimpia Vaccari (Pisa: Pisa University Press, 2005), 377–99.

46. Similar social stakes also shaped conversion experiences among women in the Venetian-Ottoman sphere: Eric R Dursteler, *Renegade Women: Gender, Identity, and Boundaries in the Early Modern Mediterranean* (Baltimore: Johns Hopkins University Press, 2011), 114–15; Rothman, *Brokering Empire*, 88–89, 102–5.

47. On Thornton, see Tazzara, *The Free Port of Livorno*, ch. 2. For Jewish converts serving as Catholic priests, see Frattarelli Fischer, *Vivere fuori dal ghetto*.

48. Frattarelli Fischer, *Vivere fuori dal ghetto*, 212.

49. Ibid., 236–38.

50. Quoted by Francesca Bregoli, *Mediterranean Enlightenment: Livornese Jews, Tuscan Culture, and Eighteenth-Century Reform* (Stanford, CA: Stanford University Press, 2014), 166.

51. See Bregoli, *Mediterranean Enlightenment*, chs. 3–5.

52. On the figure of the Muslim barber as well as on the other economic activities of the slave population, see Guillaume Calafat and Cesare Santus, "Les avatars du 'Turc.' Esclaves et commerçants musulmans à Livourne (1600–1750)," in *Les Musulmans en Europe occidentale au Moyen Âge et à l'époque moderne: une intégration invisible*, ed. Jocelyne Dakhlia and Bernard Vincent (Paris: Albin Michel, 2011), 471–522, at 486–92.

53. John Evelyn, *Diary and Correspondence* (London: Henry Colburn, 1850), 1:90–91.

54. See, for instance, ASF, MP, 2140, ff. 13–14, letter by Ugolino Barisori. The situation in Livorno is similar to Rothman's portrait of the Venetian marketplace in *Brokering Trade*, 69–77.

55. Italian translation available as Georg Christoph Martini, *Viaggio in Toscana (1725–1745)*, ed. Oscar Trumpy (Modena, Italy: Aedes Muratoriana, 1969), 59.

56. See Carlo Mangio, "Testimonianze di viaggiatori francesi su Livorno fra Seicento e Settecento," in *Livorno e il Mediterraneo nell'età medicea* (Livorno, Italy: Bastogi, 1978), 306–17; Mario Currelli, "Scrittori inglesi a Livorno nel Seicento," *Nuovi Studi Livornesi* 11 (2004): 53–82.

57. See Trivellato, *The Familiarity of Strangers*, 142–43, 328–39; and Francesca Trivellato, "Credito e tolleranza: i limiti del cosmopolitismo nella Livorno di età moderna," in *La città delle nazioni: Livorno e i limiti del cosmopolitismo (1566–1834)*, ed. Andrea Addobbati and Marcella Aglietti (Pisa: Pisa University Press, 2015), 39–50.

58. Quoted by Louis Dermigny, "Escales, échelles et ports francs au moyen âge et aux temps moderns," in *Les grandes escales* (Brussels: Recueil de la Société Jean Bodin, 1974), 213–644, at 553.

59. Savary, *Le parfait négociant* (Paris: Jean Guignard fils, 1675/1713 ed.), 1, my italics. See on the theme of divine providence, Jacob Viner, *The Role of Providence in the Social Order: An Essay in Intellectual History* (Princeton, NJ: Princeton University Press, 2015).

60. Albert O Hirschman, *The Passions and the Interests: Political Arguments for Capitalism before Its Triumph* (Princeton, NJ: Princeton University Press, 1977), 56–61. The theme of *doux commerce* was sharply contested by other Enlightenment political economists, however. See Istvan Hont, *Jealousy of Trade: International Competition and the Nation State in Historical Perspective* (Cambridge, CT: Harvard University Press, 2005); Sophus A. Reinert, *Translating Empire. Emulation and the Origins of Political Economy* (Cambridge, CT: Harvard University Press, 2011).

61. Steven Pinker, *The Better Angels of Our Nature: Why Violence Has Declined* (New York: Penguin, 2011), 31–36, 75–78.

62. Trivellato, *The Familiarity of Strangers*, 99–100.

63. Voltaire, *Letters Concerning the English Nation* (London: George Faulkner, 1733), 44, quoted by Ole Peter Grell and Roy Porter, eds., *Toleration in Enlightenment Europe* (Cambridge: Cambridge University Press, 2000), 4.

64. Sir William Temple as quoted by ibid, 20 n. 12. See also the slightly earlier comment on the Amsterdam bourse by the Dutch poet Jérémias de Decker: "[The Amsterdam Bourse is] a hall that at midday teems with people of various kind, a public garden where Moors trade with Norwegians; a temple where Jews, Turks, and Christians stand next to the other, where all languages are taught a fair rich in every product; a bourse which spurs on all the others of the universe." Quoted by Donatella Calabi, *The Market and the City: Square, Street, and Architecture in Early Modern Europe* (Burlington, VT: Ashgate, 2004), 183.

65. Adam Smith, *An Inquiry into the Nature and Causes of the Wealth of Nations* (London: W. Strahan, 1776), book 5, ch. 1, pt. 3, art. 3.

66. My view of toleration is compatible with the accounts of modernity provided by Marx and Polanyi, each of whom emphasized in different ways how contractualism eroded older ways of regulating exchange—exchange of labor, obviously, but of social reciprocity writ large.

67. See Rothman, *Brokering Empire*, 10–11; Krstić, *Contested Conversions*, 145ff. Dursteler's remarks in *Renegade Women*, 108–9 are salutary but sit ill at ease with his prior work.

68. See Daniel Goffman, "Ottoman Millets in the Early Seventeenth Century," *New Perspectives on Turkey* 11 (1994): 135–58; Maurits H. van den Boogert, *The Capitulations and the Ottoman Legal System: Qadis, Consuls, and Beratlıs in the 18th Century* (Leiden: Brill, 2005); Karen Barkey, *Empire of Difference: The Ottomans in Comparative Perspective* (Cambridge: Cambridge University Press, 2008). The Ottoman Empire had a well-organized network for managing diplomatic information, but as in Europe, such techniques were less adept at managing capillary affairs. See Gabor Agoston, "Information, Ideology, and the Limits of Imperial Policy: Ottoman Grand Strategy in the Context of Ottoman-Habsburg Rivalry," in *The Early Modern Ottomans. Remapping the Empire*, eds. Virginia H. Aksan and Daniel Goffman (Cambridge: Cambridge University Press, 2007), 75–103; and Tazzara, "Managing Free Trade."

69. Dursteler, *Venetians in Constantinople*, 155–58: quote on p. 158. For spatial segregation in Aleppo and Izmir, see Edhem Eldem, Daniel Goffman, and Bruce Alan Masters, *The Ottoman City between East and West: Aleppo, Izmir, and Istanbul* (Cambridge: Cambridge University Press, 1999), 39–40, 102–4. Occupational specialization also occurred along religious lines. See Suraiya Faroqhi, *Artisans of Empire: Crafts and Craftspeople under the Ottomans* (London: Tauris, 2009), 54, 61, 161, 177–78; cf. 92, 124.

70. See Leslie P. Pierce, *The Imperial Harem: Women and Sovereignty in the Ottoman Empire* (Oxford: Oxford University Press, 1993), 198–212; Suraiya Faroqhi, *Pilgrims and Sultans: The Hajj under the Ottomans, 1517–1683* (London: Tauris, 1994), chs. 5 and 6; Colin Imber, *Ebu's-Su'ud: The Islamic Legal Tradition* (Stanford, CA: Stanford University Press, 1997), passim; Gülru Necipoğlu, *The Age of Sinan: Architectural Culture in the Ottoman Empire* (London: Reaktion, 2005), passim. Mehmed I and Süleyman experimented with non-Islamicate forms of legitimacy: see Gülru Necipoğlu, "Süleyman the Magnificent and the Representation of Power in the Context of Ottoman-Hapsburg-Papal Rivalry," *The Art Bulletin* 71, no. 3 (1989): 401–27.

71. See Daniel Goffman, "Negotiating with the Renaissance State: The Ottoman Empire and the New Diplomacy," in *The Early Modern Ottomans*, 61–74. For the state's promotion of long-distance commerce, see Cemal Kafadar, "A Death in Venice (1575): Anatolian Muslim

Merchants Trading in the Serenissima," *Journal of Turkish Studies* 10 (1986): 191–218; Palmira Brummett, *Ottoman Seapower and Levantine Diplomacy in the Age of Discovery* (Albany, NY: SUNY Press, 1994); Kate Fleet, *European and Islamic Trade in the Early Ottoman State: The Merchants of Genoa and Turkey* (Cambridge: Cambridge University Press, 1999); Giancarlo Casale, *The Ottoman Age of Exploration* (Oxford: Oxford University Press, 2010).

72. See Colin Imber, "The Persecution of the Ottoman Shi'ites according to the Muhimme Defterleri, 1565–1585," *Islam* 56 (1979): 245–73; Dursteler, *Christians in Constantinople*, 95–98. This seems true even in light of the application of the confessionalization model to the Ottoman Empire in Krstić, *Contesting Conversions*, esp. 14–16 et passim.

73. On the effort to restrict access to the Spanish imperial sphere to Catholics, and especially the Genoese, see Céline Dauverd, *Imperial Ambition in the Early Modern Mediterranean. Genoese Merchants and the Spanish Crown* (Cambridge: Cambridge University Press, 2015), passim, esp. 2–3, 65–80, 252–61.

6

A FATHER'S CONSOLATION

Intracultural Ties and Religion in a Trans-Mediterranean Jewish Commercial Network

Francesca Bregoli

SCHOLARS HAVE ARGUED THAT FACE-TO-FACE INTERPERSONAL RELATIONSHIP AND the "family matrix" were crucial for the operations of early modern commerce, particularly when it came to access to credit.[1] The family played an especially significant role for Mediterranean Jewish trade since Jewish merchants in that area continued structuring their business in family firms even in the late eighteenth century, when joint-stock companies had become commonplace in northern Europe.[2] Hence, the continued maintenance of a sense of creditworthiness and honor in family members involved in the same commercial network were key elements to ensure trust and enable the operations of premodern trade.[3] Yet, geographical distance naturally disrupted and challenged bonds of trust among separated kin in the absence of face-to-face supervision.

This chapter asks how Mediterranean Jews engaged in long-distance trade dealt with family members who could not be directly monitored since they were stationed in faraway countries. In particular, I focus on the rearing of young merchants and the theme of their reputation. In the highly uncertain world of early modern long-distance trade, reputation was vital currency.[4] In order to make decisions about how to conduct their affairs, merchants relied on information about the past conduct and honesty of agents or fellow merchants, which circulated via hearsay and through written correspondence.[5] The flow of information within a merchant's network allowed him to assess the risks of entering into commercial deals with a potential business associate and to form expectations about his future conduct—in other words, whether he could be trusted—and to develop strategies to contain or minimize such risks.[6] Scholars disagree whether trustworthy mercantile behavior was determined by purely economic factors in a world of self-interested individuals, a position privileged by some economists,[7] or rather was shaped by ethical, social, and communal pressures, as historians emphasize.[8] Still, reputation and creditworthiness were essential to build and maintain commercial networks based on trust; early modern traders viewed them as synonymous with their ability to conduct business and with their life itself.[9]

For early modern Jewish merchants, as an ethnic and religious minority, issues surrounding reputation—above all, perceptions of creditworthiness, honor, and honesty—were especially urgent. Jewish firms were subject to higher levels of mistrust than non-Jewish ones,[10] and Jewish traders could be the objects of Judeophobic or philo-Semitic fantasies depicting them as fraudsters or as masterful merchants, respectively.[11] We know that western Sephardic merchants in Europe were deeply concerned about their *collective* reputation in the surrounding society and at times employed communitarian sanctions to avoid economic disorders.[12] But how did *individual* Jewish merchants go about handling their family's—and hence their business's—reputation in their daily dealings?

Through analysis of the correspondence of Tunis-based, Italian Jewish merchant Joseph Franchetti (1721 or 1734–ca. 1794), I aim to clarify some of the ways in which Jewish merchants in the Mediterranean approached the themes of reputation and honor discursively and pragmatically.[13] Many young Jews who engaged in long-distance Mediterranean trade left home for distant markets not long after their bar mitzvah and grew up, both as men and merchants, far away from their households of origin and the supervision of their fathers. For this reason, the management of a young man's good name could be a tricky business. What sort of educational programs, safety networks, and disciplining structures were in place to control young merchants once they had left home?

The answers to this question help nuance some assumptions that have long characterized scholarship on Mediterranean Jewish trade. Late eighteenth- and nineteenth-century Mediterranean traders belonging to ethno-religious minorities have often been portrayed as quintessentially cosmopolitan.[14] Still, as we will see, this alleged "cosmopolitanism" seems to have gone hand in hand with a strategic reliance on intra-Jewish ties and did not exclude deep mistrust of life in strange lands and fear of too close contacts with non-Jews, especially Christians.

More broadly, much historiography on the medieval and early modern Mediterranean has focused on cross-cultural trade as a way to get at questions of boundary crossing and interreligious exchange, highlighting the degree of interaction among different groups in this area, in spite of ethnic and religious differences. As Adnan Husain has remarked, Mediterranean trade can be presented "as an integrating force for the peoples of different religions and cultures ... creat[ing] secular relations among diverse peoples despite conflicting identities."[15] There are sound reasons for this scholarly emphasis on interreligious connections and cross-cultural ties. Jewish commercial networks were never limited to Jewish merchants; indeed, Jews traded with non-Jewish partners, at times relied on non-Jewish agents, and non-Jewish authorities were frequently involved as well.[16] But we should not forget that, alongside interreligious and cross-cultural connections—and even as late as the last quarter of the eighteenth century, as the world of merchants was becoming more secular—familial and extrafamilial Jewish bonds of allegiance, together with reminders about Judaism, retained a critical place, not only (unsurprisingly) as practical avenues to secure business but, more importantly for our discussion, also in the self-representation and reputation-managing practices of Mediterranean Jewish traders.

Franchetti's Correspondence

Joseph Franchetti, a successful merchant of Mantuan background,[17] was a head partner in the Salomone Enriches & Joseph Franchetti Company, with branches in Tunis, Livorno, and Smyrna.[18] The primary nodes of Joseph Franchetti's network were entirely Mediterranean; as far as it is possible to reconstruct, his business relations and affairs focused around the Middle Sea and did not reach into northern Europe and the Atlantic, nor did they go beyond the Ottoman Empire.[19] In the 1770s and 1780s, the core of Franchetti's business was the sale of Tunisian *chechias*.[20] These hats, made in Tunis with European wool acquired from Livorno, were sought after in the Ottoman Empire, with Smyrna serving as a key distribution center.[21] The tricoastal arrangement of the Enriches and Franchetti Company placed these entrepreneurs at the forefront of the *chechia* trade in the last quarter of the century.[22] But like other Jewish merchants, Franchetti did not specialize in one good only.[23] He also traded in Spanish grain and other foodstuff, weapons, and occasionally Jewish ritual objects, working with influential Livornese merchants, such as Paltiel Semach and David de Montel.[24]

Between 1776 and 1790, Franchetti wrote about four hundred letters in Italian to a number of business associates, copies of which are preserved in two folio-size letter books. Replies to Franchetti's letters have not survived. Despite the source's relatively limited scope, if we consider letters as constructs that adhere to shared cultural conventions and can thus reveal broader values and codes of communication,[25] it is possible to derive some preliminary, cautious generalizations about Jewish mercantile culture in the Mediterranean area from this material. Only future research and the discovery of comparable Jewish archives will allow us to assess more fully this correspondence's representativeness.

Among the recipients were two of Franchetti's sons, Reuben (b. 1757) and Isache (b. 1763), and his young brother-in-law, Beniamin Baruch.[26] As with many Jewish family firms, members of the immediate household were posted abroad to secure the company's commercial position in distant markets. Joseph's eldest child, Abram (b. 1754), remained in Tunis, but his three younger sons, Reuben, Jeudà (b. 1760), and Isache, were sent to learn the trade not long after reaching the age of majority.[27] Given the impossibility of bridging the geographical distance that kept them apart—Reuben and Beniamin were already stationed in Smyrna by 1776,[28] Jeudà joined them in 1778 and was later sent to Livorno, while Isache moved to Livorno in 1778[29]—letters allowed Franchetti to maintain ongoing contact with them in the hope of shaping their growth as men and traders.[30]

Although the seventy-nine letters (approximately 20% of the total) addressed to Reuben, Isache, and Beniamin contained primarily discussion of commercial matters (no letters were sent to Jeudà alone, who would have read letters addressed to his brothers during his stays in Smyrna and Livorno), Franchetti wove in lengthy personal asides, expressed in emotional tones and interspersed with simple Hebrew expressions, which included above all practical and ethical advice, blandishments, reprimands, as well as reminders of parental love and the importance of Judaism. Occasionally, correspondence to business partners and close associates also included information or requests for information about his sons, as well as appeals to supervise them, equally coached in sentimental language. These letters illuminate both the moral codes that Franchetti tried to inculcate in young Jews living and trading far away from home and specific strategies to protect his own and his sons' reputation. The next two sections will look at letters Franchetti sent to correspondents *about* his sons, out of concern for their reputation, and letters that he sent directly *to* the young men, giving advice to preserve it.

Networks of "Familial Supervision": Rumors, Reports, Monitoring

The crucial role of correspondence in enabling premodern business, by spreading news about the quality of merchants as well as about the market or political events that could affect it, cannot be overstated. Correspondence could make or break the budding career of young traders, by gathering and circulating information about their behavior. Letters were also used to summon help from older family members and other business associates in monitoring them. As we will see, Franchetti's correspondence suggests that the commercial network within which he operated was envisioned as an extended family of like-minded Jewish traders, whether connected by blood ties or not, imbued in a culture not only of dutiful mercantile reciprocity but also of familial sentimentality. This fact nuances purely economic understandings of trust-building and reputation-managing mechanisms within merchants' networks.[31]

Just as sons inherited their father's name and network after he retired, so a father's name was tied to that of his sons when the young men started out; established businessmen needed to pay close attention to their heirs' standing, since a son's reputation affected that of the entire family and its business. Rumors and hearsay played a key role in bolstering or damaging it: "I have certainly the greatest pleasure when I hear people sing your praises, and please continue behaving like you do, so that everybody may sing your praises," a satisfied Franchetti wrote Reuben in 1777.[32] Rumors and reports came from Jewish and non-Jewish sources; on a different occasion, in praising his son Reuben's wise conduct, Franchetti noted that "all Jews (*jeudim*), Christians (*harelim* [sic]) and Muslims (*turchi*) love you as the precious gem you are."

Problematic reports about Franchetti's sons' behavior were fairly common, however, causing tremendous anxiety and concerned retorts.[33] They could amount to information gathered from unnamed Jewish passengers returning from a trip,[34] although more frequently trusted Christian ship captains or traveling Jewish associates supplied oral reports once they returned to Tunis from Livorno or Smyrna.[35] These informal exchanges put in motion direct requests for information. A more precise level of detail was achieved by asking for written intelligence from business partners or associates who spent time with the young men; in these cases, Franchetti only relied on Jewish informants.[36]

In exceptional cases, written reports could be obtained from people outside of the commercial network, by relying on Jewish friends of friends. In 1782, Franchetti received disheartening news that troubled him greatly; they concerned Isache's extravagance and penchant for attending comedies and his brother Jeudà's complicity. In relaying the dismal report to Reuben, Franchetti described the letter's messenger, the local Jewish Caid Jeusuah Coen Tanugi, as "crying like a baby, telling [him] that he would have never thought he would hear this about your ... brothers, whom he loves like his own sons." To find out the truth, Franchetti reached out to his Mantuan cousin Ihiel (Yehiel) Franchetti, a correspondent of the "noble Franco house of Livorno."[37] Representatives from the Franco house had their "ministers, persons of excellent religion [and] honesty, research the behaviors of the two Franchetti youth who reside [in Livorno]." They put together a report for Ihiel, stating that there indeed was "something true" about what had been conveyed to their father ("truly, in a certain way, they let themselves be conducted to entertainments that are not so laudable.... I was assured that the elder is rather generous in spending"), although not everything was, and "to give them the praise that they deserve, they are both attentive during the hours of business." Their father in Tunis, the letter concluded, should "affect them with his paternal fear to avoid any disorder," while the Franco "ministers" would endeavor to keep an eye on them.[38]

Even within a close-knit group of associates, the flow of information could, however, be disrupted, with wider repercussions for the commercial network. Writing Abram Coen de Lara, a partner in the company who had been sent to Smyrna in the spring of 1777, Franchetti complained bitterly about the lack of news about his son: "I told you so many times before your departure to give me precise and sincere information on the conduct and ability of my son Reuben," he wrote. Instead, Coen de Lara had "not behaved towards [him] like a friend" and briefly reported that the boy had more good than bad in him. "It's useless for me to know that he has more good than bad," Franchetti continued, "but I want to know his qualities one by one, and his conduct." Coen de Lara's failure to report extensively about Reuben's character was all the more unexpected considering that the associate was "a Father, and of a single child, may God preserve you and grant you others." He should have understood that "these are not the terms to offer a Father consolation about his Son." "I am very surprised that a friend would treat me like this," Franchetti reprimanded him.[39]

Early modern commercial networks expected solidarity from their members, to safeguard bonds of reciprocity and obligation. This applied to the concepts of reputation and honor as well. These notions' ramifications extended beyond a merchant's immediate family to his circle of "friends"—namely, the partners and associates who conducted business with him. A merchant's reputation implicated the people in his network. For this reason there was, at least in theory, a vested interest on the part of commercial "friends"—who could be affinal family members and extrafamilial business associates—to manage, protect, and support a fellow trader's and his family's reputation.[40] Written reports about young men living away from home, included in business correspondence, seem to have been an aspect of the ties of "friendship" that connected long-distance merchants. Coen de Lara's apparent failure to adhere to this code of conduct not only deprived Franchetti of vital information about Reuben's behavior, but disobeying a head partner's request could also undermine Coen de Lara's position in the network. Coen de Lara's next task was a trip to Livorno to procure grain and Spanish wool. There, Franchetti reminded him, he was expected "not to hesitate a moment to second [our] common concerns—all the more so as you are aware of our intentions to increase business with your lovable person."[41]

For similar reasons, male Jewish members of the commercial network were summoned to act as supervisors for young men learning the trade and had self-interested reasons to serve as such. When it was possible, an older brother might serve as a mentor. Calling on Reuben in 1778, when Jeudà arrived in Smyrna where he was set to apprentice, Franchetti urged the more experienced son to use care, attention, and discipline to "make a good man of trade" out of his younger brother.[42] In other cases, an older affinal kin could help monitor a young man's behavior; when his son Reuben was sent to Smyrna, he was entrusted to the care of his uncle, Beniamin Baruch, who was requested to behave like a father with the boy.[43] In the absence of a direct family member, the circles of control widened to extrafamilial associates and even to "friends" who were not partners in the firm. Nonetheless, bonds of familiarity were still stressed and constructed through rhetoric; appeals were often couched in emotional language that tugged at the heartstrings, entreating fellow merchants to heed a disconsolate father's plea, on the one hand, and enjoining them to behave like *real* family members, on the other.

This process is exemplified by a web of letters that Franchetti wrote his associates after his youngest son, Isache, moved to Livorno at fifteen, in 1778. Once again, the company tasked Abram Coen de Lara with following the boy up close, living and working with him in the Tuscan port. Franchetti turned to him first, recommending Isache's well-being in an emotionally loaded letter, and enjoining Coen de Lara to be like a father for the boy: "My dear sworn brother . . . he ought to respect you as if you were me, not less and not more, it is in your right to beat him or kiss him like your own son, and raise him to be God-fearing like your own son."[44] Soon after, he wrote letters to all of his regular Jewish associates in the port, such as David de Montel, Samuel and Moise Leon, and Paltiel Semach, begging them repeatedly to watch over him, fearing for his safety and his morals in the Tuscan hub.[45]

In January 1779, Franchetti wrote again to his regular Livornese correspondents, Samuel and Moise Leon. The brothers had related a rumor about Coen de Lara's decision to return to Tunis, which would leave Isache without immediate supervision. "I cannot express the agitation, which the point in your letter about my son Isache who lives there has caused me, that I can assure you it's caused me enough agitation," he wrote. Franchetti had "constantly encouraged Coen de Lara to never let [his son] take a single step without him being at [his son's] side" and had instructed him to bring Isache back should he decide to leave, as he "absolutely [did] not want to leave [his son] to be free in such a dangerous land."

And if Coen de Lara decided to leave without Isache, he begged the Leon brothers to "welcome him":

> But in whatever shape it may happen, I beg you for God's sake not to withdraw from my aforementioned son your affectionate vigilance concerning his behaviors, in order to break off any road [leading] to bad practice. *In doing so you will console an afflicted father, that can only find repose in you Sirs for his own quiet,* and then I will be even more certain of your great propensity towards me, and so *I plead with you from the bottom of my heart, and above all take it upon your hearts,* if you want to truly favor me, *to prevent suspicious practices and [those] of people of inferior standing, which then lead to the precipice.* I am very much in your debt because of the kind precautionary notice that you give me about the matter, *but you have wounded my heart so much that I cannot be consoled,* if you think it opportune to summon Sig. Coen and have a conversation with him about this important matter of mine please do what you think is necessary, *while I place in you all my trust for the good education and salvation of my dear son.*[46]

When a boy was sent to a port where he did not come under direct familial supervision, in the absence of his blood relatives other trusted adult men from the Jewish mercantile network in which the young man's father was embedded socialized and supervised him.[47] This system shows some similarity with other forms of apprenticeship. Just as lower-class Jewish boys and girls who were sent to work as domestic servants came under the care of the master and lady of the house,[48] so young men who moved away from home to become clerks and agents were placed in the care of older business associates who worked and lived with them.[49] In the case of the Mediterranean Jewish merchants represented by Franchetti, the systems of control extended to members of a broader network of Jewish commercial relations who kept an eye on the boys even without living or working with them, compelled by the ties of solidarity and reciprocity that connected them with other members of the network.

A network of male Jewish "friends" and associates was called on to educate and protect boys and young men, imparting to them directly those values of professional self-control and mercantile honesty that faraway fathers could only impress on their children by correspondence. Established business partners were recruited alongside less close associates—often with moving calls for help stressing familial intimacy—to monitor young family members stationed far away and to report back on the qualities and behaviors of these children, creating a network of reputation control and information parallel to the commercial network itself.[50] The associates were explicitly requested to serve as surrogate brothers[51] and fathers;[52] for their part, the young men were requested to treat these people as "true" fathers and brothers.[53]

To conclude this overview, it is possible to suggest that webs of quasi-paternal and quasi-fraternal relations forged within a family-like community of Jewish merchants helped manage and bolster a young merchant's budding reputation. The prominence of intra-Jewish ties, along with the marked conceptualization of business relations as (Jewish) family relations, show that within Franchetti's network trust was not built on purely economic self-interest. Rather, it depended on social ties conceptualized as familial bonds and articulated with the sentimental language of the late-eighteenth-century household.

Good Judaism and Good Reputation

Aside from circulating information about the conduct and behaviors of traders, letters were also one of the key avenues for early modern families to teach shared values across space, reinforcing rights and stressing obligations—a tool to both monitor and offer advice, admonishing distant relatives about which ideals and habits made one a good man and a successful merchant. Merchants' personal letters helped fathers inculcate values of credit and honesty in their sons, cousins, nephews, and other young men who regarded them as figures of authority.[54] In Franchetti's letters, one of the recurring themes is the necessity for young traders to preserve a commitment to Jewish learning, piety, and observance.[55] This played out in Franchetti's correspondence on various levels.

A stress on religious piety as a marker of an honorable merchant accompanied Franchetti's admonishments and moral advice to his sons. For instance, bemoaning the firm's feared ruin in 1782 because of Isache's excessive expenses in Livorno, Joseph urged him simultaneously to be "a good son and a true Jew" by following his father's orders: "I will not have any problems in dragging you before a court, therefore behave like a good son and a true Jew (*vero jeudi*), and then I will say that you value honor and Judaism (*Jeudut*) more than any other interest and you will be like my innards ... and I will shed my blood for you."[56] To be a good Jew was synonymous with being trustworthy,[57] hence accusations of irreligion had larger implications well beyond the individual sphere: "I always pray God that, if my sons are not good Jews, God take them from the world," Franchetti intimated.[58] Religion, honor, and honesty were synonymous in his language.[59]

Franchetti's emphasis on Judaism could be explained by turning to the tradition of the early modern *ars mercatoria*, in which love and fear of God were viewed as crucial elements in the education of an apprentice trader; they were simultaneously keys to his success and safeguards for orderly affairs. Jacques Savary's *Le Parfait Négociant* (1675), a popular and much-reprinted classic of the genre, urged young men to pay the utmost attention to their Christian duties, recommending that apprentices hear Mass every day on top of attending Mass in their parishes every Sunday with their masters.[60] A lack of religious piety and observance led instead to "disorders" in commerce.[61] Such recommendations were common in other European merchant guides,[62] a genre with which Jewish merchants were familiar.[63]

At the same time, the eighteenth century has been traditionally described as a time in which attitudes to trade allegedly became more secular and cosmopolitan, and the European "commercial society" grew more tolerant and open, particularly as the century progressed.[64] Jewish merchants themselves, at least in certain areas, ostensibly became more secular and laxer in their religious observance. Granted, central-eastern European Ashkenazi merchants appear to have retained an observant and modest lifestyle,[65] but research on Sephardic traders in southern and northern Europe has stressed their degree of acculturation and aristocratic aspirations or episodes of Jewish transgression in which they participated, besides their successful engagement in cross-cultural trade.[66]

In fact, it is possible that the lack of observance on the part of Jewish merchants involved in Mediterranean trade—who were not only Sephardic but also Italian, North African, and Ottoman—may have been exaggerated.[67] Franchetti's origin and background as an Italian Jew living in Tunisia may have rendered him more traditionally inclined and set him apart from Sephardic coreligionists who were reputed to have a laxer approach to Judaism. But his overlapping fatherly and commercial concerns must have played a part too. It is worth noting that even the Prager brothers, observant but enlightened and highly acculturated Ashkenazi traders in Amsterdam and London who had little patience for rabbinic culture, were deeply preoccupied with maintaining an upstanding religious reputation; as late as the 1770s and 1780s, they regarded Jewish adherence pragmatically, as assurance of mercantile probity, an avenue for securing profitable marriage alliances, and a guarantee of sound business reputation.[68]

To his children, Franchetti prescribed regular synagogue attendance for the three Jewish daily prayers as well as daily study of biblical, rabbinic, and zoharic texts. In keeping with Savary's advice, in his view Jewish observance not only protected the virtue of his sons but also guaranteed sound business—not just for them but also for their relatives: "David tells us that you have absolutely no religion," he anxiously wrote Reuben in 1777, "and it's rare that you say *tefillah* [*shacharit*], *minchah*, *arvit*, and you do not go to the holy synagogue even on Shabbat, and if this were true . . . I gave your uncle orders that *if you don't go to the synagogue every day* [to pray] *tefillah* with a *minyan* as . . . all Jews [there] do, first he ought to beat you up and then he ought to tie you up and send you back here, because if a *talmid* of rabbi Shlomo [sic] Alfasi [like you] does this, *it is certain that you will never make any gains, neither you nor your parents and brothers*." Reuben's brothers, on the other hand, went "to the holy synagogue with a *minyan* every day, then every evening they study (*meldano*) in [his] house the Torah portion, the Prophets, and the Zohar, and at noon an hour of Talmud."[69]

Franchetti's stress on his sons' continued study and observance was intertwined with a deep concern about their *public* religious reputation, which, as in the case of other facets of a son's standing, reflected on that of his father and by extension the family business. He insisted on their display of observance in appropriate public forums such as the synagogue; active observance and piety connected the individual merchant with the larger communal sphere, where reputations were enhanced or disgraced. The synagogue was after all the place where communal norms of behaviors were reinforced. Writing Coen de Lara before his son Isache's arrival in Livorno, he requested that he let the boy pray only in the main synagogue of Livorno, "like he is used to doing here."[70] The implication seems to have been to avoid smaller, private *minyanim*, which might allow Isache to avoid communal monitoring.

Franchetti's consideration of the utility of Jewish observance for commercial success may thus have been more widespread among Mediterranean merchants than previously believed. Although many young men ostensibly abandoned their religious education once they reached the age of Jewish majority in order to pursue commerce,[71] the letters' rhetoric shows that Jewish observance and continued study could be presented not only as a path toward virtue and spiritual salvation but also as a gate to economic profit and material security. Even in the late eighteenth century, as commercial society was ostensibly secularizing, intra-Jewish networks still played a crucial role in making reputations and securing deals; to foster trust, it must have been essential for merchants participating in these networks to preserve a respectable standing as pious and observant Jews.

Occasional reports concerning Franchetti's sons' religious laxity were therefore a cause of anxiety. The danger of his sons' spiritual perdition and accompanying material ruin loomed large among Franchetti's overlapping fatherly and mercantile concerns. The allures of acculturation and the risks of estrangement in a foreign land—particularly the mingling with Christians and the pursuit of secular pleasures—led to suspicions and misunderstandings that could taint a young merchant's reputation. From Smyrna, Franchetti received word in 1783 that Reuben had fallen in with a group of Christian "freemasons," to his horror: "Signor Iacob [Enriches] ... now tells our company that you have become a freemason (*fermasson*) ... and you do not know what Judaism means, and say neither *tefillah* [*shacharit*], nor *minchah*, nor *arvit*, and you do not wash your hands before eating and do not say the blessing, and only that the *harelim* [sic] (uncircumcised) freemasons greet you all day with the sign of the cross [*il segno dello selem*] *has ve-shalom* (God forbid)."[72] He could only hope that these were all lies: "My dear joy, hearing these rumors ... for an old Father like me, and your religious brother, who is ill, you have sent us to our grave *has ve-shalom* (God forbid)."[73]

Even more than Ottoman Smyrna, it was the Tuscan port of Livorno that elicited Franchetti's trepidation. From Tunis, which Franchetti often described as a provincial backwater, Livorno represented not only the allure of a bustling, sophisticated city but also, more perilously, unmatched possibilities for unfettered freedom and dangerous interaction with Christians. Children sent to Livorno at a young age without familial supervision risked not only the perdition of their soul but also the ruin of their fathers, if they did not preserve their virtue and commitment to Jewish tradition.[74] The frequentation of "comedies" epitomized in particular all the ills of the Tuscan port for young Jewish traders.[75]

In his first letter to Isache after he had left home, Joseph stressed that the most essential of the boy's duties was to pray and study and urged him not to waste his time by going to the theater: "it is not mandatory that a young man your age remain there [in Livorno] to attend to a commercial firm *in a land of freedom*, far away from Barbary . . . so it is up to you to *show me that you behave like a religious person*, and obey everybody . . . go to the holy synagogue daily for *shacharit*, *minchah* and *arvit*, and every morning and evening in your yeshivot study with the sons of Mr. Recanati,[76] which is the essential thing, and don't go all the time to see comedies, which is what ruins youth, [for] this world and the next."[77]

Franchetti's emphasis on Judaism points to the ongoing importance of religion as a factor in keeping up a young man's name, and by extension that of his family, before Jewish public opinion, which was still crucial for maintaining good commercial reputations as late as the last quarter of the eighteenth century. At the same time, this merchant's anxious rebukes about his sons' alleged lack of religiosity signal a possible generational shift.[78] To be sure, some of the behaviors discussed by Franchetti smack of stereotypes about youth as a dangerous time of passion and lack of restraint, which were common among both Italian Jews[79] and more generally European merchants in the early modern period.[80] But aside from tensions between older and younger generations, other deviations which Franchetti worried about, such as Reuben's alleged frequentation of freemasons or Isache's love for theater, indicate the emergence of new venues of sociability for young Jewish merchants, parallel to and possibly in competition with those bonds of sociability structured around the Jewish community that had traditionally provided mercantile information and group control in the form of an extended family.

Conclusion

This chapter has focused on some of the pragmatic and discursive approaches of a Mediterranean Jewish merchant, Joseph Franchetti, to the rearing of young traders within a long-distance family business. Considering the tantamount role that maintaining a sense of honor, honesty, and creditworthiness played in making a merchant's reputation, I have concentrated on two of the efforts through which Franchetti endeavored to manage and safeguard the good name of his boys learning the trade—and, by extension, his own. Pragmatically, Franchetti gathered information about the conduct of his faraway sons through hearsay and letters, relying primarily, albeit not exclusively, on Jewish informants. He also used his correspondence to appeal for help from fellow Jewish traders within his network to raise his children properly and steer them away from dangerous behaviors. Discursively, in his letters to Reuben and Isache, Franchetti invoked the importance of good and true *Jeudut*, reminded them to study and pray, and chided them for not properly displaying their Jewish piety in the public forum of the synagogue, equating continued Jewish observance with economic success for his sons and the entire family.

These strategies highlight the ongoing importance of intra-Jewish ties for Mediterranean merchants like the Franchettis in the regime of honor and reputation that formed the basis of early modern commerce. The groundbreaking research of Francesca Trivellato on Sephardic merchants in Livorno has emphasized the facility with which they participated in the wider European commercial society and the degree to which they adopted shared codes of business communication with non-Jews.[81] Still, intracultural bonds continued to serve crucial purposes for early modern Jewish traders in the Mediterranean alongside interreligious and cross-cultural ones. And yet, these bonds were not as immediate as one may think and raise a number of questions.

In the example provided by the Franchetti family firm, "good Judaism"[82]—Jewish observance intended as a synonym of honor, honesty, and trustworthiness—appears as crucial for building and preserving commercial success. Late-eighteenth-century Italian Jewish merchants have been depicted as sophisticated cosmopolitans who not only took advantage of family ties across regional borders to foster their business but also spread European culture to North Africa and the Eastern Mediterranean.[83] Jewish traders of Italian origin—referred to as *francos* in the Ottoman Empire and *grana* in Tunisia—certainly maintained a keen connection to their roots; Joseph himself was proud of his Italian background, pointedly reminding his sons about his own "Mantuan blood."[84] And yet, identification with Italian lands did not necessarily translate into a cosmopolitan attitude, at least in Franchetti's generation. Despite the border-crossing nature of his commerce, Franchetti remained suspicious of Smyrna and Livorno, expressing concerns about his children's preparedness to navigate the attractions and dangers of life in foreign countries without parental supervision, especially when interaction with Christian society was involved. Instead, a good Jewish name translated for Franchetti into sound reputation, and relying on fellow Jews remained paramount. Simultaneously, this father's emphatic reminders do highlight a significant shift taking place in the late eighteenth century, a time in which attitudes to trade are reputed to have become more secular; indeed, young Jewish merchants could choose new venues of sociability that replaced or competed with traditional Jewish ties, as the cases of Reuben and Isache Franchetti seem to suggest.

Additionally, as we have seen, in the absence of direct paternal monitoring, concentric circles of Jewish associates—from family members, to close business partners, to regular correspondents who were not members of the firm—served as sources of control, information, and education in various Mediterranean ports. The "Jewish family matrix" thus continued to be key for enabling the success of Jewish commercial networks. Still, unlike previously believed, this matrix did not only include household members, whether immediate or extended, but also external associates who were constructed as kin and requested, through sentimental appeals, to supply bonds of solidarity in the moment in which the challenge of long distance could threaten actual family ties. Among the social obligations that bound Jewish merchants together and fostered their trustworthiness, in other words, were not only communal pressures but also *familial* ones, real and imagined, articulated through an idiom of love, fear, and anxiety.

In conclusion, intra-Jewish ties were essential, but they did not imply automatic cohesion or trust within the network. Classic historiography on the early modern Mediterranean has maintained that Jewish commercial success was based, to use Braudel's words, on "the organization of mutual confidence and cooperation throughout the world."[85] As the Franchetti case suggests, such a system of mutual confidence was not necessarily a *natural* result of the Jewishness of the network's members; it was built over time and over space, through practices of inclusion and exclusion that relied on the flow of information and circuits of surveillance. In the past, the economic success of trading diasporas was presented as an organic by-product of their shared culture and inferred cohesiveness.[86] While a correlation between shared culture, language, kinship, and trust remains entrenched in the historiography,[87] more recent scholarship increasingly recognizes that trust within merchant minorities, such as the Sephardic Jews of Amsterdam, Portuguese New Christians, or Armenians, was not immediate but needed to be nurtured and maintained through specific strategies of social control.[88] The Franchetti example highlights another facet of this phenomenon: although kinship and religion were key starting points, they were not enough on their own to ensure trust. Rather, these notions themselves needed to be painstakingly constructed, preserved, and managed in order to translate into creditworthiness, honor, and good reputation.

FRANCESCA BREGOLI is an Associate Professor of History at Queens College and The Graduate Center of the City University of New York and holds the Joseph and Oro Halegua Chair in Greek and Sephardic Jewish Studies at Queens College. She is the author of *Mediterranean Enlightenment: Livornese Jews, Tuscan Culture, and Eighteenth-Century Reform* (Stanford University Press, 2014), and coeditor of *Italian Jewish Networks from the Seventeenth to the Twentieth Century: Bridging Europe and the Mediterranean* (Palgrave, 2018) and *Connecting Histories: Jews and Their Others in Early Modern Europe* (Penn Press, 2019).

Notes

1. Peter Mathias, "Risk, Credit and Kinship in Early Modern Enterprise," in *The Early Modern Atlantic Economy*, ed. John J. McCusker and Kenneth Morgan (Cambridge: Cambridge University Press, 2000), 15–35: 16–18.

2. Frédéric Mauro, "Merchant Communities, 1350–1750," in *The Rise of Merchant Empires: Long Distance Trade in the Early Modern World*, ed. James D. Tracy (Cambridge: Cambridge University Press, 1990), 255–86; Francesca Trivellato, *The Familiarity of Strangers: The Sephardic Diaspora, Livorno, and Cross-Cultural Trade in the Early Modern Period* (New Haven, CT: Yale University Press), 132–52.

3. For the Ashkenazi sphere see Cornelia Aust, "Daily Business or an Affair of Consequence? Credit, Reputation, and Bankruptcy among Jewish Merchants in Eighteenth-Century Central Europe," in *Purchasing Power: The Economics of Modern Jewish History*, ed. Rebecca Kobrin and Adam Teller (Philadelphia: University of Pennsylvania Press, 2015), 71–90.

4. Mathias, "Risk, Credit and Kinship"; Luuc Kooijmans, "Risk and Reputation: On the Mentality of Merchants in the Early Modern Period," in *Entrepreneurs and Entrepreneurship in Early Modern Times: Merchants and Industrialists within the Orbit of the Dutch Staple Market*, ed. Clé Lesger and Leo Noordegraaf (The Hague: Gegevens Koninklijke Bibliotheek, 1995), 25–34.

5. Francesca Trivellato, "Merchants' Letters across Geographical and Social Boundaries," in *Correspondence and Cultural Exchange in Europe, 1400–1700*, ed. Francisco Bethencourt and Florike Egmond (Cambridge: Cambridge University Press, 2007), 80–103; Trivellato, *The Familiarity of Strangers*, 167–76; Sebouh David Aslanian, *From the Indian Ocean to the Mediterranean: The Global Trade Networks of Armenian Merchants from New Julfa* (Berkeley: University of California Press, 2011), 166–201.

6. See for instance the insightful remarks of David Hancock on "network memory" in his "The Trouble with Networks: Managing the Scots' Early-Modern Madeira Trade," *The Business History Review* 79 (2005): 467–91, at 478–84.

7. The position is associated with Avner Greif, "Reputation and Coalitions in Medieval Trade: Evidence on the Maghribi Traders," *The Journal of Economic History* 49 (1989): 857–82.

8. Nuala Zahedieh, "Making Mercantilism Work: London Merchants and Atlantic Trade in the Seventeenth Century," *Transactions of the Royal Historical Society* 9 (1999): 143–58; Trivellato, "Merchants' Letters across Geographical and Social Boundaries," 92; Aslanian, *From the Indian Ocean to the Mediterranean*, 166–201.

9. Mathias, "Risk, Credit and Kinship," 32.

10. Gedalia Yogev, *Diamonds and Coral: Anglo-Dutch Jews and Eighteenth-Century Trade* (New York: Leicester University Press, 1978), 260–63.

11. Francesca Trivellato, "Images and Self-Images of Sephardic Merchants in Early Modern Europe and the Mediterranean," in *The Self-Perception of Early Modern Capitalists*, ed. Margaret Jacob and Catherine Secretan (New York: Palgrave, 2008), 49–74: 55–63.

12. Ibid., 63–65.

13. Franchetti Family Archive, MS General 237, vols. 2:1 and 2:2, Columbia University Library, New York, NY. Volume 1 is paginated with a number on the left side of two facing pages. Volume 2 follows the traditional recto and verso pagination. In the following notes, references to volume 1 will be followed by "left" and "right," while references for volume 2 will be marked "r" and "v." For a preliminary description of the volumes see Amedeo Spagnoletto, "Nuove fonti sulla famiglia Franchetti a Tunisi, Smirne e Livorno fra XVIII e XIX S.," *La Rassegna Mensile di Israel* 76 (2010): 95–113, at 99–105.

14. Evridiki Sifneos, "'Cosmopolitanism' as a Feature of the Greek Commercial Diaspora," *History and Anthropology* 16 (2005): 97–111, with references to Jewish merchants as well; see also the insightful remarks in Hank Driessen, "Mediterranean Port Cities: Cosmopolitanism Reconsidered," *History and Anthropology* 16 (2005): 129–41.

15. Adnan A. Husain, "Introduction: Approaching Islam and the Religious Cultures of the Medieval and Early Modern Mediterranean," in *A Faithful Sea: The Religious Cultures of the Mediterranean, 1200–1700*, ed. Adnan A. Husain and K. E. Fleming (Oxford: Oneworld, 2007), 1–26: 15.

16. S. D. Goitein, *A Mediterranean Society: The Jewish Communities of the Arab World as Portrayed in the Documents of the Cairo Geniza*, vol. 1, *Economic Foundations* (Princeton, NJ: Princeton University Press, 2000); Trivellato, *The Familiarity of Strangers*. But these practices were not limited to the Mediterranean: see Liliane Pérez and Bernard Vaisbrot, "Le livre de comptes de Solomon Hyman. Judaïsme, culture négociant et réseaux innovateurs entre Paris, Londres et Birmingham au XVIIIe siècle," in *Langues et langages du commerce en Méditerranée et en Europe à l'époque moderne*, ed. Gilbert Buti, Michèle Janin-Thivos, Olivier Raveux (Aix-en-Provence: Presses Universitaires de Provence, 2013), 227–53; Cornelia Aust, *The Jewish Economic Elite: Making Modern Europe* (Bloomington: Indiana University Press, 2018), 50–51, 138–40.

17. I am grateful to Baron Alberto Franchetti for sharing with me his unpublished reconstruction of the family's genealogic tree; according to him Joseph was born in Tunis. Spagnoletto, on the other hand, claims that Franchetti was born in Mantua ("Nuove fonti," 96). Franchetti refers repeatedly to his brothers in Mantua: MS General 237, 2:1, 169 right (July 22, 1778); 2:2, 43v (March 22, 1782), 110v (January 30, 1783), 127v (June 20, 1783). While his birth in Mantua is possible, I have not been able to verify this fact definitively yet.

18. On Franchetti's business, see Jean-Pierre Filippini, "Gli ebrei e l'attività economica nell'area nord-africana," *Nuovi Studi Livornesi* 7 (1999): 131–49; Jean-Pierre Filippini, *Il porto di Livorno e la Toscana (1676–1814)* (Naples: Edizioni Scientifiche Italiane, 1998), 2:259–61. On the Franchetti family more generally, see Mirella Scardozzi, "Itinerari dell'integrazione: una grande famiglia ebrea tra la fine del Settecento e il primo Novecento," in *Leopoldo e Alice Franchetti e il loro tempo*, ed. Paolo Pezzino and Alvaro Tacchini (Città di Castello, Italy: Petruzzi, 2002), 271–320; Mirella Scardozzi, "Una storia di famiglia: i Franchetti dalle coste del Mediterraneo all'Italia liberale," *Quaderni storici* 38 (2003): 697–740.

19. Only from 1795 on, after Joseph's death and the move of the remaining family to Livorno, his heirs will develop business connections with Trieste and Vienna: Scardozzi, "Una storia di famiglia," 702–3. By 1832, Isache and Jeudà had enough interests in England to have their wills registered at the Prerogative Court of Canterbury in London: IT/IT1366, not numbered, Central Archives for the History of the Jewish People, Jerusalem.

20. Filippini, "Gli ebrei e l'attività economica," 140; Scardozzi, "Una storia di famiglia," 702; Scardozzi, "Itinerari dell'integrazione," 271–74.

21. Scardozzi, "Una storia di famiglia," 701–2. On European commerce in Smyrna, see Elena Frangakis-Syrett, *The Commerce of Smyrna in the Eighteenth Century, 1700–1820* (Athens: Centre for Asia Minor Studies, 1992).

22. The company had operated under the same leadership but with a different contract since 1770 (MS General 237, 2:2, 29r). The partnership with the Enriches family was dissolved around 1794. When the Tunisian hub declined in the late 1780s, with the emergence of Tuscan production centers, the Franchetti moved their center of operation to Livorno (Scardozzi, "Una storia di famiglia," 702).

23. For a survey of the goods Jewish merchants like the Franchetti exported from Tunisia to Livorno, and imported from Livorno to Tunisia, see Filippini, *Il porto di Livorno*, 2:250–55, 274–76.

24. Spagnoletto, "Nuove fonti," 98.

25. Elisheva Carlebach, "Letter into Text: Epistolarity, History, and Literature," in *Jewish Literature and History: An Interdisciplinary Conversation*, ed. Eliyana R. Adler and Sheila E. Jelen (Bethesda: University of Maryland Press, 2008), 113–33.

26. While the letters to business associates outside the family are brief and to the point, usually no longer than one manuscript page, those to Reuben, Isache, and Beniamin generally average three to six pages. In some cases, letters addressed to his sons reach fifteen, eighteen, and even twenty-three pages, composed over a period of several days and characterized by a disorderly and colorful style.

27. On Jewish apprenticeships in early modern Italy see Roni Weinstein, "'Thus Will Giovani Do': Jewish Youth Sub-Culture in Early Modern Italy," in *The Premodern Teenager: Youth in Society, 1150–1650*, ed. Konrad Eisenbichler (Toronto: Centre for Reformation and Renaissance Studies, 2002), 51–74: 67; Julia R. Lieberman, "Childhood and Family among the Western Sephardim in the Seventeenth Century," in *Sephardi Family Life in the Early Modern Diaspora*, ed. Julia R. Lieberman (Waltham, MA: Brandeis University Press, 2011), 129–66: 163; Julia R. Lieberman, "Adolescence and the Period of Apprenticeship among the Western Sephardim in the Seventeenth Century," *El Prezente: Studies in Sephardic Culture* 4 (2010): 11–23, at 14–16.

28. MS General 237, 2:1, 3 left–5 left (January 28, 1776).

29. Ibid., 165 left (July 17, 1778), 169 left (July 22, 1778).

30. Jeudà occasionally returned to Tunis.

31. This is in line with practices among other early modern merchants, for instance Dutch Protestants and Portuguese New Christians: Kooijmans, "Risk and Reputation," 31–32; Daviken Studnicki-Gizbert, *A Nation upon the Ocean Sea: Portugal's Atlantic Diaspora and the Crisis of the Spanish Empire, 1492–1640* (Oxford: Oxford University Press, 2007), 81. For a broader analysis of the overlaps between family and business in Franchetti's correspondence, see Francesca Bregoli, "'Your Father's Interests': The Business of Kinship in a Trans-Mediterranean Jewish Merchant Family, 1776–1790," *Jewish Quarterly Review* 108, no. 2 (Spring 2018): 294–324.

32. MS General 237 2:1, 103 left (March 22, 1777).

33. On August 20, 1782, for instance, Franchetti found himself resorting to evidence found in letters from his sons to defend their good name: "I will never believe that my sons in Smyrna could be ungrateful towards anybody, and especially towards your worthy house," he wrote to the Livornese Samuel and Moise Leon. Indeed, Reuben and Jeudà had recently written to him that "they had absolutely entered into a riot with a partner of theirs in Smyrna because of you," a demonstration of their loyalty to the Leon brothers. Franchetti promised that he would soon "make them aware of the real [quality] of [his] sons," discrediting in turn those "captains that dare give you these most false reports" (MS General 237, 2:2, 69r).

34. MS General 237, 2:1, 25 right (June 11, 1776).

35. Ibid., 26 right (June 11, 1776); 27 right (June 24, 1776); 2:2, 35r (March 18, 1782).

36. MS General 237, 2:2, 44v (March 22, 1782).

37. The Sephardic Franco firm was indeed one of the wealthiest and most influential Jewish companies in eighteenth-century Livorno.

38. Ihiel Franchetti had sent the delicate letter to Joseph in Tunis, who in turn copied it and enclosed it in confidence in his own letter to Reuben: MS General 237 2:2, 43v-44v (March 22, 1782).

39. MS General 237, 2:1, 106 right (May 5, 1777).

40. Kooijmans, "Risk and Reputation," 32.

41. MS General 237, 2:1, 106 right (May 5, 1777).

42. Ibid., 174 left (September 2, 1778).

43. Ibid., 26 left (June 11, 1776).

44. Ibid., 169 left (July 22, 1778). In the same letter, Franchetti promised that in return he would invite into his own house Coen de Lara's young son one hour per day to let him study with an experienced Italian teacher, "so that when he knows how to write I can send him to you there, and I await your reply to carry this out, otherwise I will say that you do not love your son."

45. Ibid., 166 right (July 17, 1778). See also ibid., 195 left-195 right (May 20, 1779), 197 left (May 19, 1779), 197 right (May 19, 1779), 211 left (July 23, 1779), 218 right (September 24, 1779); 2:2, 119r (July 4, 1783).

46. MS General 237, 2:1, 190 left (January 28, 1779), emphasis mine.

47. A similar phenomenon can be noticed for the Gradis family of Bordeaux: Richard Menkis, "The Gradis Family of Eighteenth-Century Bordeaux: A Social and Economic Study" (unpublished PhD diss., Brandeis University 1988), 106–7.

48. Weinstein, "'Thus Will *Giovani* Do,'" 67.

49. This phenomenon parallels practices of apprenticeship in the non-Jewish world.

50. MS General 237, 2:1, 106 right (May 5, 1777), 173 left (August 18, 1778), 182 right (December, 7 1778), 189 left (January 28, 1779).

51. "Dear friend, please recognize the youth of my son on my account, and love him as your own brother," he wrote the son of his partner Salomone Enriches, also called Isache, who had been sent to Livorno in 1780 to live and work with Isache Franchetti: MS General 237, 2:1, 230 right (February 1780).

52. See also ibid., 166 right (July 17, 1778), 169 left (July 22, 1778).

53. Ibid., 103 left (March 22, 1777); 2:2, 60v (July 18, 1782). For a comparable phenomenon among seventeenth-century Portuguese merchants see Studnicki-Gizbert, *A Nation upon the Ocean Sea*, 80–81.

54. David Cressy, *Coming Over: Migration and Communication between England and New England in the Seventeenth Century* (Cambridge: Cambridge University Press, 1987),

213; Sarah M. S. Pearsall, *Atlantic Families: Lives and Letters in the Later Eighteenth Century* (Oxford: Oxford University Press, 2008), 111–42.

55. This section presents a revised and modified version of arguments drawn from Bregoli, "'Your Father's Interests.'"

56. MS General 237, 2:2, 71r (August 15, 1782).

57. MS General 237, 2:1, 194 left (March 26, 1779); 2:2, 43v-44r (March 22, 1782); 70v (August 15, 1782).

58. MS General 237, 2:2, 59r (June 21, 1782).

59. MS General 237, 2:1, 197 left (May 19, 1779); 2:2, 44r (March 22, 1782).

60. Jacques Savary, *Le Parfait Négociant* (Paris: Jean Guignard fils, 1675), 55. Additionally, parents ought to carefully consider the Christian qualities of the merchant they apprenticed their sons with, as virtue, love, and fear of God were the qualities upon which their children's spiritual salvation depended (Ibid., 48).

61. Ibid., 55.

62. Giovan Domenico Peri urged young apprentices to go to mass every morning in his *Il Negotiante* (Venice: Giacomo Hertz, 1662), 27. The advice to pray daily is also found in English manuals: Donald J. Harreld, "An Education in Commerce: Transmitting Business Information in Early Modern Europe," in *Information Flows: New Approaches in the Historical Study of Business Information*, ed. Leos Müller and Jari Ojala (Helsinki: SKS Finnish Literature Society, 2007), 63–83: 78.

63. Trivellato, *The Familiarity of Strangers*, 185–89.

64. Trivellato, "Images and Self-Images," 50.

65. Glickl bas Leib famously begins her memoirs by inviting her children to "serve God from [their] heart," pray "with awe and devotions," and "put aside a fixed time for the study of the Torah." The injunction to "diligently go about your business" follows these religious prescriptions: *The Memoirs of Glückel of Hameln*, tr. Marvin Lowenthal (New York: Schocken Books, 1977), 2.

66. For Livorno see Trivellato, *The Familiarity of Strangers*, 84–92; on deviance among the Sephardim of Amsterdam see Yosef Kaplan, *An Alternative Path to Modernity: The Sephardi Diaspora in Western Europe* (Leiden: Brill, 2000).

67. For instance, although Hayim Yosef David Azulai depicts the wealthy Livornese elite as irreligious, those very same traders had a vested interest in supporting rabbinic scholars that passed through the city, like him: Francesca Bregoli, "Printing, Fundraising, and Jewish Patronage in Eighteenth-Century Livorno," in *Jewish Culture in Early Modern Europe: Essays in Honor of David B. Ruderman*, ed. Richard I. Cohen, Natalie B. Dohrmann, Adam Shear, Elchanan Reiner (Pittsburgh: University of Pittsburgh Press, 2014), 250–59.

68. Yogev, *Diamonds and Coral*, 267–70. See also Todd M. Endelman, "Secularization and the Origins of Jewish Modernity—On the Impact of Urbanization and Social Transformation," *Simon Dubnow Institute Yearbook* 6 (2007), 155–68: 165–66.

69. MS General 237, 2:1, 141 right (November 21, 1777), emphasis mine.

70. Ibid., 169 left (July 22, 1778).

71. Mordechai de Soria, *Oracion panejirico doctrinal sobre la mala tentacion . . . en Primero de Sucot* (Livorno, Italy: Fantechi, 1751).

72. MS General 237, 2:2, 122r-v (July 15, 1783).

73. Ibid., 120v (July 15, 1783).

74. Ibid., 75r, 84v (no date, but August 1782).

75. Ibid., 84r-85r (no date, but August 1782), 133r (June 20, 1783). Franchetti had heard rumors on the ruin of the Jewish firms Castro, Caravaglio, and Bonfil, all attributed to the

excessive expenses of dissolute sons chasing after secular pleasures and entertainments in Livorno.

76. The wealthy Recanati family ran one of the most prosperous firms in Livorno. They were the first Italian Jews to join the primarily Sephardic government of the community in 1715, when the grand duke allowed Italian Jews to be selected for leadership positions.

77. MS General 237, 2:1, 193 left (March 26, 1779), emphasis mine. Portions of this letter were published in Spagnoletto, "Nuove fonti," 102–3.

78. See Shmuel Feiner, *The Origins of Jewish Secularization in Eighteenth Century Europe* (Philadelphia: University of Pennsylvania Press, 2011), esp. 29–63.

79. Elliott Horowitz, "The Worlds of Jewish Youth in Europe, 1300–1800," in *A History of Young People in the West*, vol. 1, *Ancient and Medieval Rites of Passage*, ed. Giovanni Levi and Jean-Claude Schmitt (Cambridge, MA: Harvard University Press, 1997), 83–119: 93–97; Weinstein, "'Thus Will *Giovani* Do,'" 58.

80. Margaret R. Hunt, *The Middling Sort: Commerce, Gender, and the Family in England, 1680–1780* (Berkeley: University of California Press, 1996), 50–51.

81. Trivellato, *The Familiarity of Strangers*.

82. It should be noted that the "good Judaism" Franchetti hoped his children would maintain had different implications from the courtly, dignified yet ostentatious "bom Judesmo" of the Amsterdam Sephardic elites: Yosef Kaplan, "Bom Judesmo: The Western Sephardic Diaspora," in *Cultures of the Jews: A New History*, ed. David Biale (New York: Schocken Books, 2002), 639–69: 652–655.

83. Hayim Yosef David Azulai, for instance, accused the *grana* in Tunis of being impious and prone to freemasonry. On the *francos* see Anthony Molho, "Ebrei e marrani fra Italia e Levante ottomano," in *Storia d'Italia. Annali XI: Gli Ebrei in Italia*, ed. Corrado Vivanti (Torino: Einaudi, 1997), 2:1009–43; Esther Benbassa and Aron Rodrigue, *Sephardi Jewry: A History of the Judeo-Spanish Community* (Berkeley: University of California Press, 2000), 34, 46, 74–79.

84. MS General 237, 2:1, 54 left (September 8, 1776), 206 left (June 30, 1779).

85. Fernand Braudel, *The Mediterranean and the Mediterranean World in the Age of Philip II* (Berkeley: University of California Press, 1995), 2:817.

86. The classic statement of the correlation between trust and close-knit, diasporic communities can be found in Philip D. Curtin, *Cross-Cultural Trade in World History* (Cambridge: Cambridge University Press, 1984).

87. See for example Daniel M. Swetschinski, "Kinship and Commerce: The Foundations of Portuguese Jewish Life in Seventeenth-Century Holland," *Studia Rosenthaliana* 15 (1981): 52–74, at 59, 65, 73; Zahedieh, "Making Mercantilism Work," 157, which however also stresses the importance of communal control.

88. Jessica Vance Roitman, *The Same but Different?: Inter-Cultural Trade and the Sephardim, 1595–1640* (Leiden: Brill, 2011), esp. 266–67 for a discussion of network failure; Studnicki-Gizbert, *A Nation upon the Ocean Sea*, 67–89; Aslanian, *From the Indian Ocean to the Mediterranean*, 166–201.

7

SOAP AND THE MAKING OF A SHORT-DISTANCE NETWORK IN THE NINETEENTH-CENTURY ADRIATIC

Constanze Kolbe

When the French novelist and humanitarian activist Albert Cohen published the book *Solal*[1] in 1930 and *Book of My Mother*[2] in 1954, the Corfu of his grandfathers had long since disappeared. He described a world in which the Jewish community was a vital part of the vibrant urban and commercial setting. Many Jews worked in trade or in small workshops in the city's central market. The *Ebraiki*, as the Jewish quarter in Corfu was called in the Corfiote Greek-Venetian dialect, was home to the small soap workshop in which Cohen's grandfather, Abram Coen, produced soap from around 1860 until 1910. It was one of four soap factories on the Ionian Islands and had established itself as a prominent producer of soap for the wider Adriatic region, in particular for the region of Ottoman Albania just across the Ionian Sea.

Much of Coen's trade correspondence is housed today in the Albanian State Archives in Tirana. The letters span a period from the early 1880s until 1914 and include both incoming and outgoing trade letters.[3] The earliest remaining letters date back to 1882 when Abram Coen of Corfu sent soap samples to Ciobba & Bianki in the Ottoman-Albanian city of Scutari. Although these are the first letters in the archive, it is clear both parties traded with each other well before that time; in fact, Abram Coen must have run his workshop as a soap merchant from roughly the mid-1860s. From around 1885, his son Marc Coen was also involved in the business; they signed all business letters jointly.[4]

The collection of these merchant letters constitutes a rare source on a short-distance trade network connecting Corfu to the Ottoman mainland from a period that coincided with an intense reshuffling of borders. Montenegro, just a stone's throw away from Scutari, gained independence from the Ottoman Empire in 1878. The ports of Ulcinj/Dulcigno and Bar/Antivari,[5] two of the ports that Coen most commonly used to ship his soap, changed from Ottoman to Montenegrin administration. The change in political administration came with a change in trade legislation. When access to Ottoman ports (Durres/Durazzo and Shengjin/San Giovanni di Medua) became increasingly difficult for Coen because of Turco-Greek rivalries and resulting new trade treaties, Coen diverted his business to the ports of the young nation-state Montenegro, which strategically provided more favorable conditions of entry for cargo.

The focus on short-distance, coastal (cabotage) trade in the nineteenth century allows us to rethink the historiographic division of early modern and modern trade networks. While early modern Mediterranean scholarship focuses on short-distance and cross-imperial trade,[6] scholars of the nineteenth-century Mediterranean tend to emphasize national and mono-imperial dimensions.[7] The trade between the Greek island of Corfu and Ottoman Albania occurred within a border region that was not navigated by large steam liners, such as those of the Austrian Lloyd, which crisscrossed the waters of the Adriatic by the 1830s. Along with long-distance steam liners, cabotage trade remained a crucial element in the Adriatic. As the merchant letters reveal, several merchants in Scutari had invested in a small fleet, stationed at various ports such as Ulcinj/Dulcigno, part of Montenegro since 1878. These were small sailing boats, much like the ones used for early modern Adriatic trade,[8] which could navigate fluvial barriers and transport the goods into the Balkan hinterland and to the market of Scutari.

The artificial division between the early modern and modern periods is also reflected in its implicit assumption that by the nineteenth century, recourse to commercial institutions replaced alternate, oral ways of conflict resolution. The teleological historiographical perspective emphasizes economic progress in which the use of institutions becomes part of a new global trade order.[9] A close look at the Coen business correspondence shows, however, that in this inter-imperial region, noninstitutional, private methods of conflict resolution continued to coexist with institutional approaches. The analysis of trade disputes in the letters shows that suing in court was a time-consuming, expensive affair and was used only as the very last resort. This stands in stark contradiction to studies on northern European mercantile courts at the time and suggests that in this region both institutional and noninstitutional ways of conflict resolution coexisted well into the nineteenth century.

Coen's trade correspondence sheds light on a region which is not usually studied as a unit but rather from the perspective of national economic histories

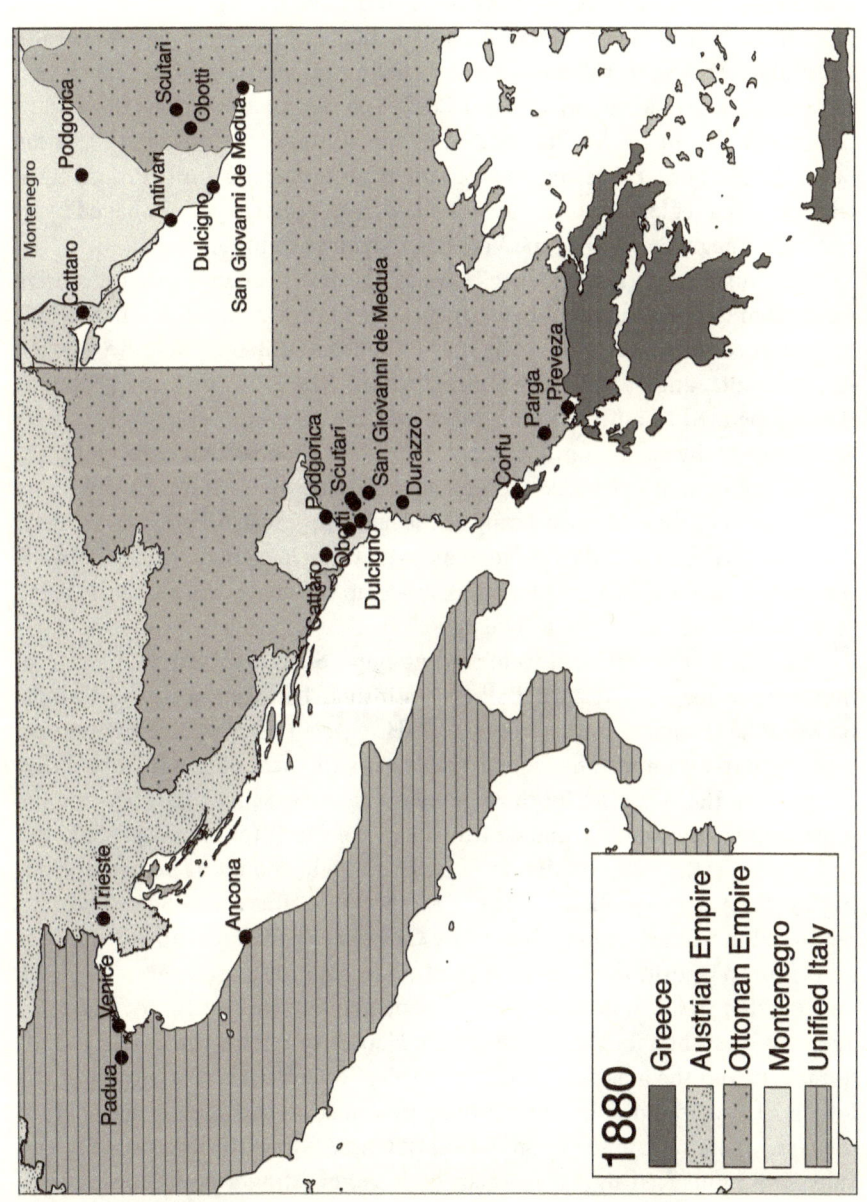

or that of imperial trade. The analytical concept of "microregion" functions here as a useful heuristic tool. Horden and Purcell used this concept to show how the ancient and medieval Mediterranean was connected through various microregions, highlighting diversity around the Mediterranean. Microregions are also a useful alternative to national and imperial narratives in the nineteenth century, as Coen's trade not only linked Corfu and the Albanian coast but also its hinterland, to which it was connected by fluvial trade. Rethinking the notion of the border, border crossing, and how merchants used legal institutions illustrate how this region is best understood as a post-Venetian space, shaped by its erstwhile integration within the Venetian maritime commonwealth.

The business correspondence between the Jewish soap merchant Abram Coen from Corfu and two of his clients in the Ottoman-Albanian market city of Scutari commenced in the early 1880s: Ciobba and Bianki were two Catholic merchants, and Saraci, a Muslim merchant. The joint company Ciobba & Bianki operated as an importing and exporting firm and was, together with Saraci, one of the most prominent firms in Scutari. Ciobba & Bianki was formed in 1798 and quickly expanded with offices in Venice and Trieste. From around 1850, Angelo Ciobba was also acting as the honorary Austro-Hungarian consul in Scutari. Already in the 1860s, together with other local merchants, Ciobba & Bianki had invested in a small merchant fleet to conduct trade along the Adriatic coast via the city of Ulcinj/Dulcigno.[10]

Both Scutari and Corfu were trading hubs. Scutari served as the central marketplace for the Western Balkan peninsula. Its location at the triangle between the Ottoman Empire, the Austro-Hungarian Empire, and Montenegro made Scutari an important center for the transshipment of goods from different parts of the Adriatic. By the eighteenth century, Scutari had become the most important economic and cultural center of the Ottoman *vilayet* Shkodra and had an estimated population of seven to eight thousand people, including Muslims and Catholics.[11] Between 1741 and 1800, there were 804 merchants registered in Scutari, 128 of whom were Catholic. By the early nineteenth century, Scutari's position as an important node for transit trade grew.[12] Corfu, on the other hand, was located at the southern entrance of the Adriatic Sea and served as a hub for the trade between Habsburg Trieste, the Eastern Mediterranean, and the adjacent Ottoman mainland. Corfu was the biggest of the Ionian Islands, and despite the fact that by the 1880s it had already been part of the Greek nation-state for roughly twenty years, it was still linguistically and culturally influenced by its Venetian heritage, boasting a multiethnic population consisting of Catholics, Greeks, and Jews. The Jewish community of roughly six thousand was mainly of Italian origin, with a smaller number of Romaniotes. While the Jews of Corfu were active in all kinds of business, they were disproportionally well represented in commerce. In 1860, they constituted 27 percent of recorded merchants, and this number further increased to 37 percent in 1862.[13]

The Venetian heritage and the persistent influence of the Italian language facilitated trade relations in this microregion. Both Corfu and Scutari had been Venetian colonies. Venice conquered Scutari in 1396 and controlled the city until roughly 1479, when it was ceded to the Ottoman Empire. Although now controlled by Istanbul, it still shared borders with the remaining Venetian parts of the Eastern Adriatic coast. Venetian control of the Ionian Islands lasted much longer, from the mid-fourteenth century until the late eighteenth century. Despite the short Venetian presence in Scutari, Italian continued to be an important language of the market, with many Scutarites opening agencies in cities around the Adriatic, such as Ragusa, Ancona, Senigallia, and Ljubljana as well as Venice and Trieste. Equally in Corfu, Italian continued to be of importance as the language of trade, especially for the Jewish community and the Catholic population.[14]

Corfu and Scutari were connected through the Bojana River, which provided an entry point into the Balkan Peninsula. While Scutari was only twenty-three kilometers away, the river's many meanders almost doubled the actual distance. Because large, heavy steamers like those of the Lloyd could not move up the shallow waters of the Bojana, the port facilities along the Ottoman coast at San Giovanni di Medua, today's Shëngjin, or the Ottoman/Montenegrin ports Ulcinj/Dulcigno and Antivari/Bar were used as major transshipment centers. Goods from Corfu were mainly shipped with smaller boats, called *trabaccoli* or *longas* (luggers), which were distinctive in particular for the early modern Adriatic trade.[15] Their use remained invaluable for short-distance trade to reach markets like Scutari, which was inaccessible for steamboat vessels. They had a capacity of around thirty to two hundred tons and were equipped with reeling sails. Singularly mobile, these boats were much better suited to navigate the rugged and shallow waters of the Bojana River until the small endpoint village of Obotti, from where the commodities could be sent deep into the Balkan hinterland. The small sailing fleet used by the Scutarite merchants was stationed at the Ottoman (from 1878 onward, Montenegrin) port of Ulcinj/Dulcigno. As the trade activities of the port of Scutari grew, encouraged by the local notables who sought new means of income, the merchants of Scutari invested in the merchant fleet of Ulcinj/Dulcigno, which was as large as 250 to 300 boats.[16] As Traian Stoianovich has documented, the Dulcignote merchant marine was formed as early as 1750 and mainly lived off the coastal trade along the Morea and Trieste.[17] In fact, the smaller local sailing boats became so successful that they could conduct coastal commerce without any competition. The Austro-Hungarian chamber of commerce noted: "Our steam liners shipped trade goods of a total of 7 million gulden out of a total trade volume of 10 million gulden. We successfully competed with our steam liners against two Ottoman steam liners on the same route. However, as for the sailing ships, we cannot even consider any competition."[18] Thus, the trade volume of the sailing boats should not be underestimated. In 1871, goods worth 2.5 million guldens were shipped between Trieste and Scutari alone, not including all the goods that came on sailing boats from the Ionian Islands or the Morea.[19] This small shipping fleet provided the backbone for the trade network of Abram Coen in Corfu.

Soap was the main item in trade between Corfu and the Scutarite merchants Ciobba & Bianki and Saraci. While the industrialized professional manufacturing of soap was concentrated in France, its production quickly spread to the eastern Mediterranean. Soap production in Greece and the Ionian Islands goes back to roughly the 1850s. By the 1890s, when Corfu was already incorporated into Greece, the number of factories across Greece had increased to thirty-seven, the Ionian Islands being the main producer with around twenty factories in Corfu, Zakynthos, and Cephalonia combined, Coen's factory being one of them. Greece exported around 6.5 million okdadas of soap per year altogether, and the "Turkish" market was one of its prime exporting destinations.[20] Apart from Coen, there was one other Jewish soap merchant on the island of Corfu, Abram Israel, and he was Coen's fiercest competitor. Together, these two workshops were among four to five factories in the city of Corfu at that time. We know that at least two of the other soap merchants were Christian. There is thus no indication that soap making was a preferred business for the Jewish community but rather an industry undertaken by both Jews and Orthodox Christians.

While the soap produced in Marseilles was based on vegetable oils, soap from the Ionian Islands used olive oil as the main ingredient as it was easily available in the Ionian Islands, the Greek markets, and the olive-rich regions of Puglia in southern Italy. (At times, a shortage of olive oil, or its high price, made production difficult.[21]) The letters indicate that a small-scale trade network across the southern Adriatic (Corfu-Bari) existed and allowed for the import of olive oil.[22] The production of soap was seasonal and dependent on the supply of olive oil, the majority of which originated from the nearby Ionian Islands or was imported from Tuscany and other areas in southern Italy.[23] The quality of the soap was low, and the olive pits, an ingredient for very low-quality soap, were imported from Crete, Lesbos, Chios, and Rhodes.[24]

While no indication exists concerning how initial contact was established between Coen and his customers Saraci and Ciobba & Bianki in Scutari, a shared language of communication was certainly beneficial. All incoming and outgoing letters were in Italian. Some exceptions were letters of instruction to captains, written in Latin script in a mix of Italian and colloquial Albanian, which until then had not been standardized as a written language. Most correspondence was sent directly from the Scutarite merchants and Coen, but often the captains, who were mainly of Muslim Albanian origin, acted as representatives. Originating from the port cities where the boats were stationed, they had long-lasting trade relations with specific merchants. Often, a captain was hired by a coalition of different merchants in Scutari, all of whom would give him detailed instructions for the purchase of the goods they needed. On their way southward, the captains pursued an almost always identical set of products from specific places of origin, for example, vinegar from Lefkada (Santa Maura), soap from Corfu, and figs from the Morea.

The captains used small sailing ships (*veliero*) or *trabaccolos*. Initially employed by the Venetians, the *trabaccolos* were slow but reliable and were mainly used for smaller cargo up to two hundred deadweight tons. Described as "efficient and frugal seafarers," the captains journeyed for several weeks along the Ottoman coastal line to the Morea.[25] The small boats were heavily dependent on the weather, and if no wind was in sight, Coen would write to his clients in Scutari that "the soap is ready, but there is no sign of the captain."[26] Shipping with smaller sailing boats not only impacted the schedule but also made the cargo sensitive to the rough weather. Although rare, complications due to the weather could destroy an entire cargo and the ship; usually the cargo was insured during the winter months, when the weather was much rougher.

The role of the captains extended beyond carrying a shipment safely from one place to the next; they also served as crucial intermediaries between Coen and the Scutari merchants. While abroad, captains maintained close contact with the merchants in Scutari and acted as negotiators upon inspection of the merchandise. They assessed the different qualities of the fresh produce, and upon receiving detailed description, Saraci or Ciobba & Bianki would inform the captain telegraphically which ones to purchase. The captains also acted as direct representatives of the party selling the goods. For example, many of the letters addressed to Saraci and Ciobba were written on the official letterhead of soap merchant Coen by the captain.[27] Captains thus performed a second role as brokers.

The correspondence reveals that trade relationships were, once formed, fiercely pursued. Long-lasting trade relations were more important than achieving the lowest price for a certain product in the short term. By the 1890s, competing soap merchants opened up new workshops, in the Ottoman provinces of Scutari but also in Corfu. Despite the increased competition, there is no indication that either Ciobba & Bianki or Saraci also purchased from another merchant. Rather, the strategy was to leverage new competition to lower prices and increase quality. In 1888, for instance, Abram Israel, a member of the Jewish community in Corfu and another Jewish soap merchant of Corfu, tried to win over Coen's customers in Scutari by offering his soap well below Coen's prices. Instead of entering a second soap business, both Ciobba & Bianki and Saraci used the offer to inform Coen of the new competitor on the market. This was a very effective way to get Coen to lower his own prices while at the same time gathering background information about the new competitor. While Coen dropped prices by a few cents, more importantly, he was able to discourage his cherished customers from going against their established trade relationship. Coen wrote, "As what regards Abram Israel, his [company] is not even worth mentioning, it is a very small company and you cannot expect great things."[28] In another letter, Coen asserted that "these are very small workshops that only want to ruin the market price, and you cannot expect any commission from them."[29] Neither Israel nor any Turkish workshop was able to win over the customers in Scutari, despite offering more competitive prices. Coen had already built up a reputation for himself as a trustworthy partner in trade, though he was forced to offer better conditions.

These close trade relationships were continually reaffirmed in the merchants' correspondence, both to reinforce the partnership and, on occasion, to secure better conditions. The words *friendship* (*amicizia*) and *friends* were paramount in the correspondence. Coen often referred to his trade contacts in Ottoman Albania as "best clients" and "best friends." Sometimes this was a bargaining tool, in which the language of friendship and preferential treatment was used to strengthen the offer made. For instance, on one occasion Coen replied to Ciobba & Bianki, "If you do not want my soap for this price, I will send it to someone else in your marketplace, as many other clients have already asked me. However, to show that I consider you one of my *best clients and best friend*, thus I give you first choice. In that way, you can also fight the competition of the soap factories in your own market."[30] On another occasion a year later, Coen rejected Ciobba & Bianki's desire to further bargain, saying that he "could sell the soap to another merchant in Scutari from whom I already have an offer. I will gain much more but, as I told you, I desire to please you and show you that *I consider you one of my best clients*."[31] As Francesca Trivellato has noted, the term *friendship* encompassed a "wide spectrum of meanings and relations, ranging from kinship ties to sentimental relationships, neighborly sociability, occupational connections, political alliances, charitable endeavors, intellectual affinities, spiritual attachments and economic ties."[32] The language of friendship in their correspondence was thus part and parcel of the utilitarian economic relationships that the merchants had formed and should not necessarily be viewed as a sign of any emotional affection.

In addition to implied amicable relations, a language of confidentiality played into creating a feeling of trust, especially during the negotiation of bilateral prices. In 1890, Coen informed Ciobba & Bianki, "I was nice enough to treat you as a close friend and give you a very favorable price; I ask you not *to disclose it to the others* because it will damage me! I insist on your seriousness!"[33] Secret deals could sometimes backfire when prices did not remain confidential. In 1890, Saraci wrote that he was "very displeased" to hear that Coen did not offer him preferential prices that he had allegedly offered to the other merchants of the market. Coen replied that he had treated Saraci in the "same way as I treat the others while I have practiced the conditions in full equality among all my friends."[34] Coen, to defend his reputation, had to adjust his price. Secret letters could also be employed to ruin trade relations and damage a reputation. On another occasion, an anonymous letter was sent to Saraci in which Coen was accused of "doing cheaper business with others."[35] Coen denounced this as calumny and replied that we "all have to understand that we have enemies and jealousies in our careers."[36] The decision to give lower prices to some merchants was always a delicate balancing act.

Since recurring trade relations formed this trade network, merchant letters also functioned as the preferred means to resolve conflicts, as opposed to bringing them to court. As Mafalda Ade has shown in her work on the trade court of Aleppo, very few cases made it to court. Suing was expensive, time-consuming, and could have detrimental effects on one's reputation. She argues that when both sides knew that one party was bankrupt, the court had little power to restore the losses.[37] This is also the impression gained from the sources from the Corfu merchant court in the 1840s and 1850s. Suing in the trade court of Corfu was very expensive, slow, and to be avoided at all cost because decisions were publicized and could ruin trade relationships.[38] This was in clear contrast to the French merchant courts, where Lemercier has argued that litigation was "extremely cheap, both for the parties and the state. . . . Also, their decisions were quick, rarely appealed and generally confirmed."[39] Not only did the case of the Corfiote merchant court show that cases took a long time to resolve and were expensive but also the inter-imperial dimension made it difficult to sue as any accused could abscond from the island.[40]

When looking at court cases, most often we do not know which extra-legal measures preceded a trial in court. The letters and the way conflict was dealt with provide insight into how commercial law was executed in this region. An example of the different resources available to merchants in arbitrating a trade conflict is presented in a long-lasting dispute between Coen and Saraci. In 1900, the customs office in Obotti stopped a small *trabaccolo* with a large load of soap that Coen had sent from Corfu to the Ottoman port San Giovanni di Medua/

Shengjin, claiming that "it is harmful to the population." Saraci accused Coen of having delivered inferior soap: not "pure" but with "harmful content," which could refer to sand or any other filling products. "Even if it were the best possible quality, your customs would still find whatever possible reason not to let the soap pass!" Coen charged in response.[41] Since roughly 1895, the usual procedure for imported soap was an investigation by a medical clerk, who would determine whether the soap was produced according to the same purity standards that were applied in the Ottoman territories. The Ottoman administration had also asked for certificates, verifying that the soap was "genuine"—unadulterated with "harmful" additives. This was in itself a standard procedure. The arbitrary confiscation of the goods at the customs check, however, was new.

As far as Coen was concerned, the problem was the result of new Ottoman trade decrees that changed the chemical ingredients for soap. The trade treaty between Greece and the Ottoman Empire had changed in 1900 and specified that the soap could only contain a half of a percent of caustic soda, which according to Coen was ridiculous as "the oil does not bind with these percentages!"[42] Coen suspected that this change was a by-product of Greco-Turkish rivalries, which increased because of the war in Crete in 1897. Although these political tensions concerned the status of Crete, an island many kilometers away from the Adriatic, they also played out in questions of trade; for example, import rules set by the Ottomans made it increasingly difficult to import soap.[43] Imports to the Ottoman Empire were at various times sabotaged or blocked, making it a frustrating endeavor for both sides to maintain their trade relations. Coen wrote to Saraci, still hoping for a release of the merchandise: "sustain towards the governor that [this] soap arrived before the *circolare* [the official law], this is the strongest argument!"[44] After the soap was prohibited from entering the Ottoman market, it was stored in "very humid storage facilities, which is damaging to the quality of the soap."[45] Storage costs were thus to be paid for a product that ultimately was of no use anymore, particularly as no time frame for its release had been set by the authorities.

Yet, Saraci's suspicion about adulterated soap was not without basis. The weight of the soap could be increased by illegally mixing different products into it, such as sand, small stones, or marbles. Fraud became so widespread that it was specifically addressed in handbooks on soap production, circulating in Corfu and Trieste. The *Handbook of Soap Making*, published in Athens in 1898, called for a standardization of this craft, with a vocational school that would teach people how to make "genuine" soap. The book was explicitly written "for soap makers and merchants" and provided clues for determining the quality of the soap. It reminded the reader that "the soap maker should not forget that the public shows a preference for the soap that looks good even if it's not pure, instead of pure soap that doesn't look good."[46] While there were ways to produce cheaper soap, the key to its production was to make it look like higher-quality soap. We do not know whether Coen's problems were the result of the war fought over Crete or an illegal ingredient in the soap. Either way, both the political tensions between the Ottoman Empire and Greece as well as the increasing bureaucratization and standardization of the trade through circulars and handbooks could make trade for Coen more difficult rather than facilitating and streamlining production and trade.

A very effective threat to force conflict resolution was to make the case public in the market of Scutari. In 1898, for example, when Ciobba was unsatisfied with the quality of the soap, he asked Coen to acknowledge his mistake: "We can even make a loss in this affair, even if it is 2000 francs, for us this is nothing, but we only want you to show reason. Otherwise, we will make it public."[47] A good reputation was part and parcel of the merchant's identity; a public disclosure of unlawful business practices could ruin one's business forever.[48] At the time, Coen was facing severe competition from Corfu-based workshops but also from Trieste. Losing the market of Scutari would have been detrimental to his business. Threatening a member of the network with public shaming was tantamount to starting a lawsuit, since in a court case the outcome of each hearing was brought before the public upon resolution.

If a resolution through letters failed, consuls residing in the city functioned as intermediaries. Coen advised Saraci that he should seek a resolution through a letter of complaint to the Ottoman consul, while he had already sent a letter of protest to the Greek consulate in Scutari "because the comportment of the medical clerk is against the Greek-Turkish trade treaty and commercial law."[49] Coen had also dispatched a letter of protest to the Turkish embassy as well as to the Greek Ministry of Foreign Affairs, which, he hoped, would talk to the Turkish government in Constantinople.[50] Coen asked Saraci to send a petition, too. These protests to institutions had been successful in the past, as Coen recalls in one of his letters; he had protested to the Greek customs office as he ordered baryte (an ingredient for the production of soap) from Marseille. When this product was tied up in the customs office, Coen successfully protested and was able to reduce the amount he was charged. Although we do not know the outcome of the official complaint to the consuls, the conflict continued for several weeks via letters. It turned out that the losses Coen would incur were substantial and could lead to his ruin: "I have lost my work, and I have to pay for expenses every day for the workshop while I do not have sufficient money to pay the workers, and other materials—the workshop is lying dead!" writes Coen, acknowledging the importance of the market of Scutari for the export of his soap.[51]

As no solution to the problems caused by the Ottoman customs inspection could be found through the intervention of the consul, another way to maintain old trading relations was to circumnavigate those ports that created the most problems for the entry of the merchandise. Montenegro had been independent since 1878 and had pursued an active policy that encouraged shipments through its ports Bar/Antivari and Dulcigno/Ulcinj, which had already served as ports of entry to the Balkan hinterland when still under Ottoman administration. As Blumi has shown, salt merchants consistently diverted their goods from Ottoman ports and customs to ship the merchandise via the Montenegrin ports.[52] Scutarite merchants exchanged information about which Ottoman ports pursued a less rigid interpretation of the new trade treaties, although in theory, of course, these treaties were identical for all of the Ottoman territories. Coen asked Saraci whether "Scutari applies any special laws that are not applied elsewhere"[53] and whether the soap could be sent "anywhere else," preferably to Durazzo, which was located south of Scutari, implying that the inspection in this southern Ottoman-Albanian port was less rigid.[54] The fear of arbitrary medical inspection of the soap or any other restrictions that might impact the merchandise made it preferable for Coen to send his merchandise many miles south of San Giovanni di Medua, increasing the overland distance that the soap had to travel to reach Scutari. Eventually, after both sides had incurred enormous losses, Coen shipped the soap to Montenegro, from where it was allowed to enter. For Coen and Saraci, the diversion of the goods from the Ottoman ports allowed them to maintain their trade relations.

There were also instances that suggest merchandise was imported illegally, bypassing customs altogether. Saraci repeatedly asked Coen to lower his prices for soap when competitors undercut him. Coen responded, "I cannot understand how others do it; I am restrained as my profits are already very limited with this order. Those who cede [the soap] at the cost price and even less, and I cannot imagine anything else than that they *perhaps introduce the soap as contraband without paying customs!*"[55] Coen added that he refused to go down this road: "and if this is what they do, I do not and will not do it!"[56] The bypassing of the Ottoman customs or the smuggling of the products were effective to avoid both taxation and the arbitrary inspection of the soap.

Coen's soap was eventually imported via Montenegro, but losses had been substantial, and no agreement could be reached concerning who should shoulder the additional cost of the transport. As Coen refused to pay for any of the losses incurred, Saraci moved to his last resort, which was to threaten to sue Coen in court. It appears that this was indeed an exceptional event; Coen writes that "we have been in business together for over 40 years and never, ever has someone threatened me with court! Moreover, I never did anything wrong to anyone!"[57] It also becomes apparent that this was really the last resort for a business relationship, as Coen writes that "your letter caused me great pain, but as one who has a pure conscience of not having done anything bad, I certainly will not fear anything in any court of the world!"[58] More than anything, Coen saw his relationship—based on trust—threatened. "I am displeased to see such a step from a person that I have always cherished for many years and still cherish, and I have always tried to satisfy! It is not my fault that if by higher force things turned out that way!"[59] While the letters were very clear in their tone, there was always an attempt to keep the moods calm: "I know you must be upset, but you should not vent against me, because it is not my fault that the Turkish government wanted to hinder the import of soap in general!!"[60]

Eventually, Saraci proposed that this case be brought before a committee of two arbitrators. Arbitration was also a common practice in the court of Corfu; it was often the preferred mode of conflict settlement as its resolutions would not be made public. Thus it provided a means to settle a conflict without the publicity that would come with a court verdict. These arbitrators, however, were not to solve the question of who was to be responsible for the money that Saraci claimed to have paid for the extra shipping and deposit fees; rather, their task was to determine whether the soap had been faulty in the first place. Upon receipt of the merchandise in Montenegro, Saraci complained that the soap "turned out not to be genuine." Coen argued that he sold "soap of prime quality."[61] For that reason, Coen refused to give in to Saraci's accusation; for him, it was "this malicious *circolare* [the new trade rules that were issued]"[62] that made him lose a significant amount of money. Moreover, although parts of the merchandise had been shipped to Montenegro, other boxes of soap that were destined for other merchants in Scutari were still tied up in customs, blocking much of Coen's trade.

Six months later, Coen wrote that his business was on the verge of bankruptcy because of the huge losses from the embargoed merchandise. The continued difficulties impeding trade relations with the Ottoman Empire destroyed the exports to his most important market. While one of his sons had been employed as a coworker in the workshop, he had since left Marseille to look for work as a commission agent. Desperate because of the conditions of trade, Coen wrote that "as soon as the new trade treaty between Turkey and Greece is signed, I promise that when our relations in soap recommence, I will do everything possible to recuperate your losses."[63] However, this was not about to happen. Trade in soap was increasingly susceptible to arbitrary regulations. Coen's soap production continued to decline, and trade relations with the Albanian coast slowly came to an end. Increasingly, Ottoman ports such as Agia Saranda or Valona were becoming restrictive. Moreover, competition from the soap merchant Patounis in Corfu and other soap factories that opened up around the Adriatic in cities such as Trieste and Scutari made trade for Coen difficult.

As trade in Corfu dwindled, new centers of opportunity were explored, building on old networks of trust. The close-knit trade relationship that had developed over the previous forty years was used to forge new ones beyond the Adriatic. Letters of recommendation sent from Coen's sons to Scutari functioned as trust-invoking mechanisms by which new trade routes opened up. Coen's son Armando turned his focus to commission agency. His letter of introduction, which he sent both in French and Greek, read, "Armand Coen, trading house, which will be responsible for exporting and importing. I will also take care of commissions and propose to execute orders of purchase and sale in the commission of any goods. I hope you will come to honor me with your confidence."[64] The efforts were successful, and Saraci wrote back that "if [Armando Coen] makes a good price for the residue of olives [*ossia d'olive*], I will deliberately deal with him. I very much enjoy having business with a person whom you know."[65] The fact that Saraci was importing *ossia d'olive* suggests that by 1897 soap was also produced in Scutari;[66] Saraci was now only importing the bulk materials.[67] Thus, this was not only a geographic reorientation but a transition from manufacturing and single commodity marketing to a diversification of trade.

Abram Coen's son Marc, the father of the writer Albert Cohen whom we encountered at the beginning of this chapter, moved west, to the port of Marseilles. Even from there, the relations with Scutari would continue by diversifying his trade to other commodities, such as flour. It appears that Marc Coen did not pursue the practice of his father but rather acted as commission agent together with Ben Battino, who was also of Corfiote Jewish origin and had settled in Marseilles.[68] Apart from soap, Battino also sent flour (*formentone*) to the Albanian market.

Another brother, Isacco, moved to Alexandria, Egypt, which already harbored a small Corfiote Jewish community. Isacco Coen, too, tapped into the connections his father had forged, telling him that "it is very likely that I will move to Alexandria to work in this market."[69] Just months before the outbreak of the Great War, when the Balkan Wars shook the region, Isacco wrote again to Ciobba informing him that the business in Corfu would close and asking for help in collecting the remaining debts from their customers. The Balkan Wars, which started in 1912, made trade in the region increasingly unfruitful if not impossible. Isacco had personally traveled to Scutari a few months earlier to collect outstanding payments, but he still missed replies from various creditors. "So can you give me any advice on how to cash these credits, even if it involves sacrificing some of the sums? Are you sure that the company of Mr. Tepeli is still functioning well?"⁷⁰ In 1914, Isacco Coen wrote to his business partners in the now Albanian city of Scutari: "As I have written to you before, the company of my father Abram M. Coen is going bankrupt. . . , and we ask you for help in collecting money from our debtors in your market."⁷¹ Already before the outbreak of the Great War, the Balkan Wars were leading to a breakup of trade relations in this region, and the Coen family used all channels to recuperate outstanding debts.

Not much is known about how the Coen family continued business in the Mediterranean from different ports. Their archive in Albania closes in June 1914, just months before the outbreak of the war, which essentially put a stop to the regional trade inside the Adriatic. In light of the political reshuffling of borders, this regional trade connecting empires and nation-states was unable to transform into a cross-national trade. By 1914, the waters between the Ionian Islands and the Albanian-Montenegrin coast had turned from a connected microregion into one where competing alliances clashed. While the Austrian navy declared naval blockages around the Montenegrin coast, Montenegro itself was an ally of France. France, together with Italy and Britain, closed off Trieste, Istria, and the Dalmatian coast.⁷² The French also used the Ionian Islands as a naval base. The Gulf of Cattaro, just north of Scutari, was one of the most important naval bases for the Austrians inside the Adriatic. Any ship that sought entry into the Montenegrin ports had to fear the Austrian naval powers just miles north.⁷³ World War I thus marked the end of the economic relations that had persisted in this area over the previous fifty years.

As more and more Jews sought lives outside the Adriatic, the interconnected Adriatic region shrank—and the Corfiote diaspora grew more dispersed. When Albert Cohen and his family abandoned Corfu for Marseilles, the island he left behind still formed part of an interconnected region uniting the Ionian Sea with the Adriatic. Fifty years later, when he published his memoirs, the seas his grandfathers crossed easily were now divided by the iron curtain.

Looking at short-distance trade in the Adriatic shows that the concept of microregion is a useful geographical unit when looking at the nineteenth century, no less than in the premodern period. The nineteenth-century Adriatic was not only a commercial space for foreign or imperial powers but equally defined by local, short-distance networks. Short-distance trading networks remained part and parcel of the nineteenth-century Adriatic trade. While the Austrian Lloyd was strong in long-distance trade through steam shipping, small-scale networks continued to link microregions that were not accessible through the Lloyd. Understanding trade connections between empires and nation-states through the study of short-distance trade shows the continuation of trading patterns that have been primarily studied in medieval and early modern contexts. Means of transportation usually associated with early modern shipping were still instrumental in the expansion and reconfiguration of trade in the nineteenth-century Adriatic. The territories that had once been connected to a wider Venetian-dominated space along the Adriatic coast and that had become part of different national, imperial, or colonial administrations after the fall of Venice continued to be connected through short-distance trading networks.

Equally, the periodization of early modern and modern ways of conflict resolution appears more fluid when looking at how conflict was arbitrated. The example of the soap trade makes it clear that letters were crucial for the arbitration of conflicts beyond political borders, fulfilling a role that is commonly ascribed to commercial institutions (such as mercantile courts). A tight and intimate trade relationship developed that tried to solve trade disputes through merchant correspondence. Only when conflicts could not be resolved in writing did official institutions become involved. The interplay of personal and institutional ways of conflict resolution in the nineteenth century complicates a teleological perspective that focuses on the gradual use of institutions as legal intermediary.

Finally, as borders in this microregion became increasingly impenetrable, merchants tried to divert their trade to alternative ports, hoping for more lenient laws for their merchandise. Especially the ports of the new nation-state Montenegro proved more attractive than the Ottoman ports farther south for the import of the soap. Only the Balkan Wars and the subsequent Great War made trade in this region impossible. Naval blockades and competing trade interests brought this small-scale trading network to its demise.

Looking at the actual functioning and day-to-day workings of the cross-border and cross-religious soap trade shows that religious ties did not play a role in how this particular network functioned. Rather, the post-Venetian heritage and the continued importance of Italian as the language of the market both in Corfu and northern Albania set the background against which trade flourished. The short-distance trade and the close cooperation with captains provided the backbone against which long-lasting trade partnerships were formed. The involvement of Corfiote Jews not only compels us to rethink the triumphal historiography of the nineteenth century as the century of the Greek Orthodox and Greek-speaking merchant marine but also shows that short-distance cross-ethnic ties continued to be of importance. Jews, but not "Jewishness," were crucial.

CONSTANZE KOLBE is a visiting scholar at the Henry M. Jackson School of International Studies at the University of Washington, Seattle, and recipient of the Ephraim Urbach Postdoctoral Fellowship by the Memorial Foundation for Jewish Culture. She was the 2017/18 Hazel Cole Postdoctoral Fellow at the University of Washington, Seattle. She defended her dissertation "Crossing Regions, Nations, Empires. The Jews of Corfu and the Making of a Jewish Adriatic, 1797–1914" in 2017 at Indiana University, Bloomington, and is currently revising her book manuscript and working on an article on the Adriatic etrog trade during the nineteenth century.

Notes

1. Albert Cohen, *Solal* (Paris: Gallimard, 1930). All translations are my own.
2. Albert Cohen, *Le livre de ma mère* (Paris: Gallimard, 1954).
3. Located in the Albanian State Archives in Tirana, hereafter ASAT. The incoming and outgoing trade letters between the merchants Saraci and Ciobba Bianki in Scutari and Coen in Corfu are preserved, covering a period from ca. 1860 until 1915. The entire correspondence (also with other cities in the Adriatic and beyond) covers tens of thousands of pages and I am only focusing on the communication between Corfu and Scutari, which spans roughly 2,300 individual letters covering the years from 1860 to 1915. For Corfu, Coen was the only permanent trade partner. The correspondence has not attracted any thorough research thus far. The following works draw on small parts of the collection: Adrian Papajani, *Veprimtaria Ekonomike E Firmave Tregtare Shkodrane Cioba Dhe Bianki (1795–1912): Monografi* (Tirana, Albania: Pegi, 1998). Blumi draws on parts of the correspondence for his comparative work on Yemen and Albania; see Isa Blumi, "Adding New Scales of History to the Eastern Mediterranean: Illicit Trade and the Albanian," in *Cities of the Mediterranean: From the Ottomans to the Present Day*, ed. Biray Kolluoğlu and Meltem Toksöz (London: Tauris, 2010), 116–229; Isa Blumi, "Thwarting the Ottoman Empire: Smuggling through the Empire's New Frontiers in Yemen and Albania, 1878–1910," *International Journal of Turkish Studies* 9, nos. 1, 2 (2003): 251–70.
4. Letter from Abram Coen to Saraci, May 20, 1885, V.10.1, Trade Archive of Saraci, ASAT.
5. Both the Italian and the Albanian terms are used in the correspondence.
6. For the early modern Mediterranean, the literature on trade is vast. See for example Francesca Trivellato, *The Familiarity of Strangers: The Sephardic Diaspora, Livorno, and Cross-Cultural Trade in the Early Modern Period* (New Haven, CT: Yale University Press, 2009); E. Natalie Rothman, *Brokering Empire: Trans-Imperial Subjects between Venice and Istanbul* (Ithaca, NY: Cornell University Press, 2011). Horden and Purcell make the same observation with regards to trade in antiquity and medieval trade networks. Comparing the ancient and medieval economies, they argue that past scholarship advanced from a false division between the ancient and medieval economies. While in the ancient Mediterranean people were engaged "in self-supporting agriculture," the medieval economy was characterized by "high commerce," creating the misleading idea of a "progressivist point of view" with a "whiggish teleoscopic intent." Peregrine Horden and Nicholas Purcell, *The Corrupting Sea: A Study of Mediterranean History* (Oxford: Blackwell, 2000), 140–46.
7. In particular, the Adriatic region of the nineteenth century thus far has been mainly analyzed from the perspective of the internal market, ignoring trans-imperial, national, and imperial trade connections. This holds true generally for the nineteenth-century

Mediterranean, though some notable exceptions are Julia Clancy-Smith, *Mediterraneans: North Africa and Europe in an Age of Migration, c. 1800–1900* (Berkeley: California University Press, 2011); Julia Clancy-Smith, "Making a Living in Pre-Colonial Tunisia: The Sea, Contraband and Other Illicit Activities, c. 1830–81," *European Review of History: Revue européenne d'histoire* 19, no. 1 (2012): 93–112. For work on the Ionian Islands see Panayiotis Kapetanakis, "The Ionian State in the 'British' Nineteenth Century, 1814–1864: From Adriatic Isolation to Atlantic Integration," *International Journal for Maritime History*, v. 22, no. 1 (2010): 163–84; Panayiotis Kapetanakis, *Nautilia Kai Emporio Hypo Vretanikē Prostasia: Ionio Kratos (1815–1864)*, Tomeas Neoellēnikōn Ereunōn (Series) (Athens: Ethniko Hidryma Ereunōn, Institouto Historikōn Ereunōn, 2015); Athanasios Gekas, *Xenocracy: State, Class, and Colonialism in the Ionian Islands, 1815–1864* (New York: Berghahn, 2017). For the history of the Greek merchant marine see Gelina Harlaftis, *A History of Greek-Owned Shipping: The Making of an International Tramp Fleet, 1830 to the Present Day* (London: Routledge, 1996). For the Habsburg Empire see Ronald Coons, *Steamships, Statesmen, and Bureaucrats: Austrian Policy towards the Steam Navigation Company of the Austrian Lloyd, 1836–1848* (Wiesbaden, Germany: Steiner, 1975).

8. Recent works on Indian Ocean networks stress the continuation of non-Western networks and maritime linkages despite the arrival of competing colonial networks and argue for a continuation of small-scale shipping networks. See Pedro Machado, *Ocean of Trade: South Asian Merchants, Africa and the Indian Ocean, c. 1750–1850* (Cambridge: Cambridge University Press, 2014).

9. Amalia D. Kessler, *A Revolution in Commerce: The Parisian Merchant Court and the Rise of Commercial Society in Eighteenth-Century France* (New Haven, CT: Yale University Press, 2007); Claire Lemercier, "How Do Businesspeople Like Their Courts? Evidence from Mid-19th Century France, England, and New York City," *Joint Michigan Legal History Workshop/Law & Economics Workshop* (2015). See also Timur Kuran, *The Long Divergence: How Islamic Law Held Back the Middle East* (Oxford: Oxford University Press, 2011), for a Middle Eastern perspective.

10. Very few secondary references are available for this; see for example Peter Bartl, "Le picciole Indie dei Veneziani. Zur Stellung Albaniens in den Handelsbeziehungen zwischen der Balkan- und der Appeninenhalbinsel," in *Münchner Zeitschrift für Balkankunde* 4 (1981–1982): 1–10, at 8–9.

11. Stavri Naci, "Le Pachalik de Shkoder considéré dans son développement économique et social au xviii s.," *Studia Albanica* 3, no. 1 (1966): 123–44; "Le facteur albanais dans le commerce balkanique au xviii siècle," *Studia Albanica* 7, no. 2 (1970): 37–42, at 40. Already in 1736, the vice consul of Venice at Scutari, Anton Duoda, wrote that there were at least a thousand shops present in Scutari. Three years later, Venetian geographers indicated that Scutari was a "great city, the main city of Albania."

12. Adrian Papajani, *Veprimtaria Ekonomike E Firmave Tregtare Shkodrane Cioba Dhe Bianki (1795–1912)* (Tirana, Albania: Pegi, 1998).

13. Athanasios Gekas, "The Merchants of the Ionian Islands between East and West: Forming International and Local Networks," in *Spinning the Commercial Web: International Trade, Merchants and Commercial Cities, 1640–1939*, ed. Margrit Schulte Beerbühl and Jörg Vögele (New York: Peter Lang, 2004), 43–63.

14. P. Mackridge, "Venise après Venise: Official Languages in the Ionian Islands, 1797–1864," *Byzantine and Modern Greek Studies* 38, no. 1 (2014): 69–90.

15. Mario Marzari, *Trabaccoli E Pieleghi Nella Marineria Tradizionale Dell'adriatico* (Milan: Mursia, 2008).

16. Stavri Naci, "Le Pachalik de Shkoder considéré dans son développement économique et social au xviii s.," *Studia Albanica* 7, no. 2 (1970): 37–42; Bartl, "Le Picciole Indie Dei Veneziani," 8–9.

17. Traian Stoianovich, "The Conquering Balkan Orthodox Merchant," *The Journal of Economic History* 20, no. 2 (1960): 234–313, at 275.

18. *Nachrichten über Industrie, Handel und Verkehr aus dem Statistischen Departement im k. k. Handels-Ministerium* 1 (1873): 53.

19. Ibid.

20. Ibid., 41.

21. Aggelos Skintzopoulos, *Handbook of Soapmaking (Eghiridion Sapwnopoieias)* (Greece: S. K. Vlastos, 1889), 40.

22. I was not able to do any research in the southern Italian archives to explore the west-east trade across the Adriatic further. As for the olive oil trade, Gekas is only concerned with its export from the Ionian Islands, and he states that the Jews were dominant in the olive oil trade. Gekas, *Xenocracy*, 133–35.

23. Skintzopoulos, *Handbook of Soapmaking (Eghiridion Sapwnopoieias)*, 67–70.

24. Ibid.

25. *Nachrichten über Industrie, Handel und Verkehr aus dem Statistischen Departement im K. K. Handels-Ministerium* 1 (1873): 53.

26. Letter from Abram Coen to Saraci, July 8, 1890, V. 10, Trade Archive of Saraci, ASAT.

27. Letter from Ciobba to Captain Begiri, October 22, 1895, V. 10, Trade Archive of Ciobba, ASAT.

28. Letter from Coen to Ciobba, March 12, 1896, V. 295, p. 37, Trade Archive of Ciobba, ASAT.

29. Letter from Coen to Ciobba, September 6, 1897, V. 306, p. 11, Trade Archive of Ciobba, ASAT.

30. Letter from Coen to Ciobba, February 22, 1890, V. 331, p. 2, Trade Archive of Ciobba, ASAT.

31. Letter from Coen to Ciobba, February 22, 1900, V. 382, p. 2, Trade Archive of Ciobba, ASAT. Emphasis mine.

32. Trivellato, *The Familiarity of Strangers*, 181.

33. Letter from Coen to Ciobba, February 28, 1890, V. 242, p. 14, ASAT. Emphasis added.

34. Letter from Coen to Saraci, September 7, 1898, V. 10, p. 18, Trade Archive of Saraci, ASAT.

35. Letter from Saraci to Coen, December 21, 1896, V. 06, p. 360, Trade Archive of Saraci, ASAT.

36. Letter from Coen to Saraci, February 21, 1898, V. 10, p. 258, Trade Archive of Saraci, ASAT.

37. Mafalda Ade, *Picknick mit den Paschas: Aleppo und die levantinische Handelsfirma Fratelli Poche (1853–1880)* (Würzburg, Germany: Ergon, 2013), 170–202.

38. For a more detailed analysis of the workings of the merchant court in Corfu see Constanze Kolbe, "Crossing Regions, Nations, Empires. The Jews of Corfu and the Making of a Jewish Adriatic, 1850–1914" (unpublished PhD diss., Indiana University, 2017).

39. Lemercier, "How Do Businesspeople Like Their Courts?," 4. For an excellent study on the functioning of a merchant court in eighteenth-century France, see Kessler, *A Revolution in Commerce*.

40. The records of the Corfu merchant court (Emporodikeion) date from the time period of the British administration of the islands (1815–1864). As they predate the time of the mercantile archive, no court records that refer to Coen and his trade partners were included.

41. Letter from Coen to Saraci, March 16, 1898, V. 10, p. 259, Trade Archive of Saraci, ASAT.

42. Ibid.

43. The boycott of Greek merchandise as a result of the Cretan question has been studied extensively by Y. Cetinkaya, *The Young Turks and the Boycott Movement: Nationalism, Protest and the Working Classes in the Formation of Modern Turkey* (London: Tauris, 2014), 90.

44. Letter from Coen to Saraci, May 2, 1900, V. 339, p. 381, Trade Archive of Saraci, ASAT.

45. Ibid.

46. Skintzopoulos, *Handbook of Soapmaking (Eghiridion Sapwnopoieias)*, 171.

47. Letter from Ciobba to Coen, February 14, 1898, V. 309, p. 220, ASAT.

48. Ade, *Picknick mit den Paschas*, 147–70.

49. Letter from Coen to Saraci, April 6, 1900, V. 10, p. 373, Trade Archive of Saraci, ASAT.

50. Ibid.

51. Letter from Coen to Ciobba, May 2, 1900, V. 10, p. 373, Trade Archive of Ciobba, ASAT.

52. Blumi, "Thwarting the Ottoman Empire," 259. Blumi claims that "Montenegrins consistently undertaxed goods to attract trade away from Ottoman ports, and Albanian merchants shifted the flow of capital away from Ottoman coffers and denied the empire cash needed to pay back European banks."

53. Letter from Coen to Saraci, May 30, 1900, V. 10.1, p. 385, Trade Archive of Saraci, ASAT; Letter from Coen to Saraci, April 4, 1900, V. 10, p. 375, Trade Archive of Saraci, ASAT.

54. Letter from Coen to Saraci, April 13, 1900, V. 10, p. 375, Trade Archive of Saraci, ASAT.

55. Letter from Saraci to Coen, September 18, 1904, V. 8, p. 287, Trade Archive of Saraci, ASAT. Emphasis in the original.

56. Ibid.

57. Letter from Coen to Saraci, May 30, 1900, V. 10.1, p. 385, Trade Archive of Saraci, ASAT.

58. Ibid.

59. Ibid.

60. Ibid.

61. Letter from Coen to Saraci, June 13, 1900, V. 10.1, p. 387, Trade Archive of Saraci, ASAT.

62. Ibid.

63. Letter from Coen to Saraci, July 12, 1900, V. 10.1, p. 390, Trade Archive of Saraci, ASAT.

64. Letter from Coen to Saraci, December 13, 1897, V. 10, p. 241, Trade Archive of Saraci, ASAT; Letter from Coen to Saraci, December 14, 1897, V. 10, p.242, Trade Archive of Saraci, ASAT.

65. Letter from Saraci to Coen, December 27, 1897, V. 6, p. 485, Trade Archive of Saraci, ASAT.

66. Letter from Saraci to Ben Battino in Marseilles, September 22, 1901, V. 7, p. 273, Trade Archive of Saraci, ASAT.

67. In fact, there is mention several times of this factory in the materials. Letter from Saraci to Ben Battino in Marseilles, September 22, 1901, V. 7, p. 273, Trade Archive of Saraci, ASAT; Letter from Saraci to Coen, January 1, 1903, V. 8, p. 192, Trade Archive of Saraci, ASAT; Letter from Saraci to Coen, March 22, 1904, V. 8, p. 238, Trade Archive of Saraci, ASAT.

68. Letter from Ben Battino, Marseilles to Saraci, June 1, 1901, V. 10.3, p. 27, Trade Archive of Ciobba, ASAT.
69. Letter from Coen to Ciobba, February 1, 1914, V. 745, p. 33, Trade Archive of Ciobba, ASAT.
70. Letter from Coen to Ciobba, June 9, 1914, V. 745, p. 34, Trade Archive of Ciobba, ASAT.
71. Ibid.
72. Charles Koburger, *The Central Powers in the Adriatic, 1914–1918: War in a Narrow Sea* (Westport, CT: Praeger, 2001), 28.
73. Paul Halpern, *The Battle of the Otranto Straits: Controlling the Gateway to the Adriatic in World War I* (Bloomington: Indiana University Press, 2004), 4–7.

8

A GUIDE TO THE JEWISH MEDITERRANEAN

Le Guide Sam *and the Shaping of an Interwar Mediterranean Diaspora*

Devi Mays

IN 1921, SAM LÉVY, ERSTWHILE EDITOR OF THE Salonica-based *Le Journal de Salonique* and *La Epoka* periodicals (appearing in French and Ladino, respectively), who was now residing in Paris, began to publish the predominately French-language *Le Guide Sam*, an annual commercial guide to "the Orient." He would continue to publish this guide until its final volume in 1930. Although drawing on a long tradition of commercial and tourist guides to Ottoman and other lands of the Mediterranean littoral geared toward western European and American importers, exporters, and tourists, Lévy's guides were notably different in scope and target.[1] Like other such commercial manuals, *Le Guide Sam* offered explanations of the different religious calendric systems of the Mediterranean, contact information for foreign consulates and banks, brief discussions of economic conditions and tourist attractions in each country, and page after page of contact information for merchants classified by country, city, and specialty. However, unlike other such publications, which focused on particular Mediterranean port cities and the surrounding hinterlands from which they drew, Lévy's guides were wider in geographical scope, articulated in the language of linking the "exporting countries" of France, Italy, and England with the "importing countries" of what he referred to alternatively as the "Mediterranean countries," "the Orient," or "the Near East."[2] But while geographically expansive, the volumes of *Le Guide Sam* were circumscribed in one notable regard: the vast majority of the merchants, brokers, and traders who contributed advertisements or were listed in the thousand pages of each edition were Jews of predominantly Ottoman and North African provenance now residing in both the "importing" and "exporting" countries. In spite of its purported purpose as a guide to the Mediterranean as a whole, it was, in content, a guide to a Jewish commercial Mediterranean, one in which non-Jews, though existing, had a peripheral role.

This chapter uses sections of the 1924, 1929, and 1930 editions of *Le Guide Sam* and its successor *Le Livre d'Or de l'Orient* to argue that Lévy's guides put forward the aspiration of a broadly Jewish—and indeed Sephardic—yet avowedly diasporic world centered around the Middle Sea.[3] This was a world whose contours were demarcated by commerce, family connections, and a shared interest in the social, political, and economic place of Jews in the quickly transforming interwar reality. This interwar period was marked by intensive processes of nation-state formation in the post-Ottoman Balkans and Anatolia, mandates and colonial projects in the Levant and North Africa, and more generally by increasing restrictions on mobility and trade. Such restrictions existed in simultaneous tension with what Michael Herzfeld has characterized as "the shrinking sea," when new technologies of communication and transportation ostensibly facilitated the hypermobility of people and goods throughout the Mediterranean and beyond.[4] Lévy's guides contended with the challenges of mobility, nationalizing processes, and trade restrictions. In doing so, they provided one means by which Jews of the Mediterranean littoral could maintain networks of individuals and communities in communication and constant interaction, crucial to the perpetuation of a cohesive diaspora.[5]

Fernand Braudel's 1949 magnum opus asserted a "common destiny" between what he identified as the "Turkish" and "Christian" Mediterranean in the early modern period. It was this shared fate, in part, that justified the Mediterranean as an analytical category. Many historians, building on Braudel, have posited that both the utility of the Mediterranean as a framework and the region's common destiny cease in the modern period. They point to an array of causes for Mediterranean decline: the northern invasion, the economic peripheralization of parts of the Mediterranean as a result of the development of a global economic system, or the fragmentation and power differentials resulting from colonial incursions and the rise of nationalizing states.[6] Those whose work on the modern period bears the mantle of Mediterranean studies tend to either examine an individual region or link together two or three cities or states—often across a north-south axis—as a synecdoche for the region as a whole.[7] Iain Chambers has called for scholars of the Mediterranean to think along "oblique axes" in order to "deepen and disturb" inherited cultural and historical mappings.[8] In a similar vein, Manuel Borutta and Sakis Gekas point to the utility of focusing on hybrid subjects, migration flows, peripheries, and cosmopolitan places in order to acquire a more polycentric view of Mediterranean power structures.[9] *Le Guide Sam* emphasized commercial and cultural concerns and relationships shared across much of the Mediterranean littoral. Those interests highlighted in the guides were cultivated in large part by Jews, like Lévy himself, who bore a varied legacy of imperial and national ties and whose lives and livelihoods were profoundly shaped by ongoing transnational connections. As such, Lévy's guides prompt us to disrupt our historiographical and historical preconceptions by taking seriously the Mediterranean as an analytical whole in the interwar period, to think *with* the Mediterranean in order to discover what new understandings of interwar Jewish experiences such an approach might yield.

Indeed, the cover image of *Le Guide Sam*'s 1924 edition disturbs the literal mapping of the Mediterranean in a number of ways. It shifts the axes of the familiar borders of the sea so that the Strait of Gibraltar rather than Europe is at the top of the page, includes Great Britain squashed into the top right corner, and gestures toward but does not strictly adhere to geographically accurate state borders. This image—simultaneously familiar and jarring—alludes to the ways in which the guides' vision points to the continuity of a shared destiny linking the shores of the Mediterranean as a whole. This was a common destiny because of the continued circulation of (Jewish) individuals and goods that contended with disparate legal, national, colonial, and economic regimes, embedded within hierarchies of power whose discursive structures Lévy and other contributors to *Le Guide Sam* at times adopted and at times rejected. The Mediterranean was the *omphalos* around which the economic and social worlds of *Le Guide Sam* revolved, but these worlds were not always bounded by the shores of the sea. In this way, the guides captured a new diasporic Sephardic reality spread from the southern and eastern Mediterranean to western Europe and beyond. Indeed, the underlying Jewishness of *Le Guide Sam* prompts us to rethink prevalent scholarly approaches to the modern Mediterranean, which often emphasize the cosmopolitanism or interreligious nature of the region.[10] Although non-Jewish merchants and writers contributed to or were featured in the guide, they existed within a framework that was overwhelmingly Jewish, one that lends itself to an inaccurate perception of commerce in the modern Mediterranean as being overwhelmingly Jewish. Here, Jews functioned as commercial connectors between different regions of the Mediterranean but largely not as cultural intermediaries, or at least not with non-Jewish spheres. *Le Guide Sam* provides a compelling example of a historical source from the interwar years that takes the regional cohesiveness of the Mediterranean seriously and

GS ANNUAIRE DE L'ORIENT

LE GUIDE *Sam*

MAROC · ALGÉRIE · TUNISIE · ÉGYPTE · PALESTINE · SYRIE · G.DE BRETAGNE · ESPAGNE · FRANCE · ITALIE · GRÈCE · BULGARIE · TURQUIE

1, Rue Frédéric Clément, GARCHES (S.&O.)

TOUS DROITS RÉSERVÉS

yet largely restricts the Mediterranean to a single religious group, through content if not through design.

* * *

Sam Lévy (Samuel Saadi Halevy), the eponymous editor of Le Guide Sam, was a colorful individual whose life was shaped by the profound transformations that shook Ottoman and post-Ottoman Jewry. His father, Bezalel Saadi Halevy, the founder of the Salonica-based periodicals La Epoka and Le Journal de Salonique, earned the ire of the Salonican rabbinical establishment through his efforts to use the press not only to keep readers abreast of the latest news but also to "enlighten the readers' minds by providing them with more progressive ideas."[11] Like many of his peers, Lévy, born in Salonica in 1870, was educated in a French-language school of the Alliance Israélite Universelle, and later, more rare among Ottoman Jews, in the Imperial Turkish Lycée. Following his father's retirement in 1898, Lévy took the helm of his periodicals. In June 1912, just prior to the outbreak of the Balkan Wars that would mark the end of Ottoman Salonica, Lévy relocated to Belgrade, followed by Switzerland, then France, where he died in 1959.[12] Throughout his life, he maintained an active interest in educating the Sephardic masses. He vociferously defended Ladino, even as he published widely in French, as an aspiring European intellectual.[13]

Le Guide Sam should be understood, in part, as a product of Lévy's background in Ladino publications. Just as Ladino periodicals, including those Lévy inherited from his father, sought to shape their readers' worldviews with a moralizing undertone buried within the narrative, so too did Lévy use Le Guide Sam to shape an interwar Mediterranean world.[14] Through contributions ranging from discussions of Jewish race and Zionism to the value of Ladino and astrology, advertisements from Jewish firms that ran the gamut of Mediterranean languages, illustrations capturing the most salient features of the various countries of the Mediterranean littoral, and page after page of mostly Jewish brokers, traders, importers, and exporters from the countries featured in the guide, Lévy articulated the boundaries of an interwar Jewish diaspora, a world that was centered around the Middle Sea. The extent of both the readership of Le Guide Sam over the course of its publication and the degree to which it was actually used as a commercial guide are unknown, as is the case with many Ladino publications of this period; while the ten editions of the guide that appeared over a decade might suggest that others valued it or found it useful, the scattered extant copies of the volumes undercut such assumptions. However, the vision that Lévy put forward of an informed and commercially connected, largely Jewish world centered around the Mediterranean can be understood in light of its aspirations, as with the Ladino press, to both reflect and shape changes in the Jewish world.[15]

The contents of the guides yield some insight into their target audience. The 1924 edition noted that the previous year's volume had been distributed to a number of notable officials throughout France, as well as its consular agents, and chambers of commerce in France, Turkey, Egypt, Palestine, Syria, Bulgaria, and elsewhere.[16] While the later editions of the guide included a wider variety of content—discussed below—the 1924 edition focused primarily on commercial interests linking countries of the Mediterranean littoral, with articles on French commercial interests in "the Orient," the French press in the Levant, relations between Italy and Turkey, and others.[17] However, the guides also served those from "the Orient" present in France, a point driven home by the pages of advertisements for firms in France operated by individuals whose names implied origins in the southern or eastern Mediterranean. Additionally, articles like that in the 1924 edition on "Foreigners in France," though not explicitly articulated as being of interest for the demographic groups the guide targeted, offered information on acquiring the requisite paperwork for traversing through or residing in France, questions of particular importance for hypermobile Mediterranean Jews.[18] The 1930 edition, in turn, made explicit the connection between the guide's target audience and the necessity of adequate paperwork: a "Notice to Oriental Turkish Subjects" in bold font explained that acquiring certificates of nationality from a Turkish consulate within six months of arrival in a new locale was necessary for Turkish subjects who wanted to retain a passport and that consuls would refuse protection to any Turkish subject lacking such a certificate.[19]

An exchange of letters provides some insight into Lévy's vision of the guide and the process by which submissions were solicited. A large number of readers had "made the very friendly remark" that the guide did not give adequate attention to Great Britain, "which possesses considerable interests in all of the Mediterranean countries," noted the 1930 edition. This edition included a number of pages devoted to Manchester, the only British city covered.[20] In an English-language letter dated from June 29, 1929, Lévy informed the secretary of the Manchester Chamber of Commerce that several weeks earlier, when he had presented himself to the chamber bearing two letters of introduction—one from the British Chamber of Commerce in Cairo and another from one Alphonso Nahum in Manchester, whose name suggests Mediterranean Jewish origins— "the right consideration" was not accorded his requests. Lévy noted that he was the editor of the *Guide Sam*, "a publication extensively known in the Near East" that acted as a "contact medium between two groups of countries, on the one hand producing and exporting countries such as England, France, and Italy, and on the other hand all the buying and importing countries of the Near East." As such, he required a list of "those of your members who are connected to or have an interest in the Near East."²¹ The secretary declined, several days later, to provide any information, noting that "I am not, myself, familiar with your publication, but if it is as you suggest extensively known in the Near East, surely all those Manchester firms who operate in the Near East will know of it and will themselves apply to you for inclusion."²² The guides, then, were perhaps indeed known and read, shared by those with connections and interests in the Near East who clamored for more information about countries with extensive economic interests in the Mediterranean. Nonetheless, it was also entirely possible that they served little functional value and were not widely known beyond the sphere of mostly Jewish advertisers with commercial, and often familial, interests in both the "importing" and "exporting" countries the guides featured.

The guides' contents revealed the slippery boundaries of the geographical region that they unified. The 1924 edition encompassed only countries bordering the Mediterranean, plus Great Britain and Bulgaria, and excluding Albania, Yugoslavia, and Libya. The 1929 edition's cover page explicitly named the countries included: France, Italy, Egypt, Turkey, Greece, Bulgaria, Syria, and Palestine.²³ The 1930 edition had similar inclusions and exclusions to that of the 1924 edition, with the addition of Czechoslovakia at the behest of "Czechoslovak friends established in the Orient" who asserted that "their country possesses vast interests in the Mediterranean countries."²⁴ But the commercial reach of the firms featured in the guides extended far beyond the shores of the Mediterranean, or even Europe. The volumes included advertisements from firms in Rio de Janeiro,²⁵ Mexico City,²⁶ and Antwerp,²⁷ even as Brazil, Mexico, and Belgium were not featured countries in the guides. And additional advertisements alluded to commercial connections in places as dispersed as Japan, China, Amsterdam, Buenos Aires, Berlin, and New York. While the Mediterranean might be the center of the guides' world, branches radiated out across the globe, mirroring the geographical dispersal of Mediterranean Jews and the central role that commerce played in maintaining a cohesive diasporic world.

Although not made explicit in the guides themselves, personal connections to Lévy were clearly at play in inclusion, with Jewish geography weaving into physical geography. This suggests that the familial and extrafamilial Jewish bonds among early modern Jewish merchants that Francesca Bregoli's contribution to this volume explores continued to hold sway in the twentieth century. The firm of Elie Alaluf of Rio de Janeiro, for example, belonged to one of Lévy's relatives who had emigrated to South America some years prior.²⁸ Meanwhile, the Manchester-based firm Ascher Salem and Son in 1924—Ascher Salem and Sons by 1930—also had personal ties to Lévy.²⁹ In a 1930 letter to the secretary of the Manchester Chamber of Commerce, Lévy explained that, though he was leaving the British manufacturing city the next week after a brief visit, communications to him could be directed to Ascher Salem and Sons.[30] The advertisements for this firm varied slightly in wording between the 1924 and 1930 editions, but both clearly marked it as Jewish and as connected to Salonica, featuring the intertwined monogram "S.A.S." inside a Star of David and an etching of Salonica's famous White Tower overlooking the Thermaic Gulf. Personal ties between Lévy and Salem, forged in their city of origin, continued long after one had emigrated to France and the other to England. The guides, in turn, exhibited this connection between these two men, their city of origin, and their Jewishness, all under the guise of facilitating commerce within the Mediterranean and beyond.

* * *

The guides exhibited a tension between the embrace and rejection of stereotypes associated with specific terminology for the Mediterranean in general, and Mediterranean Jews specifically. Herzfeld alerts us to be attentive to discourse on the Mediterranean, arguing that it is by ascribing or self-ascribing "Mediterranean" to a region or group that "the Mediterranean" has analytical value in the modern period. He cautions against the facility with which the "Mediterranean" slides into essentializing notions paralleling orientalism, noting that the designation of "Mediterranean" in a modern context is one embedded within implicit hierarchies of power, in which "the Mediterranean" in a European context is distinguished from Germany, England, and France. Simultaneously, he leaves open the possibility that people in the Mediterranean embrace negative stereotypes as means of asserting their cultural distinctiveness from northern Europeans.[31] Joelle Bahloul, meanwhile, notes that within the modern Jewish context, the designation of "Mediterranean" when applied to Jews often implies presumed inherent traditionalism, entrenched familial and gender hierarchies, and, thereby, the lack of qualities desirable in the context of the Israeli nation-state.[32] The articles in Lévy's guides certainly were shaped by the hierarchies of power, economic disparity, and colonialism so entrenched by the interwar years. However, as discussed below, the guides at times recast seemingly negative ascriptions of the Mediterranean and terms used synonymously in a positive light, seemingly as a means of proudly asserting distinction from non-Mediterranean Jewries.

Throughout the guides, the regions covered were described at times in the binary of "exporting countries"—specifically England, France, and Italy—and "importing countries," which included all other states featured, paralleling Herzfeld's regional distinctions with their implied hierarchies. While at times both regions were united under the common rubric of "Mediterranean" within the guides' articles, more often did the articles focus on the "importing countries," which were alternatively described as the "eastern Mediterranean," "the Orient," or "the Near East," with little discursive distinction between such appellations. The regional demarcations were linked to the divergent economic relationships between those countries of the economic core and peripheral areas they had colonized or semicolonized. Lévy's employment of this terminology marked his clear understanding of economic divisions between regions covered in his guide. Nonetheless, this did not obviate the continued centrality of the Mediterranean littoral in the world that the guides encompassed. Rather, the guides provided a means of contending with and even benefiting from regional economic disparities, linking the predominately Jewish businessmen of Mediterranean origins living in "exporting countries" with those in the "importing countries."

But undergirding the terminology used to describe the regions on which the guides focused were discursive structures that often exhibited an easy slippage into Saidian orientalism. Each guide featured a series of articles, many of which explained the currency, industry, and legal systems of a given country. However, by 1930, the guide also featured articles penned by an array of authors—most, but not all, Jewish of eastern Mediterranean provenance—on topics ranging from excerpts of literature to discussions of the place of Judeo-Spanish within post-Ottoman nationalizing regimes. For example, the preface of the 1930 edition, penned by famed French journalist Pierre Mille, whose acquaintance Lévy first made during the Thessaly campaign of 1897, was a thought-piece on "The Orient" that wholly embraced orientalist tropes.[33] Beginning with the exclamation "The Orient! It is a civilization. A civilization that is not ours," Mille dwelled on the submission of women to men—an orientalist fascination—which he attributed not to Islam but rather to an imagined "East" extending from "Brahmanist" India, to Taoist China, to the Russia of Peter the Great. Yes, Christianity might be of oriental origins, but it was not embraced in the region because the Greeks had modified it in "an anti-oriental sense." This region was, in his estimation, not receptive to Western interference, with one notable exception: nationalism, an ideology adopted from the West.[34] Mille's preface embraced the discursive distinction between "Occident" and "Orient," marking the latter as Other in standard orientalist tropes even as it was the focus of the guides.

Given Mille's preface to the 1930 edition, one might expect the guide's other articles to follow a similarly orientalist tack, and indeed, certain features did. It was not uncommon for Ottoman Jews to embrace orientalist motifs and merchandise, both as a means of presenting themselves to western Europe and the United States in an easily recognizable fashion and of marking their own Ottomanness.[35] While the 1924 edition of the guide offered an image of the Mediterranean on its shifted axis with the name of each country superimposed over it as a marker of transition from one country to the next, the 1930 edition featured individualized images on the cover of certain sections—Egypt, Palestine, Turkey, Greece. In an orientalist collapse of past and present, or rather, a focus on the past to the exclusion of the present, the frontispiece for the Egyptian section gestured to the "Royaume d'Egypte" but featured images of the Sphinx before one of the pyramids at Giza, several other sphinxes, and stylized hieroglyphs.[36] The cover for Greece's section likewise focused on an image from antiquity—the Acropolis—but an image that, less exotic than the Sphinx, marked Greece firmly within the tradition of Western civilization.[37] Turkey's frontispiece, in contrast, bore no photographs or gestures to political complexities as did Palestine's (discussed below) but rather a stylized vegetal motif vaguely reminiscent of Izmit tiles and a misspelling of Turkey's name as "Türkyie."[38] If orientalism subsumed the present within a legible and usable past—the Kingdom of Egypt elided into pharaonic times, Greece through the lens of Pericles's projects—the Republic of Turkey was devoid of such a history. The sections covering the "exporting countries" of Great Britain, Italy, and France bore no pictorial representation; they were irreducible into a single image.

But even as elements of the guides seemed to embrace orientalist discourse and images without critique, other elements subverted this discourse even as they adopted it. That denizens of the southern and eastern Mediterranean were superstitious, fatalist even, was a common trope justifying regional intervention from western Europe. This stereotype, further, was leveled by Jews—particularly French Jews and those connected to the schools of the Alliance Israélite Universelle—as an indication of the need for regeneration among the Jewish populace of the Orient.[39] Indeed, in an article in the 1924 edition of the guide that quoted the 1923 version, Sam Lévy noted that France was the proponent of ideas of progress and civilization and that French expansion should persist in the "countries of the Levant" in order to push the people to innovate.[40]

"To publish a *Livre d'Or de l'Orient* and to neglect the astrology that was born there would have been very nearly absurd," began a section on "What the Stars Say" in the guide's 1930 edition. Lévy interviewed Mme. Albane de Siva, "professor of occult sciences," on what the coming year held for Egypt, Palestine, Turkey, Greece, and Yugoslavia.[41] De Siva's credentials, Lévy reminded his readers, included the successful prediction in 1926 of the violent death of Turkish general Halid Pasha (who, in fact, died in 1925). In his inclusion and embrace of astrology within the guide, Lévy endorsed tropes of superstition levied against the Mediterranean populace, thereby undermining the negative valence of such discourse. But simultaneously, Mme. de Siva's prognostications offered a means of envisioning futures for the post-Ottoman eastern Mediterranean that all contained critiques of nationalism couched within worn tropes that infantilized its populace. Egypt, she predicted, should be wary of the nationalist youth who sought a governmental regime for which autochthonous elements were not sufficiently politically mature.[42] The reforms of the new Turkish state were, she opined, more inexpert than superficial, and Turkey would succeed in moving beyond its barbarous past and joining "true civilization" only once it ceased to view others as inferiors or enemies.[43] Yugoslavia was gangrenous, containing an unspecified infirm member that would need to be amputated for the well-being of the body as a whole, an analogy she broadened for the entire Orient.[44] Greece's horizon, in contrast, was "free of any cloud."[45] It was Palestine, though, that was "the epicenter of the dark region." Quick to distance herself from anti-Semitism by noting that she loved Jews, who were intelligent and studious, she nonetheless explained that the natal chart for the Balfour Declaration was full of teachings that Jews should "reflect upon for a second time before launching themselves into an adventure without result."[46] Mme. de Siva's astrological predictions decried the Zionist endeavor in Palestine as ill-advised given the mythologies of the stars composing the constellation Virgo, under which the Balfour Declaration was born. Within the guide, astrological considerations—certainly a marker of superstition—were embraced as a legitimate basis for a critique of nationalism.

Indeed, if Mille in his preface to the 1930 edition had noted that nationalism was the one ideology from the Occident that was wholeheartedly embraced in the Orient, it was an ideology with which the guide contended but ultimately rejected in favor of a vision that was both Jewish and staunchly diasporic. The 1930 guide included a number of critiques less esoteric than Mme. de Siva's of Jewish resettlement in the Levant. The frontispiece for the guide's section on Palestine included translations of *Le Guide Sam* in both Hebrew (HaMadrikh Shmuel) and Arabic (Dalil Sam), the region denoted as "Palestine" in Latin characters, *Filistin* in Arabic, and *Eretz Yisrael* in Hebrew. Occupying the upper half of the frontispiece was the royal coat of arms of Great Britain, marking the territory as under British control. But most interesting was what the frontispiece did not include—in contrast to the entries for Greece and Egypt, the page for Palestine contained no images of storied historical sites, particularly notable given both the number of recognizable structures within Palestine and the centrality of images of the land and those working it to the Zionist project.[47]

Beyond the guide's reluctance to ascribe an iconic image to its depiction of Palestine, Lévy went far further in his critique of Zionism. Indeed, his anti-Zionist position was not uncommon among the Ottoman Jewish intellectual elite, many of whom had viewed calls to establish a Jewish state within the Ottoman territory of Palestine as unpatriotic and indeed dangerously close to sedition.[48] In the post-Ottoman interwar years, Lévy remained virulently anti-Zionist, noting that "Palestine belongs to the Palestinians, who are composed of Muslims, Christians, and Jews, which the Zionist leaders have never wanted to comprehend nor admit."[49] In his estimation, the "truly culpable" for ongoing antagonism in Palestine were neither the British authorities nor the "autochthonous Hebrews and Arabs, who have always lived in harmony" but rather those at the head of the Zionist movement, who, overtly or tacitly, "have pursued a separatist, exclusivist, imperialist policy" in the mistaken belief that there was an unbridgeable abyss between Jews and non-Jews. He advocated instead for a "radical change of system" in which the Jewish Colonization Association, collaborating loyally with the British government, would transform into a wholly humanitarian organization and admit Muslim and Christian observers.[50]

The 1929 guide included an appeal concerning Zionism, which Lévy addressed in French to the Sephardim of Greece, in which he explained that he was "Salonican like you" and had devoted a large part of his life to safeguarding Judeo-Spanish. Nonetheless, he called on his "dear brothers" to be on guard in resisting the threat that Zionism posed to Hellenic Judaism in trying to deracinate them.[51] Similarly, the 1930 guide contained articles, some penned by Lévy and some unattributed, with titles like "Zionism Is Bankrupt" and "The Zionist Folly."[52] A long article by Lévy on "The Decline of Zionism," written in 1928 and submitted to the *Revue de Paris* for publication, where it languished for months before being rejected, argued—among other things—against the idea of the Jews as a unified race or nation.[53] Instead, Lévy posited the existence of three distinct Jewish peoples. First were the Sephardim, "Palestinian Jews who reached Spain" centuries before and after 1492 made their way to the Ottoman Empire, Holland, Italy, southern France, and in small numbers, to the Crimea. These were "the pure Jews," "the last Latins," phrases that clearly articulated Lévy's sense of Sephardic racial superiority to what he perceived to be other races of Jews, a view that Lévy continued to hold through the Nazi occupation of France.[54] Then there were the Ashkenazim, who were in part descended from the communities installed in central and eastern Europe prior to the Spanish Expulsion. The final group was the Alluvial Jews (*Juifs Alluvionnaires*), who formed part of the Ashkenazim but were the descendants of Khazars and other peoples of the Urals and Caucasus who converted to Judaism. In drawing on the parlance of scientific racism, Lévy explained that in the veins of these Alluvial Jews flowed "Muscovite, Tartar, Kalmyk, Turanian, and even Semitic blood," but that their souls, their mentality, their actions and gestures were all Slavic in the generic sense of the word.[55] One of Zionism's key flaws, Lévy asserted, was the attempt to "mix all these Jews in the same basket."[56] Judaism was a religious confession professed by many, but Jews were not a race. And of the peoples who professed Judaism, it was, in Lévy's estimation, the Sephardim who were the unadulterated descendants of the biblical Israelites, yet Latins rather than Semites.

Articles like these, together with the plethora of advertisements and notifications of predominately Jewish firms, traders, and businessmen from throughout the Mediterranean, helped to cement the guides' vision of a diasporic Jewish world. Although the guides also included information, though few advertisements, from non-Jewish businesses, they were a largely Jewish space. Non-Jews were present in the guide as occasional contributors of articles, the consular personnel or heads of chambers of commerce whose letters of support graced early editions of the guide, or as commercial actors, but it was Jewish contributors who dominated the pages of the guide and the world it fashioned. This Jewish centrality was underscored by the use of Jewish languages and the overt reference to Jewish spaces. The 1924 guide, for example, included an advertisement for Jerusalem-based Abraham Elmaleh's Hebrew-French dictionary, likely to be of interest only to Jews.[57] Likewise, calls to "smoke only the cigarette paper from the Or-Ahaim National Hospital" helped to mark the guide more specifically as largely Sephardic; the Jewish hospital in Istanbul, founded in 1887, raised funds through the sale of cigarette paper.[58] The "nation" the hospital served was one centered in the erstwhile Ottoman capital, composed primarily of former Ottoman subjects and supported in part by émigrés.[59]

Indeed, it was Judeo-Spanish, rather than Hebrew, that garnered the most attention within the guide, thereby revealing its vision as one of focusing on and cohering to a specific type of Sephardic world centered around Ladino-speaking Jews.[60] A French-language short story in the 1930 edition by author A. H. Navon, originally from Edirne but residing in France as the director of the École Orientale, focused on the conflict between the Rosh Yeshiva and a wealthy Jewish notable in an unnamed "city of the Orient," where the story's Ladino epigraph "El dedo que firmó esto que se llague!" ("May the finger that signed this wither!") featured prominently in the narrative itself.[61] Lévy described Navon as "Jewish-Latin in all of his fibers," underscoring the former's conception of Sephardic racial difference.[62]

The same edition featured an article on Judeo-Spanish by Élie Carmona, whom Lévy glossed as a "descendent of one of the most illustrious Spanish Jewish families of Constantinople," and who was, though unmentioned by Lévy, his brother-in-law. Carmona had spent his life teaching and directing institutions of the Alliance Israélite Universelle in Turkey, Syria, Palestine, Morocco, Greece, and Bulgaria. He asserted that Judeo-Spanish, a "veritable fruit salad with no relationship to the beautiful Castilian language," was dead, its *coup de grâce* delivered by the demise of the Ottoman Empire.[63] In his estimation,

Judeo-Spanish had served a useful purpose for Jews of the Orient by enabling them to retain a "certain culture in a *milieu* plunged into the most profound ignorance," facilitated their adaptation to Western civilization, and thereby contributed to their emancipation and prosperity in commercial endeavors.[64] Nonetheless, he opined, today Jews are "Turks in Turkey, Greeks in Greece, and Bulgarians in Bulgaria; their language is no longer Judeo-Spanish but the language of the state in which they are residents and to which they should become faithful citizens conscious of their duties and able to defend their rights."[65] Carmona's focus on the demise of Judeo-Spanish in favor of Jews speaking national languages was one that resonated among a wide swath of the post-Ottoman world, from Turkey's Jewish leadership to the popular "Citizen, Speak Turkish" campaign that began in 1928. Nonetheless, Carmona glossed over the complex series of negotiations over language usage among Sephardic Jews in post-Ottoman nationalizing states, still very much in process in 1930.[66] Further, his formulation of Jews as "Turks in Turkey" likewise did not capture the complexity of the place of non-Muslims within the Turkish Republic; Jews, like Armenians or the Greek Orthodox not subject to the population exchange, might be Turkish citizens, but, in governmental and popular discourse and policy, they were not Turks.[67]

Several other articles in the same edition of the guide were critical of the views Carmona expressed. Lévy, in introducing Carmona, explained he did not hold with the latter's view that Judeo-Spanish was dead. Perhaps Judeo-Spanish was disappearing in the Orient, but it would flourish in the Occident, where people appreciated the beautiful things of the past, as well as in America, where there was still a strong concentration of oriental Jews.[68] This language, to which Lévy had dedicated so much of his life, retained its relevance both as a beautiful vestige of history but also as a diasporic language with cohesive value. Nonetheless, in spite of Lévy's advocacy of Ladino, the guides included no articles in this language, although Ladino did feature in a number of advertisements.

Albert Fua, a prominent member of the early Young Turk movement from Salonica who had lived and published widely in Paris for many years, engaged critically with Carmona's facile assertion that Jews were "Turks in Turkey." Although scholars have argued that Fua rarely involved himself with Jewish issues in his publications advocating for the Young Turk movement, the piece he prepared for *Le Guide Sam* focused on the future of Turkey in light of the question of nationalities and the place of Turkish Jews.[69] The brief introduction to Fua's piece noted that, in spite of decades of residence in France, this "eminent author" (elsewhere in the guide he is designated an "homme de lettres") retained his Turkish citizenship, "so profound is his love for the natal soil and ardent his patriotic faith."[70] In his piece on "The Future of Turkey," Fua, who described himself as "a veteran of battles for liberty in Turkey," noted the social and political inequalities between "the Turanians [Turks] and the minorities"; in spite of official acts that erased distinctions between Turks and non-Turks, minorities were not admitted into the Grand National Assembly, nor in ranking military positions, nor in the employ of public administration.[71] Turanian ostracism of "the nationalities"—undefined but seemingly synonymous with the recognized millets of the Ottoman Empire—had led to the expatriation of, in his estimation, one hundred thousand Jews, and a substantial number of Armenians, and had closed channels of commerce linking Turkey with Europe and America.[72] He feared that Turkey's economic future would remain grim and emigration would continue unless absolute legal equality was extended to "the nationalities."[73]

* * *

While the boundaries of the region covered in *Le Guide Sam* shifted over the course of its publications, the Mediterranean remained central throughout. But beyond merely unifying a geographical region, the guides helped to cohere a group of individuals—predominately Jewish and largely involved in trades that benefited from transnational connections. Although some dwellers of Mediterranean port cities might live "with their backs turned to the sea," those featured in the guides, and to whom the guides may have been of interest, were those whose livelihoods hinged on networks and axes crossing the Middle Sea.[74] Drastic political, social, and cultural changes came in the wake of the Great War, resulting in new borders, legal regimes, mandates, and nationalizing states and an attendant necessity to negotiate the transformed power dynamics that accompanied them. The guides provided one avenue by which residents could retain commercial connections and contacts across a region increasingly divided. And the existence of the guides, containing articles on individual countries and on transnational questions, implied a Braudelian common destiny across political borders for those with, in the guide's words, "an interest in the Mediterranean." *Le Guide Sam*, then, sought to promote and reinforce a cohesive Jewish Mediterranean in the interwar period, but one that was connected by commerce rather than a national dream, particularly if that national dream was one of a Jewish state.

Indeed, a close reading of *Le Guide Sam* emphasizes that to think with the Mediterranean in a modern framework is not to adopt tropes of cosmopolitanism nor the erasure of linguistic, ethnic, and religious differences. Though Sam Lévy employed the Mediterranean in opposition to nationalism, it was, in part, the existence of new borders and the process of creating new nations that undergirded the need for his work. Economic disparities across the Sephardic diasporic world, the rise of national languages as opposed to the continued shared use of Ladino among the Sephardic Jews who formed the majority of the guide's entries, and even the project of Jewish nationalism within mandate Palestine and elsewhere that glossed over Jewish racial differences as conceived of by Lévy together motivated his publication of the guide. Lévy's Mediterranean as outlined in the guide was one that recognized and perpetuated certain types of distinctions and separations—religion, language, subethnicity—even as it countered regional and national rifts. As Constanze Kolbe's contribution to this volume demonstrates, cabotage was still a common form of commercial trade in the nineteenth century; neither did twentieth-century borders and the rising primacy of the nation prevent long-distance transnational commerce.

Indeed, even if the dream of a Jewish state was foreordained to become a nightmare, per Mme. de Siva's astrological predictions, nationalism in general curtailed the shared destiny of the Mediterranean. Lévy concluded the introductory section of the guide's 1930 edition with his own contribution, entitled simply "Epitaph." The deceased entity that his contribution honored was the "dear Orient of my childhood."[75] "Meanwhile, the Orient is dying, the Orient is dead," Lévy bemoaned, "killed, involuntarily, by the Turanians themselves, who, without suspecting it, are committing suicide too."[76] Here, the Orient was the world of Lévy's boyhood, the Ottoman world now remembered nostalgically even as Turkish nationalism threatened to destroy the very foundations of that world, and, in the process, imperiled itself. It was not, interestingly, the Hellenization of Salonica, Lévy's own natal city, that Lévy lamented; in focusing on the Turanians and their unintended murder of the Orient, Lévy implied a successive relationship between the Ottoman Empire and Turkey rather than other successor states. *Le Guide Sam* was, in some way, a last-ditch effort to preserve the world of Lévy's childhood with its extensive cross-sea connections, his lauding of Ladino and use of French subtly subverting the exclusivist language policies of many of the countries included in the guide even as it perpetuated the cultural and economic centrality of France within this Mediterranean world.

"History has become histories," continued Lévy, implying that the common destiny of the region as later defined by Braudel had now ceased to exist.[77] Nonetheless, *Le Guide Sam* itself sought to perpetuate a world in which transnational commercial connections, networks of communication and exchange, and continued affective ties contributed to a shared future. Scholars have often proclaimed that the unified Mediterranean died long before the interwar period. Lévy, however, eulogizes a world that had only just lost its cohesion. This epitaph, though, exists within *Le Guide Sam*, a body of work that reinforced interconnection and a continued common history of the Mediterranean, thereby prompting a larger question. Is a key feature of the modern Mediterranean, in fact, the premature mourning of its demise?

DEVI MAYS is an Assistant Professor of Judaic studies and history at the University of Michigan. Her research interests lie in the modern Sephardic Mediterranean and transnational Jewish networks. Her book *Forging Ties, Forging Passports: Migration and the Modern Sephardi Diaspora* (Stanford University Press, 2020) traces the histories of Ottoman Sephardi Jews who emigrated to the Americas—and especially, to Mexico—in the late nineteenth and early twentieth centuries, and the complex relationships they maintained to legal documentation as they migrated and settled into new homes.

Notes

1. Examples of other commercial guides, which were more regional and less Jewish-focused, include Joseph L. Nalpas, *Annuaire des commerçants de Smyrne et de l'Anatolie* (Izmir: Journal de Smyrne, 1894); for more on tourist guides to the Ottoman Empire, see Aytuğ Arslan and Hasan Ali Polat, "Guidance Services and Legal Regulations Aimed at Interpreters and Guides in the 19th Century Ottoman Empire," *Tourism Management Perspectives* 19 (2016): 40–47; Zafer Toprak, "İstanbul'da Turizm Çabaları: Eğlence Kültürü," https://archives.saltresearch.org/handle/123456789/158909 (accessed November 15, 2019).

2. Lévy uses these terms interchangeably throughout the guides. On the importance of Mediterranean port cities, see Fernand Braudel, *The Mediterranean and the Mediterranean World in the Age of Philip II* (New York: Harper Torchbooks, 1972), 1:312–25; Henk Driessen, "Mediterranean Port Cities: Cosmopolitanism Reconsidered," *History and Anthropology* 16, no. 1 (March 2005): 129–41.

3. I have had access to partial versions of the 1924 and 1929 editions, as well as the full 1930 edition. For clarity's sake, I cite the 1924 edition as *Le Guide Sam*, 4th edition, and the 1929 edition as *Le Guide Sam*, 9th edition; the 1930 text is cited as *Le Livre d'Or*. I am indebted to Paris Papamichos Chronakis for sharing his scans of the 1929 edition with me, and to Anya Quilitzsch for scanning a large part of the 1924 edition for me.

4. Michael Herzfeld, "Practical Mediterraneanism: Excuses for Everything, from Epistemology to Eating," in *Rethinking the Mediterranean*, ed. W. V. Harris (Oxford: Oxford University Press, 2005), pp. 45–63, at 45.

5. Matthias B. Lehmann, "Rethinking Sephardi Identity: Jews and Other Jews in Ottoman Palestine," *Jewish Social Studies* 15, no. 1 (2008): 83.

6. On the "common destiny" of the Mediterranean, see Braudel, *The Mediterranean*, 1:14; on the demise of the Mediterranean, see Braudel, *The Mediterranean*, 1:14, 19; Peregrine Horden and Nicholas Purcell, *The Corrupting Sea: A Study of Mediterranean History* (Oxford: Blackwell, 2000), 3; Sharon Kinoshita, "Mediterranean Literature," in *A Companion to Mediterranean History*, ed. Peregrine Horden and Sharon Kinoshita (Chichester, UK: Wiley Blackwell, 2014), pp. 314–29, at 324; Naor Ben-Yehoyada, "Mediterranean Modernity?," in *A Companion to Mediterranean History*, pp. 107–21; Faruk Tabak, *The Waning of the Mediterranean, 1550–1870: A Geohistorical Approach* (Baltimore: Johns Hopkins University

Press, 2008); Faruk Tabak, "Imperial Rivalry and Port-Cities: A View from Above," *Mediterranean Historical Review* 24, no. 2 (2009): 79–94.

7. Harry Kashdan, "Eating Elsewhere: Food and Migration in the Contemporary Mediterranean" (unpublished PhD diss., University of Michigan, 2018). As examples, see Julia Clancy-Smith, *Mediterraneans: North Africa and Europe in an Age of Migration, c. 1800–1900* (Berkeley: University of California Press, 2011); Lucia Carminati, "Alexandria, 1898: Nodes, Networks, and Scales in Nineteenth-Century Egypt and the Mediterranean," *Comparative Studies in History and Society* 59, no. 1 (2017): 127–53.

8. Iain Chambers, *Mediterranean Crossings: The Politics of an Interrupted Modernity* (Durham, NC: Duke University Press, 2008), 136.

9. Manuel Borutta and Sakis Gekas, "A Colonial Sea: The Mediterranean, 1798–1956," *European Review of History* 19, no. 1 (2012): 1–13, at 4.

10. Dieter Haller, "The Cosmopolitan Mediterranean: Myth and Reality," *Zeitschrift für Ethnologie* 129, no. 1 (2004): 29–47; Glenda Sluga and Julia Horne, "Cosmopolitanism: Its Pasts and Practices," *Journal of World History* 21, no. 3 (2010): 369–73; Maria Vassilikou, "Greeks and Jews in Salonika and Odessa: Inter-Ethnic Relations in Cosmopolitan Port Cities," *Jewish Culture and History* 4, no. 2 (2001): 155–72; there is now a plethora of scholarship critiquing and recontextualizing the application of the designation of "cosmopolitanism" in the Mediterranean. See Athanasios Gekas, "Class and Cosmopolitanism: The Historiographical Features of Merchants in Eastern Mediterranean Ports," *Mediterranean Historical Review* 24, no. 2 (2009): 95–114; Will Hanley, "Grieving Cosmopolitanism in Middle East Studies," *History Compass* 6, no. 5 (2008): 1346–67; Deborah A. Starr, "Recuperating Cosmopolitan Alexandria: Circulation of Narratives and Narratives of Circulation," *Cities* 22, no. 3 (2005): 217–33.

11. Bezalel Saadi Halevy, *La Epoka*, November 1, 1875, 1, as quoted in Olga Borovaya, *Modern Ladino Culture: Press, Belles Lettres, and Theater in the Late Ottoman Empire* (Bloomington: Indiana University Press, 2012), 43–44. Halevy memorializes his struggles with Salonica's religious leadership and his own excommunication in *A Jewish Voice from Ottoman Salonica: The Ladino Memoir of Sa'adi Besalel a-Levi*, eds. Aron Rodrigue and Sarah Abrevaya Stein (Stanford, CA: Stanford University Press, 2012).

12. Sam Lévy, *Le Déclin du Croissant* (Paris: Bernard Grasset, 1913), 5.

13. Olga Borovaya, "Halevy, Samuel Saadi," *Encyclopedia of Jews in the Islamic World* (Leiden: Brill, 2010), https://referenceworks.brillonline.com/entries/encyclopedia-of-jews-in-the-islamic-world/halevy-samuel-saadi-SIM_0013790?s.num=1&s.f.s2_parent=s.f.book.encyclopedia-of-jews-in-the-islamic-world&s.q=Halevy (accessed July 7, 2017).

14. Borovaya, *Modern Ladino Culture*, 9.

15. Sarah Abrevaya Stein, *Making Jews Modern: The Yiddish and Ladino Press in the Russian and Ottoman Empires* (Bloomington: Indiana University Press, 2004), 125.

16. *Le Guide Sam*, 4th ed., 43.

17. Sam Lévy, "Les intérêts de la France en Orient," *Le Guide Sam*, 4th ed., 47–50; Sam Lévy, "La presse française dans le Levant," *Le Guide Sam*, 4th ed., 65–66; "Italie et Turquie," *Le Guide Sam*, 4th ed., 51–53.

18. "Les étrangers en France," *Le Guide Sam*, 4th ed., 55–57; Sarah Abrevaya Stein, *Extraterritorial Dreams: European Citizenship, Sephardi Jews, and the Ottoman Twentieth Century* (Chicago: University of Chicago Press, 2016), 73–96.

19. *Le Livre d'Or*, 138.

20. Ibid., 389.
21. Ibid., 395.
22. Ibid., 396.
23. *Le Guide Sam, Annuaire de l'Orient*, 9th edition.
24. *Le Livre d'Or*, 439.
25. Advertisement for Elie Alaluf, *Livre d'Or*, 146.
26. Advertisement for silk and wool firm of Salem, Castoriano and Behar, *Le Livre d'Or*, 284.
27. For Antwerp, see advertisement for Navon and Misrachi, *Le Livre d'Or*, 262.
28. Advertisement for Elie Alaluf, *Le Livre d'Or*, 146. Sarah Abrevaya Stein suggests that this firm belonged to the brother-in-law of Lévy's nephew Leon. Correspondence with Sarah Abrevaya Stein.
29. Advertisement for Ascher Salem and Son, *Le Guide Sam*, 4th ed., 42; advertisement for Ascher Salem and Sons, *Le Livre d'Or*, 408.
30. Letter from Sam Lévy to E. Raymond Street, Manchester, June 29, 1929, *Le Livre d'Or*, 395.
31. Herzfeld, *Practical Mediterraneanism*, 46, 48–50.
32. Joëlle Bahloul, "The Sephardic Jew as Mediterranean: A View from Kinship and Gender," *Journal of Mediterranean Studies* 4, no. 2 (1994): 197–202.
33. Sam Lévy, *Le Livre d'Or*, 17–18.
34. Pierre Mille, "L'Orient," in *Le Livre d'Or*, 19–21.
35. Julia Phillips Cohen, "Oriental by Design: Ottoman Jews, Imperial Style, and the Performance of Heritage," *The American Historical Review* 119, no. 2 (2014): 364–98; Julia Phillips Cohen, "The East as a Career: Far Away Moses and Company in the Marketplace of Empires," *Jewish Social Studies* 21, no. 2 (2015): 35–77.
36. *Le Livre d'Or*, 486.
37. Ibid., 853.
38. Ibid., 712.
39. For a primary source example of this type of rhetoric, see "A Pastoral Letter from the Chief Rabbi of France to the Jews of Algeria Urging Reform," in Norman Stillman, *The Jews of Arab Lands in Modern Times* (Philadelphia: The Jewish Publication Society, 1991), 187–89; Aron Rodrigue, *Jews and Muslims: Images of Sephardi and Eastern Jewries in Modern Times* (Seattle: University of Washington Press, 2003), passim; Aron Rodrigue, *French Jews, Turkish Jews: The Alliance Israélite Universelle and the Politics of Jewish Schooling in Turkey, 1860–1925* (Bloomington: Indiana University Press, 1990), passim.
40. Sam Lévy, "Les intérêts de la France en Orient," *Le Guide Sam*, 4th ed., 47.
41. *Le Livre d'Or*, 59.
42. Ibid., 60.
43. Ibid., 60–61.
44. Ibid., 61.
45. Ibid., 61.
46. Ibid., 61.
47. For more on the centrality of visual images of Palestine in this period among American Jews in particular, see Jessica Carr, "Palestine in Jewish-American Life, 1901–1948" (unpublished PhD diss., Indiana University, 2013).
48. Michelle Campos, *Ottoman Brothers: Muslims, Christians, and Jews in Early Twentieth-Century Palestine* (Stanford, CA: Stanford University Press, 2011); Esther Benbassa, "Zionism and the Politics of Coalitions in the Ottoman Jewish Communities in the Early Twentieth Century," in *Ottoman and Turkish Jewry: Community and Leadership*,

ed. Aron Rodrigue (Bloomington: Indiana University Turkish Studies, 1992), 225–52; Esther Benbassa, "Le sionisme dans l'Empire ottoman à l'aube du 20e siècle," *Vingtième Siècle* 24 (1989): 69–80; Esther Benbassa, "Presse d'Istanbul et de Salonique au service du sionisme (1908–1914)," *Revue Historique* 276, no. 2 (1986): 337–65.

49. Sam Lévy, "Le Sionisme a fait faillite," *Le Livre d'Or*, 633.
50. Ibid., 633.
51. Sam Lévy, "Appel aux Séfardims de Grèce," *Le Guide Sam*, 9th ed., 35–37.
52. "Le Sionisme a fait faillite," *Le Livre d'Or*, 631–33; Sam Lévy, "La Folie Sioniste," *Le Livre d'Or*, 635–38.
53. Sam Lévy, *Le Livre d'Or*, 619.
54. Ibid., 620; Sam Lévy, "'Aryans of the Mosaic Belief': A Defense of the Sephardi Jews of Paris [1942]," in *Sephardi Lives: A Documentary History, 1700–1950*, ed. Julia Phillips Cohen and Sarah Abrevaya Stein (Stanford, CA: Stanford University Press, 2014), 263–64.
55. Sam Lévy, "Le Déclin du Sionisme," *Le Livre d'Or*, 620.
56. Sam Lévy, *Le Livre d'Or*, 621.
57. *Le Guide Sam*, 4th ed., 30.
58. Ibid., 13.
59. [No author given], *Boletino del Ospital Nasional Israelita "Or Ahayim"* (Constantinople: Fratelli Haim, 1923).
60. Although the guide did include Jews from North Africa and the Levant, both within those geographical subsections and among their expatriate communities in France and England, there were no analogous discussions of Judeo-Arabic. Likewise, in Lévy's contribution on Jewish racial divisions, he did not include a separate category for what would today often be termed as Mizrahi Jewry, nor did he even mention Jewish populations in Iran, Yemen, and elsewhere. Taken together, this seems to suggest that Lévy was perpetuating what Aron Rodrique and Esther Benbassa have referred to as a Ladino-speaking Sephardic *Kulturbereich*. See Esther Benbassa and Aron Rodrigue, *Sephardi Jewry: A History of the Judeo-Spanish Community, 14th–20th Centuries* (Berkeley: University of California Press, 2000), xix.
61. A. H. Navon, "Souvenirs des temps jadis," *Le Livre d'Or*, 36–38. For more on Navon, see Celine Piser, "How to Be a French Jew: Ottoman Immigrant Authors in Early Twentieth-Century Paris," *Prooftexts* 33, no. 2 (2014): 182–221.
62. Sam Lévy, "Le Tarraud Juif," *Le Livre d'Or*, 35.
63. Elie Carmona, "Le judéo-espagnol," *Le Livre d'Or*, 46.
64. Ibid., 46–47.
65. Ibid., 47.
66. On interwar language policies in formerly Ottoman lands, see Eyal Ginio, "'Learning the Beautiful Language of Homer': Judeo-Spanish Speaking Jews and the Greek Language and Culture between the Wars," *Jewish History* 16, no. 2 (2002): 235–62; Yesim Bayar, "The Trajectory of Nation-Building through Language Policies: The Case of Turkey during the Early Republican Period (1920–1938)," *Nations and Nationalism* 17, no. 1 (2011): 108–28, at 108–12; Senem Aslan, "'Citizen, Speak Turkish!': A Nation in the Making," *Nationalism and Ethnic Politics* 13, no. 2 (2007): 245–72, at 250–51; Devi Mays, "Transplanting Cosmopolitans: The Migrations of Sephardic Jews to Mexico, 1900–1934" (unpublished PhD diss., Indiana University, 2013), 198–99, 259–66.
67. Rıfat N. Bali, *Bir Türkleştirme Serüveni: Cumhuriyet Yıllarında Türkiye Yahudileri, 1923–1945* (Istanbul: Iletişim, 1999); Mays, "Transplanting Cosmopolitans,"

passim; Lerna Ekmekçioğlu, *Recovering Armenia: The Limits of Belonging in Post-Genocide Turkey* (Stanford, CA: Stanford University Press, 2016).

68. Sam Lévy, "Elie Carmona," *Le Livre d'Or*, 45.

69. D. Gershon Lewental, "Albert Fua," *Encyclopedia of Jews in the Islamic World*, https://referenceworks.brillonline.com/entries/encyclopedia-of-jews-in-the-islamic-world/fua-albert-SIM_0008050?s.num=0&s.f.s2_parent=s.f.book.encyclopedia-of-jews-in-the-islamic-world&s.q=fua (accessed July 7, 2017); Mehmet Şükrü Hanioğlu, "Jews in the Young Turk Movement to the 1908 Revolution," in *The Jews of the Ottoman Empire*, ed. Avigdor Levy (Princeton, NJ: Darwin Press, 1994), 519–26.

70. *Le Livre d'Or*, 759, 199.

71. Albert Fua, "L'avenir de la Turquie," *Le Livre d'Or*, 759–60, 763. Pan-Turanism was a late-nineteenth- and twentieth-century ideology that propagated attachment between all Turkic peoples, popular among leaders of the Committee of Union and Progress as a potential means of increasing Ottoman influence in the Caucasus and Central Asia. Fua, however, seems to be using the term "Touranien" as a simple synonym for "Turk." Jacob M. Landau, *Pan-Turkism: From Irredentism to Cooperation* (London: Hurst, 1995).

72. Fua, *Le Livre d'Or*, 763.

73. Ibid.

74. Driessen, "Mediterranean Port Cities," 130.

75. Sam Lévy, "Epitaph," *Le Livre d'Or*, 57.

76. Ibid., 58.

77. Ibid., 58.

9

A NEW MYTH OF COEXISTENCE?

*The Jewish Mediterranean Dream
and the Three Ages of Nostalgia*

Clémence Boulouque

"CENTRAL EUROPE IS JUST A WORD THAT SYMBOLIZES the needs for our present," wrote the Austrian poet Hugo von Hofmannsthal in 1917, during the last months of the Habsburg Empire.[1] Such a view, whereby political and cultural geographies are turned into a concept that meets the demands of the day, is also captured in the claim of Predrag Matvejevic, the late Yugoslav writer, that "the Mediterranean is inseparable from its discourse."[2] It is worth transposing Hofmannsthal's claim into a question about the Mediterranean: How did the Mediterranean become a discourse, and what does the word symbolize for our times?

This paper seeks to address these questions while pondering Michael Herzfeld's thesis of Mediterraneanism.[3] His work, "coined on the model of Orientalism,"[4] explores the implicit hierarchy of values as well as the dangers of stereotypes or self-stereotypes of the "Mediterraneans." Indeed, representations of the Mediterranean are anchored in national traditions: in Italy, the term conjures up a *Mare Nostrum* which, far from evoking a peaceful dream, as it has sometimes been made out to be, was a war cry in the Punic wars; in Germany, in the absence of coastal borders, the Mediterranean is more abstract and conjures up a Goethean romanticism; and in Turkey, the sea also means the mourning of a lost Ottoman power.[5] To these representations, I propose to add a Jewish Mediterranean, as expressed more specifically in the twentieth century; although the paper focuses on mostly Jewish Francophone literature, this operative concept exhibits a number of shared features across other Jewish literatures. Why and when did a Jewish Mediterranean imaginary become significant? What are the uses of this Mediterranean construct?

First, I would like to suggest that the Jewish Mediterranean is an iteration of the trope of a symbiosis that came to an abrupt end: because the Jews were expelled from the places of coexistence, they responded by fostering the narrative, or myth, of a golden age. With its tropes of pluralism and tolerance, the Mediterranean symbiosis bears resemblances to *convivencia*—the concept coined by Américo Castro in 1948[6] in order to describe peaceful interactions and religious coexistence in medieval Spain—which has become a staple in Spanish history and interfaith efforts, albeit a much criticized one: an ideologically charged concept that lends itself to a romantic or idealized past.[7] It is worth noting, however, that most of the Jewish idealizing description of Andalusian Spain predated by a century the historiographical notion of *convivencia*.

Sephardism (defined as an account of Jewish life in Iberia and of its intellectual heritage, written with a political agenda) became a tribute to this specific religious and cultural Iberian symbiosis but also a cautionary account since it showed the decline of this form of interreligious coexistence on the peninsula following the Reconquista and the Jewish and Morisco expulsions.[8] I argue that the myth served as an identity narrative at a time when religious observance had started dwindling and when other forms of Jewish identity—such as culture—emerged in the nineteenth century. I will then explore how the literary depictions of the Jewish Mediterranean echo Franco Cassano's definition of the Mediterranean[9] as a "pluriverse."[10] Drawing on the French writers Albert Camus and Gabriel Audisio, Cassano's work *Il Pensiero Meridiano* (*Southern Thinking*), published in 1996 to great acclaim, defines the Mediterranean as "between lands without belonging exclusively to any of them."[11] It is a space in between, of multiple sociabilities and identities—the bygone model of a world free of bigotry.

Finally, I will analyze the political overtones of the depiction of loss; over the course of the second half of the twentieth century, the Mediterranean became increasingly depicted alongside its loss and exile, turning the Jewish Mediterranean into a nexus of nostalgia. The image of the sea emerged in Jewish literature in the late 1950s as sentiment, a locus of innocence lost and of powerlessness in a fading colonial order.

The Mediterranean as a Variation on Coexistence Narratives in Jewish History

Reading the Jewish Mediterranean as an iteration on the theme of *convivencia* has been arguably turned into a foundational narrative with two other antecedents: Al-Andalus and the Habsburgian (and, to a lesser extent, Ottoman) Empires.

Sephardism

The role of the Jews under Muslim rule in Al-Andalus emerged as the first narrative of a diasporic golden age—and of coexistence. Ismar Schorsch's seminal essay, "The Myth of Sephardic Supremacy,"[12] examined the importance of the Iberian model for the scholarly study of Judaism, the *Wissenschaft des Judentums*, which originated in nineteenth-century Germany. Part of a greater rediscovery of Spain, this effort was inspired by the romantic ethos[13] and an attempt to discover alternatives to the Enlightenment.[14] From an internal Jewish standpoint, Al-Andalus was an attack against the insularity of the Ashkenazi educational model opposed to the Iberian cultural openness. It was also geared to the non-Jewish world and served as crucial demonstration of the necessary role of Judaism in building a flourishing culture and served to emphasize Jewish civic worthiness and the benefits of emancipation. It could also arguably be used by Jews to depict Islam as a countermodel of tolerance aimed at their Christian fellow citizens. Conversely, the alleged decline of Spain after the expulsion offered a cautionary tale for Germany as well as signaling to Jews their precarious status; even in such a prosperous environment, their position had never been assured.

These accounts of Sepharad were first written mostly as history or historiography; indeed, "pleasure reading," as Amos Bitzan has called it,[15] was only emerging then in Jewish life. Jewish-themed novels by Jewish authors began to appear, timidly, in the wake of Auerbach's *Spinoza* (1837) and Heine's *Rabbi of Bacherach* (1840).[16] This was followed by a wave of historical romances. With the exception of British writers Grace Aguilar and Benjamin Disraeli, both of Sephardi descent,[17] most of these stories and histories were written by Ashkenazi authors who were neither contemporary nor had any familial ties with the Iberian community but shared an apologetic agenda or tried to foster a new sense of Jewish identity. The attraction of Sepharad was also translated into praxis and esthetics with the adoption of Sephardic liturgy, architecture, and poetry.[18] Reclaiming Sephardism is part of the turn to history of the nineteenth century that functioned as the "faith of the fallen Jews," as Yosef Yerushalmi put it.[19]

Sephardism—defined as the usable account of an expulsion that abruptly ended the Iberian symbiosis—has become a lingering presence in contemporary historiography and literature.[20] As a result, Sepharad exceeds its geographic dimensions; it is "a form of literary expression that functions politically during heightened moments of historical consciousness in diverse national contexts," as aptly defined by Yael Halevi-Wise.[21] A number of Sepharad-themed novels were published at the end of the twentieth century, around the celebration of the five hundredth anniversary of the expulsion from Spain. Coinciding with the outbreak of war in former Yugoslavia, the rememoration of Jewish life in exile around the Mediterranean served as an elegy for defunct religious and ethnic coexistence and a call to resurrect both. The discovery of the richly illuminated Sarajevo Haggadah, composed in Barcelona in the fourteenth century, was turned into a symbol; escaping both the Inquisition and Nazi occupation, in the midst of the siege of Sarajevo and of ethnic conflict, it became an instance of *convivencia* as inspiration, used as a countermodel both to a "lachrymose" Jewish history—in Salo Baron's famous phrase[22]—and to modern-day bigotry.[23]

The Habsburg Empire

The second instance of an imagined golden age of coexistence and of a symbolic multiethnic political entity emerged with the end of the Habsburg Empire, which became a staple of modern European historical attention in the last two decades of the twentieth century. In 1979, Carl Schorske's *Fin de Siècle Vienna* signaled this rekindled interest;[24] in linking politics to the psyche and in showing how culture became a surrogate for politics and replaced any kind of political involvement on the part of the Jewish liberal bourgeoisie, his work proved seminal.

The role and influence of Jews, as well as the precariousness of their coexistence, was known to most who witnessed that era. Hugo Bettauer's 1922 dystopian novel, *The City without Jews*, both satirized anti-Semitism and showcased the unmistakable Jewish contribution to Viennese culture. The book chronicled the failed attempt by a politician to expel the city's Jews, a measure that led to economic and cultural wreckage, prompting him to beg them to return.[25] Overrepresented in the arts, journalism, and medicine, Viennese Jews shaped the perception of the city as a magnet of modernity—fracturing the self and its representations, fostering anxiety and dissonance. Its enduring allure stemmed from the perception of what lay below the surface of a world that seemed to offer security and coexistence.[26] Nevertheless, if Vienna's split identity was also hidden by ideology or delusion, its amalgamating power was heralded by some of its Jewish advocates who echoed the regime's agenda. Joseph Roth's description of unvarying Sunday lunches, recounted in his novels from *Radetsky's March*[27] (1932) to *The Emperor's Tomb* (1938), functions as an ironic symbol of the empire's uniformity and continuity: noodle soup, *Tafelspitz* (brisket of beef), and *Kirschknödel* (cherry dumplings), all of which were Emperor Franz Joseph's favorites.

In his introduction to *The Myth and the Empire*, Claudio Magris interprets commitment to Habsburg myth-making as participation in a delusional unity.

This contrasts with the previous interpretation of the Frankfurt school, whose thinkers seemed to envision Austrian literature as a harbinger of the dislocation of truth, unity, and narrative and as an instance of negativity "conceived of as the only authentic position in thought and art."[28] In response, Magris identified in Austrian Jewish writers a counternarrative meant "to reduce the plurality of the real into one unity, the chaos of the world into order, and the accidental fragmentation of existence into a harmony susceptible to resolution, or at least to reconciliation."[29]

The Habsburg myth thus looked backward in order to look forward and painted the *convivencia* experience as a self-portrait framed by a cautionary tale. Elevating Andalusia to a myth was a statement about the defunct flourishing empire that had blinded itself to the true source of its fortunes: ethnic and religious coexistence. This lost harmony lies at the heart of Stefan Zweig's essay collection, *Journeys*, and his depiction of spring in Sevilla.[30] The comparisons with the Habsburgian empire were quite transparent: writing about the apex of the Andalusian culture and about its cultural openness, also meant to promote the Austro-Hungarian Empire's own myth.

Joseph Roth's impassioned defense of the empire and the emperor in *Radetzky's March* cannot be explained otherwise; his apology for the dual monarchy had taken on an existential urgency—saving it meant saving a world that would protect its Jewish subjects. The tendency was only heightened in the wake of the Nazi seizure of power, in the many literary eulogies of a Jewish Vienna. Stefan Zweig's memoir, *The World of Yesterday: An Autobiography*, written in exile in 1941, magisterially epitomizes most accounts of this fated encounter between a nation and its Jews. However, the use of such words as *twilight*, as well as the oxymorons "nervous splendor" or "joyful apocalypse" in the words of Hermann Broch,[31] display a consciousness of the liminal states of Viennese politics and culture.[32]

Only the Habsburg Empire could grant a political identity to the Jews, who had no historical claim to a nation or territory and could only be protected by identifying with a transnational identity. A longing for empires and for the stability granted by a centrifugal force reemerged as a template for peaceful coexistence in the 1980s and 1990s, a time when the question of nationalism and minorities in central Europe resurfaced. Viennese Jews had by then widely come to embody cosmopolitanism, its delusion before an abyss, and the way in which they had forever defined the identity of the empire, as the doomed heralds of its culture and ironic legacy. Both Al-Andalus and the Habsburg Empire met the needs of the modern age and suggested either a political and/or cultural Jewish contribution whose short-lived nature fueled its specific nostalgia.

The Mediterranean "Pluriverse" and Its Jewish Literary Adaptations

Unlike Iberia or the Habsburg Empire, the Mediterranean was never controlled by a single political entity. Over the course of the colonial period, beginning with the 1830 French conquest of Algeria, the incursions of France, Spain, and Italy in the Maghreb, and the British Empire in Egypt and in Palestine created a north-south axis without canceling out local networks, interactions, and multiple belongings, as Jewish circulation of ideas, rabbinic personnel, and books seem to indicate.[33] This enduring web of identities echoes Horden and Purcell's famous claim of "connectivity" as a defining feature of the Mediterranean, made in *The Corrupting Sea*.[34]

Even if the first writings on the Mediterranean seem unrelated to any discourse pertaining to a Jewish identity or self-definition, the historiography of the Mediterranean further illuminates what was at stake in the discursive nature of the Mediterranean as inclusion; the literary groups and movements in and about Algeria constitute a prime case study of both, multifaceted since Mediterraneanism was also used to fend off competing narratives bent on advancing a xenophobic agenda for the region.

Although Hegel's *Philosophy of the Subjective Spirit* introduced the Mediterranean both as a center and a hyphen between cultures ("The Mediterranean around which these three continents are situated does not divide, it unites them"),[35] it is the Saint-Simonian thinker Michel Chevalier who conceptualized the Mediterranean as a locus of pluralism in a series of articles published in 1832 and collected in a pamphlet,[36] *Système de la Méditerranée*. This theorization of the Mediterranean as a peaceful articulation of identities, reminiscent of Kant's *Project of Perpetual Peace*, mirrored the hybridity of Saint-Simonianism as a religion and as a system. For our purpose, given the sympathy that the Saint-Simonian movement elicited among Jews in the nineteenth century, it is only natural that Jews should have gravitated toward the narrative of coexistence. This Saint-Simonian framing of the Middle Sea, and its agenda, did not gain much traction until the 1930s, when the representations of the sea became an ideological battleground; the theme was deployed anew by a generation of thinkers, eager to counter far-right groups, who had availed themselves of the Mediterranean as a place of "Latinity."

Even though it is often presented as the first instance of a book-length historical description of the Mediterranean as a locus of coexistence, Henri Pirenne's fraught *Mohammed and Charlemagne* (1937) posited that the catalyst of this Mediterranean unity, initially created by the Roman Empire and that outlasted him, had been the fight against Islam.[37] Pirenne's work should be understood in the context of this right-wing Algérianisme, to which Camus and others responded. Proponents of the Algérianisme such as Pirenne promoted an unambiguously aggressive, anti-Semitic, xenophobic agenda; they conceived of France and Algeria as organically connected, making Latin Algeria an extension of Europe and dismissing the Muslim presence by emphasizing the importance of Berbers, invoking the work of Charles Maurras and regionalist thinkers in France.[38]

Against such worldview and against the Algérianisme of right-wing thinkers, the *Cahiers du Sud* in Marseille, and even more visibly the essayists and novelists Gabriel Audisio and Albert Camus, responded by highlighting the multireligious, multiethnic identity of the Mediterranean.[39] While Pirenne's thesis was first formulated in 1922, his book appeared in 1937. That same year, in February, Albert Camus gave a talk entitled "La nouvelle culture méditerranéenne" ("The New Mediterranean Culture") at the newly inaugurated Maison de la Culture in Algiers. His lecture has been regarded as the manifesto of L'École d'Alger[40] as well as Camus's expression of humanism, or well-meaning colonialism. A major influence for his speech was the lesser-known writer Gabriel Audisio, whom he cited. In *Jeunesse de la Méditerranée* (*Youth of the Mediterranean*), Audisio argues that the unique strength of the Mediterranean lay in this union of cultures, the East and the West. Mediterranean unity proceeds from a common condition, the cultural syncretism of which North Africa is the epitome: "The group he [Camus] called 'My people' has multiple visages, like everything that is alive, and its authenticity rests, like every truth, on an amalgam of suspicious antecedents."[41] Audisio thus offered an alternative reading of Carthaginian culture, seeing it not as a threat to the Latin culture then dominating the Mediterranean but rather as its complement, a locus of fruitful collaboration between Orient and Occident.

For Camus, too, the Mediterranean was literally the Middle Sea, a place of balance between extremes and of solidarity with fellow humans.[42] Its nature is imagined in the present tense, not in some messianic future, religious or political. Rather, it was an embodied experience of the world, of a pantheistic or pagan nature, famously described in *Nuptials at Tipasa*.[43] Camus's Mediterranean constituted a matrix of coexistence and an intimate, sensorial experience, much as Jewish literature also came to emphasize around the middle of the century.[44] The intellectual stature of the writer, who was awarded the Nobel Prize, gave greater visibility to his quasi-pantheistic and sensual Mediterranean imagery; the sea, the sun, and the earth trumped religion and ethnicity—and Jews had a stake in such characterization.

The first novel of Greek-born Albert Cohen (1895–1981), *Solal* (published in 1930), is an early instance of fiction that portrays the Ionian island of Cephalonia as the home of a clamorous, humorous, multicolored crowd. It was followed by *Mangeclous* (*Nailcrunchers*) in 1938, which became the second part of a Solal trilogy. *Belle du Seigneur*, its third part, published in 1968, has acquired the status of a cult novel in France as the ultimate love story. In its first two installments, Solal's truculent uncles resemble caricatures of Oriental Jews in the eyes of a haughty Western world. It also raises the question of self-stereotypes as Mangeclous and Les Valeureux certainly embody the stereotypical qualities of the Mediterraneans: unreliable, imprecise, spontaneous. These "semi-imbecile Jews, first in the Greek island of Cephalonia and later in Switzerland"—in the words of an excoriating review of *Nailcrunchers* by George Orwell—will ultimately prove their ludicrous but moral grandeur. Moreover, the life-affirming presence of the characters seems to pay tribute to a soon-to-be-defunct universe. Indeed, an elegiac tone was then to prevail.

The sense of an ending is key to Leon Sciaky's seminal 1946 autobiography.[45] Recently reissued, it chronicles the stories of artisans and merchants whose ethnic or religious identity had little relevance to their everyday life. The author, who had left Salonica in 1915 and moved to the United States, claimed never to have known who was or was not Jewish. His own Jewishness became significant in the wake of World War II and the destruction of the world of his youth.

In a noteworthy parallel, the appearance of novels that explored this coexistence coincided with scholars' early interest in the Mediterranean and the interreligious fabric and economy of these societies. The resulting depiction of the Mediterranean Jewish world was, in the words of the late scholar of Moroccan Judaism Haim Zafrani, an "interdenominational symbiosis" in which religion was not central. This echoes the depiction of earlier Jewish communities by yet another towering scholar of the Jewish Mediterranean, Shlomo Goitein, who wrote that "religion formed the frame, rather than the content of daily existence."[46]

Both history and fiction seem to converge into a shared discourse: a usable Mediterranean in which ethnic belongings are toned down. Goitein's emphasis on the Mediterranean as a locus of coexistence and his highlighting of a Jewish perspective is all the more interesting as he was himself a scion of German-Jewish symbiosis. (Goitein was born in 1900 in Bavaria to a father born in Hungary.) His scholarship may appear as a response to the rift between Jews and the Arab world in the wake of the creation of the State of Israel.[47] Novelists, too, seem to have elicited a retreat into a more hospitable past and thus the evidence of possible coexistence. In *False Papers*, for example, André Aciman describes Alexandria in the 1950s and 1970s as a place "where overzealous piety was derided and where friendship was almost never based on creed."[48]

Such notions have long conveyed, in literature, a paradoxical image of religiosity free of bigotry, or of a quasi-secularized identity whose religion-based or ethnic characteristics[49] essentially displayed harmony. This is an expression of the pluriverse described in *The Southern Thought*, where rules imported by and from the metropole did not apply—between observance and indifference, tension and appeasement. For most observers, for instance, the 1934 riots in Constantine, Algeria do not appear to have been a consequence of mutual suspicion among Muslims and Jews but rather were the by-products of outside influences and of the inefficiency of the French authorities.[50] Emphasizing syncretism became all the more crucial for Jewish writers as tensions in the region steadily grew.

As a consequence, the Mediterranean was turned into a microcosm of religious coexistence, especially after 9/11, with a particular emphasis on Muslim-Jewish relations. In a graphic novel version, the multivolume saga *The Rabbi's Cat*, published by Johan Sfar in five installments from 2002 to 2015, literally illustrated this narrative. His fantasy captures a sentiment of togetherness in an inadvertent, spontaneous, joyous, and somewhat messy coexistence. Cats and youth, as witnesses deprived of agency, seem to be the chosen narrators of this world in its twilight—a place of quiet wisdom and of unassuming, but soon to be vacated, brotherhood.

Out of Guilt: Loss, History, and Memory of the Jewish Mediterranean

In one of the vignettes in *False Papers*, the recollections of return to the birthplace he left decades earlier, André Aciman gazes at the port of Alexandria, Portus Eunostos, and muses over its name: the ancients called it the harbor of good and safe return (*eu-nostos*). He ponders: "Nostalgia is the ache to return, to come home; nostophobia, the fear of returning; nostomania, the obsession with going back; nostography, writing about return."[51] The novelist, who is also a scholar of Marcel Proust, captures a key feature of this sensibility: claiming to love the memory of Alexandria more than he loved the experience, and maybe distorting that very experience along the lines that Herzfeld calls "Mediterraneanism," which I complicate by placing it within the ambit of the history of emotions.[52]

The question of homecoming, which goes back to the *Odyssey*, arguably the first Mediterranean novel, also provides insights into a literary Jewish Mediterranean. This is worth exploring against the backdrop of increased interest in the history of emotions; as a locus for nostalgia and nostography, the use of a discursive Mediterranean illuminates the slippage from history to memory and the intimate relation between memory and geography. The sea functions as a *lieu de mémoire*, as defined by Pierre Nora: "a turning point where consciousness of a break with the past is bound up with the sense that memory has been torn."[53] The shards of memory probably explain why Benjamin Stora, one of France's most prominent historians of the Maghreb and contemporary Algeria, felt compelled to explore these themes in a memoir about his departure from Algeria in his youth and then his visit, years later, accompanied by his father and son.[54] "There are *lieux de mémoire*, sites of memory, because there are no longer *milieux de mémoire*, real environments of memory."[55]

In the beginning, nostalgia was a condition. The term, coined by the Swiss physician Johannes Hofer at the end of the seventeenth century, described symptoms said to produce erroneous representations that affected their relation to the present.[56] Are these erroneous representations, triggered by nostalgia, shaping representations of the Mediterranean? In French, a portmanteau word has been coined to fuse nostalgia and Algeria: *nostalgérie* ("Nostalgeria"). Is it a case in which memory is at odds with history?

In the nostalgic fabric of a contemporary Jewish Mediterranean literature, one of the first instances of the Mediterranean as a shore of expulsions goes back to the mid-1950s. Albert Cohen's 1954 *Le livre de ma mère* (*The Book of My Mother*), written after her death, ushers in this feeling of uprootedness as he reminisces about the five-year-old child he used to be, whose family decided to leave Corfu after a pogrom, arriving in Marseille. Their final destination was Paris, where his mother's heavy accent was an idiosyncratic combination of the French she spoke in Corfu and the distinct Marseille accent that she had picked up upon her arrival in the port city. In Cohen's lament for his late mother, the sea has become a synecdoche for her and for everything he had lost: a portable essence and absence, an image, something that you carry under your eyelid when you close your eyes. It becomes the most intimate sea.

> I can see myself at the age of ten.... I was a bit cracked. I was sure that everything I saw really and truly existed inside my head, absolutely real but on a very small scale. If I was by the sea, I was sure that the Mediterranean before me was also inside my head—not a picture of the Mediterranean but the Mediterranean itself, minute and salty inside my head, in miniature but real and with all its fish, though very tiny, all its waves, and a little burning-hot sun, a real sea with all its rocks and all its ships, absolutely complete inside my head, with coal and real live sailors, each ship with the same captain as in the world outside, the same captain, dwarf-sized and delicate enough.[57]

The Book of My Mother was Cohen's third book. In the interwar period, his books had not really addressed uprootedness, but in 1954, the climate had changed and Cohen's Mediterranean tale of exile foreshadowed a number of memoirs of various—and often lesser—literary quality, which recount the many shapes of loss.

The specific nature of Mediterranean exiles is linked to the end of the established colonial or imperial order, an event in which Jews could simultaneously be seen as victims but also as complicit or bystanders. This imperial dimension of the Jewish experience has only recently come to the fore in Jewish historiography.[58] The memoirs that chronicle their lives may well reveal "postcolonial melancholy," as Gilroy puts it.[59] Indeed, the number of Jews who had acted, or been visibly used, as intermediaries was large enough to fuel resentment. The Crémieux decree, which granted French citizenship to Algerian Jews, had been used to drive a wedge between Jews and Muslims.[60] Those in the Ottoman Empire who, under the capitulations, had been given special legal status[61] could readily be identified with an external power—thus becoming an alien body in a new, nation-based political landscape. Accounts of these days are marked by anguish and hasty departures imposed by external circumstances. For those capable of showing proof of citizenship, they often involved flight to an unknown metropolis in France, England, or Italy—or to Israel for those who did not have citizenship elsewhere or were motivated by Zionist feelings. These stories share some features of the expulsion narratives found in Sephardism. But the Mediterranean tales were of a different, nostalgic nature.

The ambiguities of Jews, and of minorities in general, toward decolonization may explain the urge for a narrative that conjured up a sense of dispossession. In *The Future of Nostalgia*, Svetlana Boym revisits a proposition made by the historian Michael Kammen: "Nostalgia, with its wistful memories, is essentially history without guilt."[62] This proposition, this urge to find history without guilt, may explain why memory took on an important role—and it certainly captures the essence of a Jewish Mediterranean nostalgia. It is a way to tame the dissonances described by Memmi, this identity in between: "I knew only too well the contradictory emotions which swayed their lives."[63] Indeed, as Boym notes, "nostalgia in this sense is an abdication of personal responsibility, a guilt-free homecoming, an ethical and aesthetical failure."[64]

For the most part, urban, educated Jews had bought into a French universalism that made them less likely to embrace nationalist movements, as Albert Memmi described in *The Colonizer and the Colonized*.[65] Championing the delusion of coexistence was embedded in the colonial system. Indeed, Memmi remarks that the ruling powers "never seriously promoted religious conversion of the colonized" because it would have been a step toward assimilation and therefore "the disappearance of the colonial relationships."[66] Moreover, this universalism had also been propagated by the schools of the Alliance Israélite Universelle,[67] in which Jews received their primary and secondary education—though a majority of Moroccan Jews, for instance, continued to have a poor command of French. If some nationalist movements did include Jews (Elie Zerah in Tunisia's Destour movement or Henri Alleg[68] in Algeria), the instances of political involvement at the highest level in the Mediterranean are scarcer than in the eastern European orbit.

In *Gagou*, Tunisian-born Guy Sitbon's autobiographical novel, a dialogue sums up the impasses of hyphenated identities. As a teenager and precocious journalist, he had adhered to the Communist Party; soon deluded, he was active in the most leftist part of the nationalist Union Générale des Étudiants de Tunisie, which he had to leave on account of recurring attacks due to his Jewishness.

> LET'S BE CLEAR: are you Jewish or Arab?
> Both.
> Half and half?
> No, both, fully.
> And when they fight each other, on which side are you?
> On the wailing side.[69]

In most accounts, both political commitment and aloofness yielded the same results of loss and exile.

Written by those who left their country of birth, Jewish Mediterranean literature often presents an embellished account of lives before they got disrupted, the imperceptible cracks and the expulsion of individual lives dislodged by history; many accounts, told from a child's perspective, epitomize guiltless memory. In France, the noted writer Colette Fellous, who was forced to leave Tunisia at age seventeen, has revisited her home country in book after book in order to put the pieces of the puzzle together. Her novel *Pièces détachées* (*Spare Parts*) is missing a sense of a whole; the conflation of past and present in her writing is a way "to see how our life has been completely fabricated by political history, whereas we thought that it belonged to us, that it was personal to us."[70]

Individuals' stories are thus crushed by events they fail to foresee. As divergent voices in an Ashkenazi-dominated narrative of contemporary Jewish history, such Mediterranean chapters of exile have been overlooked and needed to be reclaimed.[71] It is no coincidence that *Les trois exils*—the title of Benjamin Stora's memoir—insists on the multiple exiles of Algerian Jews. If such returns are less common among Algerian-born writers, a slew of mostly self-published recent memoirs capture the very last moments and departures,[72] after decades of silence in the wake of the war.[73] This narrative apparatus, where crucial events go unexplained, imposed by a world of adults that does not make sense, is obviously meant to convey the arbitrary and the absurd, *l'Histoire avec sa grand hache* ("History with its capital H"), in the words of novelist Georges Perec.[74]

If the Jewish Mediterranean experience in literature can be defined by the spectrum of coexistence and expressions of nostalgia, its Israeli iteration seems to be the most delicate. For decades, the novelist A. B. Yehoshua, committed to his Moroccan origins, sought to offer a Sephardic counternarrative to the Ashkenazi cultural hegemony in Israel. As part of the effort to reshape the country's self-perception, he sought to be the voice of a past worthy of being heard in order to foster new chapters of coexistence.[75] His work seems to illustrate how a literary endeavor defined as Sephardism does not convey the sense of intimate loss or nostalgia that I have previously delineated as part of the Jewish Mediterranean. The first generation of Mizrahim[76] were pushed to embrace extreme politics by loss of status in a secular country, as described by David Grossman in *The Yellow Wind*. Mizrahim in Israel took a right-wing turn, forming the backbone of the Shas party, which offers its own version of Sephardic nostalgia ("returning the crown to its rightful place," as its slogan says), and forsaking any kind of future coexistence with the Arab world. At the same time, a turn in historiography gravitated toward a lachrymose view.[77] It has nevertheless, albeit marginally, spawned second and third generations of writers eager to recover—or reinvent—a lost Mediterranean heritage.[78]

From French-born children of Algerian Jews to Israeli-born children of Moroccan Jews, a new generation might well represent what Marianne Hirsch described—pertaining to the Holocaust—as the generation of post-memory.[79] Such transgenerational, Jewish Mediterranean nostalgia gives credence to the proposition made by French philosopher Barbara Cassin: it is "like every origin, a chosen fiction that constantly gives cues so as to be taken for what it is, an adorable, human fiction, a cultural fact.... But as with 'Homer' himself, nostalgia is not exactly what one believes it to be."[80] Indeed, nostalgia may exceed its object.

The vibrancy of urban life as well as the poignancy of abandoned lives captures a recent turn in scholarship of geography that endows it with affects, contrary to the accepted idea that "geography often presents us with an emotionally barren terrain, a world devoid of passion, spaces ordered solely by rational principles."[81] Not so with the Mediterranean. In these landscapes of memory, geography stands in the stead of history. Places tell stories; the narratives are less linear, more fragmented. Nostalgia possesses a timeless quality and tends to rely on geography as it cancels out history. "The Alexandria I knew, that part-Victorian, half-decayed, vestigial nerve center of the British Empire exists in memory alone, the way Carthage and Rome and Constantinople exist as vanished cities only—a city where the dominant languages were English and French, though everyone spoke in a medley of many more, because the principle languages were really Greek and Italian, and in my immediate world Ladino (the Spanish of the Jews who fled the Inquisition in the sixteenth century) with broken Arabic holding everything more or less together."[82]

Deleuze and Guattari claim that physical and cultural deterritorialization engenders reterritorialization in linguistic and artistic realms. For Jewish writers, this very reterritorialization happened in the language of the metropolis, which Cixous and Derrida have spelled out in their conversations:[83] "The metropolis, the City-Capitale-Motherland, the city of the mother tongue, here is a place which featured without really being a far away country, near yet distant, not foreign, that would be too simple, but strange, fantastic, ghostly."[84] In a reversal of the usual ghost story, the haunting will soon come from the place left.

In 1977, almost three decades after his seminal study, *The Mediterranean and the Mediterranean World in the Age of Philip II* (*La Méditerranée et le monde méditerranéen à l'époque de Philippe II*), Fernand Braudel characterized the Mediterranean as resisting unity in *La méditerranée: l'espace et l'histoire*: "not one civilization but civilizations stacked on top of one another."[85] What is the nature of such stacking? Are these civilizations stacked on top of one another akin to a palimpsest or to mnemonic traces? Do such traces call for an archeological approach akin to that of Freud's analysis of the unconscious? Do the various inaccessible strata of history function like a form of unconscious, and are thus timeless? This is what Predrag Matvejevic suggests in his Mediterranean breviary: "Talk of graveyard leads naturally to talk about dead languages. The Mediterranean has many, perhaps as many as it has islands. The Mediterranean is a vast archive, an immense grave."[86]

In most shores of the Jewish Mediterranean, experiences have been reduced to their archives—this *arke*, which Derrida defined as commandment and commencement. The archive, that which could seem to signal the end, is thus a beginning. Indeed, Jewish Mediterranean literature seems to be an archive and to function as a third age of the *convivencia* myth. But the nostalgia it entails is a mechanism capable of deflecting guilt in a postcolonial order. Such recollections—or reconstructions—might be puzzling unless one realizes that the way to the memory of this world functions as a dreamlike experience. In Freudian terms, displacement and condensation constitute the dynamics and mechanisms of a dream. And aspects of Mediterranean literature have a dreamlike quality. This emotional space condenses the lives and the loss of the displaced. And the dream can be haunting.

In *The Stranger*, Camus highlights the role of the sun, but it is a veiled sun, almost a dark sun. It is that very sun that leads Meursault to kill the Arab—an unnamed victim about whom the Algerian novelist Kamel Daoud wrote a counterhistorical novel in his 2014 *Mersault's Papers*.[87] The Algerian sun can also be a murderous glare. The meaning of the Mediterranean, and of a Jewish Mediterranean, has certainly evolved, maybe giving voice to more oblique, irrational narratives.[88] In *Le marabout de Blida*,[89] and in most of her work, Annie Cohen's back and forth between north and south, past and present, between France and her pre- and postwar Algerias, as well as her self-criticism bordering on schizophrenia, only betray her doomed capacity to belong to a specific place. But a more ominous Mediterranean has emerged. In light of the migrant crisis of this early twenty-first century, the Mediterranean has become both a barrier and a silent archive of anonymous death. Jews of the Mediterranean no longer constitute the waves of exiles, but they are witnesses to these new migrations. Confronting the suffering of others may call for new chapters in the attempt to salvage the elusive hope of a Mediterranean coexistence—or its tale.

CLÉMENCE BOULOUQUE is the Carl and Bernice Assistant Professor of Jewish Studies at Columbia University. Her forthcoming book is entitled *Another Modernity: Kabbalah, Jewish Universalism and Interreligious Engagement in the Work of Elia Benamozegh.*

Notes

1. David Luft, *Hugo von Hofmannsthal and the Austrian Idea: Selected Essays and Addresses, 1906–1927* (West Lafayette, IN: Purdue University Press, 2011).
2. Predrag Matvejevic, *Mediterranean: A Cultural Landscape* (Berkeley: University of California Press, 1999), 12.
3. Michael Herzfeld, "The Horns of the Mediterranean Dilemma," *American Ethnologist* 11 (1984): 439–54; Michael Herzfeld, "Practical Mediterraneanism: Excuses for Everything, from Epistemology to Eating," in *Rethinking the Mediterranean*, ed. W. V. Harris (Oxford: Oxford University Press, 2005), 45–63.
4. Herzfeld, "Practical Mediterraneanism," 48.
5. Thierry Fabre and Robert Ilbert, eds., *Les representations de la Méditerranée*, 10 vols. (Paris: Maisonneuve et Larose, 2000).
6. Initially a concept of limited scope, *convivencia* described Spanish philology in the 1926 work of Ramón Menéndez Pidal, *Orígenes del español* (1926) and more specifically the coexistence of phonetic variants among regional versions of medieval Romance. It was expanded into a whole cultural framework by Castro. See Américo Castro, *España en su historia: Cristianos, moros y judíos* (Buenos Aires: Editorial Losada, 1948) [Translation: *The Spaniards: An Introduction to Their History* (Berkeley: University of California Press, 1971)]. *Convivencia* became an ideological framework: this idealist agenda never aimed to describe a lived reality. The central concept of the book, written in exile from fascism, challenged the popular narratives emphasizing the essence of an "eternal Spain," grounded in a cultural homogeneity traceable to the antiquity and the Romano-Gothic period—a discourse prevalent in Franco's Spain. For a positive approach to *convivencia*, see Maria Menocal, *The Ornament of the World* (New York: Little, Brown, 2002); Simon Doubleday and David Coleman, eds., *In the Light of Medieval Spain* (New York: Palgrave McMillan, 2008).
7. Calling the symbiosis an instance of anti-biosis, another scholar in exile, Claudio Sánchez-Albornoz, penned scathing rebuttals of Castros's work in his *España: un enigma histórico* (1956). In the final chapter of his 1979 classic study, Thomas Glick critiqued both and rejected their essentialization of cultural and religious categories. See Thomas Glick, *Islamic and Christian Spain in the Early Middle-Ages* (Princeton, NJ: Princeton University Press, 1979)

and Thomas Glick, Vivian Mann, and Jerryline Dodds, eds., *Convivencia: Jews, Muslims, and Christians in Medieval Spain* (New York: Braziller, 2007). More recent studies have cautioned against such reifications: Brian Catlos, who replaced *convivencia* with "conveniencia," showed that sectarian differences were only one of the many aspects of these interactions. See Brian Catlos, *The Victors and the Vanquished: Kingdom of Faith* (New York: Basic Books, 2018). Focusing on religious unrest, David Nirenberg contended that *convivencia* was a self-correcting mechanism for convenience purposes in an environment where the outbursts of intercommunal violence became ritualized. See David Nirenberg, *Communities of Violence* (Princeton, NJ: Princeton University Press, 1996). For a survey of the challenges to the notion of *convicencia*, see Maya Soifer. "Beyond Convivencia: Critical Reflections on the Historiography of Interfaith Relations in Christian Spain," *Journal of Medieval Iberian Studies* 1 (2009): 1935.

8. Yael Halevi-Wise, *Sephardism: Spanish Jewish History and the Modern Literary Imagination* (Stanford, CA: Stanford University Press, 2012).

9. Cassano qualifies the relevance of this Orient-Occident axis and turns "the South" into a paradigmatic alternative to what he defines as Northern values of ethics, rationality, time, and space. His opposing categories are autonomy, slowness, moderation, and the Mediterranean.

10. Franco Cassano, *Southern Thought and Other Essays on the Mediterranean* (New York: Fordham University Press, 2011), 147.

11. Ibid., 142.

12. Ismar Schorsch, *From Text to Context* (Hanover, MA: Brandeis University Press, 1994), 71–92.

13. Barbara Becker-Cantarino, "The Rediscovery of Spain in Enlightened and Romantic Germany," *Monatshefte* 72, no. 2 (1980): 121–34.

14. Bernard Lewis, *History: Remembered, Recovered, Invented* (Princeton, NJ: Princeton University Press, 1975).

15. Amos Bitzan, "The Problem of Pleasure: Disciplining the German Jewish Reading Revolution, 1770–1870" (PhD diss., University of California, Berkeley, 2011).

16. These were inspired by the success of historical novels, such as *Ivanhoe*, a conscious reference for Heine. Jonathan Efron, *German Jewry and the Allure of the Sephardic* (Princeton, NJ: Princeton University Press, 2015), especially ch. 4.

17. Grace Aguilar's *Cedar Valley* in 1850, or Disraeli, *Alroy* and *Tancrede* in the 1860s.

18. See Efron, *Allure of the Sephardic*.

19. Yosef Haim Yerushalmi, *Zakhor* (Seattle: University of Washington Press, 1996), 86, 98.

20. Antonio Munoz-Molina, *Sepharad* (New York: Harvest, 2008). On this "imaginary Sepharad," which extends until Iran or Iraq, see Jonathan Schorsch, "Disappearing Origins: Sephardic Autobiography Today," *Prooftexts* 27, no. 1 (2007): 82–150. For Al-Andalus as a rhetorical event, see Gil Anidjar, *Our Place in Al-Andalus* (Stanford, CA: Stanford University Press, 2002).

21. Halevi-Wise, *Sephardism*. Edna Aizenberg's research on Latin American Jews discusses their use of *Sepharad*, or *neo-Sepharad*, as a concept and word meant to further their agenda of a Latin American diaspora in service of their native (or adopted) country's development and prosperity: Edna Aizenberg, *Books and Bombs in Buenos Aires: Borges, Gerchunoff and Argentine-Jewish Literature* (Hanover, MA: Brandeis University Press, 2004), 49–67.

22. Salo W. Baron, "Newer Emphases in Jewish History," *Jewish Social Studies* 25, no. 4 (1963): 245–58. See, too, Adam Teller, "Revisiting Baron's 'Lachrymose Conception': The Meanings of Violence in Jewish History," *AJS Review* 38, no. 2 (2014): 431–39.

23. Roger Cohen, "Bosnia Jews Glimpse Book and Hope," *New York Times*, April 16, 1995; Géraldine Brooks, "The Book of Exodus," *The New Yorker*, December 3, 2007.

24. Carl Schorske, *Fin de Siècle Vienna: Politics and Culture* (New York: Vintage, 1979).

25. Hugo Bettauer, *The City without Jews: A Novel of Our Time* (New York: Bloch, 1991). The book became a best seller and made Bettauer a prominent figure, which led in 1925 to his murder by a Nazi sympathizer for being a "corrupter of youth." See Murray Hall, *Der Fall Bettauer* (Vienna: Löcker, 1978).

26. Peter Gay, *Freud, Jews, and Other Germans: Masters and Victims in Modernist Culture* (Oxford: Oxford University Press, 1978).

27. Joseph Roth, *Radetzky's March* (New York: Overlook Press, 2002).

28. Claudio Magris, *Le Mythe et l'Empire dans la littérature autrichienne* (Paris: Gallimard, 1991), 15.

29. Ibid.

30. Stefan Zweig, *Journeys* (New York: Hesperus, 2010).

31. Hermann Broch, *Hofmannsthal und seine Zeit* (Frankfurt-am-Main: Suhrkamp, 2001), 46. The fourth part of the essay ("Die Fröhliche Apokalypse Wiens um 1880") is a reference to Nietzsche's "gay science" ("fröhliche Wissenschaft").

32. Similar tropes can be found in writings about the Ottoman Empire, which also fell as a consequence of World War I. The empire's diversity was part of its foundational mythology, as a key to explain its success. This mythology was, however, complicated when the empire devoured its own subjects in the Armenian genocide.

33. Most of the networks described for the eighteenth century can be found in the nineteenth century, see Évelyne Oliel-Grausz, "La Circulation du personnel rabbinique dans les communautés de la diaspora sépharade au XVIIIe siècle," in *Transmission et passages en monde juif*, ed. Esther Benbassa (Paris: Publisud, 1997), 313–34. Clémence Boulouque, "An 'Interior Occident' and the Case for an Oriental Modernity: The Livornese Printing Press and the Mediterranean Publishing Networks of Elia Benamozegh (1823–1900)," *Jewish Social Studies* 23, no. 2 (2018): 86–136.

34. Peregrine Horden and Nicholas Purcell, *The Corrupting Sea* (New York: Wiley-Blackwell, 2000).

35. Gottfried Wilhelm Friedrich Hegel, *Philosophy of Subjective Spirit*, vol. 2: *Anthropology* (Amsterdam: Reidel, 1978), 49.

36. Michel Chevalier, *Système de la Méditerranée: Articles extraits du Globe* (Paris: Le Globe, 1832); Jérôme Debrune, "Le Système de la Méditerranée de Michel Chevalier," *Confluences en Méditerranée* 36, no. 1 (2001): 187–94; Florence Deprest, "L'invention géographique de la Méditerranée: éléments de réflexion," *L'Espace géographique* 31, no. 1 (2002): 73–92.

37. This thesis has been most recently rejected by Iain Chambers; it is precisely the Arab conquests that rekindled networks and intellectual exchanges that had waned under disruptive unilateral forces imposed from the North: Rome and the Punic wars, the Crusades or even modernity. Iain Chambers, "Off the Map: A Mediterranean Journey," in *Comparative Literature Studies* 42, no. 4 (2005): 312–27, at 325.

38. Georges Fréris, "L'Algérianisme, le mouvement du Méditerranéisme et la suite," in *Méditerranée: Ruptures et Continuités. Actes du colloque tenu à Nicosie les 20–22 octobre 2001, Université Lumière-Lyon 2, Université de Chypre* (Lyon: Maison de l'Orient et de la Méditerranée Jean Pouilloux, 2003), 43–51.

39. Roger Quilliot, "Politique et culture Méditerranéennes," in *Albert in Camus: Essais* (Paris: Gallimard, 1965), 1314-20.

40. Audisio (1900–1978) was a writer and civil servant who was dispatched to Algeria. His work promoted a vision of North Africa as a site of cultural convergence; his essays *Jeunesse de la Méditerrannée* in 1935 (Paris: Gallimard, 2002) and its sequel *Sel de la mer* in 1936 (Paris: Gallimard, 2002) proved influential. After the war (during which he was imprisoned as a resistant), his publications included *Ulysse ou l'intelligence*, in 1946, an allegory of a Mediterranean mindset through the tribute to Odysseus construed as its typical hero. *Ulysse ou l'intelligence* (Paris: Gallimard, 2002). The reprinting of all these texts in 2002 indicates an appetite for such a narrative of the Mediterranean.

41. Gabriel Audisio, *Jeunesse de Méditerranée* (Paris: Gallimard, 1935), 13.

42. Camus elaborated on this theme of a multicultural Mediterranean in subsequent writings, notably the essays "Prometheus in the Underworld" (1947) and "Helen's Exile" (1948), in *The Myth of Sisyphus and Other Essays* (New York: Vintage, 2012), 185–93, as well as in "Thought at the Meridian" (1951), the last part of *The Rebel* (New York: Vintage, 2002). Edwige Tamalet Talbayev, "Between Nostalgia and Desire: L'Ecole d'Algers' Transnational Identifications and the Case for a Mediterranean Relation," *International Journal of Francophone Studies* 10, no. 3 (2007): 359–76; Franco Cassano, "Camus: The Need for Southern Thought," in *Southern Thought*, 63–85.

43. Albert Camus, "Nuptials at Tipasa," in *Lyrical and Critical Essays* (New York: Vintage, 2012), 65–73.

44. In the bleak postwar period, the Mediterranean became widely associated with cookbooks and its multitude of flavors. In Britain, Elizabeth David's *Book of Mediterranean Food* became rapidly popular. But it was Claudia Roden's *Book of Middle-Eastern Food* (1968) that really led to awareness of the region's coexistence of multiple influences. The Egyptian-born author of Syrian descent left Egypt to go to English boarding school in 1953 and was joined by her impoverished family in 1956. Memories of being taught cooking by neighbors and friends of diverse backgrounds infuse the book, which abounds with nostalgia for this lost world. An instant classic, the book has inspired many variations, including Roden's *Book of Jewish Food*. As David Abulafia highlights, with these books, the Mediterranean became everybody's possession. See David Abulafia, *The Great Sea* (New York: Oxford University Press, 2011), 650.

45. Leon Sciaky, *Farewell to Salonica: City at the Crossroads* (Philadelphia: Paul Dry Books, 2003).

46. Shlomo Goitein, *A Mediterranean Society: An Abridgement in One Volume*, ed. Jacob Lassner (Berkeley: University of California Press, 2003), 502.

47. The first volume of Goitein's five-volume study, *A Mediterranean Society*, in which he analyzed the documents of the Cairo genizah, came out in 1967, more than ten years after his *Jews and Arabs: Their Contact through the Ages*, published in 1955. Its displays of orientalism have been noted. The escalation of the Israeli-Palestinian conflict, the first and second intifadas and the post-9/11 rhetoric of a clash of civilization, in which Islam seems to have become the ultimate political enemy, fueled both an appetite for and a defiance toward Goitein's study and a reassessment of his work. That Mediterranean seems to act as a foil and a cure for the rupture between Jews and Arabs in the wake of the 1956 Suez intervention, intensifying with the Six-Day (1967) and Yom Kippur (1973) wars. See Steven Wasserstrom, "Apology for S. D. Gotein: An Essay," in *A Faithful Sea*, ed. Adnan Husain and K. E. Fleming (Oxford: Oneworld, 2007), 173–98.

48. André Aciman, *False Papers* (New York: Farrar, Strauss and Giroux, 2001).

49. In that sense, the Mediterranean could represent a postmodern understanding of religiosity. See Bruno Latour, *We Have Never Been Modern* (Cambridge, MA: Harvard University Press, 1993); Zygmunt Bauman, *Intimations of Postmodernity* (London: Routledge, 1992).

50. The pogroms, which resulted in thirty deaths and two hundred stores sacked, were instigated by the extremist French Social Party, which published tracts in Arabic in order to incite Muslims' hatred of the Jews. On this episode, see Ethan Katz, *The Burdens of Brotherhood* (Cambridge, MA: Harvard University Press, 2015), 85–97.

51. Aciman, *False Papers*.

52. History or anthropology may indeed contradict or nuance literary memoirs: Joseph Viscomi's work "Out of Time: History, Presence, and the Departure of the Italians of Egypt, 1933–present" (unpublished PhD diss., University of Michigan, 2016), details the ways in which the community experienced and remembered their life in, and departure from, Egypt, leading to different conclusions and a less idealized portrayal of the community—Jewish and non-Jewish alike.

53. Pierre Nora, "Between Memory and History: Les lieux de mémoire," *Représentations* 26 (1989): 7–24.

54. Benjamin Stora, *Les Trois Exils: Juifs d'Algérie* (Paris: Stock, 2006).

55. Nora, "Between Memory and History," 7.

56. Svetlana Boym, *The Future of Nostalgia* (New York: Basic Books, 2002), 3.

57. Albert Cohen, *The Book of My Mother* (New York: Archipelago Books, 2012), 33 (first published in 1954).

58. See Ethan Katz, Lisa Leff, and Maud Mandel, eds., *Colonialism and the Jews* (Bloomington: Indiana University Press, 2017).

59. Paul Gilroy, *Postcolonial Melancholy* (New York: Columbia University Press, 2004).

60. This is one of the consequences of the Crémieux decree, also conceived by the ruling power as a wedge between Muslims and "Arabs of the Jewish faith," which Joshua Schreier explores in *Arabs of the Jewish Faith: The Civilizing Mission in Colonial Algeria* (New Brunswick, NJ: Rutgers University Press, 2010).

61. On exceptions and privileges in the Ottoman Empire, see Sarah Stein, *Extraterritorial Dreams: Jews, Citizenship, and the Calamitous Twentieth Century* (Chicago: University of Chicago Press, 2016).

62. Boym, *The Future of Nostalgia*, 3. The context of American history in the aftermath of World War II is evidently different; see Michael Kammen, *Mystic Chords of Memory* (New York: Vintage, 1991), 688.

63. Albert Memmi, *The Colonizer and the Colonized* (New York: Routledge, 2014), 10.

64. Boym, *The Future of Nostalgia*, xiv.

65. "Unlike the Muslims, they passionately endeavored to identify themselves with the French. To them the West was the paragon of all civilization, all culture" (Memmi, *The Colonizer and the Colonized*, xiv).

66. Ibid., 40.

67. Lisa Leff, *Sacred Bonds of Solidarity* (Stanford, CA: Stanford University Press, 2006), 159–99.

68. Alleg (1921–2013) is the famed author of *La Question*, published in 1958 and prefaced by Jean-Paul Sartre, which, from personal experience, addressed for the first time the French army's use of torture in the Algerian war. The book became a rallying cry for a soul-searching

moment in France. Hiding from the French authorities until the end of the Algerian war in 1962, Alleg was declared *persona non-grata* in Algeria in 1965 after the military coup and had to settle in France.

69. Guy Sitbon, *Gagou* (Paris: Grasset, 1995).

70. Colette Fellous, *Pièces détachées* (Paris: Gallimard, 2017), 77.

71. It is remarkable to note that until recently scholarship could still address the question of exile in the "modern Jewish imagination" without mentioning the Sephardic/Mizrahi experience beyond Judah Halevi. See, for instance, Sidra DeKoven Ezrahi, *Booking Passage: Exile and Homecoming in the Modern Jewish Imagination* (Berkeley: University of California Press, 2000).

72. This is especially true of self-published novels or memoirs. Nicole Squinazi-Teboul, *Petite musique d'une déchirure: Une petite fille dans la Guerre d'Algérie* (Paris: L'Harmattan, 2010). There is no specificity in the description of this exile. See Jean-Louis Yaiche, *Alger sans moi* (Paris: Editions Maurice Nadeau, 2016). Social media and websites seem to have eased the memory process and the reconstitution—or the creation of new forms of (nostalgic) sociabilities. See www.judaicalgeria.com, where memoirs are compiled as well as videos.

73. Raphaëlle Branche, "The State, the Historians and the Algerian War in French Memory, 1991–2004," in *Contemporary History on Trial: Europe since 1989 and the Role of the Expert Historian*, eds. Harriet Jones, Kjell Östberg, and Nico Randeraad (Manchester: Manchester University Press, 2007), 159–73.

74. The pun appears in *W or a childhood's memory*, the tale of Perec, orphaned by the Holocaust. It is a play on words between the later *h* (masculine in French) and its homophone *hatchet*, a feminine word. History is thus spelled with a capital *H* as in *hatchet*.

75. With *The Lover*, A. B. Yehoshua is credited for giving voice to the first Arab character in Hebrew novels. In spite of being—arguably—condescending, A. B. Yehoshua's work still raises the question of the "other" as part of a multiple identity. See Gila Ramras-Rauch, "A. B. Yehoshua and the Sephardic Experience," *World Literature Today* 65, no. 1 (1991): 8–13; Bernard Horn, "Sephardic Identity and Its Discontents: The Novels of A. B. Yehoshua," in Yael Halevi Wise, ed., *Sephardism: Spanish Jewish History and the Modern Literary Imagination* (Stanford, CA: Stanford University Press, 2012), 189–212.

76. Mizrahim ("orientals") as an umbrella term in Israeli society that typically designates Jews from Arab countries, from Morocco to Yemen (though can also include Jews from other parts of the "Orient," including Iran and India).

77. Mark R. Cohen, "The Neo-Lachrymose Conception of Jewish-Arab History," *Tikkun* 6, no. 3 (1991): 55–60.

78. Dario Micoli, ed., *Contemporary Sephardic and Mizrahi Literature* (New York: Routledge, 2017).

79. Marianne Hirsch, *The Generation of Post-memory* (New York: Columbia University Press, 2012). The noted author Brigitte Giraud, who is not Jewish, used this setting of minute interviews of her parents for the first time in *Un loup pour l'homme* (Paris: Flammarion, 2017). The historical reconstitution—alongside the reclaiming of a legacy—is present in Valérie Zenatti's novel, *Jacob Jacob* (Paris: Editions de l'Olivier, 2014), the story of a Constantine-born great-uncle, enamored with French ideals, enrolled in World War II alongside his Muslim brethren and duped by history. Sfar's work, and his already mentioned *Rabbi's Cat*, also, belong to that generation.

80. Barbara Cassin, *Nostalgia: When Are We Ever at Home?* (New York: Fordham University Press, 2016), 3.

81. Liz Bondi, Joyce Davidson, and Mick Smith, "Introduction: Geography's 'Emotional Turn,'" in *Emotional Geographies*, ed. Liz Bondi, Joyce Davidson, and Mick Smith (London: Routledge, 2007), 1.

82. Aciman, *False papers*, 4. On Alexandria as palimpsest, see also: Veronica Della Dora, "The Rhetoric of Nostalgia: Postcolonial Alexandria between Uncanny Memories and Global Geographies," *Cultural Geographies* 13, no. 2 (2006): 207–38.

83. Jacques Derrida, *Le monolinguisme de l'autre ou la prothèse d'origine* (Paris: Éditions Galilée, 1996), 73.

84. Hélène Cixous, *Insister of Jacques Derrida*, trans. Peggy Kamuf (Stanford, CA: Stanford University Press, 2007), 47. The same can be said of Annie Cohen.

85. Fernand Braudel, *La Méditerranée. L'Espace et l'Histoire* (Paris: Flammarion, 1999), 8. ("Non pas une civilisation, mais des civilisations entassées les unes sur les autres.") In spite of this mention of civilizations, the human element comes second in the work of Braudel. This is one of the main criticisms of David Abulafia's *The Great Sea*; according to Abulafia, Braudel emphasized the environment at the expense of the specifically human element that Abulafia made central to his project, as the title of his work indicates. See David Abulafia, *The Great Sea; A Human History of the Mediterranean*, xx.

86. Matvejevic, *Mediterranean*, 15.

87. Kamel Daoud, *Meursault's Papers* (New York: The Other Press, 2015).

88. In Jewish and non-Jewish fiction; see Assia Djebar, *Femmes d'Alger dans leur appartement* (Paris: Editions des Femmes, 1980).

89. Annie Cohen, *Le Marabout de Blida* (Paris: Actes Sud, 1996).

INDEX

Page numbers in italics indicate figures.

Aaron of Baghdad, 32
Abraham ibn Daud, 32
Abulafia, David, 7, 22n9, 53, 208n44, 211n85
acculturation, 14, 138, 139
Aciman, André, 198, 199
Ackerman-Lieberman, Phillip, 57
Ade, Mafalda, 157
Adriatic region, 149, 165n3, 165n7; cabotage trade in, 150; Great War and, 163; olive oil trade in, 154; as Venetian-dominated space, 164
Africa, 9
agency, 2, 10, 15, 44, 45, 57, 199
agriculture, 32, 71; dry-farming economies, 36, 47n17; north–south agricultural axis in Europe, 68, 77; trinity of wheat, olives, and grapes, 12
"agro-literate" regimes, 40, 48n26
Aguilar, Grace, 193
Ahmed ben al-Hadji, Hadji, 103n35
Ahmed Paşa, Grand Vizier, 108
Aizenberg, Edna, 206n21
Alaluf, Elie, 176
Alashkar, Moses, 55
Alashkar, Solomon, 55
Albania, 1, 20, 153, 163, 176; Italian as language of trade in, 164; in Ottoman Empire, 149, 150, 156, 160
Albanian language, 155
Albanian State Archives (ASAT), 149
Alexandria (Egypt), port of, 162, 198, 199, 203
Algeria, 52, 196–97, 199; Algerian Divan, 95; Crémieux decree, 201, 209n60
Algérienisme, right-wing ideology of, 196–97
Algiers, 86, 87, 95, 102n25, 112; ransom market for captives in, 96–97; two Jewish communities in, 105n61
Alia, Mordecai (Mordafay), 91
Alleg, Henri, 201, 209–10n68

Alliance Israélite Universelle, 174, 179, 182, 201
Alluvial Jews, 181
Alps, 32
Amsterdam, 33, 138, 142, 148n82, 176
Anatolia, 171
Ancient Economy, The (Finley), 30
anthropology, 8, 35, 66n42
Antiochus IV, 42
anti-Semitism, 180, 194, 197
Appiah, Kwame Anthony, 51
Arabic language, 14, 85, 86, 180, 203
Arabs, 1, 117
Armenians, 110, 115, 117, 121, 142, 183
ars mercatoria, 137
artisans, 34, 72, 73, 110, 198
Artom, Elias, 71
Ascher Salem and Son, 176, 177
Asher ben Yeḥiel, Rabbi ("Rosh"), 75–76
Ashkenazim, 2, 18, 58, 60, 64n18; Alluvial Jews and, 181; contemporary Jewish history dominated by, 202; insular educational model of, 193; merchants, 138
Asia Minor, 34
assimilation, 50, 98, 201
Astren, Fred, 7, 9, 11
astrology, 174, 179–80, 185
Atlantic Ocean, 32
Audisio, Gabriel, 192, 197
Auerbach, Berthold, 193
Austrian Lloyd steamship company, 150, 153, 163
Austro-Hungarian (Habsburg) Empire, *151*, 152, 154, 163, 191, 194–95
Azulai, Hayim Yosef David, 147n67

Bahloul, Joelle, 177
Balfour Declaration, 180
Balkan Wars, 162, 163, 164, 174

213

Baltic Sea, 15
Bar/Antivari, port of, 150, *151*, 153, 160
Baron, Salo, 76, 77, 194
Baruch, Beniamin, 132, 135, 145n26
Battino, Ben, 162
Bayezid II, Sultan, 108
Belle du Seigneur (Cohen, 1968), 198
belonging, 60, 61, 196, 198
Benbassa, Esther, 189n60
Ben Sira (*Wisdom of Ben Sira*), 38–39, 41
Berab, Jacob, 55
Berbers, 1, 197
berit ahavah (covenant of friendship/love), 38
Berns, Andrew, 19
Bettauer, Hugo, 194, 207n25
Bible, Greek, 34, 43
Bible, Hebrew, 15, 36–37; Deuteronomy, 38, 70; Ecclesiastes, 38; Leviticus, 41, 70, 71; prohibition on *sha'atenez* garments, 68, 70; Proverbs, 38; Samuel, 38
Bitzan, Amos, 193
Black Sea, 32
Blumi, Isa, 160, 168n52
Book of Mediterranean Food (David), 208n44
Book of Middle-Eastern Food (Roden, 1968), 208n44
Book of My Mother (Cohen, 1954), 149
borderlands, 120–21
Botero, Giovanni, 108–9, 119
Boulouque, Clémence, 20
Boym, Svetlana, 201
Braudel, Fernand, 3, 4–5, 7, 12, 15, 30, 211n85; at École Pratique des Hautes Études, 9; on ecological unity of Mediterranean, 19, 74, 76; in German prison camp, 23n24; historians of premodernity and, 44–45; impressionism of, 31; on Judaism as a civilization, 5, 24n28, 69; on Mediterranean as multiplicity of civilizations, 204; on Mediterranean unity ("common destiny"), 69, 171, 185; on religions as "warring" civilizations, 107
Bregoli, Francesca, 17, 18, 20
Bricuela, Pedro de, 86
Britain (England), 74, 163, 175, 176, 203; as exporting country, 170, 177, 179; Palestine under mandate of, 180, 185

Broch, Hermann, 195, 207n31
Broggia, Carlo, 110
Brubaker, Rogers, 29n106
Bulgaria, 175, 176, 182, 183
Byzantine Jewry in the Mediterranean Economy (Holo), 13
Byzantium, 2, 70

cabotage (short-distance coastal trade), 6, 15, 31, 150; port cities and, 55; in Roman world, 32
Cahiers du Sud (journal), 197
Cairo genizah, 9, 10, 12, 19, 27n79, 32; image of Jewish/Mediterranean history and, 52; lives of Mediterranean Jews recorded in, 57
Calvinism, 99, 109
Camus, Albert, 192, 196–97, 204
Cansino, Rabbi Abraham, 93
Cansino, Jacob, 92, 93, 94, 98
Cansino family, 86, 88, 89, 92
capitalism (proto-capitalism), 33
Capsali, Elia, 71, 72–73
Carmona, Élie, 182–83
Caro, Joseph, 55
Cassano, Franco, 192, 206n9
Cassin, Barbara, 203
Cassuto, Umberto, 71
Castro, Américo, 8, 192, 205n6
Catholics/Catholicism, 8, 9, 96, 107, 108; in Corfu, 152; Counter-Reformation, 113; French Catholics in Ottoman cities, 121; Greek Uniates, 113, 114–15; Jewish and Protestant refugees from Catholic persecution, 109; Jewish converts to, 17, 116; in Livorno, 112, 113–14; marriages with non-Catholics, 115; in Ottoman Albania, 152
Catlos, Brian, 8
Central Asia, 11, 12
Ceuta garrison, 86, 90–91, 95
Chambers, Iain, 171–72, 207n37
charity, 40, 43
chechia trade, 131
Chevalier, Michel, 196
China, 36, 176, 178
"Christendom," 1, 107, 110

Christianity, 9, 59, 89; as a "civilization," 69; early sectarian communities, 43; Jews as intermediaries and, 5; Muslim slaves converted to, 92, 95–97; oriental origins of, 178; in the Roman Empire, 34; Spanish Muslims forced to convert to, 85

Christians, 1, 16, 17, 40, 57, 77; boundaries between different confessions, 108; Christian tailors and *sha'atenez* prohibition, 72; enslavement of, 81, 83; friars' collaboration with Jewish merchants to redeem captives, 85–89; in medieval Iberia, 8; merchants, 83, 84, 85; narrative of Jewish symbiosis with, 20; New Christians, 116, 142, 145n31; Palestinian, 181; religious boundaries in Livorno and, 111; as slave owners, 91–92, 99; in Spanish North Africa, 86. *See also* Catholics/Catholicism; Orthodox Christians; Protestants/Protestantism

Ciobba, Angelo, 152, 159, 162
Ciobba & Bianki, 149, 152, 154, 155, 156, 157
City without Jews, The (Bettauer, 1922), 194, 207n25
Cixous, Hélène, 204
class divisions, 6, 115
Clear Standard, The (al-Wansharīsī), 91
climate, 4, 6, 68, 76
Coen, Abram, 149, 165n3; customers in Scutari, 152, 156; decline of soap business, 161–62, 163; dispute with Saraci, 157–61; merchant court of Corfu and, 168n40; rivalry with Abram Israel, 154, 156; ship captains and, 155; soap factory of, 154; trade correspondence of, 150, 152, 155; trade with Montenegro, 150
Coen, Armando, 162
Coen, Isacco, 162–63
Coen, Marc, 149, 162
Coen de Lara, Abram, 134, 135–36, 139, 146n44
Cohen, Albert, 20, 162, 163, 197–98, 200
Cohen, Annie, 204–5
Cohen, Mark, 27n79, 52
Cohen, Rabbi Moses, 74
Colbert, Jean-Baptiste, 118
Cold War, 30

colonialism, 53, 177
Colonizer and the Colonized, The (Memmi), 201
communication technologies, 171
Companion to Mediterranean History, A (Horden and Kinoshita, eds.), 7
connectivity, 28n95, 31, 37, 59; cross-cultural, 50; diversity and, 56; fragmentation-plus connectivity, 15; Mediterranean Sea and, 49; North Africa outside zone of, 46n6; questioning concept of, 61; transregional networks and, 54
Constantine (Algeria) pogroms (1934), 199, 209n50
conveniencia (convenience principle), 8
conversion, religious, 116, 126n46
conversos, 8, 24n28, 58, 125n43
convivencia model, 8, 18, 20, 59, 194; absence of single model in Mediterranean, 122; Habsburg myth and, 195; history of, 205n6; as idealizing description of Andalusian Spain, 192; Jewish Mediterranean literature and, 204
Corfu, 20, 55, 163, 200; Bojana River connection to Scutari, 153; *Ebraiki* (Jewish quarter), 149; Italian as language of trade in, 164; Jews of, 152–53; map, 151; merchant court (Emporodikeion), 157, 168n40; short-distance trade with Ottoman mainland, 149–50
Corrupting Sea, The: A Study of Mediterranean History (Horden and Purcell, 2000), 5–7, 9, 14, 30, 59, 69; on "connectivity" as defining feature of Mediterranean, 196; on religious landscape and Mediterranean geography, 78n5
cosmopolitanism, 2, 14, 16, 21, 49, 172; communitarian, 9; intra-Jewish networks and, 130; liberal cosmopolitanism of port cities, 118; Maimonides and, 49–50; Mediterraneanism and, 56; "melting pot" and, 50, 53; nationalism and waning of, 56; "Oriental" influence and, 3, 23n15; pluralism contrasted with, 50; Sephardic Jews and, 52; Viennese Jews as embodiment of, 195

Costa, Abram, 115
court Jews, 14
creditworthiness, 129, 130, 142
Crémieux decree, 201, 209n60
Crete, 68, 69; botanical cultivation and nomenclature in, 74; Greco-Turkish war in (1897), 158, 159; identification and use of plant fibers in, 70–74
criminalization, religious boundaries and, 111–12
Crónica de Almançor (Saldaña), 103n33
Crudo, Jacob, 87, 90, 91, 102n25
Crusade, Fourth (1204), 13, 28n93, 71
Crusades, 3
culturalism, 1
"culturalogical" approach, 8, 9
culture, 12, 45; cultural symbiosis, 14; "Mediterranean culture," 35–36; socioeconomic structures and, 31
Czechoslovakia, 176

Daoud, Kamel, 204
Dati identity, 61
David, Elizabeth, 208n44
Davis, John, 35, 36
De Beneficiis (Seneca), 38
De Brosses, Charles, 110
debt bondage, restriction of, 41
Decker, Jérémias de, 127n64
"Decline of Zionism, The" (Lévy, 1928), 181
Deleuze, Gilles, 203
"Democracy versus the Melting Pot" (Kallen), 50
Derrida, Jacques, 204
Destour movement, in Tunisia, 201
deterritorialization, 203
dhimmis (protected non-Muslims under Muslim rule), 90, 91
difference, religious, 8, 16, 17, 82
Disraeli, Benjamin, 193
divorce, as manumission from servitude, 43
doux commerce ("gentle commerce"), 118, 126n60
Driessen, Henk, 55, 56, 61
Dubin, Lois, 14, 98
Duoda, Anton, 166n11
Durres/Durazzo (Albania), port of, 150, 151, 160

"East–West" (Orient–Occident) division, 9, 60, 178, 197, 206n9
Egypt, 12, 27n85, 33, 34, 175, 176; British Empire in, 196; Hellenistic, 42; Mamluk control of, 14; Nagid of, 55; nationalism in, 180; orientalist image of, 179; slave owning in, 94
Elmaleh, Abraham, 182
Emperor's Tomb, The (Roth, 1938), 194
endogamy, religious, 115
England. *See* Britain (England)
Enlightenment, 108, 117, 118, 193
Enriches, Iacob, 139
Ephraim of Regensburg, Rabbi, 79n28
episteme, 15, 45
Epoka, La (periodical), 170, 174
España: un enigma histórico (Sánchez-Albornoz, 1956), 205n7
ethnography, 35
euergetism, 37, 39–40, 42, 43–44
Europe, western, 12, 178
Evelyn, John, 117

False Papers (Aciman), 198, 199
Fancy, Hussein, 58
fatwas, Muslim, 83, 91, 94
Fellous, Colette, 202
Fez, city of, 86
Fin de Siècle Vienna (Schorske, 1979), 194
Finley, Moses, 30, 31, 32, 36
Fischer, Theobald, 1
flax, 68, 70, 75, 78n7, 78n9; botanical nomenclature and, 76; confusion over definition of, 71; equated with hemp, 74, 79n28
fluidity, 2, 8, 16, 18; in borderlands, 120–21; erasure of boundaries and, 108; of personal identity, 107; questioning concept of, 61; Sephardic Jews as stereotyped marker of, 9
France, 13, 74, 83, 175, 176, 196; Algeria as extension of, 196–97; effort to drive Protestants from, 109; as exporting country, 170, 177, 179; Great War and, 163; Jewish North African exiles in, 202
Franchetti, Abram, 132
Franchetti, Baron Alberto, 144n17

Franchetti, Ihiel (Yehiel), 133, 146n38
Franchetti, Isache, 132, 133, 142, 145n26, 146n51; cautioned against theater attendance, 140; father's letters emphasizing Jewish observance, 132, 141; move to Livorno, 135, 136, 137, 139
Franchetti, Jeudà, 132, 133, 135, 145n30
Franchetti, Joseph, correspondence of, 130, 131–32, 140–42, 145n19, 145n26; Judaic values and reputation emphasized, 137–40, 141–42, 148n82; networks of "familial supervision" and, 132–37, 146n33, 146n44
Franchetti, Reuben, 132, 133, 135, 142, 145n26; in company of Christian "freemasons," 139, 140; father's letters emphasizing Jewish observance, 132, 141
Franchetti family, 17, 18
Franco, Francisco, 205n6
Frankfurt school, 195
freemasons, 139, 140, 148n83
free ports, 110, 113, 114, 118
French language, 170, 174, 185, 201
Freud, Sigmund, 204
Fua, Albert, 183–84
Future of Nostalgia, The (Boym), 201
"Future of Turkey, The" (Fua), 183–84

Gagou (Sitbon), 202
Galilee, 40
Ganucci, Filippo, 125n44
Gellner, Ernest, 48n26
gender, 6, 177
genizah studies, "Princeton school" of, 27n79
Genoa, 95
geography, 4, 176; culture in tension with, 1; Jewish agricultural laws and, 75; memory and, 199; microregions, 6, 9, 69, 77, 163
Germany, 74, 112, 177, 193; German historians, 4; idea of the Mediterranean in, 191
Giaccaria, Paolo, 61
Gibraltar, 90, 96
gift exchange, 31
Gilroy, Paul, 201
Giraud, Brigitte, 210n79
Glick, Thomas, 205n6

Glickl bas Leib, 147n65
globalism, 15
globalization, 30, 35
Goitein, Shlomo Dov, 9–12, 14, 19, 27n72, 53, 60; Arab-Israeli conflict and, 198, 208n47; influence on Jewish studies, 49
Goldberg, Jessica, 10, 12–13, 27n72, 27n85; on importance of flax in Islamicate world, 78n9; on zones of agricultural macro-ecology, 78n3
Goodman, Martin, 37
Gravier, Anna, 116
Great Sea., The: A Human History of the Mediterranean (Abulafia), 7, 22n9, 211n85
Great War (World War I), 162, 163, 164, 184
Greece, 34, 152, 176, 180; Alliance Israélite Universelle in, 182; map, *151*; orientalist image of, 179. See also Corfu; Ionian Islands
Greek language, 203
Greeks, 1, 3, 33; in Corfu, 152; *xenia* (interethnic friendship), 38
Greene, Molly, 8
Greif, Avner, 10
Gritti, Andrea, 108
Grossman, David, 203
Guattari, Félix, 203
Guide Sam, Le (commercial guide, 1920s–30s), 17, 18, 170–71, 183, 184–86; cover image (1924 edition), 172, *173*; editions of, 171, 186n3; Jewishness of, 172; Ladino publications and, 174. See also Lévy, Sam
Gulf of Aden, 51

Halevi, Judah, 210n71
Halevi-Wise, Yael, 194
Halevy, Bezalel Saadi, 174, 187n11
Halid Pasha, 179
Handbook of Soap Making (1898), 158–59
Haredi identity, 61
Haskalah, 14
Hasmonean dynasty, 44
Hebrew language, 13, 14, 180
Hegel, G.W.F., 196
Heine, Heinrich, 193, 206n16
Hellenism, 40

Hellenistic culture/period, 11, 36, 37, 41
hemp, 68, 70, 71, 75, 78n7; botanical nomenclature and, 76; equated with flax, 74, 79n28
Herodian family, 33, 47n12
Hershenzon, Daniel, 17, 19
Herzfeld, Michael, 20, 21, 35, 171; on ethnography of masculine honor, 37; on Mediterranean as discursive space, 7, 80n37, 177; Mediterraneanism thesis, 191, 199
Hess, Andrew C., 63n5
Hierro, Maria de, 106n67
Hillel, 41
Hirsch, Marianne, 203
Hirschman, Albert, 118
Hodgson, Marshall, 11
Hofer, Johannes, 200
Hofmannsthal, Hugo von, 191
Holo, Joshua, 13, 28n93
Holocaust, 203, 210n74
Holy Land, 55
honor, 39, 41, 43; Mediterranean culture and, 8, 37, 49; of merchants, 129, 130, 137, 141
Hopkins, Keith, 32, 36
Horden, Peregrine, 2, 3, 5–7, 12, 14, 22n9, 60; on ancient and medieval economies, 165n6; approach to culture, 31; on connectivity, 15; on "culturalogical" approach, 8; on disunity in Mediterranean region, 69, 74–75; on fragility of dry-farming economies, 36; on Mediterranean as zone of net introversion, 58; on micro-regions, 12, 69, 76, 152; on "New Thalassology," 49; predecessors in Mediterranean studies, 9; on unity-out-of-diversity, 50–51, 63n6; on unity-through-fragmentation, 53. See also *Corrupting Sea, The*
Horowitz, Elliott, 14
hybridity, 2, 8, 18, 21, 56; cultural, 55, 56; limits of, 16; Mediterranean studies and, 59

Iberia, 2, 20, 52, 83, 196
Iberian studies, medieval, 8
Ibn Habib, Levi, 55
Ibn Tibbon, Jacob, 55

"ideal type," Weberian, 15, 45
identity, cultural, 30
identity, religious, 2, 20, 21, 58, 60; centrality to Jewish self-understanding, 59; construction of, 61; of slaves, 99; slave trade and, 82; toleration in borderlands and, 120–21
ideology, 45
Imperial Turkish Lycée, 174
India, 178
Indian Ocean, 32, 33, 121, 166n8
Inquisition, Roman, 116
Inquisition, Spanish, 87, 89, 103n35, 194, 203
Interdict (1606–1607), 124n22
interfaith sociability, 117
intermediaries, Jews as, 4, 5, 6, 172, 201; "impression management" and, 86–87; linguistic intermediaries, 86; ransom of captives and, 93, 96, 97; slave trade and, 89
intra-Jewish networks, 7, 17, 18
Ionian Islands, 154, 163; Corfu as largest island, 152; olive oil exported from, 167n22; soap factories on, 149, 154; Venetian control of, 153
Iran, 11, 12, 121, 189n60
Iraq, 11, 32
Iron Age, 38
Islam, 1, 4, 9, 59, 84, 178; Christian slaves converted to, 91, 92; as a "civilization," 69; "clash of civilizations" rhetoric and, 208n47; Jews as intermediaries and, 5; Mediterranean unity and, 196; Muslim conquest of seventh century, 12; Muslim legal scholarship (*fiqh*), 13; Pirenne Thesis and, 3, 4; tolerance of Al-Andalus and, 193. See also Muslims
"Islamicate" world, 11, 13, 78n9, 121
Israel, Abram, 154, 156
Israel, modern state of, 59, 60, 177, 198, 201; Ashkenazi cultural hegemony in, 203; Mizrahim ("orientals") in, 203, 210n76; post-Zionist scholarship on, 14
Israelites, biblical, 36, 37, 40, 41, 182
Istanbul, 33, 121, 182
Italian language, 153, 155, 164, 203
Italy, 14, 32, 34, 55, 175, 176; in Adriatic region (map), *151*; botanical cultivation

and nomenclature in, 69, 74; commercial toleration in, 108–10, 124n22; Counter-Reformation, 58; effort to drive Protestants from, 109; as exporting country, 170, 177, 179; Great War and, 163; incursions in the Maghreb, 196; landholding arrangements in, 35; reduction in customs barriers, 110; spatial religious boundaries in, 113; toleration of religious minorities, 108. *See also* Livorno; Venice/Venetian Republic

Jacob Jacob (Zenatti, 2014), 210n79
Jerusalem, 34, 38, 43; (post) Herodian, 40; Hellenistic, 41; yeshivot of, 55
Jerusalem School, 27n72
Jeunesse de la Méditerranée [Youth of the Mediterranean] (Audisio), 197
Jewish Colonization Association, 181
Jewish diaspora, 5, 11, 40, 47n12; Byzantine, 13, 28n93; Corfiote, 163; interwar, 174; Jewish communal life and diasporic networks, 34; *sha'atenez* prohibition and, 70, 74, 75; social networks and, 57. *See also* Sephardic diaspora
Jewish law (halakha), 13, 54, 57, 72, 74
Jewish studies, 49, 51, 57, 60, 61; Mediterraneanism and, 50; Mediterranean studies in confluence with, 58; slavery in Mediterranean and, 81; transnational versus local/regional Jewish society, 53
Jews: absence from Mediterranean studies, 1–2, 6; Algerian, 85, 94, 201–3, 209n60; Corfiote, 162, 163, 164; Egyptian, 42; as farmers, 34; in-group solidarity among, 45; Jewish distinctiveness, 2, 16, 19; "Jews of Islam," 2; in medieval Iberia, 8; in Mediterranean history, 2–9; as merchants, 3–4, 6; mobility of, 54, 175; of the Muslim world, 60; narrative of symbiosis with Muslims and Christians, 20; "orientalization" of, 60; in Ottoman cities, 121, 174, 178, 201; of Palestine, 42; "port Jews," 14, 49, 56, 98; in Roman Mediterranean world, 32–35; slave trade associated with, 4, 17; Viennese, 194–95. *See also* Ashkenazim; intermediaries, Jews as; merchants, Jewish; Mizrahim; Sephardim
Jews and Arabs: Their Contact through the Ages (Goitein, 1955), 208n47
Jews and Modern Capitalism, The (Sombart), 4
Joseph ibn Abitur, 64n17
Josephus, 33, 39, 42, 44
Journal de Salonique, Le, 170, 174
Journal of Levantine Studies, 66n47
Journeys (Zweig), 195
Judaea, 39, 40, 42, 44
Judaica scholars, 58
Judaism, 9, 24n29, 33, 51, 56, 132; anti-Judaism of Catholic lower classes, 114; as a "civilization," 5, 24n28, 69, 107; in education of apprentice traders, 137–40; former *conversos'* reversion to, 17, 58, 116; Mediterranean studies and, 58; Zionism and, 181
Judeo-Arabic language, 13, 189n60

kabbalah, 54
Kallen, Horace, 50
Kalonymids, 32
Kammen, Michael, 201
Kant, Immanuel, 196
Kaplan, Benjamin, 107, 122n2
Katz, Jacob, 65n35
Khazars, 181
kilayyim ("diverse kinds"), laws of, 74
Kinoshita, Sharon, 7, 15
kinship, 2, 20, 40, 57, 142, 156
Kolbe, Constanze, 20, 185
Krakow, 33
Kymlicka, Will, 107, 122, 122n2

Ladino (Judeo-Spanish) language, 170, 174, 203; Lévy's advocacy for, 181, 182, 183, 185; in post-Ottoman regimes, 178; viewed as dead language, 182–83
"Latinity," 196
Lehmann, Matthias, 69, 76–77, 78n5
Lemercier, Claire, 157
Leon, Samuel and Moise, 135, 136, 146n33
Levant, 69, 109, 175, 179

Levantines, 58, 61, 117
Levi, Sima di Giuseppe, 102n25
Lévy, Sam (Samuel Saadi Halevy), 18, 170, 175, 184–85, 186n2; belief in Sephardim as "pure Jews," 181–82; critique of Zionism, 180–81; family and biography of, 173; geography and personal connections of, 176–77; on racial divisions among Jews, 18, 181, 182, 185, 189n60; terminology used by, 178. See also *Guide Sam, Le*
liberalism, invention of, 118–20
Libya, 34, 176
Lieberman, Phillip, 27n79
Livornina letter patent (1591, 1593), 111, 114, 116
Livorno, city of, 20, 87, 102n25, 108, 148n76; *bagno* building, 112–13, 124n25; cross-cultural trade in, 115–18; Franchetti family in, 131, 135, 137, 140, 145n22; freedom and risks for Jewish merchant youth in, 140, 147–48n75; as free port, 110; Jews as slave owners and slave traders, 94, 98; mechanisms of social discipline in, 111–15; Piazza Grande as stock exchange, 117, 119; religious tolerance in, 17; slavery/slave trade in, 95; Statue of the Four Moors, 113
Livre de ma mère, Le [*The Book of My Mother*] (Cohen, 1954), 200
Livre d'Or de l'Orient, Le (Lévy guide), 171, 179, 186n3
London, 119, 138
longue durée, la (Braudel's concept), 2, 4, 36, 46n6
Loup pour l'homme, Un (Giraud), 210n79
Lover, The (Yehoshua), 210n75

macro-ecology, agricultural, 12
Maghreb, 83, 84, 94, 99; French historians of, 199–200; Jews of, 82; Maghrebi culture, 19; Spanish garrisons in, 85, 86. See also North Africa
Magris, Claudio, 194–95
Maimonides, Moses, 13, 14, 49–50
Maimonides in His World (Stroumsa), 13
Majares, Diego de, 86
Malachi, Yehuda (Judas Malaqui), 88–89, 90
Malinowski, Bronislaw, 46n2

Malta, 112
Mamluks, 14
Manasseh (Menagi), Abraham, 91
Mangeclous [*Nailcrunchers*] (Cohen, 1938), 198
Al-Mansur, Ahmad, 103n33
Maque family, 92
Marabout de Blida, Le (Cohen), 204–5
Marakesh, city of, 86
Marglin, Jessica, 69, 76–77, 78n5
Marrakech, 103n33
Marranos, 108
Marseilles, port of, 118, 154, 162, 163
Martini, George Christoph, 117, 119
Marx, Karl, 127n66
Matvejevic, Predrag, 191, 204
Maurras, Charles, 197
Mauss, Marcel, 46n2
Mays, Devi, 17
Medici family/regime, 17, 110, 112; flow of power through intermediaries, 114; religious toleration in Livorno and, 116
medievalists, 8
Medina, Pedro de, 105–6n67
Mediterranean (Middle Sea) region, 1, 21n1; biome of, 74, 77; "Christian" divided from "Muslim," 2; climate and growing conditions, 68–69; connectivity of, 6, 9; cross-cultural trade in, 130–31; as discursive construct, 7, 191; ecological unity of, 4, 7, 69; employed against nationalism, 184; environmental unity of, 19; in European context, 177; "importing countries" associated with, 170, 177; in Jewish history, 9–14, 62; meaning of, 62; memory and exile, 199–205; microregions in, 152; north-south axis in, 171, 196; as "pluriverse" in Jewish literary adaptations, 192, 196–99; redemption of captives in, 83–85; toleration in, 120–22; as variation on coexistence narratives, 192–95
Mediterranean, The [*La Méditerranée et le monde méditerranéen à l'époque de Philippe II*] (Braudel, 1949), 4, 5, 23n24, 24nn28–31, 69, 204; English paperback edition (1972), 9; scholars of ancient history and, 44–45

Mediterranean Historical Review (journal), 14
Mediterraneanism, 7, 12, 14, 30, 56; ancient Jewish history and, 35; canon of, 3, 7, 22n9; history of emotions and, 199; Jewish studies and, 50; new moral geography and, 49; religious identity and, 60; used to fend off xenophobic narratives, 196
Mediterranean Sea, 2, 49, 68
Mediterranean Society, A (Goitein, 1967–1988), 9, 10, 26n68, 208n47
Mediterranean studies, 1–2, 4, 15, 22n6, 52, 57, 61; "hybrid" turn in, 16; integration of Jews into, 50; Jewish history and, 51, 56; Pirenne Thesis and, 3
Mediterranean unity, 69, 197; Braudel's concept of "common destiny" and, 69, 171, 185; Islam and, 196; Turkic "invasion" and, 12
Méditerranée, La: L'espace et l'histoire (Braudel), 204
Megillat Ahima'az, 32
Mehmed I, Sultan, 127n70
Mejía, Joseph (José), 90–91
Mejía, Moses (Moisés), 91
"melting pot," 50, 53, 56
Memmi, Albert, 201
Menéndez Pidal, Ramón, 205n6
mercantilism, 33
Mercedarians (Order of Our Lady of Mercy), 83, 85–88, 91, 95, 96
merchants: Christian, 83, 84, 85; European guide literature for Christian merchants, 137–38, 147n60, 147n62; Greek and Armenian Orthodox, 110; Livornina and, 111; Muslim, 83, 84, 96, 97; socializing in Piazza Grande of Livorno, 117
merchants, Jewish, 3–4, 6, 9, 57; apprenticeship and, 136, 137, 146n49; Cairene, 10; in Corfu, 20, 153; cosmopolitanism and, 17; family firms and, 129; legal status of, 11; Livornese, 52; in Livorno, 110, 147n67, 148n76; "port Jews," 98; redemption of captives and, 83–89, 96; reputation of, 129–30, 133, 134, 136, 159; role of correspondence in premodern business, 132; soap manufacturing and, 149–64

Mersault's Papers (Daoud, 2014), 204
Mesopotamia, 33
Middle Ages, 33, 34, 52, 53, 54; in Crete, 72; as period of incomplete secularism, 58
Middle East, 5, 7, 9, 14, 57, 61
Middle Eastern studies, 2, 22n6
Middle Sea, The (Norwich), 22n9
migration crisis, 1, 205
Mille, Pierre, 178, 180
Miller, Peter, 10, 27n72
Minca, Claudio, 61
Mizrahim, 60, 61, 189n60, 203, 210n76
Mizrahiyut, 60
mobility, 7, 33, 54, 85, 99; effort involved in, 30; expulsions and, 34; hypermobility, 171, 175; naturally fostered by Mediterranean Sea, 49; between religious communities, 58; restrictions on, 171
Mohammed and Charlemagne (Pirenne, 1937), 3, 196
Monroy, Bernardo, 86
Montel, David de, 131, 135
Montenegro, 20, 150, 152, 161, 164; Great War and, 163; map, 151; Ottoman trade policy undermined by, 160, 168n52
Montesquieu, 118
Moriscos, 85, 90, 192
Moroccan Jews, 81, 87, 90, 100n4, 103n35, 201; Israeli-born children of, 203
Morocco, 27n85, 81, 88, 103n35, 182
Morris, Ian, 21–22
Mosaic allotments, 41
Moses of Greece, 79n28
Mulay Zidan, 88
Muslims, 1, 16, 57, 77; Algerian Jews and Crémieux decree, 201, 209n60; converted to Catholicism, 116; enslavement of, 81, 83, 84, 95–97, 112, 117, 124n25; in Livorno, 112, 117; in medieval Iberia, 8; merchants, 83, 84, 96, 97; Muslim civilization, 10; narrative of Jewish symbiosis with, 20; Ottoman, 8, 152; Palestinian, 181; in Renaissance Italy, 110; Shia, 121; as slave owners, 92. *See also* Islam
Mustarab Jews, 58
Myers, David N., 4–5
Myth and the Empire, The (Magris), 194

nationalism, 14, 50, 56, 65n31, 179–80; Jewish, 185; Turkish, 185
nation-states, 2, 14, 49, 163
Navon, A. H., 182
Nazism, 194, 195, 207n25
"Near East," 170, 175–76, 178
Netherlands, 112
network theory, 35
Neusner, Jacob, 27n72
"New Thalassology," 49
Nietzsche, Friedrich, 207n31
Nile Valley, 32
9/11 (September 11, 2001) terrorist attacks, 199, 208n47
Nirenberg, David, 206n7
Nora, Pierre, 199
North Africa, 2, 7, 19, 69, 95, 171; Castilian and Portuguese conquests in, 84; cultural syncretism in, 197; European culture spread to, 141; Judaism in, 58; outside zone of connectivity, 46n6; Spanish and Moroccan Jews in, 82, 100n4. *See also* Maghreb
North Sea, 15
Norwich, John Julius, 22n9
nostalgia, 8, 20, 192, 195, 199–203, 210n72
"Nouvelle culture méditerranéenne, La" ["The New Mediterranean Culture"] (Camus), 197
Nuptials at Tipasa (Camus), 197

Odyssey (Homeric epic), 199
olive oil trade, 154, 162, 167n22
On the Greatness of Cities (Botero, 1588), 108–9
Oran, city of, 82, 83; Castilian conquest of (1509), 84; as Christian community, 97; Jewish community of, 86, 88, 98; Muslim slaves sent to Spain from, 92, 104n48; slave population of, 92, 104n52
"Orient, the," 170, 175, 178, 185
Orientalism, 7, 177, 178, 179, 191
Orígenes del español (Menéndez Pidal), 205n6
Orthodox Christians, 8, 108, 110, 114; Armenian, 125n43; Greek, 108, 110, 121, 125n43, 164, 183; in Ottoman cities, 121; soap manufacturing and, 154

Orwell, George, 198
Ottoman Empire, 14, 18, 20, 25n42, 131, 185, 201; in Adriatic region (map), *151*; *'ahdname* (capitulation agreements) and, 121; commercial and tourist guides to, 170; commercial toleration in, 108; demise of, 182; *francos* (Jewish Italian traders) in, 141; Islamic legitimacy of, 121, 127n70; Jewish slave owners in, 94; Judaism in, 58; millet system, 107, 114, 122, 122n2, 184; naval battles with Spanish Empire, 84; Pan-Turanism in, 190n71; refugees from Catholic persecution in, 109; slavery in Algiers, 81; toleration in, 119, 121–22; trade in eastern Mediterranean and, 51; trade treaty with Greece, 158. *See also* Turkey

Pact of 'Umar (ninth century), 91, 94
paganism, 6, 197
Palestine, 18, 32, 34, 42, 175, 176, 179; Alliance Israélite Universelle in, 182; British mandate over, 180, 185, 196; land tenure patterns in, 35; slave owning in, 94; Zionist project in, 180
Parfait Négociant, Le (Savary, 1675), 137, 147n60
Parthian Empire, 33
Passions and the Interests, The (Hirschman), 118
"Past & Present School," 36
patronage, 37, 38, 39, 40, 43
Pensiero meridian, Il [*Southern Thinking*] (Cassano, 1996), 192, 199
"people of the genizah," 9, 10, 13
Perec, Georges, 202, 210n74
Peristiany, John G., 35
Persian Gulf, 33
Persians, 117
Philip II, king of Spain, 88
Philip III, king of Spain, 89, 96
Philo of Alexandria, 33, 42, 47n9
philo-Semitism, 130
Philosophy of the Subjective Spirit (Hegel), 196
Pièces détachées [*Spare Parts*] (Fellous), 202
pilgrimage: Christian and Muslim, 7; Jewish, 6, 47n12

piracy, 31, 56, 81, 83, 90
Pirenne, Henri, 3–4, 11, 23n15; Algérienisme and, 196–97; in German prison camp, 23n24; on western Europe under Roman rule, 12
Pirenne Thesis, 3, 12
Pitt-Rivers, Julian, 37
Plato, 40
pluralism, 16, 18, 50, 56, 192
Polanyi, Karl, 30, 46n2, 127n66
"Ponentines," 58
poor relief, 64n18
"port Jews," 14, 49, 56, 98
Portugal, 58
post-Marxism, 36
post-structuralism, 36
Prager brothers, 138
Prague, 33
Project of Perpetual Peace (Kant), 196
prostitutes, 115, 125n41
Protestants/Protestantism, 107, 110, 145n31; converted to Catholicism, 116; driven out of France and Italy, 109; in Livorno, 112, 113
Proust, Marcel, 199
Provence, 74
prozbol loophole, 41
Ptolemaic dynasty, 42
Purcell, Nicholas, 2, 3, 5–7, 12, 14, 22n9, 60; on ancient and medieval economies, 165n6; approach to culture, 31; on connectivity, 15; on disunity in Mediterranean region, 69, 74–75; on micro-regions, 12, 69, 76, 152; on "New Thalassology," 49; predecessors in Mediterranean studies, 9; on unity-out-of-diversity, 50–51, 63n6; on unity-through-fragmentation, 53. See also *Corrupting Sea, The*

Question, La (Alleg, 1958), 209–10n68
Qur'an, 91

Rabbi of Bacharach (Heine, 1840), 193
rabbis, 59, 105n54; patronage and, 39, 43; rabbinic ordination (*semikhah*), 55; "Republic of Letters" among, 54; *sha'atenez* prohibition and, 68, 72–73

Rabbi's Cat, The (Sfar, 2002–2015), 199, 210n79
racism, scientific, 181
Radetzky's March (Roth, 1932), 194, 195
Ray, Jonathan, 16, 18, 19
Recanati family, 140, 148n76
reciprocity, 37, 38, 40, 42, 43, 44
Reconquista, 192
redistribution, 9, 15, 45; cabotage and, 31, 32; cellular, 31; institutions of, 36–37
Red Sea, 32
Renaissance, Italian, 108, 119
responsa, rabbinic, 75, 83, 94
reterritorialization, 203–4
Robertson, William, 118
Roden, Claudia, 208n44
Rodrique, Aron, 189n60
Roman Empire, 2, 4, 11, 196; fall of, 3; historians of, 5; Jewish revolts (66–135 CE), 33, 47n12; Jews in Roman world, 32–35; patronage and friendship in, 39; three economies in, 31–32
Romaniote Jews, 58, 152
Roman Republic, 44
Rostovtzeff, Mikhail, 22n9
Roth, Joseph, 194, 195
Rothman, Natalie, 8, 16
Russia, 178

Sacripandi, Caludio, 116
Sahara, 15
Sahlins, Marshal, 43
Said, Edward, 7
Saint-Simonianism, 196
Saldaña, Antónion de, 103n33
Salomone Enriches & Joseph Franchetti Company, 131, 145n22
Salonica, city of, 33, 55, 170, 198; Halevy family in, 174, 187n11; Hellenization of, 185; White Tower, 177
Sánchez-Albornoz, Claudio, 205n6
Saraci (Muslim merchant in Scutari), 152, 154, 155, 156, 162; correspondence with Coen, 157, 158, 160–61; dispute with Coen, 157–61
Sarajevo Haggadah, 194
Sartre, Jean-Paul, 209n68

Sasportas, Yaho, 86–87, 92
Sasportas family, 86, 88, 92
Savary, Jacques, 118, 137, 138, 147n60
Schorsch, Ismar, 193
Schorske, Carl, 194
Schreier, Joshua, 209n60
Schwartz, Seth, 14–16, 66n47, 76
Sciaky, Leon, 198
Scutari (Albania), city of, 149, 150, 165n3; Bojana River connection to Corfu, 153; Coen's clients in, 152, 156; map, *151*; soap factories in, 162; Venice and, 153, 166n11
Second Temple period, 40
Sefer Ha-Qabalah (Abraham ibn Daud), 32
Seleucids, 42
Semach, Paltiel, 131, 135
Seneca, 38
Sepharad, 193, 206n21
Sephardic diaspora, 2, 14, 51, 53; Lévy's guides and, 171, 172, 184–85; rabbinic leaders, 55; social networks and, 57
Sephardim, 52, 64n18, 181; acculturation of traders, 138; Algerian Jews, 85, 94, 201–3; of Amsterdam, 142, 148n82; collective reputation of merchants, 130; expulsion narratives and, 201; Ladino (Judeo-Spanish) language and, 185; *Le Guide Sam* and, 16, 18; Livornina and, 111; in Livorno, 112; Mediterranean fluidity and, 9; *Megorashim* (expelled Moroccan Jews), 100n4; merchants from Livorno, 24n30; in Muslim and Christian societies, 58; narrative of diasporic golden age in Al-Andalus, 193–94; nostalgia and exile, 199–205, 210n71; "port Jews," 98; trading networks of, 53. See also Moroccan Jews
sexuality/sexual relations, 111, 115, 116, 121–22
Sfar, Johan, 199, 210n79
sha'atenez garments, prohibition on, 19, 68, 75–77; in Crete, 71–74; north–south agricultural axis in Europe and, 69
Shaw, Brent, 44
Shengjin/San Giovanni di Medusa, port of, 150, *151*, 153, 157–58, 160
Shibbole ha-Leket [*Ears of Gleaning*] (Tzidkiyahu ha-Rofe), 74, 75
Sholal, Isaac, 55, 64n24

Sitbon, Guy, 202
Siva, Mme. Albane de, 179, 185
slave trade, Jews and, 4, 17, 81–83, 97–99; enslavement of Jews, 81; friction with Maghrebi rulers, 94–97; Jews as slave owners and slave traders, 89–94, 104n52, 106n76; "port Jews," 98; racialization of trans-Atlantic slave trade, 99; redemption (ransom) of captives, 83–89; regional perspective on, 82
Slavs, 1
Smith, Adam, 119–20
Smyrna, 131–35, 139, 140, 141, 146n33
Social and Economic History of the Roman Empire, The (Rostovtzeff), 22n9
social network analysis, 108, 123n7
Solal (Cohen, 1930), 149, 197
Sombart, Werner, 4, 23n19
Sorkin, David, 14, 98
Spain, Christian, 13, 19, 58, 68, 76; botanical cultivation and nomenclature in, 69, 74; incursions in the Maghreb, 196; Jews expelled from, 85, 109, 192, 194; precarious tolerance in, 122; *Reconquista*, 75, 192; slavery/slave trade and, 81, 92, 95–96
Spain, Muslim (al-Andalus), 5, 12, 27n85, 64n17, 76, 193, 195
Spanish Jews, 81, 88, 89, 100n4
Spanish language, 86, 116
spatialization, religious boundaries and, 111, 112–13, 121
Spinoza (Auerbach, 1837), 193
Stein, Sarah Abrevaya, 52, 188n28
stereotypes, 6, 9, 177, 179; about youth, 140; Jews' ties to commerce, 5; self-stereotypes, 191, 198
Stoianovich, Traian, 153
Stora, Benjamin, 199, 202
Stranger, The (Camus), 204
Stroumsa, Sarah, 13, 14
structural functionalist social theory, 36, 45
Süleyman, Sultan, 127n70
symbiosis, 21, 192, 198
synagogues, 34, 43, 112, 138, 139, 140
Syria/Syrians, 3, 23n15, 34, 175, 176; Alliance Israélite Universelle and, 182; slave owning in Syria, 94

Tacitus, 39
takkanot (communal ordinances), 79n25
Takkanot Kandiyah (Artom and Cassuto, eds., 1943), 71, 72
"Tale of the Four Captives, The," 32
Talmud, 39, 138
Tangiers, city of, 86
Tanugi, Jesuuah Coen, 133
taxes, 32, 54, 64n24, 94, 160
Tazzara, Corey, 17–18, 19
Tétouan, city of, 82, 83, 87, 88; Jewish community of, 90–91, 93, 98; as Muslim community, 97; redemption (ransom) of captives in, 95
textile industry, 70
Theognidea, 39
Thornton, Richard, 116
Toch, Michael, 5, 77
tolerance/toleration: commerce and invention of liberalism, 118–20, 127n64; commercial, 108–10; Italy compared to Mediterranean as a whole, 120–22; religious, 17, 55, 107, 108
Torah, 39, 40, 42–43, 138
Trade and Institutions in the Medieval Mediterranean (Goldberg), 12
Trani, Moses, 55
transnationalism, 52, 53, 172
transportation technologies, 171
Trevinos, Juan, 86
Trieste, city of, 151, 152, 153; Great War and, 163; soap manufacturing in, 159, 162
Trinitarians (Order of the Holy Trinity), 83, 85, 86, 88, 95–96
Trivellato, Francesca, 5, 8, 24n30, 98; on meaning of term *friendship*, 156; on methods of poor relief, 64n18; on relation of trade and tolerance, 97; on Sephardic merchants in Livorno, 141
Trois exils, Les (Stora), 202
Tunis, city of, 55, 130, 131, 134; Italian merchants in, 17; as provincial backwater, 140
Tunisia, 201, 202

Turkey, 175, 176, 179, 180, 183–84; Alliance Israélite Universelle in, 182; "Citizen, Speak Turkish" campaign, 183; idea of the Mediterranean in, 191. *See also* Ottoman Empire
Turkish language, Ottoman, 85
Turks/Turkic peoples, 1, 12
Tzidkiyahu ben Avraham Anav (Tzidkiyahu ha-Rofe), 74–75

Udovitch, Abraham, 10
Ulcinj/Dulcigno, port of, 150, 151, 152, 153, 160
usury, 5

Venice/Venetian Republic, 33, 51, 69; fall of, 164; Fondaco dei Turchi, 112, 113; Jewish ghetto in, 109–10; Jews of Crete and, 73
Voltaire, 119

al-Wansharīsī, Aḥmad ibn Yaḥyā, 91
Weber, Max, 36, 46n2
Weitzman, Steven, 42
Were the Jews a Mediterranean Society? (Schwartz, 2010), 14–15
Wissenschaft des Judentums, 193
World of Yesterday, The: An Autobiography (Zweig, 1941), 195

Yam Tikhoniyut, 60
Yehoshua, A. B., 202–3, 210n75
Yellow Wind, The (Grossman), 203
Yemen, 189n60
Yerushalmi, Yosef, 193
Young Turk movement, 183
Yugoslavia, 176, 179, 180, 194

Zafrani, Haim, 198
Zenatti, Valérie, 210n79
Zerah, Elie, 201
Zionism, 18, 60, 174, 180–81, 201
Zohar, 138
Zúñiga, Melchor de, 94
Zweig, Stefan, 195

MATTHIAS B. LEHMANN is Professor of History at the University of California, Irvine, where he holds the Teller Family Chair in Jewish History. He is the author of *Ladino Rabbinic Literature and Ottoman Sephardic Culture*, *Emissaries from the Holy Land*, and (with John Efron and Steve Weitzman) *The Jews: A History*.

JESSICA M. MARGLIN is Associate Professor of Religion and Law at the University of Southern California, where she holds the Ruth Ziegler Early Career Chair in Jewish Studies. She is the author of *Across Legal Lines: Jews and Muslims in Modern Morocco*.

www.ingramcontent.com/pod-product-compliance
Lightning Source LLC
Chambersburg PA
CBHW030648230426
43665CB00011B/1001